Mental Representations

OXFORD PSYCHOLOGY SERIES

EDITORS
DONALD E. BROADBENT
JAMES L. MCGAUGH
NICHOLAS J. MACKINTOSH
MICHAEL I. POSNER
ENDEL TULVING
LAWRENCE WEISKRANTZ

Mental Representations

A Dual Coding Approach

ALLAN PAIVIO
Professor of Psychology
University of Western Ontario

OXFORD PSYCHOLOGY SERIES NO. 9

OXFORD UNIVERSITY PRESS • NEW YORK
CLARENDON PRESS • OXFORD
1986

Oxford University Press

Oxford   New York   Toronto
Delhi   Bombay   Calcutta   Madras   Karachi
Petaling Jaya   Singapore   Hong Kong   Tokyo
Nairobi   Dar es Salaam   Cape Town
Melbourne   Auckland

and associated companies in
Beirut   Berlin   Ibadan   Nicosia

Copyright © 1986 by Oxford University Press, Inc.

Published by Oxford University Press, Inc.,
200 Madison Avenue, New York, New York 10016

Oxford is a registered trademark of Oxford University Press.

Library of Congress Cataloging-in-Publication Data
Paivio, Allan.
Mental representations.
(Oxford psychology series; no. 9)
  Bibliography: p.   Includes index.
  1. Cognition.   2. Human information processing.
3. Imagery (Psychology).   4. Psycholinguistics.
5. Nonverbal communication (Psychology).   6. Verbal behavior.
I. Title.   II. Series.
BF311.P27   1986   153   85-18743
ISBN 0-19-503936-X

Printing (last digit): 9 8 7 6 5 4 3 2 1

Printed in the United States of America
on acid free paper

To Kathleen

Preface

In this book I have tried to present a systematic analysis of the psychological phenomena associated with the concept of mental representations—equivalently, cognitive or internal representations. The analysis is based on an updated version of a dual coding theory of cognition that I began to develop more than twenty years ago. Described comprehensively in my 1971 book, *Imagery and verbal processes,* the theory was applied to perceptual, memory, and language-processing tasks that were the focus of the empirical and theoretical issues of the day. Since then I have reported modifications and extensions designed to accommodate new observations (e.g., Paivio, 1978b, 1983b), but not in the context of a comprehensive restatement of the entire modified theory and the philosophy of science associated with it. This book is that restatement. Its coverage includes phenomena from the earlier period that remain relevant and challenging today, but the emphasis is on cognitive problems and paradigms that had not yet appeared or were only beginning to emerge when I was writing *Imagery and verbal processes.*

Although the conceptual and empirical developments in the interim have been remarkable, the two books are linked by recurrent conceptual issues. Research and theory up to the early 1960s had been dominated by the view that performance in memory and other cognitive tasks was mediated by processes that are primarily verbal or linguistic. From its inception, the dual coding approach was a reaction against that singular view in that it emphasized the importance of nonverbal imagery as a mode of thought that was distinct from, though coordinated with, verbal processes. However, dual coding and other imagery-based approaches promptly found themselves in competition with a computational analogue of verbal mediation: The "language of mind" became the logical proposition. Asserted to be amodal and abstract, propositions were nonetheless described as if they were mental sentences, which served as basic elements in cognitive models much as verbal mediators had done earlier. Propositional theorists were, if anything, even more singleminded in insisting that all information, whether verbal or nonverbal, was transformed into this common descriptive format and then operated on by processes of a similar form. And so, in regard to this fundamental conceptual issue, *Plus ça change plus c'est la même chose.*

Certain continuities also appear at a meta-theoretical level. Verbal mediation theory reflected the operational empiricism of the logical positivist era. Although differing in its theoretical assumptions, the early dual coding approach shared the empiricist philosophy of science and applied an explicit form of operationism to its major concepts. The propositional-computational approaches, on the other hand, were accompanied by a contrasting emphasis on a rationalist philosophy essentially continuous with the classical, nativistic form that had dominated Western philosophy prior to the advent of empiricism.

The updated dual coding approach presented here retains much of the constructive empiricism and the basic theoretical assumptions of the earlier version. In defense of those views, I spell out the advantages of an empiricist approach to the study of cognitive phenomena and show that the fundamentals of dual coding theory have stood up well to the empirical challenges over the years. Indeed, the supportive evidence is apparently so compelling that some propositional theorists have been motivated to adopt structural and processing assumptions essentially like those of dual coding theory, although expressed in a more abstract meta-language. As I have already indicated, however, the stable theoretical foundation has also been augmented by modified assumptions designed to account for new findings. The entire theoretical approach is presented here in a more integrated and explicit form than was the 1971 version, so that its strengths and shortcomings can be more easily assessed.

I have attempted throughout to evaluate the theory and its major competitors in the context of relevant evidence, including findings that seem to be more problematic for dual coding theory than for some propositional alternatives, as well as findings that are not easily handled by any of the approaches except by means of ad hoc assumptions. The review also reveals that the evidence necessary to evaluate the alternative theories is simply lacking in many research areas because relevant variables have not yet been considered. These remain rich areas for systematic study.

Although I have written this book from a personal perspective, I intend its contents to be relevant to all students of cognition, regardless of their disciplinary background or their particular theoretical or philosophical orientation. Thus, I am hopeful that not only cognitive psychologists, but also those who identify with cognitive science, linguistics, philosophy, and other disciplines concerned with the representation of knowledge will find something of interest in one or more of these chapters.

The twelve chapters cover three general topics, including (a) meta-theoretical and theoretical issues (chapters 1–3), (b) dual coding theory (chapter 4), and (c) empirical implications and evidence (chapters 5–12). Chapter 1 deals with empiricistic versus rationalistic philosophies of science and such related issues as the role of formalism, the nature of scientific language, and operationism in representational research and theory. Chapter 2 is an analysis of representational concepts, and chapter 3 discusses sceptical, empirical, and rational views regarding mental representations, including the shortcomings of each. Because of the current prominence of rationalism, the section on it includes critical analyses of nativism, formalism, and conceptual reification, the topics that usually accompany computational approaches.

Chapter 4 is a self-contained description of dual coding theory, including its basic assumptions, hypotheses, and general implications. The remaining chapters flesh out the theory in terms of its specific implications for different psychological problems and provide relevant evidence, both pro and con. Chapters 5 and 6 deal respectively with the development of representational systems and with individual differences in cognitive abilities and cognitive habits or styles. Chapter 7 addresses problems of meaning and semantic memory. Chapter 8 presents a detailed and comprehensive treatment of episodic memory as viewed from the dual coding perspective. Chapter 9 deals with the manipulation and use of representational information in such tasks as mental comparisons, mental rotations, cognitive mapping, and a variety of other problem-solving tasks. Chapter 10 shows how the theory handles language comprehension and production, including its potential as an alternative to schema approaches to text and discourse processing. Chapter 11 presents a bilingual version of dual coding theory and applies it to bilingual memory and other tasks, as well as second-language learning. Chapter 12 closes the book with a review of neuropyschological evidence and theoretical views that bear on representational issues and dual coding theory.

I would like, finally, to express my appreciation to the many friends and colleagues who have helped me in the preparation of this book. Above all, I am grateful to my wife Kathleen and my family for their continued encouragement and for their understanding during those long periods when I was either directly occupied with writing or my blank expression said, "Mental representations otherwise engaged." Others have provided helpful suggestions and technical assistance. Jim Clark commented on most of an early draft of the book, especially chapters 1 to 8, and my writing has also benefited from the many stimulating theoretical discussions we have had over the years. I have taken advantage of the suggestions on specific chapters offered by Mike Pressley (chapter 5), Wilma Bucci and Carole Ernest (chapter 6), Ian Begg (chapter 8), Mark Sadoski (chapter 10), and Mel Goodale (chapter 12). Conversations with Joanne Harbluk, Mary Walsh, Bill Yovetich, and Carla Johnson helped me to clarify my thinking concerning aspects of bilingual memory, metaphor processing, the functional properties of pictorial symbol systems, and developmental factors, respectively. Various chapters have been improved as a result of comments made by a group of graduate students with whom I discussed the penultimate draft in a seminar in the spring of 1985. They include Terry Biggs, Patricia Devolder, Nancy Digdon, Mustaq Khan, Edward Manukian (his unique expertise in the philosophy and history of science was especially relevant to chapter 1), Debbie Stuart, and Sue West. The last two also helped with the completion of the reference list. In addition to her continuous contribution as research assistant, Trudy Bons provided stylistic suggestions and helped compile the references and the index. Elizabeth Henderson was responsible for typing the entire text using a computerized system that made revisions and publication easier than would otherwise have been the case. The copy editing was done skillfully by Marie Milton and Joan Bossert of Oxford University Press. To all, my warmest thanks.

This book would not have been possible without the years of research support that I have received from the Natural Sciences and Engineering Research Council of Canada (grant A0087). The final stages of my work on the book were also aided by a Research Professorship and an accompanying research stipend awarded to me by the Social Science Faculty of the University of Western Ontario.

October 1985   A.P.
London, Ontario

Contents

Mental Representations

1
Meta-theoretical Issues and Perspectives

This book is about the form and functions of individual knowledge. How do we represent information mentally and how do we use that information to interact with the world in adaptive ways? The problem is old and persistent. Our distant ancestors must have wondered about it long before they knew how to represent information on the walls of caves or on wax tablets; and we still wonder, though we know how to represent information in computers and use it with lightning speed.

The problem persists because it is extraordinarily difficult, perhaps the most difficult one in all of science. It is essentially the question of the nature of knowledge and of thought, and all that these imply in terms of observable behavior, brain activity, developmental origins, environmental effects, and so on. Because it is so complex, we lack agreement on how to approach the problem theoretically, and even empirically. Of course, controversy is a normal part of science, so it is not surprising that it accompanies the study of mental representations. What is unusual is its current intensity and the fact that it is polarized around an old philosophical issue that seemed to have been largely resolved in the history of science, namely, empiricism versus rationalism as ways of arriving at a scientific understanding of natural phenomena. The revival has been sparked especially by a resurgence of logical rationalism, which warrants more than a footnote here because it is closely tied to a new discipline, called cognitive science, which takes the problem of mental representations as its main domain. But empiricists are also concerned with internal representations as natural phenomena, so we have a meta-scientific dilemma that needs to be resolved even as we try to understand the phenomena themselves.

I address those general issues here from the perspective of an empiricist philosophy of science, that is, an empiricist approach to theories and theory construction. The stand is reflected in an empiricist approach to the study of mental representations. Or, more correctly stated, the general philosophical stance is itself a consequence of the empirical approach to mental phenomena, including philosophical beliefs. The approach is empirical in the sense that inferences about mental processes are based on observable behavior. It is appropriate, therefore, to refer to it as *objective mentalism* or *behavioral mentalism* (Paivio, 1975c). The mentalistic or cognitive emphasis distinguishes it from behaviorism, although how it does that needs explanation because behaviorists can claim the same territory in principle, by referring to mental phenomena as covert responses or private events. This crucial distinction is discussed in chapter 3 along with the behavioristic dilemma that it entails.

The objective emphasis distinguishes the present approach from the rationalistic ones mentioned above, but this distinction, too, will need careful scrutiny because it raises a two-sided paradox. On the one hand, scientists, whatever their philosophical beliefs, must be methodological empiricists because they deal with observable phenomena. The most rationalistic of cognitive scientists must therefore confront and explain behavioral data even as they seek to construct formal models of mental representations. On the other hand, the empiricist approach has a rational side in that logical reasoning is a necessary part of systematic research, drawing inferences from data, theory construction, and so on. Accordingly, the objective mentalism advocated here is both a rational and an empirical enterprise. Does this mean that the empiricist-rationalist distinction is simply a difference in emphasis? This is partly true, but in addition it entails fundamental differences in attitudes toward particular issues in the philosophy of science, the nature of descriptive and explanatory concepts used in theories, and the kind of research that is done.

The rest of this chapter expands on the more philosophical of those issues as they apply to the study of mental representations. The focus is on the general contrast between rationalism and empiricism and certain specific issues that are usually associated with it, including formalism versus informalism in theory construction and explanation, the distinction between observational and theoretical terms, the terminal meta-postulate as a logical limitation of certain empiricistic theories, and the role of operationism in contemporary research and theory.

RATIONALISM VERSUS EMPIRICISM

Rationalism is a way of discovering or formulating general truths by means of logical reasoning alone. Its origins and development in Western culture were due in large measure to its success in mathematical reasoning, where one begins with "known truths" or premises, such as the axioms in Euclidian geometry, and goes through a series of logically consistent arguments to arrive at a final conclusion. Syllogistic reasoning is a general example of such a process. Rationalism is accordingly linked intimately to formal logic, which is considered in more detail in the next section. Here, we are concerned only with the general procedure and problems associated with it.

One of the problems is the origin of the "known truths." It is clearly illustrated by Bertrand Russell's first lessons on Euclid from his brother Frank, as told by R. W. Clark (1975). The pupil had no difficulty with the Definitions.

> The trouble came with the Axioms. What was the proof of these, the young pupil asked with naive innocence. Everything apparently rested on them, so it was surely essential that their validity was beyond the slightest doubt. Frank's statement that the Axioms had to be taken for granted was one of Russell's early disillusionments. "At these words my hopes crumbled . . . why should I admit those things if they can't be proved?" His brother warned that unless he accepted them it would be impossible to continue. (p. 31)

We shall see later that the problem has its counterpart in rationalistic approaches to mental representations and that it has been handled by resorting to a classical, nativistic argument.

The origin of axioms or premises was not the only problem. Despite its apparent success in mathematics and logic, rationalism did not advance the development of science and scientific understanding. A historical verdict has been that it fostered ignorance and hampered science for 2,000 years. Whether that severe judgment is justified or not, the fact is that rationalism was largely displaced by empiricism as a result of the successes of observational (especially experimental) procedures in the physical and biological sciences. The shift also occurred in psychology, beginning with the associationism of the British empiricists and reaching its peak with twentieth-century behaviorism. The radical turn to empiricism was reflected also in the development of various positions in the philosophy of science, including logical positivism.

Now the *philosophical* winds have shifted once again toward a rationalist pole in philosophy of science and some areas of science. Logical positivism in its extreme form lost its force and it has been largely replaced by various forms of scientific realism with a distinctly rationalistic bent. In scientific areas most relevant to us, rationalism made its reappearance in linguistics and cognitive psychology, in each case through the influence of computer science and the formal computational procedures associated with it. The movement was initiated and promoted by Chomsky, who relied more on his intuitions about linguistic structures than on objective linguistic data as a basis for theory development, and proposed a rule-bound, formal grammar as the model of human language. The rationalistic emphasis continues in the work of certain theorists in cognitive psychology (and cognitive science) who adopt a computational approach to the conceptualization of mental representations.

The general rationalistic emphasis is clearly illustrated by Pylyshyn's (1979a) argument for a "top-down" (computational) strategy in research and theory development, which he contrasted with the empiricist method (p. 429), and his stated preference for theoretical completeness, consistency, coherence, logical soundness, intrinsic constraints—all hallmarks of rationalism—as opposed to attempts at empirical rigor through operational definitions and "sticking close to the experimental data." The choice was motivated by a general "wait and see strategy" according to which one "postpones certain crucial commitments (such as entailed by operational definitions) with the intention of avoiding the most costly potential dead ends" (p. 429).

The strategy described by Pylyshyn is reasonable up to a point and all theorists follow it in that they suspend definitive judgments about the correctness (predictive value, etc.) of a theory until sufficient data have been accumulated, or they will wait and see before rejecting a theory on the basis of isolated facts that appear to be inconsistent with the theory. A full-blown, top-down, wait-and-see strategy is risky, however, for it could lead to the most costly dead end of all, where the whole structure built from the top down eventually collapses for want of empirical support.

The rationalist approach has been justified in other ways in contemporary cognitive science, and subsequent chapters will touch on those aspects that are relevant to specific empirical and theoretical questions. The main point to be noted here is that the other arguments are all secondary to and motivated by the commitment to a computational approach to psychological issues, which entails a formal rationalistic attitude because the computer *can* only operate according to formal rules. We turn now to the implications of that point.

FORMAL VERSUS INFORMAL APPROACHES

The rationalist-empiricist distinction is closely tied to the contrast between formal and informal approaches to problem solving in logic and science. We have already seen that rationalism in the classical sense depends on a formal logic that permits one to argue from some point of departure (the initial premise) through a series of logically consistent arguments to a final conclusion. Such formal systems are rule-bound and basically syntactic in that they deal with relations between symbols. The symbols also have meaning, but the meaning must be fixed for the purposes of any logical argument if the chain of reasoning is to remain intact. Thus, formal logic in its pure form uses a closed symbol system that cannot depend on external input. For example, it cannot be influenced by the pragmatic concerns of the user of the symbolic system.

Informal approaches, on the other hand, make use of input from outside of the symbol system, including evidence based on observation of external events or imagination of possible events. Of course it is not *illogical,* since the informally derived information must be used systematically if a problem is to be solved. This means that an overriding general logic may guide informal reasoning in whatever field. Nonetheless, it is not pure formal logic because it permits external input that can modify the argument at any moment. In brief, informal reasoning is psychological and empirical as well as logical and rational. We can now concretize the above argument by reviewing developments in the traditionally formal disciplines of philosophy of science and mathematics, and then by considering their relevance for representational issues.

It has been accepted for some time that formalism as a strong methodological program does not hold in the natural sciences. Philosophers of science have discussed the problem in the context of a distinction between discovery and justification of scientific theories. The classical argument was that theory generation or discovery depended on psychological, sociological, and chance factors that defy analysis in purely logical terms, whereas justification entailed reasoning that could be characterized in terms of formal logic. This sharp distinction is being challenged in contemporary philosophy of science in ways that also liberalize the very concept of rationalism so that it is equated broadly with reasoning and problem solving rather than being identified narrowly with formal logic. Interested readers can find an informative overview of these developments in Nickles (1982). The point for present purposes is that philosophers of science recognize the restrictiveness of formal logic in the interpretation of scientific thinking and are attempting to develop a broader view of reasoning because scientific inference is simply not reducible to logical implication.

The limitations of formalism are recognized even in the domain of mathematical logic, the most formal of all disciplines. The definitive statement on this point was Gödel's (see Rucker, 1982) famous incompleteness theorem, which demonstrated that mathematics is necessarily incomplete because certain mathematical propositions in axiomatic systems, like that presented in the *Principia Mathematica* by Russell and Whitehead, can never be proved or disproved. More pertinent here are the actual practices of philosophers and mathematicians because they illustrate how informal processes impinge on formal ones. I will describe a specific example and then show how it is relevant to the study of cognitive representations.

The example concerns problems in the methodology of mathematics that arose from clashes between formal and informal philosophies of mathematics. Told in a dialogue form by Lakatos (1963–1964), the study recapitulates the history of proofs and refutations applied to a theorem concerning the relation between the number of vertices (V), the number of edges (E), and the number of faces (F) of three-dimensional forms (polyhedra). The mathematician Euler was attempting to classify polyhedra when he noticed that $V - E + F = 2$. He and others sought a proof for the theorem. One approach was to imagine a polyhedron to be hollow, with a surface made of thin rubber. By cutting out one of the faces, the remaining surface could be stretched out flat without tearing it. A procedure applied to this surface appeared to prove the theorem. The refutations of this and other proofs were by means of counterexamples that showed some subconjecture or lemma to be false, or global counterexamples that refuted the theorem itself. The counterexamples consisted of solid figures that satisfy the definition of polyhedra but do not conform to Euler's theorem in that $V - E + F \neq 2$. Thus, for a crested cube (a large cube with a smaller cube sitting on top of it), $V - E + F = 3$. Such counterexamples were met by redefinitions of the polyhedron or its defining terms so as to rule out the nonconforming exceptions to the theorem. At each turn, however, new counterexamples were discovered that satisfied the "improved" definition and yet did not conform to Euler's theorem. Moreover, there was no reason to hope that the cycle would come to an end with any particular redefinition or refutation because each new version of the conjecture (theorem) was merely an *ad hoc* elimination of a counterexample that had just cropped up, and one could never be sure that *all* exceptions had been enumerated.

The dialogue is relevant here because it reveals the psychological nature of the *informal* processes in mathematical logic. These processes include the use of *concrete examples and situations*, and *conceptual shifts* in proofs and refutations. Thought experiments using concrete examples is an ancient method of mathematical proof, and it is illustrated in the present case by the imagined rubber surface and other procedures, such as imagining a polyhedron to be hollow with an inward-viewing camera attached to one surface. The counterexamples similarly consisted of such real or imagined forms as the crested cube, picture frames, and star-shaped polyhedra. The point is that the discovery and use of such examples in proofs and refutations lie outside the bounds of formal logic because the process does not rely on conceptual entities with fixed meaning and rule-determined arguments applied to those entities. It depends instead on informal psychological processes of perception, imagery, and creative discovery. Biographical data (see Strømnes, 1979, p. 262) confirm that logicians over the ages consistently relied on informal processes and especially imagined spatial analogues in their work. Our analysis suggests that they had no alternative.

The conceptual shifts included both *concept contraction* and *concept stretching*. The former were the redefinitions of polyhedra or its defining terms that were designed to eliminate counterexamples to Euler's theorem. Concept stretching consisted of the expansion of the concept of polyhedron to include increasingly complex forms. The process evolved so that more and more concepts were stretched, with a consequent reduction in the number of (as-yet) unstretched terms. The process apparently slowed down in the 1930s so that the demarcation line between unstretchable (logical) and stretchable (descriptive) terms seemed to become stable. The former were viewed as logical constants that were deemed to be essential to rational discussion. Lakatos concluded, however, that mathematicians eventually accepted unlimited concept stretching in mathematical criticism and that their acceptance was a turning point in the history of mathematics.

A major conclusion from Lakatos is that formalism is limited in its applicability, "that no conjecture is generally valid, but only valid in a certain restricted domain that excludes the *exceptions*" (p. 26). A formalist response might be that theorems can be generalized to encompass a broader empirical domain. Another response would be to accept the limitation as being inevitable, since all theoretical generalizations in mathematics and science have boundary conditions. Both comments are valid, but the point to be recognized is that the tests (proofs and refutations) of theorems require empirical procedures and psychological processes that are not formal, and that the pressure for *changes* in formal theories is a result of discoveries due to such informal procedures. This analysis has important implications in regard to theoretical approaches to mental representations, which will be discussed in more detail in chapter 3. At this point, we need only show that the mathematical problem discussed by Lakatos is indeed relevant to our concerns.

The mediating link is the concept of *proposition* and its use as a descriptive and theoretical unit in computational approaches to the study of mental representation. A proposition is generally defined as an abstract subject-predicate statement that can be evaluated for its truth value within the bounds of a logical theoretical system. That is, the truth of a proposition is defined by its logical consequences within a symbol system rather than in terms of its correspondence with objects and events outside of the system. The theorem is a prototypical proposition whose truth is evaluated by a system of formal reasoning based on already established truths. Propositional approaches to mental representations have similar properties in that formalizability and internal consistency (where propositional statements are true within the system) are important criteria for the acceptability of a propositional theory.

The formal similarities are matched by analogous controversies between proponents of formalist and informalist approaches in psychology. These controversies have entailed problems as diverse as the representation of general concepts and performance on such tasks as sentence verification and syllogistic reasoning. Thus, formalists have proposed that general concepts are represented in the form of rules of construction, that a sentence is verified as true or false with respect to a referent picture by encoding both sentence and picture as propositions and then comparing the components of each according to a set of rules, and that syllogistic reasoning depends on similar rule-determined encoding and comparison operations. On the informal side, some have suggested that concepts may be represented as image-like exemplars, and that sentence verification and syllogistic reasoning involve comparisons of images generated to sentences or premises. The term paralogic has been used to describe such reasoning (DeSoto, London, & Handel, 1965) and it could be applied equally appropriately to the exemplar-based proofs and refutations in the historical debate concerning Euler's theorem.

The representational controversy also includes examples of concept contraction and concept stretching. The former is illustrated by Pylyshyn's (1973) critique of the concept of mental imagery. His point of departure was the premise that imagery researchers interpreted mental images essentially as pictures in the head. He then followed up the consequences of this premise by an analysis of logical problems entailed by the metaphor and why images cannot be like static pictures. The rationalistic nature of the argument is clear from the fact that it all hinged on the acceptance of the original premise that the received interpretation of mental images among experimental psychologists was the picture metaphor. That, however, was a contracted definition because experimentalists were guided by a broader view of imagery. Thus, Bugelski (1971a), one of the targets of the attack, had explicitly urged researchers to think of imagery in terms of the process of imaging rather than as pictures in the head. I had similarly interpreted imagery as a dynamic process that included motor as well as sensory components, and one that needed to be defined by several objective indicators rather than by subjective reports of "mental pictures" alone (Paivio, 1971). For that reason and others, Pylyshyn's picture-metaphor premise was characterized as a straw man (Kosslyn & Pomerantz, 1977; Paivio, 1974a).

To summarize the point, modern researchers had stretched the concept of imagery relative to earlier definitions of the concept, and Pylyshyn's critique was applicable only to the earlier ones. He contracted the current definitions in order to proceed with his rational arguments, which simply are not applicable to the stretched concept. Moreover, it seems likely that the critique itself was used as a rationale for reinterpreting the concept of imagery (and cognition generally) in propositional-computational terms. Or so I will argue in chapter 3, along with the argument that the criticisms in fact turn back on the computational approach itself.

OBSERVATIONAL VERSUS THEORETICAL TERMS

The distinction between observational and theoretical terms, a disputed issue in the philosophy of science, warrants some attention here because it has recently shown up in discussions of representational issues in cognitive science. The question is whether there is any meaningful distinction between the two kinds of terms. The dominant philosophical position is that such a distinction cannot be drawn sharply because hypothetical, theoretical entities are potentially observable and tend to become so as scientific technology advances (for a review of the arguments, see van Fraassen, 1980). The molecule, for example, was originally an unobserved theoretical entity but has become observable with the advent of electron microscopy. Others argue that the distinction is real and important. Thus, van Fraassen maintains that some theoretical terms simply have no potentially observable empirical referents and that, even where the distinction is only one of degree, it is nonetheless real.

The distinction seems clearer in psychology because so many of its concepts refer to unobservable processes—emotions, motives, beliefs, attitudes, thoughts, and the like. These have been traditionally designated as inferential concepts, in contrast to the directly observable behaviors of organisms.

One way to bypass the difficulties associated with the distinction was to avoid the use of nonobservable theoretical concepts altogether, as the radical behaviorists have tried to do—rather unsuccessfully, as we shall see later. The other way is to accept the conceptual-equivalence position, as some cognitive scientists are beginning to do.

My perspective on the issue is pragmatic and psychological. The basic assumption is that the observational-theoretical distinction becomes psychologically real when interpreted in terms of the correlated difference between concrete and abstract terms (Clark & Paivio, unpublished). The former are terms like *horse* and *wagon*, with direct, observable referents whereas the latter are terms like *truth* and *beauty* that have no direct referents although they can be illustrated by pointing to examples. The relevant point is that concrete and abstract terms differ psychologically in terms of such criteria as memorability, image arousal, and ease of communication. Thus, at some point in theory construction, we cannot be indifferent to the distinction between concrete observational terms and abstract theoretical ones because they entail behavioral differences relevant to the practitioner of science. Of course, observational and theoretical terms cannot always be distinguished because theories can include the former, but it is important to recognize when they can and should be distinguished because it will help us avoid the pitfalls of reification that have plagued mentalistic psychology throughout its history. Chapter 3 elaborates on this point with respect to some recent approaches to the study of cognitive representations.

THE TERMINAL META-POSTULATE

The observational-theoretical distinction is directly implicated in arguments concerning the so-called terminal meta-postulate, which warrants our attention because it has been proposed as a fatal limitation of associationistic (empiricistic) theories. Bever, Fodor, and Garrett (1968) stated that associative principles are rules defined over the "terminal vocabulary of a theory, i.e., over the vocabulary in which behavior is described" (p. 583). Anderson and Bower (1973, p. 12) divided the postulate into three "associative metafeatures." The first is the *sensationalist statement* according to which all explanatory elements can be matched with potentially observable elements (stimuli or responses) or with elements derived from such observable (intervening variables, mediating responses, sensations, perceptions, images, ideas). The second is the *connectionist statement* that the potentially observable elements become associated only if they occur contiguously. The third is the *mechanistic statement* that all behavior can be explained by concatenating the associative links established through contiguity.

The general argument against the terminal meta-postulate is that many learnable behaviors cannot be described by principles that permit associations only between contiguous elements ("left and right members") of a behavior chain. One such behavior is learning to recognize or construct mirror-image languages, that is, any sequence followed immediately by the reverse of the sequence (e.g., aa, abba, aabbaa, etc.). Such learning violates the terminal meta-postulate because dependencies are allowed to nest within dependencies (e.g., bb sandwiched within aa). Chomsky (1957) had originally made this argument specifically in regard to the inadequacy of finite state (Markov process) grammars to account for center-embedded sentences, such as "The boy who broke his arm went to the store," where the associative dependency is between "boy" and "went." Other relevant examples include anticipatory errors of speech where a later member in a sequence shifts forward (e.g., "Smoyked oysters") distinguishing between different parts of speech, or between sentences and nonsentences, and so on.

The critics argue that such behaviors compel theorists to postulate structures and processes that are only abstractly related to external observables. For example, phrase-structure grammars make use of nonterminal symbols that stand for a sentence and its hierarchical structural constituents, and rewrite rules that translate higher level symbols into lower level ones. The corresponding psychological hypothesis is that individuals make use of analogous abstract symbols and rules. These processes are intended to account for such troublesome phenomena as the production of center-embedded sentences. They also provide for descriptive parsimony in semantic memory models in that the defining attributes of a concept need be specified only once (at the type node), and every individual occurrence (the token) of the concept can be processed simply by accessing the information stored at the type level.

Various rejoinders are possible. The most general one from the standpoint of empirical science is that the arguments against the terminal meta-postulate are to be evaluated empirically and not only logically. What exactly are the observable behaviors that really demand abstract entities for their explanation? Some of the typical examples, such as center-embedded constructions in language behavior, are relatively infrequent and it has not been demonstrated that the actual behaviors cannot be explained in terms of situational factors, traditional associative mechanisms, and the fact that people have a memory. Another response hinges on the definition of abstractness: How abstract must the postulated processes be to account for the troublesome facts? Must they be totally abstract and amodal, not corresponding even in an indirect way to observable entities such as stimuli and responses, as some propositional theorists suggest? Such an extreme view seems unnecessary. Many of the relevant phenomena can be handled by assuming nothing more abstract than internalized verbal labels that correspond to the members of a class. Thus, the word *dog* is a perfectly good type whose defining attributes are specified partly by the verbal descriptions evoked by the word. The type label may be sufficient for some behavioral purposes but for others it may be necessary to "refer to" the defining associates. An image of a dog (any dog) may have a similar abstract type function, perhaps by virtue of its association with the generic term *dog* and contextual conditions that make that association salient (likely to be activated). Under other conditions, a dog image may "stand for" a particular dog. The image in either case can be said to be "interpreted" (cf. Pylyshyn, 1973) by virtue of the particular verbal associations that it evokes in particular circumstances, or by the verbal and other contextual cues that generate the imagery in the first place. I return to such possibilities in more detail in chapter 4, where I show how dual coding theory copes with issues associated with the terminal meta-postulate.

THE OPERATIONAL APPROACH TO SCIENTIFIC CONCEPTS

All of the discussion up to this point leads naturally to a consideration of operationism in science. We saw earlier that operational procedures have low priority among some computationally oriented theorists, whereas they have high priority in the present approach. Operationism as advocated by the logical positivists once had a great influence on psychology, particularly in the theoretical approaches of Hull and Spence. The extreme positivistic doctrine was that scientific concepts are to be defined only in terms of the procedures that are used to measure them. A familiar example in psychology was that intelligence is only what the intelligence test measures. Operationism in that narrow sense was sharply attacked in philosophy of science and it has no force today.

The position adopted here is that operational definitions are indispensable in science and that we should be explicit about the nature and source (logical or empirical) of the relation between operations and concepts. Operational procedures are to be viewed as empirical indicators of concepts rather than as sufficient definitions of them, much as originally intended by Bridgman (1928; see Dubin, 1969, chap. 8). The relation between the operations and the concepts is always tentative and subject to modification in light of new empirical data. The modification, when required, could be imposed on the operational procedures (one tries different ones), the target concept itself (some property is changed or, in the extreme case, the concept is rejected), or some aspect of the theoretical model to which the concept is related. Finally, more than one operational procedure is necessary to avoid circularity in the defining relation. Thus, the operational approach is tied to *convergent* operations where several *different* empirical indicators or manipulation procedures converge, or potentially converge, on a given concept (for general discussions of the logic of converging operations in psychology, see Garner, Hake, & Eriksen, 1956; Roediger, 1980, pp. 243–244).

The above statement represents my own operational approach to the concepts of imagery and verbal symbolic processes (e.g., Paivio, 1969, 1971). I explicitly adopted the strategy of distinguishing the two concepts empirically by relating each to different kinds of item attributes, experimental manipulations, and individual difference measures. The operational procedures for imagery included use of pictures and words that are high in imagery value according to subjects' ratings, experimental instructions to use nonverbal imagery to remember verbal material, and tests designed to measure individual differences in imagery abilities. A parallel but different set of procedures were intended to converge on verbal processes. Chapter 4 presents an updated version of this approach in the context of the general theory to which it is related. At this point, we need only consider the general characteristics of the approach.

First, the convergent operations approach to imagery is tentative because different procedures may not provide satisfactory convergent evidence. For example, although item imagery and imagery instructions have comparable effects on performance in certain memory tasks, individual differences in imagery ability as measured by a number of tests have less consistently shown comparable relations to performance. Such discrepancies call for some modifications in the empirical-theoretical approach to imagery. The question is how radical the modifications should be. Because there is considerable convergence of at least two classes of variables on the imagery construct, a complete rejection of the concept itself is not warranted. Instead, we can look for possible problems in the discrepant operational area involving individual difference tests. For example, a large number of such measures are nominally related to the imagery construct in that they pertain to the processing of nonverbal, figural information, and yet many of them are essentially uncorrelated with each other (see chap. 6). The low correlations mean that the concept of imagery ability cannot refer to a unitary dimension, and that the most relevant dimension may not have been operationalized by the measures used in a particular study. This leads in turn to a more detailed consideration of the operational relations between particular ability measures and target tasks for which they are to serve as predictors. The general consequence is that our conceptualization of imagery is thereby broadened (an example of concept stretching), and empirical research designed to increase our understanding can take new directions.

The operational approach makes contact with concepts associated with widely different positions in psychology. At one extreme, it is related to Skinner's concept of controlling variables as the basis for classifying behaviors. For example, the mand, tact, echoic, and intraverbal are different classes of verbal operants defined in terms of different controlling variables (Skinner, 1957). It is fair to say that the behavioral classes are defined operationally by such variables. At the other pole, the approach bears a family relationship to the concept of processing operations in computational models of mental representations (see chap. 2), where representational information is defined by algorithmic procedures.

THE APPROACH SUMMARIZED: CONSTRUCTIVE EMPIRICISM

I began by saying that the present approach reflects an empiricist philosophy of science. To tell the truth, the underlying philosophy doesn't much matter because the scientific approach preceded any philosophical considerations on my part and it could continue without them now. On the other hand, scientific activity always entails some attitudes about the conduct of science, and no harm can come from analyzing one's implicit views on the matter as long as the philosophical tail doesn't begin to wag the scientific dog. It is difficult in any case to avoid facing the philosophical issues head on when mental representations are the subject of scientific inquiry, and when a prominent group of students of that subject are so openly rationalistic in their approach to it. And so, I am expressing my contrasting empiricistic and pragmatic position.

The tentative nature of theoretical concepts and operational procedures mark the present enterprise as a pragmatic one, consisting of working hypotheses and procedures that are retained as long as they serve explanatory, predictive, and heuristic functions. Van Fraassen (1980) has referred to such an approach to science as *constructive empiricism*, according to which "*Science aims to give us theories which are empirically adequate: and acceptance of a theory involves a belief only that it is empirically adequate* (p. 12). By empirically adequate, he means that the theory "Saves the phenomena," that is, that what it says about observable things and events in this world, is true. The acceptance of a theory is, therefore, based partly on pragmatic considerations related to the aims of the theorist and the context in which the theory is applied. Theoretical truth is tentative and dependent on empirical outcomes in particular contexts. I am not sure that my approach matches van Fraassen's definition of constructive empiricism in all repects, but it does so at least in the sense that empirical adequacy is the main criterion by which I attempt to evaluate the merits of different theoretical approaches to cognitive representation. That evaluation begins in the next two chapters with a detailed consideration of the concept of representation itself and different attitudes toward it as a research topic. Subsequent chapters deal with specific cognitive phenomena and research evidence relevant to their interpretation in terms of representational theory.

2
The Concept of Representation

This chapter and the next review the concept of representation from a psychological perspective. We begin here with a discussion of defining characteristics and controversial issues associated with the concept, followed by a summary of the various forms that it has taken in the history of psychology. This conceptual analysis provides the background for an evaluation in the next chapter of three general attitudes and approaches to cognitive representations among contemporary researchers. We shall see that the meta-theoretical issues discussed in chapter 1 also become relevant to the analysis.

CHARACTERISTICS OF PHYSICAL AND MENTAL REPRESENTATIONS

Dictionaries typically define representation as: Something exhibited to the mind; a likeness, portrait, image, or description; a sign or symbol, picture, plastic art or statue; and type or example. Such definitions indicate that representations can be physical or mental, that they are symbolic (they stand for something else), and that they vary in abstractness (e.g., from pictures to linguistic descriptions). The physical-mental comparison is a useful point of departure for our analysis because, historically, mental representations have been interpreted by analogy with physical representations, which can be easily described and classified in terms of the kinds of distinguishing characteristics that are specified in the dictionary definition as well as others identified by psychologists.

The most obvious distinction is that some physical representations are *picture-like* and others are *language-like*. Picture-like representations include photographs, drawings, maps, and diagrams. Language-like representations include natural human languages as well as such formal systems as mathematics, symbolic logic, and computer languages. Representational theorists have tried to identify the features that distinguish these two classes of representation. Picture-like representations are variously described as having analogue, iconic, continuous, and referentially isomorphic properties, whereas language-like representations are characterized as being non-analogue, noniconic, digital or discrete (as opposed to continuous), referentially arbitrary, and propositional or Fregian.

The distinctions have been the subject of much discussion and disagreement (e.g., Palmer, 1978; Shepard, 1978; Sloman, 1971) although a consensus seems to be developing around the idea that the fundamental distinguishing dimension is the degree of arbitrariness of the mapping relation between the form of the representation and the form of the represented world. Thus, the terms picture-like, analogue, iconic, and isomorphic all imply that such representations map onto represented objects or events in a nonarbitrary way. In the case of language-like representations, on the other hand, the relation is completely arbitrary. This arbitrariness is so fundamental that it was explicitly recognized by Hockett (1963) as one of the design features of human languages. At a more general level, Palmer (1978) expressed the distinction as a contrast between intrinsic and extrinsic representations. The representing relation in the former has the same "inherent constraints" as the relation that it represents (e.g., differences in object height might be represented by differences in size). The structure of a representational relation in the extrinsic case, however, is totally arbitrary whereas that of its represented relation is not. Referring specifically to cognitive representations, Palmer suggested that the analogue-propositional distinction makes sense if it is interpreted in terms of the intrinsic-extrinsic (nonarbitrary-arbitrary) representational contrast. Johnson-Laird (1983, p. 156) relies similarly on degree of representational arbitrariness to distinguish between mental (analogue) models and propositional representations.

Representations can also be described as varying in *concreteness-abstractness*, a dimension that correlates with the distinction between picture-like and language-like symbols. Thus, at one extreme we have highly concrete, iconic, modality-specific representations of objects and events. A three-dimensional colored motion picture with a sound track could be indistinguishable perceptually from real world events. At the other extreme we have completely abstract, amodal (or at least not modality-dependent) representations that are only arbitrarily related to real world objects and events. Human language is a clear case, but artificial languages such as those used by computers are, if anything, even more abstract.

The correlation is imperfect, however, because picture-like and language-like representations can both vary in abstractness in a structural or functional sense. For example, drawings of objects are structurally more abstract than photographs because they have fewer details. Caricatures are even more abstract and their symbolic function can be highly arbitrary and governed by convention. For example, structurally abstract silhouettes of a man or woman serve to indicate toilets, curves on road signs represent curves on a road, and so on, but they could be used equally well to represent any number of other situations. Such symbols have some degree of structural iconicity but they are functionally abstract and rather arbitrary in their relation to the represented world. Language-like representations also vary in their referential abstractness from concrete nouns at one extreme to abstract terms that lack specific objective correlates at the other.

Physical representations also permit us to address the issue of representational structures or systems. Here we find that a *componential-holistic* dimension cuts across the picture versus language and concrete-abstract dimensions. Thus, a representational system can be highly iconic but componential, as are the identi-kits used by police for the construction of faces. Each of the components—eyes, ears, nose, and so on—is a pictorial representation of part of a face, which can take different values on such variables as size, shape, and length-width ratio. The system would be even more abstract if the holistic components were decomposed further into simple perceptual features, such as lines differing in curvature and orientation. Completely abstract symbol systems, such as human languages, are typically viewed as componential (built up from phonemes or, in the case of writing, graphemes), but they also include onomatopoeic features and such holistic yet abstract visual symbols as numbers and other logograms.

All of the above characteristics of physical representations have been used in theoretical analyses of mental representations, where they have become especially contentious because such representations are not directly observable. Thus, theorists differ widely in their views concerning abstractness, isomorphism, modality-specificity, and the componential or holistic character of such representations. The problems have been accentuated because different levels of representational concepts have been confounded in theoretical discussions. At least three levels of usage can be distinguished: (a) mental representations that are psychologically "real" in that they are directly expressed as publicly or privately observable events (language, imagery, etc.), (b) mental structures and processes that are assumed to underlie the observable representations, and (c) representations as theoretical constructs (models) that are used to *describe* the structure and function of observable representations or their underlying mental mechanisms, or both. The next section expands on the analytic problem and its implications.

MENTAL REPRESENTATIONS AND MODELS

Palmer (1978) presented an analysis of cognitive representations in which he distinguished between the real world, the mental world (that is, the cognitive representation of the real world), and the mental model (the representation of the mental world). He reasoned that the mental model, being a model of the mental world, is also a model of the real world and, further, that a representational theory "should simultaneously be the proper description of both the mental world and the mental model" (p. 276). Accordingly, here, too, we have three levels of representational concepts: mental world, mental model, and the theorists' descriptive representation of mental world and model. Palmer's analysis differs from mine in that he does not explicitly use the term representation to refer to observable psychological phenomena that have a representational function. His discussion of mental models includes mental representations that are like images or language, but this is not the same as recognizing that images and language themselves have real representational functions that are yet to be fully understood. The same gap occurs at least with respect to language in Johnson-Laird's (1983) analysis of mental representations. Along with mental models and images, he proposed the existence of propositional representations, which he defined as "symbols that correspond to natural language" (p. 165), but he made no reference to the representational role of natural language itself. The adoption or omission, theoretically, of the manifest level of representations is relevant to later discussions because it distinguishes between relatively empirical and relatively rationalistic representational theorists.

Note that the different levels of usage of the concept of representation can be characterized in terms of the abstractness dimension. The most concrete level is when it is used as a label for publicly or privately observable behaviors that have a representational function. A more abstract level is the use of the term to refer to nonobservable cognitive processes presumed to underlie the observable phenomena. Still more abstract is the idea of representation as a mental model and, at the most abstract level of all, we have the representational theory that serves to describe the structural or functional properties of representations in the other senses of the term.

The above analysis highlights the self-embedded nature and, therefore, the complexity of the problem entailed by mental representations. Such phenomena as images and language have representational functions but, by one account at least, they are themselves *caused* by mental representations, and both are then characterized by the theorist in terms of a theoretical description that is intended to represent the mental representations! Finally, however else they might be characterized, the "psychologically real" mental representations of the individual can be viewed as a kind of theory of the world and one's interaction with it. For example, anticipatory imagery is a model precisely in the sense that it permits one to predict objects and events in the real world before they actually occur, to plan one's reactions to them, and to anticipate the outcome of those reactions. This implicit theoretical function of cognitive processes has been recognized by those who have described behavior as being determined by hypotheses or expectations ever since the time of the Hull-Tolman controversy. Recent versions of this view have been presented by Rock (1975) and Bregman (1977).

We shall see in chapter 3 how the different levels of usage have been confused in some theoretical approaches to mental representations. The focus of the confusion is that the properties of the units and structures of theoretical models tend to be reified and attributed to mental representations. The controversies have also included the important conceptual distinction between representations and processes, to which we now turn.

REPRESENTATION VERSUS PROCESS

Palmer's (1978) analysis includes the point that representations depend on processing operations in the sense that such operations determine the relations that hold among the (represented) object elements. For example, a matrix of distances among cities produced by multidimensional scaling procedures also contains information about the locations of the cities, but it can only be extracted by performing the necessary scaling algorithms on the matrix. Palmer concludes that the only information contained in a representation is that for which operations are defined to obtain it.

The representation-process distinction is closely related to the classical distinction between structure and function. The term representation refers to a structural entity on which processes or procedures can operate, whereas process refers to the activities involved in making functional use of the structural information. The term function refers variously to a mathematical relation between variables, a biological function as in evolutionary theory, and the individual psychological function of achieving a behavioral goal. The last sense is most relevant here because representational processes are meaningful, psychologically, only if they play a mediating role in behavior. Imagery, for example, can serve a mnemonic function for the individual.

The main point to be emphasized here is that it is difficult to distinguish representational structure from representational function or process, as already noted above in relation to computational models. The problem is further illustrated by the following imagery task. Imagine a two-dimensional block letter E , then count the inner and outer corners beginning at the upper right-hand corner of the letter and proceeding clockwise. Subjectively, the task seems to implicate a structural entity (the imagined letter) that is distinct from processing operations (mental scanning and counting). However, the structure of the E image is revealed only by the counting operation. It could also be revealed by other operations, such as having a person draw its shape, but again we could argue that the structure is the drawing procedure or process. More behaviorally expressed, the structure of the capital letter is equivalent to the activity (overt or covert) of tracing its outline.

We encounter a parallel problem in attempting to distinguish representational structure from behavioral function. Imagery will again serve as an example. My own research approach to the concept has been openly functional in the sense that it puts the emphasis on understanding the function of imagery in memory, thought, and language. This functional emphasis has been criticized on the grounds that it is insufficient in the absence of a theory of the structure of the mental image. Let us bypass for the moment the question of what might constitute a theory of the structure of a mental image and concentrate instead on the difficulty *in principle* of drawing a distinction. The functional argument is that imagery can mediate performance in memory and other tasks. It has been shown, for example, that imaging the referents of a pair of concrete nouns in some kind of interactive relation facilitates associative memory for the pair. Through such findings, we have come to know something about the functional properties of imagery. Structure is also implied by the idea that an interactive relation between the imagined element is important to recall, but we only know it through the observed functional relations. The structure of imagery has not been directly revealed by such research nor has it led to a theory of such structure.

In contrast, others have explicitly set out to study the structure of mental images using different procedures. Shepard and his colleagues (e.g., Shepard, 1978) have done the most elegant research on the problem using mental rotation and other tasks. The rationale is that such tasks permit one to infer that mental images share a high degree of isomorphism with perceptual structures—for example, that an imaged letter R *looks like* the perceived letter, and that it can be rotated mentally as a holistic entity. It can be argued, even in this case, however, that all we have gained is functional knowledge. That is, we know that experimental procedures designed to arouse imagery permits one to answer the questions in the mental rotation task (e.g., to say whether a rotated letter R is correctly oriented or a mirror-image reversal) with a speed that is systematically related to the degree of rotation. The structural inference is no more direct or compelling than it is in the case of superior associative learning when subjects are asked to construct interactive as compared to structurally separate images to word pairs. From the entire set of operational procedures and resulting behaviors, we can make inferences either about function or structure, or both, depending on the precise manipulations involved and on our theoretical goal.

The pragmatic position to be taken here is that it is theoretically useful to distinguish between structure and function (or representation and process) to the extent that it helps explain facts associated with such phenomena as imagery and generates new research that might add to the understanding. In brief, the theoretical constructs are useful fictions. The specific consequences of that belief are spelled out in subsequent chapters, but a concrete example will provide a hint of the direction to be followed.

Consider once again the task of counting the corners of an imaged letter E. The instruction to image the letter can be followed by any number of further instructions and questions: Rotate the letter mentally, reverse it to its mirror-image position, count the corners in any of these representations clockwise or counterclockwise or in a random order, and so on. It is useful and parsimonious to assume that we have one structural representation over which we can operate in many different ways. At the same time, we must be willing to entertain the procedural counterargument that the different instructions simply activate different processes or procedures, provided that the two interpretations can be empirically distinguished so that we may determine which one accounts for the broader range of relevant data.

BIOLOGICAL VERSUS CULTURAL SOURCES
OF REPRESENTATIONS

A biological-cultural distinction adds yet another perspective to the conceptual problem. The distinction has both a literal and a metaphorical interpretation. The literal interpretation is that some representational processes are biologically determined and others are culturally determined. The biological ones are products of evolution and are probably shared with other animals (see Griffin, 1976; Premack, 1983; Roitblatt, 1982). Examples are nonverbal memory, imagery, and action schema of some kind. The others are a product of cultural evolution and are primarily learned—for example, drawing behavior, language, mathematics, and scientific theorizing. The distinction isn't sharp because the biologically determined processes are modified by experience in that representational *content* must be acquired, so that, for example, one can imagine particular situations or behavioral outcomes but not others. Conversely, language is species-specific, so in that sense it has a biological component. The metaphorical sense of the distinction is that some representational concepts to be reviewed in the next section are essentially biological or psychobiological metaphors, expressed in behavioral or physiological terminology, whereas others are culturally derived metaphors based on artifacts used to record and communicate information. Others are ambiguous in this regard or have changed their metaphorical status over time—a form of concept stretching.

REPRESENTATIONAL CONCEPTS

We now consider specific representational concepts in some detail because they have been the basis of various representational theories and are accordingly relevant to subsequent topics. It would be convenient if the concepts could be classified systematically in relation to the distinguishing characteristics just reviewed as well as the meta-theoretical distinctions discussed in chapter 1, but this is difficult because many concepts cut across the analytic dimensions in unsystematic ways. Nonetheless, a few of them can be grouped together as being psychobiological in origin and staying close to observables in that they are interpreted as having perceptual, behavioral, or natural-language properties. These include imagery as used by some researchers, Osgood's concept of the representational mediation process, verbal mediators, and Hebb's cell-assembly constructs. These concepts tend also to enter into relatively informal theories. Others are more abstract and purely theoretical in that they have no direct observational or substantive correlates, are culturally derived, and tend to be associated with formal models. The proposition and structural descriptions are clear examples. Most of the remainder are mixed, neutral, or variable in their attributes (e.g., memory trace, features, prototype, schema, and logogen). In any case, the most relevant attributes and their implications will be identified.

Mental image

Imagery may be the oldest and is certainly the most persistent of all specific representational concepts. It has been the subject of discussion and study by philosophers and psychologists in Western culture from the time of Plato and Aristotle to the present. Its history has been marked by repeated controversy, first during the Protestant Reformation (see Paivio, 1971, chap. 5; Yates, 1966), then the behaviorist period in America, and, as already noted in chapter 1, contemporary cognitive psychology. Too compelling experientially to be denied or ignored, it has ranged in its explanatory status from that of a representational medium attributed with magical powers in memory and thought, to an epiphenomenon without functional significance. The swings occurred during each of the controversies, during which an imagery period was followed by a theoretical reaction associated with the rise of another representational concept, usually language-like in its form (inner speech, verbal mediator, proposition).

Why this conceptual persistence coupled with controversy? The simple answer to the first part is that imagery refers to an important psychological phenomenon of universal scope. Phenomenologically, it is experienced by people in all cultures in dreams as well as waking imagery. Its linkage with memory, thought, and language is compelling because people often image during those activities. It is natural, therefore, that early philosophers and psychologists would assign a causal role to imagery. However, such a view could not escape criticism because experienced images seem too specific in form to "stand for" abstract ideas and, as the Würzburg imageless-thought experiments demonstrated, they do not always accompany thinking. These and other objections were countered in various ways accompanied by the general conceptual stretching we have already noted. The major shift was from the original picture metaphor to a more psychological metaphor in which imagery was viewed as essentially equivalent to or at least similar to perceptual activity. Processing assumptions are necessary in both interpretations. Thus, the classical picture metaphor was accompanied by another metaphor, the Shakespearean mind's eye, so that we have the familiar idea of mental pictures that can be viewed by an inner eye in the same way as real pictures or scenes are viewed by the real eye. The subsequent perceptual metaphor was more of a processing interpretation in that imagery was equated with the conditioned activity of sensory and perceptual response systems rather than with mental pictures. Curiously, the swing of the conceptual pendulum has gone back to the picture-plus-inner eye metaphor, especially in the case of Kosslyn's (1980) theory, where it appears in the guise of a television set that permits an image to be generated on a screen and processed further by scanning, zooming, rotating, and other mechanisms, all under the control of a computer program. This sophisticated contemporary metaphor was itself a reaction to criticisms by other theorists who sought to replace the picture metaphor entirely by a propositional-computational metaphor. Kosslyn's solution essentially was to mix metaphors. I return to a further discussion of the implications of that approach in a later section, and a psychological alternative will be spelled out in the next chapter.

Memory trace

The mental image overlaps historically with the concept of the memory trace. In fact, the two concepts were once treated essentially as synonyms in the context of the metaphorical view that memories are images and images are like the impressions left by a signet ring on a wax tablet. The term memory trace is now used in a general theoretical sense to refer to any kind of psychological record or representation of past episodic experience. Moreover, the concept has undergone considerable stretching in that the trace is commonly viewed as having various components or attributes that correspond to spatial, temporal, associative, and other properties of the remembered event (e.g., Bower, 1967; Eich, 1982; Murdock, 1982; Underwood, 1969; Wickens, 1970). Finally, the hope persists that one day it might become an observational term identified with particular brain processes. If that happens, the concept will have shifted its metaphorical status completely from recording artifacts (wax tablets, etc.) to a physiological base. What will persist, however, is its fundamental status as a psychological representational concept to be defined and studied by behavioral procedure, as exemplified here in chapter 8.

Nonverbal mediators

The nonverbal mediator is a neobehavioristic concept that refers to processes that intervene between observable stimulus and response, and was introduced to account for S-R relations that seemed inexplicable in direct S-R terms alone. Behaviorists have generally described this mediating process in terms of covert stimulus-response chains that have exactly the same functional properties as overt S-R sequences. Osgood (1953) proposed a more complex theoretical construct with representational as well as mediational functions. This *representational mediation process* presumably consists of fractional response components that have been "detached" from overt responses and retain stimulus properties. Bundles of such fractional r_m-s_m components become conditioned to words or other stimuli and constitute their meaning. Analytically, therefore, Osgood's representational concept refers to processes that are psychologically real, highly abstract (detached from overt responses), and componential or atomic (rather than holistic) in nature.

Verbal mediators and the logogen

The terms verbal mediator and its conceptual equivalent, natural-language mediator, were used extensively as explanatory concepts in the context of verbal learning and memory research in the 1960s. The concepts are essentially specific versions of S-R mediators in that they refer to covert events that have the structural and functional properties of language (words, phrases, sentences) as perceived or produced. More abstract variants have also been proposed. The most important of these is Morton's (1969) concept of the *logogen*, which refers to a completely hypothetical mental representation that registers perceptual word information and makes a word response available when enough relevant information has accumulated. Thus, it is functionally like a word template or feature pattern (discussed further below) that is intended to account for word-recognition performance.

The original conception was that a logogen reacts to word information regardless of sensory modality and even to semantically relevant, contextual information. More recently, however, Morton (1979) found it necessary to redefine the concept in response to the observation that perceptual experience in one modality did not facilitate recognition of words presented in another modality. Morton accordingly expanded the logogen concept into modality-specific representations: visual-word logogens, auditory-word logogens, and output logogens. Moreover, he distinguished these from representations that are involved in picture recognition ("pictogens"). These empirical and theoretical developments are highly relevant to the theme of this book and I will say more about them later. Here, the important point to notice is that the logogen concept was stretched in order to accommodate empirical findings and that the stretching made the concept less abstract and more language-like, specifically in that it now has modality-specific functional properties.

Cell assembly

Various neuropsychological representational concepts have been proposed in the history of psychology and physiology. Hebb's (1949) cell-assembly construct is the best known and the most completely defined of those in terms of its hypothetical neurophysiological structure as well as its psychological (behavioral) origins and functions. Hebb has always insisted that the cell assembly is a hypothetical construct (see Hebb, 1980), but it nonetheless had a plausible observational base in the closed neuronal loops discovered by Lorente de Nó. Cell-assembly systems presumably arise from perceptual-motor experience and constitute the neuronal basis of thought and organized behavior. These systems are assumed to be hierarchically organized, with lower order assemblies corresponding to simple percepts, images, and so on, and higher order assemblies corresponding to more abstract ideas.

The theory had a liberating influence on physiological psychology and indirectly influenced the development of cognitive psychology. Moreover, references to its applicability to cognitive problems continue to appear in the literature. An especially relevant example is Barbara Hayes-Roth's (1977) extension of the theory to explain the acquisition, representation, and processing of knowledge. My own view (Paivio, 1982b), too, is that cell-assembly theory could be the basis of a plausible alternative to the computational models that constitute the dominant theoretical idiom in cognitive psychology today.

We turn next to a series of concepts that differ widely on specific characteristics (abstractness, holistic-componential, picturelike-languagelike) but all are intended to account for our ability to recognize and otherwise respond to specific instances as members of a general class (concepts, categories, stereotypical situations). Moreover, they do so using a matching process of some kind. These representational concepts are template, prototype, schema, and feature patterns.

Template

The concept of template was first applied to the analysis of pattern recognition (see Neisser, 1967, for a review), the idea being that recognition occurs when a perceptual pattern can be matched with a corresponding representation of such a pattern in long-term memory. Initially, the concept had connotations of high concreteness, specificity, and rigidity, much like the wax tablet model of the mental image. This version fell into disfavor because it could not account for findings that seemed to show that recognition accuracy was relatively unaffected by the orientation and retinal locus of the perceptual pattern. More recent studies suggest that the negative conclusion needs to be qualified. For example, Jolicoeur and Landau (1984) reported that they found strong and systematic effects of orientation on the identification of alphabetic characters. Such findings justify a reevaluation of the template concept, but in the meantime it has been largely replaced by the following "stretched" versions that are structurally and functionally more abstract than the earlier ones.

Prototype

The concept of prototype refers to representations of conceptual categories that correspond to such general terms as bird, animal, and furniture. One classical general interpretation was that the prototypical representation is some kind of composite of specific instances. A modern version of this idea is that the prototype is a statistical averaging of some kind, as in Posner and Keele's (1968) research on the generation of a prototype from exposure to specific instances of dot patterns. Another interpretation was that it is the specific instances themselves that stand for the category. The best known contemporary version of this exemplar view is Eleanor Rosch's idea (e.g., see Rosch, 1975b; Mervis & Pani, 1980) that categories are represented by "best examples"—redness by a particular "good" red, bird by robin or sparrow rather than turkey or penguin, and so on. Exemplar goodness is defined empirically by subjects' ratings and other responses, such as the speed with which they indicate that a particular instance is a member of a category. Rosch concluded from her research that good prototypes best combine the features that define a general category. She also suggested that the prototypes for perceptual categories like animal are somewhat more like images than they are like words, although she emphasized that they are mainly like neither but, rather, quite abstract in character. In any case, a prototype presumably can be accessed by either linguistic or nonlinguistic stimuli, since an experimental task may require a comparison between items of each class. This implies, too, that while the term refers to a generic representation that functions like a template, the processing assumptions go beyond that of simple perceptual matching. We shall have occasion to discuss alternative interpretations of performance on such tasks in chapter 7.

Schema

The term schema came into modern psychology through the writings of Head (1920), Piaget (1926), and Bartlett (1932). Schemata refer to mental structures that represent our general knowledge of objects, situations, and events. Current variants of the concept include frames (Minsky, 1975), scripts (Schank & Abelson, 1977), and ideals (Bregman, 1977). These concepts refer to perceptual knowledge as well as schematic descriptions, much like a verbal summary of the theme and main points of a scene. Models based on the script concept in particular have been applied to the analysis of reactions to passages that describe typical behavioral situations, such as dining in a restaurant or visits to doctors or dentists. The assumption is that a script includes general perceptual knowledge of the objects and events in such settings, as well as knowledge of how one typically behaves in relation to them. Such knowledge structures are usually assumed to be hierarchically organized, so that the restaurant script, for example, might include general knowledge pertaining to ordering and eating a meal, and more specific, lower-level verbal and behavioral components such as asking for the wine menu and using a fork. Alternatively, scripts could be viewed simply as sequentially organized event structures without any assumption of levels of generality, although this is not the usual interpretation.

Variants of the schema concept have been used in the analysis of perceptual recognition, memory, motor skills, and understanding of discourse. In the case of perception, a specific stimulus pattern is compared with a schematic representation, much as in template matching. Recognition is achieved if the stimulus represents a possible "instantiation" of the schematic pattern. Similar processes are assumed to occur in memory and comprehension. Memory for a particular stimulus would involve activation of a schematic representation plus storage of additional information corresponding to unique aspects of the stimulus—a process Woodworth (1938) described as "schema plus correction." Comprehension is similarly achieved when a text passage activates a schema and the specific content of the text can be interpreted as an appropriate instantiation of the schema. The schema concept would be supported by such evidence as subjects filling in missing information in systematic ways, as though a more complete, stereotypical schema had been activated by the incomplete input. Bartlett's (1932) idea that memory is constructive was based on such observations.

Concepts of this class have been useful but rather vague in regard to the form of representation (perceptual or descriptive) as well as its function in various tasks. How exactly is plausible instantiation evaluated? How is information about specific detail (the "correction" to schema) stored and retrieved along with the generic schema? Such questions arose in connection with a similar idea (G. Miller, 1962), derived from transformational grammar, that sentences are stored in memory as kernel strings (sentence schemata) together with grammatical tags. The "script pointer plus tag" (Graesser, Gordon, & Sawyer, 1979) and "ideal plus transformation" (Bregman, 1977) hypotheses are specific examples of the same idea applied to schema concepts. The linguistic hypothesis failed for lack of consistent empirical support (see Paivio, 1971, chap. 12), and the schema version has already been questioned on the same grounds (Alba & Hasher, 1983; for a response to their critique, see J. Mandler, 1984, pp. 109–113).

Chapter 10 presents an alternative interpretation of schema as applied to text processing.

Features

We have already seen that feature representations were first used systematically in the analysis of speech sounds (Jakobson, Fant, & Halle, 1951). Phonemes are described in terms of *articulatory* features (e.g., consonantal, labial) or *acoustic* features (e.g., resonant, spirant), which are usually treated as binary dimensions. A given phoneme is viewed as a pattern of such features, so that b, for example, is +consonantal, +stop, +labial, and +voice. This approach allows for descriptive parsimony in that a relatively small set of features can be used to classify all of the phonemes of a language, and it reveals the systematic relations between different sounds in terms of the number and kind of distinctive features in their descriptions.

Phonemic features have empirical correlates in that articulatory and acoustic patterns can be directly observed. The observational status of the features concept is less clear when it is extended to other phenomena. In the case of visual pattern perception, the discovery of feature detectors in the visual cortex of the cat (Hubel & Wiesel, 1962) provided a possible neurophysiological base for visual features. However, the original concept has been progressively stretched when applied to such problems as reading. E. J. Gibson's (1969) distinctive feature approach to reading is patterned after phonological feature theory in that letters are defined in terms of simple binary features such as having horizontal or vertical lines, closedness, and symmetry. Others postulate more complex features that result from combinations of simpler ones into higher-order patterns in a hierarchical manner.

Further extensions of the concept are even more complex. One is the extension from discrete to continuous features. Another is the shift from features that are physically measurable to ones that are defined entirely by psychological scaling techniques and are essentially semantic in nature. Discreteness and semanticity are combined in traditional componential models of semantic representation, which describe lexical units in terms of such features as animate, human, and the like. Continuous dimensions are assumed in other semantic models, such as Osgood's. Different levels of complexity can also be found in the structural assumptions of feature theories. The simplest structural model is the unordered feature list where such entities as phonemes and letters are assumed to be represented as plus or minus values on all of the features needed to describe such entities. A more complex structure is the feature "stack" in which the features are ordered in terms of some measure of saliency or importance. Still more complex is the spatial representation that is generated by factor-analytic and multidimensional scaling procedures, where an object is assumed to be mentally represented as a point in a multidimensional space (e.g., Osgood, Suci, & Tannenbaum, 1957; Shepard, 1962).

Finally, a different order of complexity was introduced by the use of relational features in semantic and perceptual analyses. The rationale in the case of semantic models was that the relationship between terms like *father* and *son* cannot be described adequately by any simple distinguishing feature such as old versus young, but requires instead some relational designation such as *is parent of* versus *is child of* (e.g., Bierwisch, 1970). Perceptual models based on structural descriptions use similar relational features to represent perceptual patterns (e.g., the letter H might be described as the connection of a horizontal line to the middle of two vertical lines). When the structural description includes both simple features expressed in terms of unitary dimensional values and relational descriptions, the result is a hybrid called *augmented structural descriptions* (Palmer, 1978). These permit one to describe such "emergent properties" as size and symmetry that result when lines are combined to form a square. Palmer suggests that such models are so powerful that they are no longer a theory because there are no principled limits on what kind of information can be represented. We can have atomic features such as lines or points, relational information such as middle-top connected, and even such global or holistic descriptive information as size and symmetry.

Feature representations are functionally similar to templates in that theories based on them assume that a feature-coded input pattern is compared against similarly coded representations of pattern types (feature templates, descriptions, etc.) in long-term memory. The input pattern is classified as being a member of the representational category to which it is most similar, depending on the match criterion used by the model. Such models accordingly need to specify how features are represented psychologically, and the nature of the processing mechanisms in the analysis of an input pattern into a feature list or description and its subsequent comparison against the stored representations. All representational models have similar requirements, but the componential nature of feature-based models makes them particularly problematic in this regard. For example, feature components could be defined as modality-specific, perceptual building blocks in the Hubel and Wiesel sense, or more generally as any property of an object "that can be deduced from our general knowledge of the world" (A. Tversky, 1977), or they could be viewed as completely amodal theoretical entities that are defined only in terms of descriptive labels. Such problems come up again in chapter 3 in the context of representational theories and in chapter 4 in relation to dual coding theory.

Proposition

We turn, finally, to the proposition, which is the most abstract and theoretical (least observational) representational concept of all. It is also the most widely used one in computational models of cognition. At one level, it serves as a kind of *lingua franca* that can be used to characterize psychological phenomena or redefine other theoretical constructs. For example, it is popular today to describe mental images and to recast feature representations, structural descriptions, and schema in propositional terms. At another level, it is treated as a "real" mental representational unit that serves as the basic building block of general knowledge structures. In view of its popularity, generality, and flexibility, this representational concept deserves careful examination.

Recall from the last chapter that a proposition is basically a truth statement. It was given that meaning in the context of symbolic logic, where truth refers to the internal consistency of a statement within the set of statements that constitute a logical system. Accordingly, the truth value of a proposition is evaluated in terms of its logical consistency: It is true if it follows logically from other statements, otherwise it is false. This definition applies as well to the concept as used in formal scientific models. It follows that such a "definition of a proposition of a scientific model rules out of consideration all truth statements having to do with the correspondence between the predictions of the model and the empirical domain it purports to represent" (Dubin, 1969, p. 166).

The concept has been stretched in cognitive psychology as well as philosophy so that propositional truth is now taken to refer specifically to the correspondence between a proposition and the "empirical domain it purports to represent." For example, Palmer (1978) asserted that *"whatever structure there is in a propositional representation exists solely by virtue of the extrinsic constraints placed on it by the truth-preserving informational correspondence with the represented world"* (1978, p. 296). Thus, in that respect at least, propositions are like natural-language statements that correspond semantically to external objects and events. Unlike languages, however, propositional representations are assumed to be completely amodal, abstract conceptual structures that represent information in the same way regardless of whether the information is experienced verbally, as a spoken or written sentence in whatever language, or nonverbally, as a perceptual scene.

Propositions play a theoretical role in information-processing models, in which they are associated with different processing assumptions. For example, models of sentence comprehension vary in their assumptions concerning the order in which the units of the (propositional) sentence-information are processed. One view is that active and passive sentences alike are processed in the order, logical subject-verb-logical object (Chase & Clark, 1972); another is that the processing sequence varies with the surface structure of the sentence (Olson & Filby, 1972); and a third is that the relational information (i.e., the verb) is processed first (J. Glucksberg, Trabasso, & Wald, 1973). The point is that propositional representations are neutral with respect to how the information is processed psychologically, and that processing assumptions must be included if such models are to have any predictive or explanatory value.

The proposition is the most versatile of representational concepts because it can be used to describe any kind of information, but such versatility also invites confusion when the concept is used in an explanatory sense. Its application to mental imagery is an apt example because of the variety of forms the propositional interpretation has taken. An extreme view is that images are nothing but propositions. A less extreme view is that images are psychologically real, much like perceptual experiences, but *generated from* propositional representations. A third proposal is that images are independent, nonpropositional representations, but they are *interpreted* propositionally. The reverse relation has also been implied, viz., that propositional representations might be interpreted with respect to images. These contrasting views and their sources are discussed in detail in the next chapter.

The proposition is also versatile in the sense that other representational concepts can be recast in propositional terms. This possibility was already mentioned above in regard to features, templates, schemata, and prototypes, and further applications can be found in the psychological literature. For example, Wilson (1980, p. 110) proposed that Tolman's concept of expectancy, interpreted as an S-R structure (MacCorquodale & Meehl, 1954), is essentially a proposition of the form "if response R is made when state S holds, then state S will result." These examples illustrate just how far the original concept of proposition has been stretched by cognitive theorists, and we might wonder whether there are any principled limits to such expansions. Such concerns come up repeatedly in subsequent discussions, particularly when rationalist-computational approaches to cognition are contrasted with empiricist ones.

This concludes our summary of representational concepts. It will serve as a background for subsequent topics, including the discussion in the following chapter of three general attitudes and approaches to such concepts as well as the psychological phenomena that purportedly require their adoption.

3
Attitudes and Approaches to Representation

Theorists who have used or commented on representational concepts and models can be classified as *sceptics, empiricists,* or *rationalists.* A fourth category includes those who have tried to adopt the best of empiricist and rationalist approaches, and their views will be identified. We begin with scepticism because the concerns of the sceptics need to be understood if representational theorists are to avoid serious theoretical and empirical errors. Empiricism follows because modern rationalism arose as a reaction to perceived shortcomings in the empiricists' approach and is understandable only against that background. We shall see that the three approaches contact each other in rather curious and surprising ways.

REPRESENTATIONAL SCEPTICS

The main sceptics are the radical behaviorists as represented particularly by B. F. Skinner. A less radical form was expressed by the perceptual theorist, J. J. Gibson (1966; 1979), and still less extreme is the hint of scepticism in Kolers's (e.g., 1978) theory of representations as skills.

Scepticism may be too mild a label for Skinner's blunt rejection of all mentalistic concepts, which is historically continuous with Watson's (1913) critique of mentalism.

Skinner (e.g., 1953, 1963, 1975) directs his arguments specifically against self-observation and models of the conceptual nervous system or mind. He insists that the events observed as the life of the mind play no causal or explanatory role in behavior. They are simply "collateral products" of that behavior, themselves in need of explanation. Moreover, this "fascination with an inner life has allayed curiosity about the further steps to be taken" (1975, p. 46) in the study of the organism as a behaving system. Information theory, cybernetics, systems analyses, mathematical models, and cognitive psychology are singled out as contemporary examples of such mind-modelling enterprises, based on the computer as the dominant metaphor. Skinner adds that his comment "about the introspectively observed mind applies as well to the mind that is constructed from observations of the behavior of others" (pp. 45–46). Thus, the status of mentalistic concepts is the same whether they are derived from introspective, rational-computational, or empirical procedures.

These devastating assertions might be valid if his premise concerning causality were acceptable, but we shall see that it appears to be too restrictive even for Skinner. The following task will concretize the argument: "Think of a cube, all six surfaces of which are painted red. Divide the cube into 27 equal cubes making two horizontal cuts and two vertical cuts each. How many resulting cubes will have three faces painted red, how many two, how many one, and how many none?" A quotation from some mentalistic psychologist, perhaps from the introspective era? Surprisingly not. It comes instead from Skinner's (1953) analysis of private problem solving. He goes on to say that "one may see the larger cube, *cut* it covertly, *separate* the smaller cubes covertly, *see* their faces, *count* them subvocally, and so on, seeing the result in each case, until the solution is reached. Presumably much of the covert behavior is similar in form to the overt manipulation of pencil and paper, the rest is discriminative behavior in the form of seeing numbers, letters, signs, and so on, which is similar to the behavior which would result from overt manipulation" (1953, p. 273).

It could be argued that Skinner is being inconsistent in using such examples and assuming at the same time that the private events play no causal role in the solution of the problem, but that would be missing his point. Skinner's reasoning is that the private event "is at best no more than a link in a causal chain, and it is usually not even that. We may think before we act in the sense that we behave covertly before we behave overtly, but our action is not an 'expression' of the covert response or the consequence of it. The two are attributable to the same variables" (1953, p. 279). Those variables are to be found in the stimulus situation and the person's prior (reinforced) experiences with cubes, colors, slicing, counting, and so on.

Skinner's otherwise reasonable argument is based on the questionable premise that a causal explanation should be restricted to historical factors alone. This restriction excludes too much from the explanation, particularly if the problem solver has never encountered the task before. In that case, private events play a direct causal role in that they must function in a creative way if the problem is to be solved. Skinner admitted as much when he remarked that the "private response may produce discriminative stimuli which prove useful in executing further behavior of either a private or public nature" (1953, p. 273). If they are useful, then the private events cannot be *trivial* links in the causal chain.

The cube visualization problem is relevant here because Skinner used it to illustrate his behavioristic analysis of private problem solving and to support his arguments concerning causality. I have argued that the example negates Skinner's claims, but experimental tasks discussed in subsequent chapters do so even more persuasively because some of the crucial antecedent conditions are under experimental control. We shall see, for example, that contrasting effects of apparently trivial instructional cues *cause* participants to generate different kinds of functionally useful mental representation, or at least behave as if they had done so.

I conclude that radical behaviorists are trying to have their cake and eat it too when it comes to the analysis of mental representations. They are fascinated enough with an "inner life" to try to interpret it in behavioristic terms and yet they deny it any causal role in behavior. The denial is possible only because they adopt a narrow view of causality whereby all effective causes are *asserted* to lie in the experiential history of the individual rather than in the current "mental life" that has resulted from that history. It would be more consistent with the radical behaviorist philosophy simply to avoid discussing private events altogether, but then the domain of a science of behavior would be narrow indeed.

There is, however, another aspect to the Skinnerian argument that deserves to be heeded by representational theorists. Whereas Skinner is too extreme in denying a causal role to all mental events, he is absolutely right in emphasizing that the hypothetical inner determiners are themselves in need of explanation and that an important part of that explanation is to be found in the learning history of the individual. For example, how does one learn to image to verbal instructions as in the cube visualization task or, conversely, to describe one's images? What precisely are the controlling variables involved in such language-to-image and image-to-language interchanges and how do they originate developmentally? Such skills obviously must originate somehow from associative experiences with language and the child's perceptual-motor reactions to things, but how? We have no precise answers to such questions concerning imagery and other phenomena at the moment.

James Gibson's (1966) rejection of representational concepts was based on his theory that perception is information pickup and that the stimulus situation contains the necessary information. Because that information is already organized, the brain does not need to *impose* organization on the input by any process. Thus, one is relieved of the need to postulate ideas, images, traces, or storehouses of memory left behind by sensations. Recognition is not the successful matching of a new percept with the trace of an old one, but rather "the tuning of a perceptual system to the invariants of stimulus information" that allow for the judgment that a place, object, or person is the same. Conversely, the absence of invariants leads to the judgment "different" (p. 278). By the same account, associations are not learned in the traditional sense for they are already there, in the invariance of stimulus combinations, and the organism learns to detect those invariants (p. 272). Expectancies, too, can be explained as cases of perceiving sequential invariants or contingencies in the environment. The learning process in all such cases is based on an "education of attention to the information in available stimulation" (p. 270), a kind of tuning of the perceptual systems to the invariants in a changing environment. The mechanisms include learning to detect the distinct features of objects so they can be differentiated (cf. E. J. Gibson, 1969), to register covariation of inputs from different systems (haptic, visual, etc.), to learn the "affordances" (values, uses, meanings) of objects, and so on. Similar arguments appear in Gibson (1979).

Gibson's theory is important and influential. Nonetheless, I am left in the end with the feeling that in one respect it simply rephrases the problem of representation in such terms as "registering of invariants," or "tuning of a perceptual system to the invariants." Such statements beg the question of the nature of the registering and tuning system, and in particular the modifications that make it possible for the perceiver to attend and respond selectively to environmental objects, relations, and events. We could argue alternatively that such changes in the perceptual system *are* the traces or representations that result from past experience. This interpretation is particularly compelling in the case of such experiences as hallucinations, which Gibson (1966) reinterpreted as a "search for meaning" under conditions of impoverished stimulation and inadequate information (pp. 303–304). But if the information necessary for meaningful hallucinations is not in the environment, where can it be if not in the mind of the perceiver? And so, Gibson has given us a novel way of conceptualizing the problems of perception and memory, but he has not relieved us of the problem of representation of information.

Kolers (1978; Kolers & Roediger, 1984; Kolers & Smythe, 1979, 1984) holds a theoretical view somewhat like Gibson's in that its emphasis is on the means by which knowledge is acquired rather than on the storage of representational entities. Thus, Kolers and Smythe (1979, p. 158) "develop the notion that rather than in a representation-process sort of theory, cognitive processes be understood in terms of skills in the manipulation of symbols and in the relating of symbols to the semantic domains that they map." Still, this approach does not call for a complete rejection of the concept of representation but only of its currently popular computational versions. Moreover, Kolers's preferred alternative is empirically based, and for that reason he should be grouped with the theorists considered in the next section.

REPRESENTATIONAL EMPIRICISTS

Representational empiricism characterizes those approaches that Skinner described (and rejected) as "the mind that is constructed from observations of the behavior of others," or what I referred to as objective or behavioral mentalism (Paivio, 1975c). It stems from British empiricism and the theory that knowledge derives from experience and is based on associations between ideas. American structuralism and functionalism were part of the historical chain because images and other forms of mental representation constituted their subject matter, but their reliance on subjective (introspective) methods removes them somewhat from my definition. Specific antecedents that do fit the definition include Galton's (1883) studies of mental imagery and mental words, and the objective studies of memory by Binet (1894) and Ebbinghaus (1885/1964) and Hunter's (1913) delayed-reaction experiments, in which an animal's choice behavior seemed explainable only in terms of some kind of cognitive representation of the situation. Leeper (1951) provided a useful review of such behavioral evidence for cognitive processes in both animals and humans.

Hebb's (1949) neuropsychological theory is another landmark in behavioral mentalism. According to Hebb, the behavioral evidence for attention and mental set demanded a mechanism for maintaining activity in the brain between stimulus input and response output. The closed neural circuits of cell-assembly theory provided that mechanism. Assumed to result from perceptual exploration of objects, cell assemblies and their activity constitute the neural basis of perception, imagery, abstract ideas, and whatever else is involved in thinking. The theory served to integrate seemingly contradictory facts about perception and learning, provide a physiological basis for the distinction between short-term and long-term memory, and so on. It also generated some unusual predictions and experiments on the effects of early experience on perceptual development, and on the nature of perceptual fluctuation when the retinal image is stablized.

The experimental results supported aspects of the theory and refuted others. Such findings together with new neurophysiological discoveries motivated changes in the model (see Hebb, 1980) that were intended to account for the discrepancies and for other recent observations. The details are not necessary for present purposes. The general point is that this was the first comprehensive theory of the representational units and structures that are the hypothetical basis of conceptual activity at different levels of abstractness. The approach is empiricist because the theoretical concepts were based on inferences from the facts of behavior and neurophysiology. Moreover, the empiricism is constructive in that Hebb views his model as a working hypothesis that is to be believed only to the extent that it is empirically adequate.

Behaviorism also branched out into a variety of empirically based representational approaches. Osgood's (1953) mediational theory is a clear example because its r_m-s_m units are assumed to be derived, via conditioning, from behaviors to things and to retain some of the functional properties of those behaviors. Other cognitive behaviorists have relied similarly on such experientially based representational-mediational constructs as cognitive maps (Tolman, 1948), and images viewed as conditioned sensory responses (Mowrer, 1960; Sheffield, 1961; Staats, 1968). These are all examples of behavioral mentalism by my definition, with behavioristic concepts replacing mentalistic ones.

Two other empirical-theoretical streams have had a major influence on the development of this neomentalism. One is the rote-memory tradition that began with Ebbinghaus (1885/1964) and the other is the information-processing approach to perception and memory launched by Broadbent (1958). Mediational concepts were introduced into the rote-memory tradition when it became apparent that even nonsense syllables were not meaningless. Thus, memory researchers (e.g., Noble, 1952; Underwood & Schulz, 1960) interpreted the meanings of nonsense syllables and their effects on memory in terms of verbal mediators, which are assumed to be activated by stimulus words in a probabilistic fashion determined by past experience and predictable from word-association norms.

The memory tradition took on an even more mentalistic flavor with Bousfield's (1953) research on category clustering in free recall. The fact that subjects recalled randomly ordered words in conceptually related clusters implied that they had reorganized the input list mentally in a systematic fashion. Bousfield originally suggested, in Hebbian terms, that categories correspond to higher-order cell assemblies and category members correspond to lower-order assemblies. Presentation of the category instances activated both levels of assemblies and recall was mediated beginning at the category level—a top-down processing interpretation by some current accounts. During the same period, Jenkins and Russell (1952) observed pairwise-clustering in the recall of associatively related words that had been randomly ordered during presentation. This finding permitted a more traditional verbal-mediational interpretation of organization. The general implication of both findings nonetheless was the same, namely, that memory is not rote reproduction but involves active reorganization of the input material by the memorizer, a view that was in essential agreement with Bartlett's (1932) earlier constructivist approach to memory.

Broadbent's (1958) information processing approach to perception and memory inspired other similar models that varied in their processing assumptions and the range of memory phenomena they were intended to explain (e.g., Atkinson & Shiffrin, 1968; Sperling, 1960; Sternberg, 1967). Again, it is unnecessary to go into the details of these developments here. The important point to note is that the theories became progressively more mentalistic, incorporating assumptions about memory structures and the processes that operate on them as information passes through different stages (sensory, short-term, and long-term memory "boxes") of the structural system. The memory models were clearly representational models— entirely hypothetical, but constructed on the basis of experimental data, used for generating predictions about memory performance under novel conditions, and modified as necessary to account for new findings. The approach accordingly qualifies as behavioral mentalism and, more generally, as a constructive empiricist enterprise.

The storage-boxes structural metaphor is no longer in vogue. The newer developments include an increasing emphasis on the analysis of the nature of the information contained in the memory trace, and on memory processing rather than structure. As we have already seen, the analysis has culminated in the view that the memory trace is a componential representation that includes information about different attributes of the stimulus: modality, sequence, associative relations, and so on. The second development was the processing-depth approach advocated by Craik and Lockhart (1972). These two empirically driven approaches differ in that the attention in one is on memory representation and in the other, on process. I will have more to say about them in relation to the dual coding approach to memory proposed in subsequent chapters.

The most clearly mentalistic of the empiricist developments also evolved out of the memory tradition. This is the study of mental imagery. Its roots in Western culture go back to the use of imagery as a mnemonic aid as proposed originally by Simonides around 500 B.C.E. (for a detailed history, see Yates, 1966; a briefer account appears in Paivio, 1971). It reemerged in the modern era as part of the general movement away from behaviorism and, more specifically, as a reaction against the verbal emphasis that continued to dominate the Ebbinghaus tradition, even in its mediational forms. The general assumption was that memory performance could be mediated by nonverbal images even when the information to be remembered was verbal. Powerful effects attributable to imagery were demonstrated in an increasing number of experimental studies beginning in the early 1960s (e.g., see Bower, 1972; Bugelski, 1970; Paivio, 1969; Reese, 1970; Rohwer, 1970; comprehensive reviews are available in several languages: Cornoldi, 1976; Denis, 1979; Paivio, 1971; J. Richardson, 1980). This empirical-theoretical work is a prototypical example of behavioral mentalism. Mental imagery was manipulated empirically by imagery instructions and by varying the image-evoking value of items. The functions of imagery were inferred from performance in tasks that differentially emphasized memory for items, associations, sequential order, and so on. The results led to specific analyses of the memory functions of imagery and to the more general dual coding theory of cognition to be described in its updated form in the next chapter.

The studies of the functions of imagery in memory were followed by studies designed to reveal the structural properties of mental images. These began with Shepard's multidimensional scaling studies of the structure of mental maps (Shepard & Chipman, 1970) and his elegant, reaction-time experiments on mental rotations (e.g., Cooper & Shepard, 1973; Shepard & Metzler, 1971). The reaction-time approach was subsequently extended to mental comparisons of object names or pictures on such symbolic (memory) attributes as size (e.g., Moyer, 1973; Paivio, 1975d), and the time to "scan" mental images (Kosslyn, 1973). The results permitted inferences to be made about the structure of mental images at a relatively fine-grained level, and the nature of the processes that operate on such images. These inferences were expressed as models of specific tasks, such as mental rotation (e.g., Shepard, 1978), and a more general theory of mental images (Kosslyn, 1980). The research represents constructive empiricism inasmuch as the models were based on behavioral data. We shall see in the next section, however, that Kosslyn has also tried to capture the best of both the empiricist and rationalist approaches by expressing his theory in computational terms.

A specific feature of the empiricist approaches deserves special emphasis because it contrasts sharply with its parallel in current rationalist theories. This feature is the assumption that mental representations are ultimately modality specific in character. Thus, verbal mediational theorists assumed that the effective mediators are implicit verbal responses. Empiricist approaches to imagery assume that images are analogue representations in the sense that the represented information is modality specific (e.g., visual) and isomorphic with perceptual information in a strong sense. The attribute approaches to memory imply that representations are multimodal. We might note, too, that Kolers (1978), though critical of current structural approaches to the representation of knowledge, nonetheless assumes in his procedural approach that representations are means dependent rather than totally abstract.

The stage models of memory also included modality-specific representational assumptions. Thus, the sensory store was assumed to store information about the input modality of items for a brief period and the short-term store was generally assumed to be auditory-motor-linguistic in character. However, the theorists were vague with respect to long-term memory representation and simply assumed on empirical grounds that the stored information was semantic. This assumption raised the question of what "semantic" means, and opened the way for the development of semantic-memory models that incorporated computational-rationalistic assumptions, including the view that semantic representations are amodal.

An evaluation of the empiricist approaches will lead us appropriately into rationalistic views. As already mentioned, the main evaluative criterion was predictive and explanatory success, and many of the empirically derived representational constructs proved to be inadequate on those grounds. For example, verbal mediational approaches to memory had difficulty with organizational phenomena and simply failed to account for the mnemonic effects of imagery variables. A logical criterion was added to the picture from the rationalist side. It began with Chomsky's view that stimulus-response theories of language are essentially finite-state models, and that such models cannot account for syntactic creativity. Fodor (1965) argued similarly that meaning cannot be explained by covert responses (r_m's) because they have the same properties as the overt responses from which they are derived, and so they also suffer from the inadequacies of nonmediational S-R theories. This line of reasoning was generalized and formalized as the so-called *terminal-meta-postulate* (see chap. 1), which was asserted to be the downfall of any theory that describes mediational or representational processes in the same language that is used to describe overt behavior. I leave further discussion of that issue to chapter 4, where I hope to show that, whatever the general merits of the critique, it does not apply to certain classes of empiricist theories, and in particular the dual coding theory described in that chapter.

RATIONALISTIC APPROACHES

The rationalism to be discussed here is closely tied to computational ideas. In view of this association, it is important to recognize that reliance on the computer does not necessarily imply rationalism. Some researchers simply use the computer to *simulate* information-processing models of intellectual activities, which they also test against human performance. Simulation was the aim in the early work by Simon and Feigenbaum (1964) on the "elementary problem solver and memorizer" (EPAM) program, and subsequently by Newell and Simon (1972) on human problem solving generally. This is true also of some computational models of long-term or semantic memory (e.g., J. Anderson, 1983; J. Anderson & Bower, 1973). Johnson-Laird's (1983) approach is an especially clear example because he stresses computability (implementation in the form of a computer program) as a criterion for psychological theories but insists at the same time that adopting this criterion does not imply that human beings are "nothing but computers" or that they are "computable" (p. 8). Moreover, he explicitly departs from classical rationalism in his theoretical approach to the psychology of reasoning. Because such theories are both computational and tested against observable facts and revised as necessary, it might be appropriate to say that they entail "computational empiricism" rather than computational rationalism. Nonetheless, most computational approaches tend to have a stronger rationalistic flavor than do the noncomputational forms of behavioral mentalism discussed in the preceding section.

We noted at the outset that rationalism as a dominant movement in modern philosophy of science began as a reaction to logical positivism (e.g., see van Fraassen, 1980). In psychology, the reaction began with Chomsky's (1959) critique of Skinner's (1957) book, *Verbal behavior*, and progressed into theoretical and research approaches in which innate determinants of behavior were increasingly emphasized. The developing rationalism was accompanied and, indeed, fostered by the explosive development of computer science and technology, whose rationalist connection lies in the formalism that is basic both to computational systems and the logical reasoning process by which rationalists hoped to arrive at true knowledge. The connection goes deeper than that, however, and implicates all of the tenets of classical rationalism. Let us examine these and see how they apply to particular representational ideas.

Classical rationalism from Plato to Descartes included at least the following assumptions: (a) that true knowledge can be arrived at by reasoning, (b) that the reasoning must follow logical procedures, (c) that elementary or basic true ideas (from which other truths follow by logical argument) are derived through intuition and not through sense data, and (d) that such ideas, not being empirically derived, must therefore be innate.

These assumptions show up in the following ways in contemporary rationalistic approaches to the study of mental representations. First, the emphasis on logical reasoning is essential if the computer is to be used as a model of mind. It follows that a computational mind must use descriptive units and elementary statements (propositions) to build logically organized knowledge structures. These features are the basis of computational models of language and semantic memory. The classical reliance on intuition and rejection of empiricism reemerges today as a relative emphasis on intuitive and speculative approaches coupled with a relative neglect of experimental and other observational procedures and data. Finally, the doctrine of innate ideas reemerges essentially in its pristine form but with its implications more fully developed: The basis of knowledge is found in innate mental structures, which function as filters for sense data and determine their manifest form in observable language or other behavior.

Plato and Descartes used geometric knowledge to illustrate their arguments concerning innate ideas. Since we never experience perfect circles or triangles but nonetheless have the idea of such perfect forms or ideals, the ideal must be innately given. The modern concepts of prototype, schema, deep structure, and the like, are all related to this idea. Bregman (1977) even adopted the term "ideal" and related it approvingly to the Platonic original. Of course, a nativist view is not logically necessary for the acceptance of the idea of schema, and Piaget (e.g., 1980) and others have explicitly adopted a constructivist approach according to which schemata are cognitively constructed on the basis of sense data.

Representational theorists vary in the degree to which they adopt the classical rationalist assumptions. Chomsky is clearly at the upper extreme because he argues strongly for the doctrine of innate mental structures, shows a relatively strong preference for intuitive or speculative methods, rejects empiricist philosophy, and deemphasizes empiricist methodology. For example, following an approving discussion of Descartes's views concerning innate ideas, Chomsky outlined its implications for a universal generative grammar and then concluded as follows: "I believe that these proposals can be properly regarded as a further development of classical rationalist doctrine, as an elaboration of some of its main ideas regarding language and mind. Of course, such a theory will be repugnant to one who accepts empiricist doctrine and regards it as immune to question or challenge" (1968, p. 73). Chomsky thereby affirmed both his rationalist approach and its contrast with empiricism. His nativistic theory of language acquisition, the so-called language-acquisition device, or LAD (Chomsky, 1965) explicitly reflected that philosophy. The rationalism extends to methodology in that Chomsky has argued that the essential facts about language are available to everyone and, therefore, it suffices for theorists to draw on their linguistic intuitions as the data base for analysis of language. Subsequent writings (e.g., Caplan & Chomsky, 1982) indicate that these views remain essentially unchanged.

Fodor's (1975) views are in some respects even more extremely rationalistic. First, he asserts that "The only psychological models of cognitive processes that seem even remotely plausible represent such processes as computational" (1975, p. 27). Second, he reasoned that one can learn a natural language only if one already knows a language rich enough to express what can be expressed in the natural language. Thus, the original (internal) language or, more generally, the first conceptual system must be innately determined (pp. 79–97). However, Fodor is more empirical than Chomsky in that he relies relatively more on objective data to support his "speculative psychology."

The extreme forms of nativistic rationalism are stultifying in regard to the growth of empirical and theoretical understanding of the wide variety of cognitive and behavioral phenomena that must be learned in some way. For example, the great variety of surface forms of human language cannot be explained by any explicit nativistic hypothesis such as Chomsky's LAD. The crucial and complex question of how the various linguistic performance skills are acquired is relegated to a secondary and relatively minor position in the Chomskyan program. Its reliance on formal constraints to define the possible linguistic structures that can be learned by a child leaves it open to charges of circularity and other limitations of formal rationalism described below. These charges apply as well to recent developmental elaborations of Chomsky's ideas by others (see chap. 5).

Weaker forms of rationalism appear in other contemporary approaches to mental representation. For example, J. Anderson and Bower (1973) suggest that their theory of human associative memory is partly rationalistic (nativistic) and partly empiricistic. The rationalistic components of their model are the perceptual and linguistic parsers that encode sensory information so that it can be used by the long-term (associative) memory system. The latter is the empirical component that stores the experientially determined information in the form of propositional networks. Anderson's and Bower's rationalism is quite weak because they have not attempted to specify the nature of the innate structural properties of the parsers in HAM and no predictive consequences arise from them. Only the empirically acquired properties of the long-term memory component are spelled out in the detail necessary to use it as an explanatory and predictive model.

The Anderson and Bower position is essentially like that of all psychologists concerned with learning and memory. All accept the idea that organisms come to a learning situation with biologically determined capacities that limit what can be learned, but their strategy is to focus on learning because such complex skills as speaking and tying shoe laces are obviously a product of experience.

Other computational theorists are committed to the rationalistic assumption that the mind is a logical device that operates according to formal rules.

As noted in the preceding chapter, such a view entails a preference for a "top-down" theoretical strategy in which empirical tests are postponed while attention is devoted to the development of internally consistent models of representational processes. The representations are viewed as descriptive or propositional entities that are abstract and neutral (amodal) with respect to stimulus modality and specific response systems. Thus, the general approach contrasts sharply with the empiricist ones that make use of representational concepts that are defined in terms of modality-specific properties of some kind. The differences show up most clearly in the analysis of mental images, as illustrated by the following quotation:

> The *propositional representation* position on the nature of imagery has been proposed by J. Anderson and Bower (1973, p. 451ff.), Pylyshyn (1973), and Simon (1972), and is related to proposals made by Schank (1972), Palmer (1975), and others. This position is based on the argument that all knowledge, regardless of its source modality, can be expressed in a single uniform, abstract, type of representation, the *proposition*. Unlike the dual-code position, there is no fundamental difference in how perceptually based and verbally based information is represented in memory. (Kieras, 1978, pp. 533–534)

The strong contrast between the propositional and (image-based) dual coding positions was initially adopted relatively uncritically by propositional theorists. Perhaps as a result of logical and empirical counterarguments (Kosslyn & Pomerantz, 1977; Paivio, 1974a, 1977), the debate subsequently took a new turn in that some propositional theorists compromised their own position while some imagery researchers moved partly into the propositional camp.

J. Anderson (1978) compared a theory identified as "basically the dual-coding model of Paivio (1971)" with propositional theories and concluded on logical and empirical grounds that the controversy is at an impasse in that either model can be constructed to accommodate existing data. The logical argument was only possible, however, because Anderson assumed that both theories could be completely formalized. Consistent with that position, he ended up suggesting a common representational format for dual coding, namely, spatial and linguistic propositions. Kieras (1978) reviewed the two approaches in the context of verbal-memory data and conceded that imagery *variables* are effective in such tasks. Like Anderson, however, he compromised by proposing that there are two kinds of propositional descriptions, one appropriate for nonverbal perceptual information and the other, for linguistic information. Subsequent exchanges between the defenders of different views (e.g., Kosslyn, 1981; Pylyshyn, 1981) did not resolve the differences.

The compromising imagery position came from Kosslyn and his collaborators (e.g., Kosslyn, 1980; Kosslyn, Pinker, Smith, & Schwartz, 1979), who proposed a computer simulation model in which mental images are assumed to function like pictures generated by a television set in that they can be scanned, rotated, and otherwise operated on by various processing components in the system. The important point to note here is that images are assumed to be generated from abstract propositional descriptions. It follows that the strengths and limitations of Kosslyn's model must rest on the strengths and limitations of propositional representations; otherwise, the propositional-base assumption plays no functional role in the model. I will return to the last possibility following a detailed evaluation of the propositional approach.

From the constructive-empiricist viewpoint, the ultimate evaluative criteria are empirical. The empirical case is made in subsequent chapters and at this point I primarily address certain conceptual problems. First, what exactly *are* propositions—are they descriptions of the properties of mental representations or are they reified and identified with them? Second, are propositions any more adequate logically than images and verbal representations as primitive explanatory constructs? Finally, do we have a mechanistic realization of the propositional approach in the form of computer simulations of imagery phenomena? The last question is important because it bears directly on the idea that images are generated from propositions.

Propositional representations: Model or reality?

At issue here is whether the term proposition, or such conceptual equivalents as structured description, are simply used as notational devices for *describing* mental representations and their properties or whether they refer to the *form* of the representations themselves. The terms have been used in both senses, often by the same writer. For example, in the context of a discussion of imagery, Zenon Pylyshyn wrote that he prefers "to speak of cognitive representations . . . as structured descriptions instead of images . . . . The point is not that there is no such object as an image, only that an adequate theory of the mental representation will depict it as having a distinctly non-pictorial character" (1978, p. 19). And, further, "even when visual imagery seems clearly implicated the underlying representation is best *characterized* as abstract and conceptual" (p. 29, italics added). Description seems to be used here in a theoretical sense that distinguishes it from the entity described, that is, there is a separate object or phenomenon called an image. At other times, the concept of description is apparently reified, as when Pylyshyn (1978, p. 25) refers to "children's internal vocabulary of descriptive concepts" (which, he is careful to point out, is not to be equated with human language), and when he asserts that the mental representation of a chessboard "*consists of* a compact descriptive structure constructed from a rich vocabulary appropriate to the game of chess" (p. 29, italics added).

Similar contrasting statements appear in Pylyshyn's (1984) recent book. Thus, at one point he emphasizes "that the notion of representation is necessary only in the context of explanation; it is needed to state generalizations concerning the behavior of systems under certain descriptions" (p. 26). Representation appears to be intended here as a descriptive convenience. Elsewhere, however, cognitive representations become reified as "concrete entities" (p. 193), now described variously as "sentence analogues," "mentalese sentences," or "discrete sentencelike symbolic expressions" (pp. 194–196)—conceptual equivalents of propositions but viewed as less abstract. The interpretive ambiguity is there, but I don't wish to belabor the point because Pylyshyn clearly intends to equate sentence-like representations with "real" psychological processes as part of his commitment to a literal or "strong equivalence" (as opposed to a metaphorical) view of the mind as a computational device (Pylyshyn, 1984).

The statements of other key figures in the debate have also been ambiguous. In the quotation cited earlier, Kieras first refers to all knowledge being *expressed* in propositional terms and then goes on to say that there is no fundamental difference in how perceptually based and verbally based information is represented in memory. These are quite different assertions. The first implies that all information can be described in propositional terms; the second characterizes memory as being amodal. J. Anderson (1978) at times discusses the proposition as a theoretical construct whose function it is to represent "information in an image or in a sentence or information from any other source" (p. 257). At other times, he gives the concept psychological and even physiological status, as when he concludes that "studies on hemispheric specialization provide very little evidence on the form of information representation. One could propose that all information has a propositional form, but that propositions encoding visual information are stored in the right hemisphere and propositions encoding verbal in the left (p. 271)."

As a final example, Olson and Bialystok (1983) launched their inquiry into spatial cognition with the stated intention of using a propositional "representational format" as a way of describing the structure of mental representations involved in spatial cognitive tasks (see their Preface). This "propositional way of talking and thinking" (p. ix) changed quickly into a reified view of a structural description as "a propositional representation of the properties or features and their relations constructed by the mind which permits the recognition of and assignment of meaning to objects" (p. 8). The theory developed on that basis is explicitly "intended as a contribution to a computational theory of mind" according to which propositional structural descriptions "are the internal structures used to model reality" (pp. 258–259). The treatise is a contribution but it also leaves us wondering whether the reification of computational terminology is really intended.

The conceptual ambiguity just described seems to be quite unlike that in other sciences. For example, physicists are guided by a theory that describes the behavior of atoms and subatomic particles in abstract, mathematical terms. They do not equate the description with the entities nor with their behavior. They postulate entities whose behaviors involve regularities that can be described as laws, and they aim to account for those laws in terms of a mathematical theory. Thus, "a physical theory . . . is a system of mathematical propositions, deduced from a small number of principles, which aim to represent as simply, as completely, and as exactly as possible a set of experimental laws" (Duhem, 1974 translation). Such a theory represents simple properties with mathematical symbols, numbers, and magnitudes. These symbols have no intrinsic connection with the properties they represent; they bear to those properties only the relation of sign to things signified. The physical theorist does not assert that the descriptive elements (i.e., the mathematical symbols) are the underlying entities, as propositional theorists have tended to do with their descriptive units (for a general discussion of reification in cognitive science, see R. Hoffman & Nead, 1983).

Propositional descriptions as primitive explanatory constructs

Let us nonetheless assume that propositional terminology is simply being used entirely theoretically in models dealing with the functional properties of mental representations. Is the concept adequate in that sense? Pylyshyn (1973) raised a parallel question when he asked "whether the concept of image can be used as a primitive explanatory construct (i.e., one not requiring further reduction) in psychological theories of cognition" (p. 2). He argued that it cannot and that abstract (propositional) descriptions are superior on that account. Here I turn the argument around and attempt to show that the descriptive approach has no explanatory advantage over the image even on logical grounds, and that in some important respects it suffers by comparison.

Limitations of formalism

The first argument follows from the formal definition of the proposition as a descriptive unit which enters into symbol systems that are intended to be completely rule-bound and internally consistent. Accordingly, propositional approaches run into the kinds of problems that were discussed in chapter 1 in connection with mathematical formalisms. Recall that Euler's theorem failed repeatedly to account for counterexamples, even when the concept of polyhedra and various terms in the theorem were re-defined so as to exclude the most recent exception to the generalization. The important conclusions were that formal systems are applicable only to a limited domain, that the tests of such systems rely on informal (psychological) procedures, and that basic (logical) concepts are constantly being redefined rather than retaining the fixed meanings required in formal logic. The implication is that propositional representational theories, which aim to be so completely formal and internally consistent that they could be simulated by a computer, are motivated by a standard that has not been achieved even in mathematical logic. Such a goal is unrealistic in the psychological domain, where the phenomena to be explained lie outside of the descriptive system and are highly variable in nature. This means that a propositionally based model must at the very least provide for considerable uncertainty rather than relying on invariant concepts and rules. Without such provisions, propositional descriptions are bound to be inadequate as explanatory constructs.

Circularity of descriptive systems

No representational theory can provide a satisfactory explanation of psychological phenomena if the basic descriptive units of the theory are defined entirely in a circular fashion. The circularity problem has plagued propositionally based theories in which the conceptual units are characterized as labelled nodes that represent objects and their properties as well as relations among the objects and properties. Thus, a labelled entity such as *bird* is defined in terms of labelled properties such as *has wings, has feathers, can fly*. These properties are in turn defined by reference to *their* labelled properties, and so on, ad infinitum. Such a description provides an illusory explanation because we know the meanings of the descriptive labels, just as we can discover the meaning of a word in a dictionary provided that the defining terms are already familiar. The illusion is shattered, however, if we try the *reductio ad absurdum* of labelling the nodes and relations in a foreign language, which is essentially equivalent to looking up the meanings of foreign words in a dictionary in that language. Ultimately, the elemental units must be meaningful in some more direct psychological sense, and we must have a language-independent (and computer-independent) way of identifying them; otherwise, we are simply caught in an infinite descriptive regress.

Some theorists (e.g., J. Anderson & Bower, 1973; Pylyshyn, 1973) sought to escape the circularity, at least in principle, by suggesting that the ultimate defining units are perceptual features, but they proposed no independent means for identifying such features. Pylyshyn (1984) recognizes the circularity inherent in describing mental activity in terms of semantically interpreted representations alone, and he gets out of it by postulating a psychological or cognitive transducer whose purpose is to "map physical events into cognitive, or computational events" (p. 178)—essentially the functional equivalent of sense organs and effector systems. He proposed a series of criteria or design specifications for these cognitive transducers, but how they are discovered remains mysterious since Pylyshyn explicitly argued that they cannot be identified by neurophysiological methods, psychophysical methods, or functional analysis. In any case, the circularity problem cannot be solved by transducers that only provide an interface between physical events and cognitive events if the latter are characterized only as "discrete sentencelike symbolic expressions." We can think about the environment even when we are not overtly interacting with it, so the *cognitive system itself* must represent the environment and our ways of interacting with it in some form that is different from and independent of the sentence-like representational system and its discrete atomic symbols. If not, we are back in the descriptive cognitive circle in which the only referents for meaningless descriptions are other descriptions.

The circularity problem does not exist in dual coding theory or other approaches in which perceptual and behavioral knowledge of the world is represented in a nondescriptive, analogue fashion. Computational theorists have also begun to recognize the need for analogue representations. For example, J. Anderson (1983) incorporated nonpropositional cognitive units (phrases and spatial images) into the latest version of his general theory, although most of his analyses still rely on propositional representations. Johnson-Laird's (1983) theory includes mental models (structural analogues of the world) and mental images along with propositional symbol strings that correspond to natural language. The analogue or image systems of such theories provide the essential cognitive-referential interface between the physical world and a descriptive-symbol system.

Computation and parsimony of explanation

Computational theories of cognition ultimately rely on a componential approach in which atomic elements of some kind (semantic features, perceptual features) are used along with rules of composition in the interpretation and construction of more complex patterns. Examples are visual pattern recognition and generation (including generation of mental images) and speech perception and generation. Such systems are hierarchical in that the output of one level (e.g., a letter or face constructed from features) can serve as the input to another processing level. The approach is computationally convenient and it makes for descriptive parsimony. Explanatory parsimony is also claimed in that one mediating mechanism (features and rules of composition) is more parsimonious in terms of memory space than a multicoding system that stores separate representations for patterns of different levels of complexity. Let us examine the logical case for the claim. The argument is that the componential approach is parsimonious because the same atomic units can be combined in various ways to construct higher order representations. Thus, a separate representation is not needed for every object or event that can be recognized or constructed, as would be required in the case of a template model. Note, however, that a separate *program* would now be required for each combination or patterning of the old elements that can be recognized or constructed. Memory for faces will serve as a concrete example. Faces can be characterized componentially in terms of such perceptual features as the shapes, sizes, and colors of eyes, ears, nose, mouth, and hair. Obviously, however, we must have a separate set of feature values for every face that we can identify or discriminate as distinct. In other words, instead of a pattern template, we would need a separate feature list and construction-rule template for every face. In addition, a propositional level of description must be added to the perceptual feature level. Thus, the componential approach appears to have no advantage in terms of parsimony over ones that propose multiple structural representations of different levels of complexity, at least where perception and memory are concerned.

The above is not a denial of the reality of compositional skills that are used in the construction or generation of novel linguistic strings, images, and behavior patterns. Constructive skills are ubiquitous and they are explicitly revealed in such tasks as anagrams and jigsaw puzzles, in which a meaningful complex pattern is generated from smaller components, and in simple multiplication, in which a small set of rote habits (including recursive acts) are used to generate a novel sequence of symbols. Such skills require explanation, but they need not themselves form the metaphorical basis of a more atomic compositional approach to the understanding of perception, language, and even imagery.

Computational models and the simulation of imagery

The next issue to be considered arises from the claim that "The notion of a description gains its greatest advantage from the fact that it has been formalized in a number of areas (e.g., in computer-simulation models)" (Pylyshyn, 1973, p. 11). Let us examine that assertion in regard to imagery: Does the descriptive approach permit image simulation in a rigorous, formal sense? A positive answer seems plausible because simple images, such as diagrams, can be generated and displayed on a CRT scope or TV screen by a digital computer driven by a descriptive program. But the situation is not quite as it seems because the system that actually constructs the diagram is an engineering heuristic that lies outside of the descriptive theory. The "interlingua" is in the mind of the engineer, who interprets the programming language and constructs a machine so that it can move a pen 2 cm. to the right, or position dots in space in a certain way, and so forth. The symbols in the programming language must be behaviorally interpreted by a behaving mechanism—an analogue machine that also lies outside the formal descriptive system. The resulting system that can construct images is certainly interesting, but descriptions are only one component of it.

Propositional theorists may respond by pointing to apparently successful computer simulations of imagery, but a careful examination again shows that this is not the case. The examples are simulation studies reported by George Baylor (1972) and Thomas Moran (1973). Baylor constructed an information-processing simulation model of the cube-visualization problem, in which a subject slices up a cube of a certain color in various ways and then answers questions concerning the number of cubes that have two faces of that color, three faces of that color, and so on. The crucial point is that, although the study was presented as "a treatise on the mind's eye," the simulation was based entirely on subjects' *verbal descriptions* of their mental processes during imagery. Therefore, the resulting model pertains to those descriptions and not to the imagery itself. The transformation from image to description was made by the subject, and the nature of the original imagery and its interface with the verbal description are lost. The same conclusion applies to Moran's simulation. The problem was the "spatial understanding" of a two-dimensional configuration (a path) presented as a verbal sequence of compass directions, and the data consisted of verbal protocols from a single subject. In his case as in Baylor's, the simulation consisted of the translation of verbal descriptions into a more formal language that could be handled by a computer.

The critique of computational-descriptive approaches extends to general theoretical views concerning imagery. Kosslyn's (1980) imagery theory includes the assumption that images are generated from propositional descriptions. However, the precise way in which such generation could occur is not specified and no directly relevant evidence is presented. The evidence reviewed by Kosslyn shows instead that complex images can be generated piecemeal from verbal descriptions, which are not conceptually equivalent to abstract propositions even in Kosslyn's approach. In fact, the propositional assumption plays no indispensable explanatory or predictive role in the theory, which is concerned primarily with the spatial and other properties of conscious imagery and the processes (scanning, rotation, etc.) that operate on the imaginal information. The actual propositional genera- tion of images is simply assumed for most purposes of the theory. If that assumption were taken seriously, it would run into all of the problems dis- cussed above in regard to formal theories in general, with restrictive con- sequences that Kosslyn avoids by excluding propositions from the func- tional component of the model. The suggestion that images are generated from propositions seems to be a hand-waving concession to the computa- tional approach, giving the illusion that the theory is formal and simulata- ble, at least in principle. Fortunately, the empirical tests and their outcomes in Kosslyn's productive research program have not been constrained by the assumption.

Some of the arguments apply as well to a variety of models based on the assumption that both language and nonverbal knowledge are represented in a common, conceptual format, even if the format is not assumed to be prop- ositional. All such theories assume that images and verbal responses are gen- erated from some other conceptual system. Osgood (1973), for example, suggested that images are generated by feedback into perceptual systems of information coded as abstract r_m-s_m components in the representational sys- tem. However, the properties of the perceptual system that allow for image- generation remain as mysterious in that approach as they do in the propo- sitional approaches to image-generation. I refer to Osgood's brief analysis of imagery simply to emphasize that a common-coding approach could be based on neobehavioristic principles rather than on propositional descrip- tions. Other variants of that approach will be discussed in later chapters to the extent that they are implicated by research findings.

THE EMPIRICAL ISSUE

Despite the logical problems that have been raised here in regard to propo- sitional approaches, they are currently the major alternative to empiricist theories of mental representations, including especially the dual coding theory to be presented in the next chapter. Accordingly, we shall evaluate the alternatives in terms of their empirical adequacy. Here, too, we encounter a logical problem at the outset: Are propositional and imagery-based theories really distinguishable? J. Anderson (1978) argued persuasively that they are not because imagery models could be expressed in propositional terms and vice versa. As mentioned earlier, the argument assumes that imagery models are formalized, which I believe to be unnecessary and undesirable for reasons already discussed. But, no matter—Anderson ends up conceding that perhaps a distinction could be made in terms of the *number* of codes that need to be postulated in order to account for data, and J. Anderson (1983) in fact opted for a triple-coding approach to the representation of knowledge in order to accommodate certain functional distinctions. The important point here is that it is possible to contrast single-code and multicode theories on empirical grounds. This we shall do in subsequent chapters.

4
Dual Coding Theory

The theory presented in this chapter is a modification and an extension of the version originally proposed in its most comprehensive form in *Imagery and verbal processes* (Paivio, 1971). Many of the basic assumptions remain unchanged but the present treatment is more systematic and it incorporates additions and qualifications required to accommodate new data as well as theoretical issues that have become prominent since 1971. Some important misinterpretations of the original theory are also identified and clarified.

The theory is presented as a set of assumptions and hypotheses concerning the origins and the structural and functional properties of representational systems, along with examples of the empirical implications of those hypotheses. Subsequent chapters expand on those implications and present a more detailed review of relevant evidence, thereby adding operational precision to the ideas that are introduced here. The empiricist nature of the approach also forces us to confront a number of related issues that have been problematic for traditional empiricist theories, namely, the nature of abstract ideas and the so-called terminal meta-postulate, described in chapter 1. We shall see how such issues can be handled in terms of the theory.

The theory is based on the general view that cognition consists of the activity of symbolic representational systems that are specialized for dealing with environmental information in a manner that serves functional or adaptive behavioral goals. This view implies that representational systems must incorporate perceptual, affective, and behavioral knowledge. Human cognition is unique in that it has become specialized for dealing simultaneously with language and with nonverbal objects and events. Moreover, the language system is peculiar in that it deals directly with linguistic input and output (in the form of speech or writing) while at the same time serving a symbolic function with respect to nonverbal objects, events, and behaviors. Any representational theory must accommodate this functional duality.

The most general assumption in dual coding theory is that there are two classes of phenomena handled cognitively by separate subsystems, one specialized for the representation and processing of information concerning nonverbal objects and events, the other specialized for dealing with language. In keeping with my earlier usage, I will often refer to the nonverbal (symbolic) subsystem as the imagery system because its critical functions include the analysis of scenes and the generation of mental images (both functions encompassing other sensory modalities in addition to visual). The language-specialized system will be referred to as the verbal system.

The idea of separate subsystems means that the two systems are assumed to be structurally and functionally distinct. Structurally, they differ in the nature of representational units and the way the units are organized into higher order structures. Functionally, they are independent in the sense that either system can be active without the other or both can be active in parallel. At the same time, they are functionally interconnected so that activity in one system can initiate activity in the other. The structural and functional distinctions combine to produce qualitative differences in the kinds of processing for which the two systems are specialized.

The representation-processing (or structure-function) distinction in the preceding account is difficult to draw in any clear sense for reasons discussed in chapter 2, but it serves a useful purpose at least at an initial descriptive level. The structural representations of dual coding theory refer to relatively stable long-term memory information corresponding to perceptually identifiable objects and activities, both verbal and nonverbal. Processing refers to functional activities that engage the two classes of representation, including activation of either by appropriate stimuli (encoding), activation of one by the other (recoding), organization and elaboration of information within each, as well as transformation, manipulation, and retrieval of information from either class. The remainder of the chapter fleshes out the details of this theoretical sketch.

OVERALL CONCEPTUAL STRUCTURE OF THE THEORY

Dual coding theory has a hierarchical conceptual structure. At the most general level, the theory is about symbolic systems, that is, cognitive systems that serve a symbolic or representational function. The general level divides into verbal and nonverbal symbolic subsystems, which in turn expand into sensorimotor (visual, auditory, haptic) subsystems at the next level. Finally, the lowest level consists of the representational units of each system, called logogens and imagens in the interests of descriptive parsimony. We shall see that the operative cognitive mechanisms are assumed to be at the unit level so that, for example, activation of the verbal system is by specific (contextual or task relevant) verbal stimuli. There is no "top-down" activating mechanism except in the sense that specific input may activate complex representational structures from which component information can be retrieved, if necessary, or activate units that have a general control function on subsequent processing. For example, the instruction to image to words maximizes the probability that nonverbal representations will be activated by subsequent verbal cues.

The classes of general and specific assumptions (hypotheses, postulates) of the theory are summarized in Table 4–1 along with the information-pro-

Table 4-1. Summary of theoretical and empirical assumptions and phenomenal domain of dual coding theory

General empiricist assumption
Cognition is served by two modality-specific symbolic systems that are experientially derived and differentially specialized for representing and processing information concerning nonverbal objects, events, and language.

Distinctions between symbolic and sensorimotor systems

Unit-level properties
Representational units are modality-specific perceptual motor analogues
Units vary hierarchically in size
Synchronous versus sequential intraunit organizational structure

System-level properties
Functional independence and partial interconnectedness of systems
Interunit connections between systems and within systems
Processing operations
Activation of representations
Representational, referential, and associative levels of processing
Synchronous versus sequential organizational processing
Transformational processing
Conscious and automatic processing

Basic functions
Evaluative functions
Mnemonic functions
Motivational and emotional functions

Empirical variables
Theoretical assumptions are linked to classes of operational indicators and procedures:
Stimulus attributes, experimental manipulations, individual differences in cognitive habits and skills, and subjective reports

Phenomenal domain
Processing of verbal and nonverbal information in perceptual, memory, language, and complex problem-solving tasks; neuropsychology; issues in epistemology and philosophy of science

cessing functions that are served by the symbolic systems. Also listed are the empirical or operational procedures that make it possible to evaluate the theory, and the classes of psychological phenomena to which it is particularly relevant. The following sections expand on the outline.

THE BASIC EMPIRICIST ASSUMPTION

The guiding theoretical assumption is that internal (mental) representations have their developmental origin in perceptual, motor, and affective experience and that they retain those experientially derived characteristics so that representational structures and processes are modality specific rather than amodal. The assumption implies continuity between perception and memory as well as between behavioral skills and cognitive skills. It means, too, that internal representations are multimodal and varied in structure and function rather than being unimodal and neutral with respect to input and output modality distinctions, as assumed in propositional theories. The empiricist claim also implies that mental representations cannot be completely abstract although they can deal with abstract information and behavior in ways to be discussed in a later section.

The empiricist assumption pertains to the perceptual and behavioral information that is *contained* in (can be made available for use by) representational structures and processes. It does not deny an innate contribution in the uncontroversial sense that the human brain is a product of biological evolution and that some of its functional properties therefore are species specific. The capacity to learn a spoken language is the most salient of the properties that characterize humans. The capacity to image may not be uniquely human but it certainly has a hereditary base. The overriding empiricist hypothesis, however, is that the innate contribution is very general and that the functionally useful content of language and imagery can vary enormously, depending on specific experiences. Thus our ability to generate, manipulate, and transform images of objects and events depends largely on perceptual-motor experiences with such objects. In any case, I assume with others that one practical way to determine the contribution of innate factors (if that is one's scientific aim) is to begin by investigating the relations between experiential factors and cognitive skills, for these are directly observable and will define the outer bound of what *might* be innate.

THE DISTINCTION BETWEEN SYMBOLIC AND SENSORIMOTOR SYSTEMS

Dual coding theory is basically about the nature of *symbolic systems*. The interpretation of the term system is complicated by the empiricist assumption that the symbolic representations retain the properties of different sensory and response modalities. The conceptual difficulty is resolved by assuming that the verbal-nonverbal symbolic distinction is orthogonal to the sensorimotor modalities in the manner illustrated by the examples shown in Table 4–2. This analysis was originally proposed specifically to accommodate episodic memory phenomena (Paivio, 1972) but it is applicable to cognition in general. It represents a kind of modularity position without the exclusive nativism associated with recent computational views on the modularity of mind (Fodor, 1983). It is more closely related to empirically based approaches that emphasize a high degree of functional specificity between and within sensory subsystems. For example, rather than being viewed as a single system for producing an integrated representation of the external world, the visual system appears to consist of a network of independent sensorimotor channels (Goodale, 1983). The present position

Table 4-2. Orthogonal conceptual relation between symbolic systems and sensorimotor systems with examples of types of modality-specific information represented in each subsystem

Sensorimotor	Symbolic Systems	
	Verbal	Nonverbal
Visual	Visual words	Visual objects
Auditory	Auditory words	Environmental sounds
Haptic	Writing patterns	"Feel" of objects
Taste	—	Taste memories
Smell	—	Olfactory memories

extends such a view to the symbolic systems, which are assumed to be derived from and retain the functional properties of sensorimotor systems.

The analysis focuses on the concept of system. A dictionary defines system as a combination of things or parts forming a complex or unitary whole. Familiar examples include railroad system, solar system, nervous system, and circulatory system. Such systems are defined by structural integration as well as functional coordination. Other systems are mainly functional in character, or at least the structural integrity is not obvious. For example, language is generally viewed as a functional system, although it actually consists of a number of subsystems, especially in literate societies. Thus, in addition to the auditory-vocal system, it also includes the coordinated activities related to reading and writing. For the deaf, it is a system of manual gestures, perhaps accompanied by reading skills. Hearing signers may have all of these functional subsystems—for comprehension and production of speech, writing, and sign language. Still other variants include systems specialized for processing braille, semaphore signals, morse code, and typing. A further example is the bilingual or multilingual individual, who has two or more functional language systems, each comprising a set of subsystems for speaking, understanding, reading, and writing.

The different subsystems comprise an integrated whole in the sense that each can be functionally mapped onto any other. For example, each could be expressed in some common form such as speech or writing, or in one language or the other in the case of the bilingual. At the same time, each is a separate, integrated subsystem that can function more-or-less independently, as evidenced, for example, by the selective effects of focal brain lesions, which might impair one subsystem while leaving others functionally intact (see chapter 12). The relative functional dominance of any subsystem presumably depends on experiential dominance. Thus, the auditory-vocal speech system is the dominant language system for most people under most but not necessarily all circumstances. For example, current evidence suggests that reading may or may not be accompanied by covert auditory-motor (phonemic) activity, depending on the individual's experience with reading, the difficulty of the material, and so on.

The idea of a general language system composed of separate subsystems raises the issue of an integrating mechanism. Is it necessary to postulate a single control system for language-related activities of all kinds, or can the facts be handled simply by assuming that the subsystems share interconnections with each other, so that we can switch from one system to another (e.g., from speech to writing) under specifiable conditions? More about that shortly.

Similar assumptions apply in the case of the nonverbal (imagery) system. It consists of a set of interconnected (functional) parts specialized for dealing with environmental information. It must include representations of the sensory properties of things, relations among them, and their behavioral "affordances," to borrow a Gibsonian term. It must be complex, for a thing can be known by more than one modality—by appearance, haptic feel, sound, smell, and taste. The component information may be integrated into a whole for some purposes, but be separable for other purposes. For example, one may visualize a telephone with or without concurrently imaging its ring or how it feels when handled. Thus, like the verbal system, the nonverbal system presumably consists of subsystems that correspond to different sensory modalities and are capable of functioning independently.

Here, too, questions arise concerning the dominance of subsystems and the necessity of postulating a single control system to integrate the activities of the sensory subsystems. The evidence suggests that the visual system is dominant for normal-sighted individuals. For example, transfer of discriminative responding from sight to touch or vice versa seems to be guided or mediated by the visual system (see Paivio, 1971, chap. 5). But vision is absent in the blind, and the degree of visual dominance varies among sighted individuals as well. Finally, the alternative to a common control system once again is the idea of interconnected subsystems, so that processing can be switched from one system to another under appropriate conditions.

A final question is whether it is also necessary to postulate an Aristotelian common sense that is completely amodal and capable of representing all sense modalities and accommodating the relation between nonverbal and verbal representations—a kind of interlingua that mediates transfer from one system to the other. Such a common representational system is precisely what propositional theorists propose, but dual coding theory incorporates a different view. The experiential derivation of the sensorimotor subsystems implies that they must be interconnected because of co-occurrences in experience and yet capable of functioning independently. The functional interconnections permit activation of one subsystem by another. The mediating interlingua is unnecessary and logically undesirable because it is unparsimonious and leads to an infinite regress of mediating interlingua. The interconnections are between representational units, so we must understand how those are interpreted in the theory before we deal with the structural and functional relations between them.

UNIT-LEVEL ASSUMPTIONS

This section deals with three interrelated assumptions: (a) the representational units in each system are modality-specific perceptual-motor analogues, (b) units are hierarchically organized structures, and (c) intraunit functional structure differs so that component information in higher-order nonverbal units is synchronously organized (permitting parallel processing up to some informational limit), whereas verbal components are sequentially organized (implying sequential constraints on intraunit processing). The modality-specific analogue assumption follows from the general empiricist postulate, and the two organizational assumptions are corollaries of the analogue assumption. The three assumptions are necessarily intertwined in the following discussion.

I have previously referred to the hypothetical nonverbal and verbal representational units as *imagens* and *logogens* (Paivio, 1978f). The logogen concept is borrowed from John Morton (1969) who introduced it to account for perceptual word-recognition results. The present usage is more general in that it does not imply acceptance of all of the features of Morton's logogen model, but the functional properties are essentially parallel. Morton's (1979) revision of the model is particularly pertinent because empirical evidence compelled him to postulate modality-specific (e.g., auditory and visual) logogens, as well as separate input and output logogens. The concept of *imagen* refers similarly to representations from which mental images are generated under appropriate conditions (cf. "iconogen"; Attneave, 1974). The detailed analysis of representational units given below implies that the imagen, too, must be viewed as a multimodal concept.

The two terms are problematic because they imply fixed entities corresponding to static objects and words. While those are appropriate referent classes, the present usage is intended to be broader and more flexible. The terms serve mainly to distinguish the underlying (hypothetical) cognitive representations from their expressions as consciously experienced images and inner speech, or overt behaviors such as drawing and speech. The term unit can also be misleading because it falsely implies a discrete entity of some fixed size and character. Nonetheless, it can be interpreted in a way that is consistent with such psychological units as the chunk (G. Miller, 1956), integral stimulus (Garner, 1974), or "blob" (Lockhead, 1972). Thus, imagens and logogens are assumed to vary in size but they are nonetheless unitary in the sense that they can function as integrated informational structures or response generators for some purposes. This is a kind of componential approach in which the components are concrete, modality-specific entities that can also combine to form more complex entities.

The two classes of units differ in the nature of their internal structure in a way that reflects their perceptual-motor origins. Thus, imagens correspond to natural objects, holistic parts of objects, and natural groupings of objects. The represented information includes not only static appearance but

dynamic and variable properties as well. The structural information is characteristically organized in a *synchronous or simultaneous* manner into perceptual hierarchies or nested sets (Paivio, 1971, p. 58). An example is the human face, which consists of eyes, nose, lips, and other holistic components that are themselves composed of still smaller parts—iris, pupil, nostrils, and so on. All are part of a synchronously organized hierarchical structure, and that structure is itself part of a larger structure, the human body. This conceptualization of internal structure of images corresponds generally to recent analyses of basic level objects as configurations of parts ("partonomy"; B. Tversky & Hemenway, 1984) and of imaginal representations as composites of figural features (Denis, 1982b; Hoffmann, Denis, & Ziessler, 1983).

The meaning of simultaneous or synchronous organization is apparent at the perceptual level: The organized elements of a face are seen together in time because that is the nature of the visual system. At the cognitive level, this characteristic is illustrated by mental images of complex objects, the parts of which are simultaneously *available* for processing (Paivio, 1975b). For example, my mental image of my living room is synchronously available in the sense that I can describe its contents beginning at any point and from any perspective in my mental space. This implies that the mental representation of my living room "contains" information that is simultaneously available. It does *not* mean that all the information can be accessed or processed simultaneously. For example, I cannot image the entire living room at once from any perspective let alone all possible viewpoints. This is a limitation of the perceptual systems on which the symbolic system is based: Like visual perception, visual imagery has a limited span and different parts of a synchronously available representation may have to be imaged successively or "scanned." The part that is initially imaged and the ordered scanning will depend on the contextual cues that activate the representation (about which more later), so that the processing order is not random. The important point is that it is not sequentially constrained by the representational structure itself.

The above examples also illustrate what is meant by a variable-sized functional unit. In the face example, eyes, nose, and mouth are units in the sense that they can be separately imaged, as can larger units. The maximum size of a functional unit is an empirical question, but presumably it can encompass whatever has been experienced sufficiently often as a unitary perception—"sufficiently often" also requiring empirical specification.

The analysis of visual representations applies as well to representations corresponding to other sensory attributes of natural objects—environmental sounds, the feel of objects, and so on. The ring of a telephone must be represented mentally as a unit, for we can imagine it or imitate it vocally. Presumably, it is closely associated with the visual representation of a telephone and both aspects might be activated in parallel but not necessarily so because the perceptual experiences on which they are based are sometimes conjoint and sometimes separate.

Logogens, too, are assumed to vary in size, but they differ from imagens in internal structure so that smaller units are organized into larger units in a sequential or successive fashion. This structure is most apparent in the case of auditory-motor representations corresponding to heard or spoken language, where phonemic units are organized in syllables, syllables into words, and so on, up to sequential structures as extensive as poems or entire plays. Similarly, writing is a sequential motor activity that must have its own sequentially organized representational base. The visual logogens that correspond to print differ in that, up to some limit, they are functionally equivalent to linear spatial structures than can be processed as visual units. Thus, we can image letters and short words, perhaps up to a limit of three or four letters in length (Weber & Harnish, 1974). Such visual word representations presumably do not differ from those that correspond to the representations of nonverbal objects except in the linear arrangement of smaller units into larger ones, which is itself dictated by the fact that written language maps onto the sequential structure of speech and, hence, is subject to the same sequential processing constraints.

The synchronous-sequential structural contrast was originally made by the British empiricists, Berkeley and James Mill, who distinguished between simultaneous and successive order in the association of ideas. Simultaneity implied simultaneous availability and freedom from sequential constraints, but was more specifically defined by the property of *redintegration* whereby the occurrence of an idea is simultaneously accompanied by other ideas that derive from perceptual experiences in which the component elements occurred together. Although not described in those terms, the synchronous-sequential contrast reemerged during the behavioristic era in the form of a controversy concerning the nature of maze learning, with Hull arguing that the animal learns response sequences and Tolman arguing that the animal learns spatial structures or "cognitive maps" that permit it to take a short cut to a goal in a spatial maze (see Tolman, 1948). Thus, Hull's theory implied sequential representational structures and Tolman's theory explicitly relied on synchronous representations in which component information is simultaneously available. In retrospect, the present analysis is a synthesis and extension of these antecedents as applied specifically to the structural properties of verbal and nonverbal representations, as defined functionally by different indices of sequential constraints and simultaneous availability.

SYSTEM-LEVEL ASSUMPTIONS

The discussion now turns to the structural and functional properties of the symbolic systems as a whole, involving relations among representational units within and between verbal and nonverbal systems. The principal assumptions concern (a) the functional independence but interconnectedness of the two systems, (b) the probabilistic nature of interunit relations between and within systems, (c) processing mechanisms and different levels of processing (representational, referential, associative) within and between systems, (d) differential specialization for synchronous and sequential interunit processing within systems, and (e) automatic and conscious processing in both systems. The assumptions are closely tied to empirical procedures, so the operational assumptions listed in Table 4–1 are also introduced into the discussion.

Between-system relations

The nonverbal and verbal symbolic systems are assumed to be functionally independent in the sense that one system can be active without the other, or both can be active in parallel. They are also independent in the information processing sense of independent stages, although the preferred metaphor in dual coding is that one system triggers activity in the other, rather than the idea that information flows from one to the other. The activation of one system by the other implies that representations in the two systems must be interconnected. The interconnections are incomplete or partial in the sense that "access routes" are only available between certain representations in each system. Thus, a *structural* connection exists between those representations, but interunit processing is nonetheless optional in the metaphorical sense that the pathways are only "used" or activated under certain conditions but not others. This means, for example, that picture naming is not automatic although it is highly likely to occur under some circumstances. Similarly, one can but need not image to concrete nouns or descriptions. This conceptualization of the structural-functional relation between systems is important theoretically because it provides for the possibility of flexible yet organized processing activity of the symbolic systems, so that they can function independently and additively for some purposes and coordinate their activities for others.

The points of functional contact between systems are between imagens and logogens—usually auditory-motor logogens, although direct connections to other modalities of verbal representations are not ruled out. The simple case is the relation between the representations corresponding to an object and its name. The most direct evidence of such interconnections are acts of reference—for example, naming objects and pointing to named objects. Clear evidence is also found at the internal level in the occurrence of images to names and names to images. Thus, if I am asked to describe my dining room table, I first experience an image of that table, which I can then describe by naming its components and adjectival attributes. Note that the referent object in this case is a particular table and the name that evokes the corresponding image is the compound expression, my dining room table. The latter is not necessarily represented cognitively as a well-integrated logogen unit in the way that compound words (e.g., armchair) presumably are, but it nonetheless evokes a unitary representation of a particular object. Such functional semantic units can be freely created in speech, just as they can in imagery, which is a problem for a later section. The important point here is that the relations between images and descriptions, however complex these may be, depend on functional connections between some elements in the verbal system and the image-generating system.

It should be emphasized, too, that the interconnections are not assumed to be one-to-one but, rather, one-to-many, in both directions. The assumption parallels the familiar fact that a thing can be called by many names and a name has many specific referents. This translates into the dual coding assumption that a given word can evoke any of a number of images, corresponding to different exemplars of a referent class (e.g., different tables) or different versions of a particular class member (e.g., my dining room table imaged from different perspectives). Conversely, a given object (or imaged object) can evoke different descriptions.

Precisely which images or descriptions will be activated at any moment depends on the stimulus context interacting with the relative functional strength of the different referential interconnections. Functional strength is determined by prior objective experiences with referent class members and verbal descriptions associated with them, and strength translates operationally into the probability distribution of overt referential responses. This analysis obviously has its roots in the analysis of associative probabilities in word-association data (e.g., Deese, 1962; Kiss, 1975). The present conception generalizes the analysis to the relations between objects and their verbal descriptions or, theoretically, imagens and logogens. Labeling data show that pictures of common objects elicit a range of names that vary in their probability. Similar data have been obtained for labeling of environmental sounds. The reverse relation, imaging to words, has not been studied as systematically but exploratory experiments have shown that names elicit drawn images that vary in type and orientation in a probabilistic way. For example, just as *shirt* is a highly probable (and prototypical) associate to the stimulus word *clothing*, subjects are likely to draw a shirt when given clothing as a stimulus word. Moreover, they are most likely to draw it in a particular orientation, as though viewed from the front with the arms out to the sides. Ratings have also been used to measure variability in the type and number of different images elicited by words (Snodgrass & Vanderwart, 1980). Various procedures of this kind need to be used to obtain systematic empirical data on the precise nature of the distribution of different images to words and vice versa.

Note that the assumptions are similar to those associated with semantic memory models (e.g., Collins & Loftus, 1975) that distinguish between conceptual representations and lexical representations. However, such models assume that the conceptual representations are abstract and descriptive (propositional) in nature and (in the interests of cognitive economy) that the relations are between type nodes rather than between specific instances, or tokens. Neither assumption is necessary in the present approach, as I will indicate more fully later on.

This analysis of between-system relations emphasizes internal representations for discrete objects and their names. The analysis is more complex in the case of the relations between attributes of objects and motor activities on the one hand, and their adjectival and verbal descriptions on the other. The relations appear to be relatively direct between focal colors and their names in that such colors can be named quickly and reliably and the names are rated high in imagery value. This observation suggests some kind of discrete representational base for colors (color imagens?) despite their perceptually continuous character, and indeed some color-processing data are consistent with such a view (Kolers & von Grünau, 1976; Paivio & te Linde, 1980). On the other hand, it is not clear that the referential relations are symmetrical: Individuals can name focal colors as quickly as familiar objects, but can they image as quickly to color names as to object names? And when they image colors, do they image colors alone or concrete objects for which the named color is a typical attribute?

Some motor reactions can be similarly interpreted. For example, verbal commands to walk, run, or jump can elicit corresponding activities quite promptly, as though referential interconnections exist between verb logogens and well-integrated motor schemata. However, imaging to such verbs may require concretization of the referent (e.g., "run" imaged as a boy running). Other classes of properties and activities are even less independent of concrete objects and the property-name relations may be relatively indirect, implicating within-system associative connections (discussed below) as well as between-system referential connections. Such complications come up again in specific empirical contexts (e.g., chap. 7) and a more detailed theoretical analysis will depend on new data.

Within-system relations

We turn next to the relations between units within each of the two symbolic systems. The verbal system is assumed to be structured in an associative fashion that can be inferred from word-association data and other procedures. A probabilistic network of relations describes the overall structure, so that auditory-motor logogens are linked to each other in a many-to-many fashion as determined by associative experience. The terms *link* and *association* again refer to functionally defined relations, that is, the probability that logogens will activate each other given initial activation by a specific target word and its accompanying context. The elements of the system are assumed to correspond to words or unitized word groups as discussed earlier in connection with the logogen concept. Thus, no abstract *entities* are postulated, although words themselves vary in denotative abstractness and generality. It is possible, accordingly, to describe aspects of the structure as a hierarchy consisting of connections between a category label such as *animal* and the instances or exemplars of the category. Such hierarchical structures arise naturally from the nature of associative experience and no special abstracting mechanism is required to account for them.

Associative hierarchies presumably can be entirely linguistic in the sense that the *referents* of the represented words are themselves verbal objects. Thus, the word *sentence* is a superordinate term for subordinates such as *subject* and *predicate* (or noun phrase and verb phrase), which in turn "dominate" such word class labels as *noun, verb*, and so on. Thus, given a cultural-linguistic context in which language is analyzed and described, hierarchical-phrase structures are built into our verbal associative networks just as naturally as are hierarchies based on natural categories. The intralinguistic hierarchies are simply a consequence of what Hockett (1963) described as the reflexive design feature of language.

But what if grammar is not analysed and category labels are not used, as in the case of young children? Does their language behavior nonetheless compel us to postulate abstract functional entities corresponding to grammatical classes? This is ultimately an empirical question and I do not believe that existing data provide a strong basis for a choice. Jenkins and Palermo (1964) proposed a verbal mediational account of word-class formation that did not depend on abstract entities, but they subsequently abandoned the associative approach completely. Kiss (1973) resurrected their approach to word-class formation but, in doing so, he introduced the concept of abstract cognitive representations that are generated as a function of associative-linguistic experience. The model was tested and supported by a computer simulation but it has not been tested experimentally and it remains uncertain whether its assumptions are necessary to account for language development even if they are sufficient to do so. The results of empirical tests might require a change in the assumption, but, in the meantime, the structure of the verbal system within dual coding theory includes only symbolic representations that correspond to actual language units. It is important to note, however, that the facts of language behavior are not to be explained solely in terms of the verbal-associative network, but rather by the properties of verbal and imaginal systems considered together. Thus, the dual coding analysis goes beyond purely verbal-associative accounts of language phenomena.

Whereas the structure of the verbal system can be appropriately characterized in terms of relations among discrete entities, the nonverbal system cannot. Our knowledge of the world must reflect the continuous nature of organized objects and events. The structure of that knowledge can be viewed simply as an extension of the hierarchical structure of imagens as described earlier. For example, my summer cottage is part of a larger setting that includes a nearby lake together with surrounding hills, roads, and neighboring dwellings. This continuity is revealed in conscious imagery so that, when I think of my cottage, I imagine it as part of its immediate environment.

Moreover, the imagery can expand and shift continuously to portions of the broader setting.

The continuity is not unbroken, however, for my perspective can shift suddenly to my home, my work setting, or to another country. Moreover, some of my knowledge of the world is inherently discrete, derived from photographs of objects or settings that I have never visited nor even seen from the perspective of a motion picture camera. My static imagery of such information reflects that discreteness. How are these discrete aspects of one's world knowledge organized? Any answer would be pure speculation because the problem has not been studied empirically, but we can be more confident about the conditions that determine the activation of the discrete chunks. One determinant is the verbal system and its interconnections with the imagery system: Questions about my cottage, my house, or the Leaning Tower of Pisa evoke images of those objects and their immediate settings in the probabilistic fashion already discussed in the context of the imagen concept. Such activation is presumably governed by processing mechanisms to be considered in the next section, following a summary of the structural assumptions.

The structural assumptions of dual coding are summarized in Figure 4–1, which illustrates the idea of separate but interconnected systems, representational units within systems, and the organization structure of the represented information. The interconnections are between referentially concrete representations, with abstract logogens and "unnamed imagens" represented within their respective systems but not directly interconnected. The figure also symbolizes the associative and logically hierarchical nature of the assumed organizational structure of the verbal system, and the nested-set character of the organization of nonverbal information. Finally, the figure indicates that the symbolic systems are connected to sensory input and response output systems, whose characteristics will be discussed only to the extent necessary to explicate the behavioral functions of the symbolic systems.

Processing operations

This section deals with the basic functional properties of the representational systems that make it possible for representational information to be used in cognitive tasks and the guidance of behavior generally. These properties consist of cognitive processing mechanisms for accessing and activating mental representations directly or indirectly (implicating different levels of processing), and for manipulating them in various ways at a conscious and unconscious level. These hypothetical processes implicate all of the operational indicators and procedures that have been used traditionally to define symbolic processes. These are conceptually related on the one hand to the behavioristic concept of controlling variables and on the other to the cognitive psychological concept of control processes. The former translates

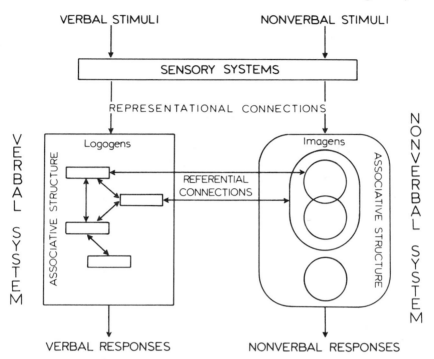

Figure 4-1. Schematic depiction of the structure of verbal and nonverbal symbolic systems, showing the representational units and their referential (between system) and associative (within system) interconnections as well as connections to input and output systems. The referentially unconnected units correspond to abstract-word logogens and "nameless" imagens, respectively.

into the assumption that nonverbal and verbal representational activity is controlled by present stimulus conditions interacting with existing properties of the symbolic systems as determined by prior experience. Control processes are the hypothetical mechanisms or operators that mediate the controlling function of stimuli. I emphasize once again that these mechanisms do *not* include a *separate* executive or controller. Instead, they consist entirely of the probabilistic activation of particular representations by environmental stimuli or by previously activated representations. Especially relevant as a paradigmatic example is the control that can be exerted by verbal instructions on subsequent verbal or nonverbal processing under ordinary conditions (e.g., Luria, 1961) and more dramatically under hypnotic induction conditions (Hilgard, 1977).

Activation of representations

The activation of verbal and nonverbal representations is a joint function of variables in the stimulus situation and relevant individual difference variables. The stimulus variables include attributes of target stimuli and contextual stimuli in a given task. The target stimuli are those that are presented for processing, such as items to be remembered, compared, comprehended, or mentally manipulated in some way. Examples of contextual stimuli are experimental instructions that arouse a task set (the *Aufgabe* and *Einstellung* of the Würzburg school) and the general context in which the experimental task is presented.

More specifically, empirical observations have supported the assumption that the activation of nonverbal representations as manifested in imagery processing is a function of the (independently determined) concreteness or image-arousing value of stimuli. Thus, imagery is more likely to be evoked and used with objects or pictures as stimuli than with words as stimuli, and with concrete than with abstract words, even in the absence of specific instructional sets. Image arousal and processing is also increased by instructions to image to target stimuli or to use imagery in the task. Conversely, verbal representational activation and processing (implying continuous representational activity) are maximized when (a) words serve as stimuli, especially ones that are high in their acquired capacity to arouse verbal associations, (b) the task demands verbal processing, and (c) instructions are given to carry out a task verbally.

Note that stimulus attributes and instructional sets are both aspects of the stimulus situation. The effects of these variables can be summarized by saying that they simply modify the probability with which verbal and nonverbal representations are activated in a given situation. The empiricist basis of the theoretical statements is apparent from the fact that the hypothetical mental processes are inferred directly from relevant variables—imagery from the imagery-value of stimuli and instructions, and verbal processing from the verbal emphasis in either class of input. We shall see later that this approach has interesting and strong empirical implications, especially when combined with other experimental task variables—implications that are not suggested by any approach (such as radical behaviorism) that assumes that the inferred processes are redundant, nor by cognitive theories that assume a single, amodal (propositional) representational base.

Individual differences, which presumably reflect innate factors and the experiential history of the individual, are specified operationally by performance on tests of symbolic habits and abilities. The former include measures of cognitive style, preferences for thinking verbally or imaginally, and so on. The latter include tests of spatial, figural, or imagery abilities on the one hand and a variety of verbal abilities on the other. The functional role of individual difference variables, like those of stimulus and contextual variables, can be expressed in probabilistic terms: They influence the probability with which verbal and nonverbal representations will be aroused (and used successfully) in a given task.

To summarize, the overall probability of the activation and use of verbal and nonverbal representations is a function of the combined effect of stimulus attributes, instructions and other contextual stimuli, and individual differences. The precise nature of the combination (whether additive or interactive, for example) is an empirical question. The activation resulting from the specified factors could involve one or both symbolic systems. For example, the arousal of images by high imagery words implies a "crossover" from verbal to imaginal system. This implication is made explicit in the following processing assumptions, which are essentially a specific conceptualization of the activation processes just discussed in operational terms.

Levels of processing

The present treatment is modified from one that I introduced earlier (Paivio, 1971, pp. 52–59) in the context of the analysis of meaning. Three different kinds of processing can be identified, namely, *representational, referential, and associative.* Representational processing refers to the relatively direct activation of verbal representations by linguistic stimuli and of nonverbal representations by nonlinguistic stimuli. The activation is only *relatively* direct because of the complications associated with perceptual analysis of linguistic stimuli of different modalities, which implicate representations corresponding to those modalities. Thus, naming (reading) printed words takes longer than naming (repeating) spoken words, suggesting that the former uses a "longer" route. Nonetheless, the representational processing of visual words takes less time and is presumably more direct than either referential or associative processing.

Referential processing refers to the activation of the nonverbal system by verbal stimuli or the verbal system by nonverbal stimuli. Imaging to words and naming objects are paradigmatic examples of tasks that require referential processing. Theoretically, these are indirect because they require a crossover of activity from one symbolic system to the other, so that objects must first activate imagens before logogens are activated and naming can occur, and words initiate activity in logogens before imagens can be activated and experienced as images. Note, too, that image generation and object-naming tasks often implicate other processes as well. For example, as discussed below, the generation of complex, novel images to verbal cues requires organizational processing of referentially activated image components to produce an integrated image. Such constructive processes are given special emphasis in Kosslyn's (1980) model of image generation.

Associative processing refers to the activation of representations within either system by other representations within the same system. This kind of processing corresponds to what is ordinarily assumed to occur during word associations and when nonverbal situations trigger nonverbal memories (images) of related situations. Associative processing and referential processing need not differ in any quantitative sense (e.g., reaction time for referential and associative responding) but they do differ theoretically in type.

A given task may require any or all of the three kinds of processing. Simple perceptual recognition or judgments of the familiarity of stimuli requires representational processing. Naming pictures and imaging to words require referential processing, which presupposes prior representational processing of the target stimulus. Free verbal associating requires verbal representational processing and then verbal associative processing, although it could also involve referential processing (e.g., the word knife elicits an image of a knife, which evokes a fork image as well, which then elicits the verbal referential response, "fork"). Finally, asking subjects to respond with a verbal associate to a picture (e.g., saying "boy" to a picture of a girl) presumably requires representational, referential, and associative processing. We shall see in later chapters that reaction time, neuropsychological, and other data support predictions from the theory.

The dual coding processing analysis is related to other approaches and concepts. It is similar to the levels of processing approach introduced by Craik and Lockhart (1972), but differs from theirs in its emphasis on qualitative distinctions and the specific nature of its processing assumptions. Moreover, these can be operationally specified or defined quite independently of performance in memory tasks, contrary to what has been viewed as a persistent problem with the levels approach (see Baddeley, 1978). The dual coding approach also implicates the concept of elaboration or elaborative coding in much the same general sense as the concept has been used by Rohwer (1973), Craik and Tulving (1975), and Stein and Bransford (1979), among others. Again, however, dual coding stands apart by virtue of its special emphasis on the importance of qualitative differences between representational codes and processes that operate on them, so that it is theoretically necessary to specify whether the elaboration is verbal, nonverbal, or some combination of both. At the same time, the dual coding approach readily accommodates quantitative effects of the different kinds of elaboration. The nature of elaborative processing and its effects would differ in ways dictated by the structural and processing capacities of the two systems, such as the way they organize and reorganize information as discussed in the next section.

Organizational processes

The reference here is to the active organization (or reorganization) of incoming verbal or nonverbal information. This process was recognized by Bartlett in his constructivist approach to memory, and later by Bousfield and others in the context of organizational processes in free recall. Organization of memory raised the question of the organizing mechanisms, to which both structural and processing interpretations have been applied. The former includes the idea of semantic memory structures or schemata to which new (episodic) information is made to conform by means of an accommodating process of some kind. Alternatively, organization could be viewed entirely as a process, such as a retrieval scheme, without any change of storage structure. The important point to note in any case is that organization of verbal memory clearly demands some kind of constructive process that operates on the input structure. The productive output mechanisms that impose syntactic structure on language behavior must also be capable of functioning constructively.

The evidence for nonverbal organizational processes is equally compelling. Bizarre dreams differ in their organizational structure from perceptual experiences, although the elements may be familiar. Dynamic organizational processes must be responsible, though we know little about their nature. We know somewhat more about the organizational structure that can be imposed on mental images by mnemonic instructions. For example, subjects can be asked to construct either interactive or noninteractive (separate) images of the referents of a pair of words or pictured objects, such as *tree-window*, with striking effects on recall. Imaging a *tree* growing out of a *window* is a constructive process, and we know that the verbal instruction to generate such an interactive image plays an essential part in initiating the constructive mental program. This process can be seen as a creative extension of the referential encoding process discussed earlier in that the end product can be a novel and complex mental structure. A simple implication of the analysis is that the time required to construct complex images should vary directly with the number of named components that are to be combined in the image (cf. Beech & Allport, 1978).

The main theoretical distinction to be noted here is that verbal and nonverbal organizational processes differ in ways already implied in the earlier discussion of the structural organization of lower-order representational units into higher-order units in the two systems. The distinction is extended here to interunit organizational processing, the hypothesis being that the verbal system is specialized for sequential processing whereas the nonverbal system is specialized for synchronous or parallel processing of multiple representational units. The verbal system generates sequential structures and the nonverbal system generates synchronous (including spatial) structures, with the paradigm cases being their manifestation in speech and compound visual images, respectively. These structures are defined by their functional properties (sequential constraints on processing, simultaneous availability of information, etc.) as discussed earlier with reference to the internal structure of representational units. The processing mechanisms themselves are internalized derivations of the perceptual-motor activity involved in listening and speaking on the one hand, and observing and reacting to nonverbal perceptual information on the other. Thus, both processes include a motor component appropriate for generating the kinds of organized structures that characterize verbal and nonverbal representations.

Transformational processes

This section deals with the hypothetical processes that account for our ability to manipulate symbolic information actively so as to change the order of representational components or otherwise transform representational structures. I discussed such processes previously (Paivio, 1971) in terms of transformational thinking and concluded that imagery is more efficient than verbal processes in that regard. The present analysis is based on the modified hypothesis that both systems are capable of transforming symbolic representations, but they do so in different ways, following the constraints imposed by the organizational structure of verbal and nonverbal information and the processes that operate on them.

Verbal transformations presumably operate on a sequential frame, imposing changes in temporal order or substitution of new elements for ones that occupy a particular temporal slot. These sequential changes could entail simple reordering of a randomly ordered list of words, or syntactic transformations analogous to those described by Chomsky (1957). The concept of transformational rules is equivalent, therefore, to one kind of verbal transformational process. This characterization implies that such processes can operate at a rather abstract level, since syntactic transformations apply to word classes. The present interpretation is that they operate at different levels—a specific level based on experiences with verbal units in many different contexts, and a more abstract level generally described as internalized grammatical rules but viewed here as being essentially equivalent to verbal statements concerning permissible combinations of verbal units (a special case of the reflexivity of language). We shall see later that linguistic transformations are also influenced by nonlinguistic (nonsequential) information, but the effects of the latter are nonetheless constrained by sequential verbal processes.

Nonverbal transformations, on the other hand, are governed by the structural and processing constraints associated with nonverbal representations. Thus, they can include spatial transformations and changes in the sensory properties of representational content. For example, spatial transformations as manifested in imagery include mental rotations on any plane, changes in imaged size, distortions of shape, and changes in the relative position of two or more objects. All of these are dynamic changes, so they could be regarded as imagined movements of different kinds. However, they also imply covert manipulation by the person doing the imaging, which may differ from the processing required for imagining an object moving on its own. In any case, the present hypothesis is that all mental transformations engage motor processes that derive originally from active manipulation of the referent objects and observations of perceptual changes in objects as they move or are manipulated by others.

This theoretical analysis of transformational processes has a number of historical precedents. The most obvious is the motor theory of thought. The present view differs from the peripheralist version of motor theory in that the processes need not be reflected in detectable overt motor activity. More importantly, I assume that the covert motor processes operate on mental representations with synchronously organized sensory properties. It is more difficult to distinguish the theoretical assumptions from Osgood's theory of representational mediation processes, although important differences in detail will be addressed later. Other precedents include behavioral views incorporating the idea of conditioned perceptual responses (e.g., Sheffield, 1961), Piaget's concept of action schemata, and Hebb's theory of the role of eye movements and other behaviors in the development and functioning of cell assemblies. Finally, viewed from the perspective of individual differences, the present hypotheses are conceptually related to figural transformational abilities in Guilford's (1967) model of the structure of the intellect. These historical antecedents are discussed in more detail in the next two chapters.

Conscious and automatic processing

The concept of consciousness has had an ambiguous position in dual coding theory. It is clear on the one hand that mental images are usually interpreted as consciously experienced internal events, and that verbal processes, too, can be experienced as mental words or inner speech when we "talk to ourselves." The conscious quality of both kinds of symbolic activity was recognized by early mentalistic psychologists who identified both with mental imagery, differentiated according to sensory modality. Thus, visual imagery referred to images of objects and printed words alike, whereas auditory-kinesthetic or speech imagery referred to what introspective psychologists experienced when they talked to themselves. Such experiences are important manifestations of imaginal and verbal symbolic activity, and this was taken into account in dual coding research by the use of postexperimental and individual difference questionnaires that ask respondents to describe the verbal and nonverbal mental activity that they consciously experienced during the performance of a prior task.

I have argued on the other hand that consciousness is not a sufficient basis for identifying the functional differences between imaginal and verbal systems, although it may indicate with some validity that the content of consciously experienced mental events was either verbal or nonverbal and of a particular sensory modality. The reported distinctions themselves need to be validated by independent behavioral evidence, and specific functional characteristics of the systems can only be inferred from performance under experimentally controlled conditions. This position was justified by the early Würzburg demonstrations of imageless thought and more specifically by the failure of tests of reported vividness of mental imagery to predict performance on objective tests of memory and other mental functions. Such observations also supported the general hypothesis that nonverbal and verbal symbolic systems can function at an unconscious as well as a conscious level.

The present position remains unchanged in regard to the limitations of introspective reports as a source of information concerning the precise functions of mental representations in cognition. However, more stress is now placed on identifying representational skills that are under conscious control. This added emphasis is motivated mainly by research discoveries that have appeared since the original version of dual coding theory was presented in 1971, although some relevant findings were already available at that time. For example, H. Reed (1918) found that subjects reported using mental images and other associative aids to learn novel paired associates. The associative aids dropped out and responding became automatic as learning progressed, but subjects returned to their use when the pair members were reshuffled so that the task was again novel. However, such findings did not go very far toward revealing the range and detailed nature of conscious mental processes.

The picture has changed enormously with the work of Shepard, Kosslyn, Moyer, and others on such problems as mental rotations, image scanning, and symbolic comparisons, and correlations that are being increasingly found between individual differences in vividness of imagery and objective performance (e.g., Finke, 1980; for a general review and a proposed model of imagery and consciousness, see Morris & Hampson, 1983). Moreover, memory theorists have introduced conscious memory processes into their memory models under such labels as working memory. Consistent with such views, imagery has been conceptualized metaphorically as a work space in which cognitive processes can operate. Finally, theoretical and research attention has been given to the distinction between conscious and automatic processes, including the idea that the same processes can operate at both levels in different tasks (e.g., Posner & Warren, 1972). Such developments are taken into account in the following theoretical analyses.

BASIC FUNCTIONS SERVED BY THE REPRESENTATIONAL SYSTEMS

The following three sections deal with the mediating functions of cognitive processes, that is, the adaptive uses of mental representations and processes in the performance of specific cognitive tasks and generally in the guidance of behavior. The functions implicate the structural properties and processing operations already discussed, with the addition of some task-specific hypotheses concerning the relative degree of involvement and effectiveness of one or the other of the representational systems. The topic is covered under the general headings of evaluative, mnemonic, and motivational-emotional functions. These are assumed to be basic functional categories, all of which are implicated to some degree in complex tasks, such as problem solving (see chap. 9).

Evaluative functions

The term evaluation refers literally to the determination of quantitative values of objects and events. Thus, it implicates whatever processes are used in the analysis and computation of absolute or relative values, with reference here to the information contained in mental representations. Some examples from the research literature are: (a) scanning mental images to determine the relative distances between locations on imaged maps, (b) counting the corners of an imagined block letter, (c) "reading out" the information in an imagined matrix, and (d) symbolic comparisons of objects on any perceptual dimension (size, color, weight, and so on). In the case of verbal representations, we have such tasks as mental arithmetic, analysis of the structure of a mental word (e.g., the number of syllables, number of vowels and consonants, etc.) or sentences (e.g., classifying the words sequentially into nouns or non-nouns).

Most of these tasks implicate both symbolic systems. For example, counting the windows in one's home requires verbally cued generation of visual images of the house as viewed from different perspectives, entailing verbal representational and verbal-to-imaginal referential processing. Counting the windows is a verbal process operating over the encoded nonverbal representations. Moreover, some evaluative activities depend on transformational processes. For example, the cube visualization task may include imagining the cube being cut into smaller cubes, separating them, then determining the number of colored faces on each small cube.

These examples suggest that the functional processes are largely under conscious control of verbal mechanisms. Thus, verbal instructions initiate image generation, scanning, counting, comparison, etc., and these mental activities are kept "on track" at least partly by the subject's own covert verbalization during the task. This suggestion does not imply that all such processes must operate at the conscious level. We might carry out mental scanning or comparison in the service of everyday problems without being aware of what we are doing and without verbal directives of any kind, but we lack evidence on the issue and need not pursue it here. We know at least that verbal cues can initiate and guide evaluative processing. It seems likely, therefore, that this control originates in similar overt processing of perceptual information as a response to verbal instructions, paralleling what is assumed to occur in the case of mental transformations.

Mnemonic functions

The relations between imaginal and verbal processes and memory are among the most intensively investigated problems in psychology. Imagery was the key element in the ancient mnemonic technique called the method of loci, and it has been a focus of research attention in the modern era since the early 1960s. The role of verbal mediation processes in verbal memory attracted similar research attention for a number of decades. The implication has always been that imaginal and verbal systems have important functions in the encoding, storage, and retrieval of episodic information.

The present analysis is based on the theoretical assumption that the memory trace is a modality-specific encoded representation of verbal or nonverbal input information. Words activate logogens, objects or their pictures activate imagens, motor movements activate motor patterns, and so on. Some portion of the total encoded perceptual-motor reaction pattern constitutes the episodic memory trace. The encoding could be entirely at the representational level or it could include elaborative coding to referential or associative levels. Representational encoding is automatic and is sufficient for some level of accuracy in recognition and recall tests of memory. Referential encoding can occur with high probability given appropriate contextual cues, and the probability of such encoding is increased by instructions to image to words or name pictures. The result is a dual trace consisting of the representation that is automatically activated by the input item and the referentially related representation that the subject generates to the input item. Associative encoding refers to activation of associated representations in the same symbolic modality as the input item, such as verbal associates, phrases, or sentences to verbal items and imaginal associates or contexts to pictures. The trace could be elaborated to any degree, depending on the encoding cues that accompany the information to be remembered. Thus, a word as a target item could be imaginally and associatively recoded, and the resulting memory trace consists of the total elaborated encoding. The encoding activity could also include transformations of input information and the memory trace would contain some record of the transformational activity and the representational structure that results from that activity.

Retrieval also entails recoding activity, which could be similar though not identical to the encoding that accompanied the original episodic information because the retrieval context is never identical to the input context. Encoding and recoding processes are likely to be most similar in recognition tests, although research on the effects of contextual changes has shown that considerable variability can be introduced even in recognition. The encoding-recoding differences are sharper and more explicit in associative recall tasks where only part of the original input information is re-presented during the recall test. The classical associative learning problem is to understand how the presented cue can elicit a response corresponding to the missing member of the original pair. The answers have varied with the theory in vogue at a given time. The present view is that the cue generates an encoding that corresponds in a probabilistic fashion to a portion of the original encoding pattern. For example, if one imaged to the pair *horse-clock*, one is more likely to image to the cue-word *horse* during recall than if no image encoding occurred during pair presentation. This simply means that recoding is itself a memory act and is subject to the same influences as memory for the target episode itself.

The effect of recoding during retrieval also depends on the structure of the representation that was generated in response to the original episode. The structural differences between imaginal and verbal representations become crucial at this point. The synchronous and integrative properties of imaginal representations imply that relevant components of the input pattern can be encoded and stored as an integrated representation under appropriate conditions. For example, the probability that *horse-clock* will be integrated is increased by instructions to imagine the referents interacting in some way (a horse winding a clock, say). Presentation of *horse* during recall may then redintegrate the entire compound, permitting the memorizer to analyze the recoded representation and then respond with the word *clock*. The sequential structure of verbal representations makes it more difficult to generate a functionally integrated verbal trace in a single trial, so that a partial verbal cue is less likely to redintegrate the pair as a verbal structure.

This analysis is intended only to indicate some of the mnemonic implications of the dual coding distinctions discussed earlier without getting into such general memory issues as the nature of retrieval processes. For example, is retrieval based on some kind of matching operation and, if so, what is matched with what? Such questions will be considered in chapter 8 in the context of the empirical implications and evidence relevant to the dual coding memory assumptions. Another qualification relates to the apparent vagueness suggested by the repeated use of such terms as "some" in the description of the mnemonic assumptions: *Some* portion of the encoding pattern constitutes the memory trace, *some* level of recall accuracy, encoding and retrieval are *probabilistic*, and so on. This vagueness is deliberate and intended to forestall such misinterpretations as the idea that what is encoded is a detailed and faithful ("raw") reproduction of the episodic information, especially in the case of pictorial information and imaginal memory coding. Even in simple recognition memory for pictures or words, the original encoding is not a detailed mental isomorph of the presented items. In the case of imaginal encoding to word pairs, the representation may be fragmentary and schematic in varying degree, and the retrieval cue may generate a representation that corresponds only partially and inaccurately to a relevant portion of the original encoded trace. All is incomplete and probabilistic to some degree.

A final qualification is that the functional assumptions rest entirely on empirical evidence. Thus, the relative integrative and redintegrative properties of nonverbal and verbal memory representations are supported by so much experimental evidence that the distinction can be included in the theory with considerable confidence. Similarly, the related hypotheses that the memory trace is modality-specific and that referential encoding results in a dual or multimodal trace are justified by empirical evidence. These ideas also have implications in regard to the degree of independence of the components of a dually coded trace. The evidence to date suggests that imaginal and verbal codes are functionally independent in the strong sense that activation of both can have additive effects on recall. Moreover, the evidence suggests that imaginal and verbal codes are unequal in mnemonic value, perhaps by a 2:1 ratio favoring the image code. These and other generalizations are firm enough to be incorporated into dual coding theory and they in turn provide the basis for interpreting a wide range of experimental findings about memory. Still, in keeping with the constructive empirical nature of the present theoretical enterprise, *all* of the theoretical assumptions that I have presented are tentative and subject to modifications if the weight of empirical evidence presses for change. The assumptions are retained as long as they "save the phenomena."

Motivational and emotional functions

The motivational and emotional functions of representational systems are viewed here from the perspective of dual coding theory. We begin with a brief reminder of the phenomena at issue. Motivation refers generally to arousal and goal-oriented aspects of behavior. Arousal includes an intensity dimension as well as qualitative features described as positive or negative affect and different emotions. Goal-oriented behaviors are approach or withdrawal (or avoidance) responses vis-à-vis objects, situations, or behavioral outcomes that have positive or negative incentive value. A common theoretical view is that the affective and goal-oriented reactions are related, so that approach and withdrawal may be mediated by, or at least accompanied by, positive and negative affect. That view is complicated by such discordant reactions as anger, which is generally regarded as a negative emotion and yet may be accompanied by approach behavior in the form of attack. The inconsistency can be resolved by interpreting withdrawal as any behavior that increases the distance between the person and the negative goal, which attack might achieve by causing the goal-object to withdraw. The details of such analyses are not essential for our purposes.

We are concerned here with learned motivational reactions to previously neutral stimuli and their relation to verbal and nonverbal representation systems. Affective and emotional reactions, being nonverbal by definition, must be identified theoretically with the nonverbal representational system and, therefore, they would be expected to accompany such nonverbal cognitive reactions as imagery. The intimate relation is familiar in nightmares and in less extreme forms in pleasant or unpleasant daydreams. The conceptual relation is so close that G. Mandler (1975, p. 194) referred to centrally (cognitively) represented emotional reactions as autonomic imagery (for related views, see Lang, 1979; Leventhal, 1980). In the present approach, however, affect is also related to the verbal system in ways to be described presently.

Goal-oriented reactions also occur in a symbolic form in imagery, commonly experienced as daydream fantasies in which one achieves success in love, sports, professional career, and so on. Singer (1966) recognized the ubiquitousness and functional importance of such goal-oriented daydreams, and Freud attributed similar functions to imagery in his analysis of primary process thinking. Other theorists have provided functionally equivalent analyses without referring explicitly to imagery. For example, Tolman's concept of expectancy, defined as an SRS' unit (see chap. 3), refers to a mental representation of a goal-object and the behavior that would provide access to that object, both components being activated by a given stimulus situation. Lewin's (e.g., see Cartwright, 1959) life-space model includes representations of goal-objects as regions in a cognitive life-space, and a process called locomotion, whereby the self (also a region in life-space) can symbolically access a positive goal region or move away from a negative one. These examples illustrate the widespread acceptance of a conceptual relation between goal-oriented aspects of motivation and cognitive representations and processes, including their conscious expression in imagery.

It is equally obvious that the verbal system can be implicated in motivational reactions. For example, words and descriptions can be highly effective in arousing emotions and goal-oriented reactions, as illustrated dramatically by what happens in a crowded theatre if someone shouts "Fire!" On the response side, motivational reactions are commonly expressed symbolically in language, as verbal descriptions of goals, achievements, and affective reactions associated with them. McClelland (e.g., 1961) capitalized on such relations in his adaptation of projective techniques to the measurement of achievement motivation through content analyses of stories, both as written by subjects under controlled conditions and as they occur naturally in the literature of a people, which are scored for achievement-related themes.

The relations between motivational reactions and verbal and nonverbal events described above translate readily into dual coding theory (for another view of these relations, see Rogers, 1983). The theory implies generally that learned emotional and motivational reactions are mediated by prior activation of nonverbal or verbal cognitive representations, that is, imagens or logogens. The analysis implies that objects or words must be processed at least up to the representational level before affective reactions can occur to them. The cognitive route can be relatively direct in the case of emotion-arousing objects and events, which presumably are represented as imagens with high-probability connections to affective systems. Direct affective arousal by the logogen system is more problematic theoretically but nonetheless compelling because of the observation that affective reactions, as measured by ratings or psychophysiological techniques, can be elicited by abstract (low imagery) words (see Paivio, 1971, p. 83). Such direct access from logogens to affective systems would be analogous to referential processing, in which the nonverbal referential reaction is a feeling or an emotion, presumably resulting from learning experiences in which particular words are reliably associated with a variety of affective situations, so that the words acquire generalized affect-arousing qualities. Ordinarily, however, words would elicit affective reactions through intervening referential and associative levels of processing in the cognitive sense, as when a description of a pleasant or an unpleasant incident evokes images which in turn arouse emotions. The analysis implies, among other things, that affective reactions would ordinarily occur more quickly to pictures than to words because the former have more direct access to affect-mediating imagens. Some relevant evidence is presented in chapters 9 and 12.

The above analysis suggests a particular viewpoint on the general relation between cognition and affect, which is currently a controversial issue. The more traditional view (e.g., Arnold, 1960; Lazarus, 1984) is that the two are separate phenomena, with affective responses following prior cognitive (not necessarily verbal) identification and interpretation of a stimulus. The opposing view, recently defended by Zajonc (1984), is that affect is part of cognition and that relevant affective reactions can occur to stimuli even when the stimuli cannot be identified by such traditional cognitive responses as naming or form-matching. The interpretation suggested by dual coding theory is closer to the traditional view, although the theory also readily handles the reverse causal relationship in which an emotional state, however aroused, increases the probability that relevant images or verbal reactions will also be activated. Such activation is no different in principle from any other experientially determined and probabilistic associative reaction. It reflects a specific (cognitive) form of state-dependent learning, which accounts for such phenomena as the selective effect of mood on verbal recall (e.g., G. H. Bower, 1981; Gage & Safer, 1985; Leight & Ellis, 1981).

The functions of the representational systems in goal-directed behavior have direct parallels in such cognitive behavioristic concepts as means-end readiness and vicarious trial-and-error as described particularly by Tolman. Imagery provides the primary cognitive medium for representing end states (goal-objects, situations, behavioral outcomes) and "trying out" different behaviors that might achieve those ends. The verbal system plays a secondary but no less important role in that the goal-oriented imagery may be initiated by specific words and descriptions that refer to ends and means. The image-evoking verbalization can be self-initiated, or provided by another person in the form of suggestions or commands—essentially, if-then conditionals of the form, if you do x, you will get y. In theoretical terms, these goal-oriented symbolic activities include referential and associative levels of processing, followed by whatever image transformations may be required as part of the means for achieving the goal. Such transformations have a historical precedent in the Gestalt concept of cognitive reorganization of a situation, accounting for the "insight" shown by Köhler's chimpanzees when they put sticks together or used boxes in order to reach otherwise unattainable goals. The cognitive (imaginal?) transformations were initiated by the situation itself in that case as they often are in the case of human problem solving, but the verbal system provides a powerful additional means for humans.

The motivational functions of imaginal and verbal processes have been explored most directly in relation to practical problems. A prominent example is the use of imagery in cognitive therapies, which began with Wolpe's (1958) systematic desensitization approach to the treatment of phobias and which has since expanded to other behavioral problems and imagery techniques (e.g., see Sheikh & Jordan, 1983; Singer, 1974). All such techniques make use of verbal instructions intended to elicit images of attractive or aversive goal-objects or situations, and adaptive behaviors vis-à-vis those situations, with the assumption (or hope) that the imagined activities will transfer to real situations as altered behaviors and emotional reactions. Another example is the use of verbal suggestions and imagery to improve athletic performance by optimizing arousal level as well as reinforcing specific perceptual-motor skills through mental rehearsal (e.g., see reviews by Denis, in press; Feltz & Landers, 1983; Hall, in press; Paivio, in press; Suinn, 1983). Some of the specific issues and findings from such research are discussed in subsequent chapters.

CONCEPTUAL ISSUES RECONSIDERED

Before turning to the empirical phenomena, let us briefly reconsider two meta-theoretical issues discussed in chapter 1 and entailed by the empiricist dual coding approach, namely, the terminal meta-postulate and operationalism.

The terminal meta-postulate and dual coding theory

Whatever their merits otherwise, the rationalistic arguments concerning the limitations of the terminal meta-postulate on associationistic theories do not apply to dual coding theory, for general and more specific reasons. The general reason is essentially a corollary of the basic theoretical point that the explanation of particular behaviors is always in terms of two interconnected symbolic systems, with the relative emphasis sometimes being more on one or the other, and sometimes on their continual interplay. Thus, verbal behavior is not interpreted solely in terms of internalized verbal stimulus and response elements that bear a one-to-one sequential relationship to the verbal behavior itself, but rather in terms of an external and internal (imaginal) situational context together with an external verbal context and activity of the internal verbal system. Only the latter is described in the same language as the terminal behavioral elements. It is interesting to note in this connection that the roles of situational factors and of imagery have not been directly considered by the critics of the terminal meta-postulate. The examples that are typically used to illustrate the problem are drawn from language behavior or from artificial grammars. Center-embedded sentences provide the paradigm case, analyzed as though associative theories rely entirely on verbal-sequential habits to explain verbal behavior. J. Anderson and Bower (1973, p. 12) assert that other mediating processes such as ideas and images run into the same difficulties if they can be matched with observables. However, they do not go on to show formally why such concepts are inadequate even individually, let alone in the kinds of combinations that are envisaged within dual coding theory.

The more specific reason for rejecting the rationalist critique is that some postulates of dual coding theory directly violate the connectionist and mechanistic statements of the terminal meta-postulate. First, the connectionist statement is violated by the assumption that the imagery system can construct novel representations that do not correspond directly to contiguities of experience. For example, I can imagine an elephant riding on top of an ambulance (an interactive image) although I have never actually seen such an event. These novel constructions are reflected in such behavioral consequences as the striking superiority of verbal-associative recall following interactive as compared to separate imagery instructions. A similar analysis can be applied to the constructive nature of verbal processes. A second violation of the connectionist statement is the assumption that similarity can play a role in associative behavior independent of experiential contiguity. For example, a perceptual stimulus can evoke a memory image of a previous experience that somehow resembles the current situation. These and other experimental examples of the role of similarity in associative reactions will be considered in the chapters to follow.

In summary, the so-called terminal meta-postulate does not pose a problem for dual coding theory for general as well as specific reasons. The general reasons relate to the failure of critics of traditional empiricist-associative approaches to consider the role of all relevant associative variables and situational contexts in the explanation of particular behaviors—factors that are taken into account in dual coding theory. The specific reasons are that a number of the assumptions of the theory violate aspects of the terminal meta-postulate.

Operationism and dual coding theory

The theoretical significance of the evidence reviewed in subsequent chapters hinges on the adequacy of the procedures that are used to operationalize concepts and statements. Accordingly, a brief recapitulation of the present position will be useful. The main point is that the operational procedures are viewed as empirical indicators or ways of manipulating the structures and processes that are postulated in the theory. The empirical-theoretical relations are close because of the empiricist nature of the theory-building enterprise itself. The procedures initially were guesses based on some experimental data, some informal observations, and a lot of traditional wisdom. The experimental data included effects of stimulus attributes and individual difference variables. The informal observations were based on reports of imagery and verbal thinking in various tasks. The traditional wisdom is the set of teachings associated with the art of memory from Simonides to the present, which hinged especially on the efficacy of mnemonic instructions. All of these procedures have become more refined and rigorous as experimental evidence accumulated. The result is that item attributes, instructions and other experimental procedures, and individual difference variables are now viewed as different ways of manipulating the probability that imaginal or verbal processes will be activated and used in a given task. The probabilities are related to both structures and processes. Thus, high imagery words encourage an image-encoding process that generates structural representations that can be used for various purposes. Instructions increase the probability that a particular kind of encoding process will be activated and that a particular representational structure will result. For example, interactive imagery instructions encourage the generation of particular kinds of imaginal structures. Instructions to rotate, scan, or otherwise manipulate imaginal information similarly arouse transformational processes of various kinds, and so on.

Such an approach is iterative and self-corrective. The operational procedures tentatively define the theoretical entities and processes and the results of the procedures serve to confirm or disconfirm the validity of the operations. When "enough" disconfirming evidence has accumulated, one must either seek new operational procedures or change the theoretical assumptions. It was on empirical grounds that I originally rejected measures of imagery vividness as an operational approach to the concept. The tentative nature of such decisions is indicated by the fact that I now believe that vividness tests may after all have some operational validity—implying, too, that vividness may be an effective attribute of imaginal representations. The inherent circularity of the process is ameliorated by the use of multiple convergent (meaning *potentially* convergent) operations, as described in chapter 1, and one's confidence in the approach depends continually on predictive and explanatory successes. That is the operational empiricism on which the scientific enterprise is based: The adequacy of dual coding theory hinges on the degree to which it "saves the phenomena," and does so better than other relevant approaches.

5

Development of
Representational Systems

We now touch on the development of internal representations and processes as viewed from the perspective of dual coding theory (for a more general and detailed review of representational development, see J. Mandler, 1983). Relevant available data are interpreted in terms of the assumptions of the theory and, where such data are not available, some testable implications are proposed. We begin with some views concerning developmental mechanisms and then turn to evidence that bears on the verbal-nonverbal representational distinction, functional interconnections between and within the two systems, and the different functional properties associated with them individually and jointly.

BASIC DEVELOPMENTAL MECHANISMS

In considering developmental mechanisms, we must deal initially with the heredity-environment problem. How much weight should be given to each and what kind of acquisition mechanism should we postulate to account for developmental changes? The problem continues to be especially controversial in the field of cognitive development, where the favored positions range from Chomskyan nativism at one extreme, through Piagetian constructivism, to learning theory at the other (e.g., see the contributions to the volume on the debate between Piaget and Chomsky concerning learning and language, edited by Piattelli-Palmarini, 1980). The controversy stems from conflicting philosophical views and persists because it is extraordinarily difficult to get an empirical handle on hereditary contributions to cognition. It is unnecessary for our purposes to review the contentious issues or the relevant evidence in detail, but some general comments are in order. Following those comments I will simply take for granted that genetic factors are involved in the development of both representational systems, and then go on to emphasize the role of experience.

The development of representational structures and skills is presumably dependent on such basic processes as short-term or working memory (e.g.,

Brainerd, 1983; Case, 1978; Chi, 1976), which are genetically constrained although learning plays a role in the rate of reaching the genetic limit. Infants might also begin life with some built in perceptual "preferences" (e.g., Field, 1982) and genetic factors presumably contribute to more complex nonverbal skills, such as spatial ability (McGee, 1982). We know, too, that language is a species-specific skill, although we remain uncertain about what aspects of it are genetically determined. The genetic determinants have been viewed traditionally as biological constraints on what can be learned. Chomsky (1965) conceptualized these limitations as formal constraints on language acquisition, and the implications of this view have been explored in detail recently in the context of cognitive development generally (e.g., Keil, 1981) and language acquisition in particular (e.g., Pinker, 1984; Wexler & Culicover, 1980).

The eventual contribution of the formal constraints approach to the scientific understanding of cognitive development remains to be seen, but at the moment it runs into all of the problems associated with formal computational approaches that we reviewed in chapter 3. For example, the learnability theory proposed by Wexler and Culicover (1980) consists of a language-learning mechanism that uses a trial and error process to test hypotheses about possible formal grammars, rather than observable properties of natural languages. The child obviously receives speech but the datum received by Wexler's and Culicover's learning device is a formal description consisting of a deep structure phrase marker and a surface string derived by a transformational component applied to the former. They could have developed the theory using some other formal grammar, but this would not change the argument. The problem is that formal grammars are not natural languages, they are theories that attempt to characterize natural languages. The step from natural language to the formal description is not bridged by formal learnability theory, it is simply assumed. The theory might show how a computer could be programmed to choose among alternative formal grammars but as an explanation it appears to be circular and irrelevant to the question of how a child learns a vocabulary and how it uses it for communicative purposes in particular situations. Wexler and Culicover (1980, p. 493) recognize that language learnability theory is not a theory of language development in children, but they do suggest that the constraints that operate in linguistic theory also operate in the grammars of children. There is no evidence to justify such an assumption and there seems to be no way to test it because formal constraints apply only within a formal system. The formal constraints approach to other areas of cognitive development is similarly circular and limited as an explanatory theory to the extent that it remains wedded to formal criteria.

The approach taken here is guided by the general empiricist assumption that the specific things that individuals know and can do with that knowledge (the content and functional properties of internal representations) must result from experience. Thus, from a theoretical and practical viewpoint, experiential factors must have priority in our inquiry into basic mechanisms

Learning mechanisms

The development of mental representations that correspond to environmental objects and events and linguistic patterns obviously requires exposure to such stimuli, but the precise nature of the effective experience is less clear. The candidates are classical and operant conditioning, which depend on reinforcement, and sensory conditioning and perceptual learning, which do not. In fact, sensory conditioning and perceptual (or observational) learning can be considered as variants of simple experiential contiguity, with the addition that perceptual learning implies an active observer (Bandura, 1977; I. Brown, 1979). What relevant evidence do we have?

Beritoff (1965) emphasized the role of sensory and classical conditioning in the development of imaginal representations ("psychoneural complexes"), supported by evidence from animal studies. More recent studies of animal behavior provide strong evidence for conditioned representations that are image-like in the sense that they can be aroused by their associates and function as the original stimuli in a variety of situations (e.g., see Holland, 1983; Rescorla, Grau, & Durlach, 1985). Some human studies also suggest that imagery can be classically conditioned to nonverbal and verbal stimuli (e.g., Ellson, 1941; Leuba, 1940; Lohr, 1976). Sensory conditioning (object-word pairing) may also be sufficient (Begg, 1976), although it has been surprisingly difficult to demonstrate such effects experimentally (Philipchalk, 1971). The proponents of the classical conditioning approach refer to images as conditioned sensations or perceptions (e.g., King, 1973; Mowrer, 1960; Sheffield, 1961; Staats, 1961). Skinner (1953, 1957), on the other hand, emphasized the response characteristics of perception itself and accordingly interpreted visual imagery in terms of operant conditioning, referring to it as operant seeing.

Bugelski (1982) presented a thoughtful review of the relation between learning and imagery in which he highlights the continued importance of understanding learning mechanisms if we are to understand imagery, and vice versa. He views images as associations formed between neural events as a result of co-occurrence over a sufficient time period. Thus, images are conditioned, sensory neural activities that normally occur on the occasion of some conditioned stimulus. Moreover, the relation between imagery and conditioning is reciprocal, so, that all imagery is said to be conditioning and all conditioning is the formation of images with or without accompanying subjective experience. An interesting feature, based on proposals by Mowrer (1960) on the function of proprioceptive stimuli and Greenwald (1970) on ideomotor action, is the suggestion that proprioception, or kinesthetic neural activity, is qualitatively the same as imagery and that such activity can move forward in time to serve as a conditioned stimulus to initiate behavior that the proprioceptive stimulation formerly followed. This analysis is intended to account for instrumental behavior as a by-product of the association of neural activities. A similar account of anticipatory behavior was proposed earlier by Sheffield (1961; for a relevant summary, see Crowder, 1976, pp. 435–439).

Bugelski's article is accompanied by critical commentaries by reviewers who point to problems associated with the conditioning approach, the explanatory status of neurological concepts, the priority attached to images as symbols, and so on. Together with Bugelski's rejoinder, the exchange highlights the problems associated not only with conditioning accounts of the acquisition of imagery but alternative accounts as well, simply because available empirical data are insufficient to resolve the issues.

The same learning mechanisms have been proposed for the acquisition of linguistic representations and skills, and similar shortcomings have been noted, beginning with Chomsky's (1959) cricitisms of stimulus-response learning theories as applied to language acquisition. Such criticisms have been directed especially at the concept of reinforcement, since no one denies that particular languages are learned in some way. As a consequence, the explanatory load has fallen on some form of perceptual learning, based simply on hearing speech and observing the circumstances in which it occurs. The child presumably attempts to sort out what is going on and, according to Chomsky (1965), tests grammatical "hypotheses." The outcome is a representational base for language, namely, linguistic competence. This approach draws attention to the nature of the input, about which something is known through the study of "motherese" and situational contexts in language acquisition (e.g., see de Villiers & de Villiers, 1978; Paivio, 1983a). However, relevant data on the issues are still sparse and reinforcement cannot be totally rejected at this time because experimental studies (e.g., see Zimmerman & Rosenthal, 1974) have at least demonstrated that language skills can be shaped by operant conditioning procedures.

DEVELOPMENTAL SEQUENCE

This section deals with evidence pertaining to the sequence of development of nonverbal and verbal representations and associative structures, interconnections between them, and the processes that make it possible to use the representational information skillfully and productively. We begin with nonverbal functional units and structures because they are assumed to be necessary for the initial stages of language development. That dependency implies that language development entails establishment of referential interconnections at the same time as representations for the first content words are formed, so verbal representations and referential relations are discussed next. Finally, we consider the complex associative structures and generative processes that are brought into play when the child's language skills extend beyond the one-word stage.

Nonverbal representations and skills

Some available evidence supports the obvious assumption that nonverbal representations begin to be established very early. The inferences are based on memory data, some of it obtained in relation to the Piagetian concept of object permanence. Initially, episodic memory for faces and objects is demonstrated by the infant's surprise reaction when an object is hidden from view behind a screen and is absent when the screen is removed, a reaction that does not occur if the object reappears. Some contend that the surprise reaction occurs in infants as young as 20 days provided that the occlusion is not more than six seconds (T. G. R. Bower, 1966). From such data, Bower and others (e.g., see Bremner, 1982; Harris, 1975, 1983) argue that these infants understand the permanence of the hidden object. However, those observations could be explained entirely in terms of an episodic memory trace that is functionally useful for six seconds. They need not be interpreted to mean that the infant has begun to develop long-term memory representations (imagens) corresponding to the objects.

The evidence for such representations is more convincing at six months of age. Bower and Paterson (1973) observed that infants of that age showed surprise when an object they were following was exchanged behind the screen, so that a different one emerged. The reaction suggests that the infants had an expectancy for an identified object, which was not confirmed. The interpretation is supported by the observation that shyness with strangers begins at about the same age, presumably because the appearance of an unfamiliar person contrasts sharply with the infants' mental representations of familiar persons. Of course, other observations indicate that infants know close family members and objects in the home quite well before the age of six months, so the conservative conclusion is that by that age the infant has a considerable repertoire of internal representations for objects and persons. The development of such representations is presumably continuous from birth onward and involves enrichment of the representations corresponding to familiar objects as well as addition of new ones. Enrichment means that objects are known perceptually in different orientations and by different senses, together with knowledge about their behaviors and what behavioral reactions they afford.

In one sense, such representational enrichment means increased elaboration of an integrated representation that incorporates information corresponding to different modalities. A conditioning approach provides a useful account of how that might come about, as in the following example from Sheffield (1961):

If a set of *n* sensory responses, R_{s1}, R_{s2}, R_{s3}, ... R_{sn}, are elicited by different aspects of a given stimulus *object*, they will become conditioned to each other in the course of exploration of the object ... Thus an object like an orange is smelled, touched, hefted, peeled, tasted, etc., giving rise to a succession of distinctive sensory responses which become conditioned to each other as cues. In the great variety of experience provided when a child becomes familiar with an orange, practically every stimulus aspect has sometimes preceded, sometimes followed, and sometimes occurred simultaneously with every other aspect, giving rise to a conditioned (perceptual) response pattern which is unique for oranges as objects and which can be elicited in relatively complete form by only one unique aspect of the orange.... This "cross-conditioning" mechanism accounts for the "filling-in" property of perceptual behavior in which a fragment of a total stimulus-pattern "redintegrates" the whole. (1961, pp. 16–17)

The conditioning analysis provides a possible basis for the development of complex integrated representations and associated mechanisms that permit them to be redintegrated by specific cues. The analysis would need to be extended to account for multiple representations corresponding to a given object or classes of objects. The problem confronts all representational theories, which generally handle it by some form of type-token distinction, such as a concept node that could be instantiated by activating other specific information relevant to a particular context. However, as noted in chapter 1, the type-token approach simply pushes the problem to another level, since we still need some differentiated representational base to account for our varied knowledge of objects in different orientations as perceived or imagined. All theories must rely on contextual factors to account for such differentiation. Conditioning theory does so in terms of experiences with objects in different contexts, so that relevant contextual cues can activate particular conditioned perceptual-motor patterns rather than others. In representational terms, the contextual interpretation translates into the idea that representational variants are differentiated by representational contexts corresponding to the perceptual and behavioral settings in which the objects have been experienced.

The inescapable general conclusion is that representational development involves the formation of an indefinitely large (and expanding) set of representational variants, or tokens, all of which are complex, integrated structures that incorporate information from different modalities in varying degrees. This conclusion is a version of the exemplar approach to nonverbal concepts, together with the idea that some narrow range of representational variants may be more typical or prototypical than others because of high frequency of experience with the represented objects in particular orientations and, sometimes, in particular settings. The most relevant evidence has come from experimental studies of the effect of experience with exemplars on the formation of representations to perceptual concepts (e.g., Salthouse, 1977; Solso & Raynis, 1979).

Verbal representations and referential skills

The present view that the development of the verbal system is based initially on a nonverbal representational substrate is in general agreement with Piaget and others who emphasize the primacy of general perceptual and other skills in language development (an especially relevant specific example is H. Clark's, 1973, analysis of how a child might learn spatial and temporal terms on the basis of a prior understanding of perceptual space). The reference is to meaningful language, since memory representations corresponding to speech sounds presumably begin to be established early through exposure to the speech of family members. Similarly, sounds produced by the infant increasingly take on the general characteristics of the child's linguistic community. The development of meaningful verbal representations (initially concrete nouns, then adjectives, action verbs, etc.) presumably occurs in relation to salient referent objects that are discriminated first as holistic entities and known later by their variable and invariant properties (cf. Macnamara, 1972; Nelson, 1974). In dual coding terms, this analysis implies that development of the verbal representational system begins essentially at the referential level, so that verbal representations are established in relation to object representations that have already attained some degree of elaboration in terms of their static and dynamic properties. In theory, therefore, the verbal system is not independent of the nonverbal system during its early development, though at some point it becomes capable of functioning independently. Moreover, verbal and nonverbal representations would be formed concurrently and interdependently when new objects are first experienced along with their names. Dissociation and functional independence would result when object and name are experienced separately as well as together. Finally, verbal representations and referential interconnections would be further strengthened by the child's own referential activity as soon as he or she begins naming objects, attributes, actions, etc., without verbal prompting from others.

The developmental priority of nonverbal representations during the initial stages of cognitive development can hardly be in doubt. However, the evidence is less clear on the stronger claim that the growth of the verbal representational system *depends on* a nonverbal representational base. Some researchers have investigated the general problem by comparing measures of nonverbal cognitive development with one-word vocabulary development. The results have been suggestive in that the two classes of behaviors tend to be correlated (e.g., McCune-Nicolich, 1981). It has also been shown that controlled experience with objects accelerates the acquisition of nonverbal communicative behaviors (Steckol & Leonard, 1981). Whether the effect also transfers to verbal skills remains to be determined. Thus, there is some support for the causal claim that development of the verbal system, at least in its early stages, is dependent on prior development of the nonverbal system but more and stronger evidence is needed before we can be confident about the causal factors (for a relevant review, see Terrace, 1985). The general problem comes up again later in connection with the role of nonverbal experience in the development of grammatical skills.

More on referential development: Imaging to words

The above discussion of the role of referential experience in the development of verbal representations implicates functional interconnections that permit objects to be named. The relevant evidence does not justify the further inference that the functional relation is reciprocal, whereby the child is also able to image to words. There is no firm developmental evidence on this difficult problem and about all that can be said is that referential imagery may be involved when children behave as though they are looking for something when they hear the name of an absent object or person. Verbal-to-nonverbal referential interconnections are also implicated when the child can pick out the correct object from several alternatives when the name is spoken, but this is a recognition test and it cannot be accepted as evidence that the child can generate an image to the name. What would be required instead is some kind of successive comparison test that would prompt the child to image to a name before an object is shown, and some response, analogous to the surprise reaction used with infants, that would indicate a match or mismatch between name-generated image and object. Such possibilities are yet to be explored.

Apparent differences in imaginal and verbal referential encoding reactions have been observed with older children. Memory studies suggest that children can use verbal strategies to aid picture recall before they can use instructionally induced imagery strategies to aid word recall (see Pressley, 1977). Again, however, the findings may reflect differences in the detectability of the two kinds of referential activity, or difficulty in getting young children to respond appropriately to imagery instructions. Such responding implicates complex control processes at the verbal-associative and referential levels. For example, the instruction to "picture in your mind a *horse* and a *bicycle* doing something together" requires that the child understand what is meant by "picture in your mind." They then must hold the to-be-remembered objects in memory while generating a relationship which is then imagined internally (Pressley & Levin, 1978). The capacity to respond appropriately in that case entails productive cognitive skills (see below) that presumably develop later than the ability to imagine objects or events suggested by words or stories that children hear, ones in which relationships between objects are already determined for the child (Levin, 1982). This passive referential capacity explains why young children enjoy having stories read to them and seem to react imaginally to such stories. Be that as it may, the experimental evidence indicates that the effective application of imagery mnemonics can be pushed to younger and younger ages by carefully programmed training and instructions (e.g., Yuille & Catchpole, 1973).

Thus, if anything, image-encoding skills in young children are probably better than present research techniques are able to reveal.

Associative structures and processes

Our earlier discussion of the progressive elaboration of nonverbal representational units and their association with particular settings suggests that imagens ordinarily develop in the context of larger associative structures comprised of representations for all of the objects that have been repeatedly and variably associated in experience. The problem here is to identify and measure the growth of such probabilistic structures and processes, particularly as manifested in such nonverbal associative reactions as imagining other objects when presented with a particular object as a cue. The necessary methodology and early developmental evidence are once again generally lacking in regard to this straightforward question as in the case of the others already examined. Some indication of nonverbal-associative structures in children old enough to draw is provided by their drawings of such complex objects as people and houses. These drawings reveal systematic distortions in the shapes, proportions, locations of parts, and so on. These are partly a function of limited drawing skills, but their systematic nature and the fact that they also occur in recognition tests suggest that they reflect stages in the development of representational structures and processes (e.g., Goodnow, 1977; Selfe, 1983).

Somewhat more evidence is available on the development of verbal associative structures. The shift from one- to two-word utterances is relevant because some of the latter appear to be repetitive, possibly reflecting associative habits. Others appear to be novel, indicating a productive capacity of some kind. Classification schemes (e.g., Braine, 1963; R. Brown, 1973, pp. 172–187) are generally in terms of syntactic or semantic structures or relations, rather than in terms of the structural relations specified by dual coding theory. Thus, we have no way of knowing from the data whether two-word utterances reflect verbal associations, compound referential reactions to complex stimuli, or productive reactions based on extension by analogy or mediated generalization of some kind.

Word-association studies with older children provide more direct evidence, particularly in relation to the distinction between syntagmatic and paradigmatic associations. The classical generalization is that children show a relatively greater proportion of syntagmatic associations than do adults up to about age seven, after which they shift to adult-like paradigmatic responding. This shift has been used as a basis for theoretical interpretations of language development in terms of verbal-mediational theory (e.g., Palermo & Jenkins, 1964) and other theories, but the regularity of the shift and its interpretation are in doubt (Nelson, 1977).

Manipulative and productive cognitive skills

We turn next to the complex cognitive skills involved in the capacity to manipulate and transform representational information and to generate novel representations in imagination and language.

The developmental study of imagery by Piaget and Inhelder (1966; for reviews, see Paivio, 1971, chap. 2; J. Mandler, 1983) suggests that anticipatory and transformational imagery do not appear in the child's mental repertoire until the transition to operational thinking at around the age of seven years. Prior to that, during the preoperational stage, imagery appeared to be predominantly static and nonanticipatory. This conclusion has not been uniformly supported by subsequent studies. For example, Marmor (1975, 1977), using the Cooper and Shepard (1973) method for studying mental rotations, found that children as young as four years showed the typical linear relation between amount of rotation and reaction time to indicate whether pairs of pictures are the same or mirror images of each other. They differed from adults only in that the slopes of the function were steeper for children, suggesting slower rotation rates. We need more evidence on the problem, obtained with various procedures, before we can generalize about the age of onset of different nonverbal mental transformational skills. For the moment, Marmor's data suggests that the ability to rotate imaginal information is present by at least the age of four years.

Next, we consider the processes responsible for the production of novel images and active imagination on the one hand, and grammatical language on the other. Both implicate generative mechanisms whose nature is unknown in the case of imagery and remains a puzzle in the case of language. Kosslyn (1980) handled the problem in his imagery model by including a "generate" operator that initiates the construction of a visual image from a propositional description. The construction system is assumed to function in principle like a picture-generation routine in artificial intelligence programs. However, as pointed out earlier, such systems are presently restricted to very simple patterns, and the construction component itself is an engineering heuristic that has no theoretical counterpart in mental models that goes beyond a hand waving stage.

The problem has been the focus of attention in language theories since the Chomskyan revolution. Such theories handle the production problem by the use of rules that operate on structural units to create permissible but novel constructions. The same general idea would be applicable in principle to imagery, given a formal definition of units and higher-order abstract structures that would correspond to those used in linguistic grammars. Case grammars and other semantically based systems (e.g., Chafe, 1970; Fillmore, 1977; Lakoff, 1977) may be particularly appropriate because their basic constructs (e.g., case relations and linguistic gestalts) have experiential correlates in perceptual scenes. Language development has been studied from such perspectives, specifically by combining case grammar with Piagetian ideas about the development of sensorimotor intelligence (e.g., Edwards, 1973; Sinclair-de Zwart, 1973), although the nature of generative mechanisms is taken for granted more than it is explicated by such approaches.

The present approach to nonverbal productive skills puts the major emphasis on extension by analogy in regard to both production and recognition of novel instances of object classes or novel relational combinations of familiar instances. This analogical approach is essentially like exemplar-based interpretations of concept learning (e.g., Brooks, 1978; Hintzman & Ludlam, 1980). Children's early years are filled with experiences with familiar objects viewed from various perspectives and in various combinations. Moreover, they increasingly manipulate objects or behave in relation to them in various ways. New objects are related to familiar ones analogically, that is, they are perceived and responded to in ways that are similar to perceptual-motor responses to the familiar ones. Or, familiar objects not previously experienced together are put into static or active relations according to possibilities already associated with one or both. Thus, a child might spontaneously "drive" a toy car into a box as though the latter were a garage even without having experienced the two objects together simply by virtue of prior separate experiences with toy cars, boxes as containers, and real cars being driven into garages. The creative act is mediated by the nonverbal-associative meanings already learned to each object. This still leaves the analysis of similarity (e.g., between garages and boxes) open to analysis in terms of feature patterns or any other theory, but the creative aspect of nonverbal cognition can be generally explained as analogical and associatively mediated extensions of nonverbal representations, associative relations among them, and behavioral patterns associated with them. Such analogic extensions can also be the basis of semantic productivity in language use as reflected in overextensions in object naming by young children (Hudson & Nelson, 1984).

A final consideration here is the relation between syntax and nonverbal representational patterns during language learning. As we have seen, experientially based theories emphasize the role of nonverbal situations and responses in language behavior. The present version of that view is that the learning of syntax depends initially on perceptual-motor and imaginal correlates based on experiences involving static and dynamic relations between objects, with later syntactic learning being possible at an intraverbal level alone (Paivio, 1971, pp. 437–438). This hypothesis has been directly supported by the results of the following miniature language acquisition experiments.

Moeser and Bregman (1972, 1973) had their participants learn miniature grammars with or without accompanying perceptual referents. Thus, a series of "sentences" constructed from nonsense words according to a phrase-structure grammar were presented alone or accompanied by pictures related to the grammars in various ways. The most relevant of these was a syntax-correlated condition, in which the syntactic constraints of the language were also mirrored in the logical constraints of the pictures. For example, the "words" in the 1973 experiment were grouped into classes so that some words referred to rectangles of different colors, others to various nonrectangular forms, others to changes in orientation or shape of the rectangle, and still others to variations in the borders of the shapes.

The results showed that learning was generally best under the syntax-correlated conditions. The effect was particularly striking in the 1973 study, where subjects in a words-only condition were unable to learn a complex grammar even when they had seen a total of 3,200 instances of correct sentences. In contrast, subjects in the syntax-correlated condition did very well. The experiment showed in addition that, once the syntax had been learned in the context of pictures, the syntactic class membership of new words could be learned in a purely verbal context. The dependence of initial syntactic learning on correlated referents and the freedom of later learning from such dependence are both consistent with the dual coding hypothesis. It is relevant, too, that a later study (Mori & Moeser, 1983) showed that subjects learning an artificial language ignored syntactic markers when the language was learned in the context of semantic referents, as in the earlier studies, but subjects were able to use the syntactic markers effectively when referents were not used during learning.

This completes our survey of developmental issues and evidence from the dual coding perspective. Further relevant evidence will be mentioned in the context of the following chapter, which deals with individual differences in representational skills.

6
Individual Differences

We focus here on individual differences in representational habits and skills, which presumably result from the developmental processes discussed in the last chapter. The principal aim is to interpret relevant evidence in terms of dual coding theory and, where such data are not available, to propose testable implications of the theory. My hope is that the approach will lead progressively to a better understanding of differences in cognitive abilities and, reciprocally, enrichment of the guiding theory. Indeed, individual differences could serve as a crucible in theory construction (Underwood, 1975). We begin with a brief overview of general theoretical issues and then turn to the present approach.

GENERAL THEORETICAL ORIENTATION

It is axiomatic that individual differences in cognitive abilities and habits are a product of experience interacting with genetic variability. Most of the theoretical discussion in this area has focused on "general" intelligence and the central issues go beyond what is most relevant for our purposes (discussions of currently salient approaches appear in a set of articles edited by Fry, 1984; see also R. Sternberg, 1984, and the accompanying commentaries). Ferguson (1954, 1956) proposed a theory of cognitive abilities that is compatible with the approach taken here and has also been favorably viewed by other students of intellectual abilities (Guilford, 1967; J. M. Hunt, 1961), so it will serve as a general orienting framework.

Ferguson defined abilities as patterns of behavior which, through overlearning, have reached a crude limit of performance in adults and show considerable stability over shorter time periods in children. Biological factors fix limiting conditions but learning has a substantial influence within those limits. Cultural and other environmental factors determine what will be learned at what age and variation in these factors leads to the development of different patterns of ability. Abilities emerge through transfer of learning that has different effects in different situations and at different stages of learning. Thus, positive transfer of specific skills across similar situations produces the high correlations between tests that define abilities of some level of generality. Ferguson elaborates on the concept of transfer, problems associated with the definition of similarity, and other issues that need not detain us here. As evidence for the theory, Ferguson (1956, pp. 127–129) cited experiments showing substantial and systematic changes in the factor structure of a learning task with continued practice, so that abilities involved at one stage differ from those involved at another stage. Other studies showed markedly different ability patterns for children reared in relatively isolated regions as compared to urban communities.

The emphasis on experiential factors in Ferguson's theory is especially compatible with the present approach, and transfer as interpreted by him provides a possible mechanism whereby experience has its differential cumulative effects. However, the specific theoretical approach to which we now turn does not depend on the validity of Ferguson's general theory. It simply provides an acceptable point of departure.

SPECIFIC THEORETICAL ORIENTATION

Our specific goal is to evaluate individual differences in terms of the general assumptions of dual coding theory. To what extent are the data consistent with the verbal-nonverbal symbolic distinction, the orthogonal relation between symbolic and sensory systems, the different structural and processing levels, and differences in the various functional properties of the two systems as specified by the theory? The emphasis will be on cognitive abilities, with some attention as well to symbolic habits or cognitive styles from the perspective of dual coding.

Since much of the evidence comes from factor-analytic studies of human abilities, it behooves us to consider the differences between the present approach and some of the models that guide those studies. The most systematic and general of these is Guilford's (1967) structure-of-intellect (SI) model. It consists of a three-way classification of intellectual factors into content, operation, and product categories. Content refers to the kind of information involved in ability tests, and the SI model includes four types, namely, figural, symbolic, semantic, and behavioral. The operation categories include evaluation, convergent production, divergent production, memory, and cognition. The product categories are units, classes, relations, systems, transformations, and implications. Overall, then, the SI model is a 4 by 5 by 6 cubic structure whose intersecting cells define a total of 120 identified or potential factors. More recent versions include modifications that add to the number of potential factors. For example, the figural category has been replaced by visual and auditory information categories (Guilford, 1982).

Guilford's approach has been criticized on a number of conceptual and methodological grounds (e.g., Carroll, 1983; Eysenck, 1967; Horn & Knapp, 1973) as well as on the more substantive grounds that the model does not include enough detail on cognitive-processing mechanisms (Royce, Kearsley, & Klare, 1978). Guilford (1974) has defended his general approach, and he is increasingly sensitive to the need for a combination of multivariate experimental and factor-analytic research in order to better identify information-processing functions (Guilford, 1982). In any case, the important point for our purposes is that the SI model is the most general of existing approaches to the study of individual differences and the richest source of data for evaluating dual coding theory. A conceptual comparison of the two approaches is accordingly warranted without getting into the methodological issues that others have addressed.

First of all, there is no one-to-one correspondence in the conceptual categories used in the two theories. Instead, dual coding categories generally map onto two or more SI categories, and vice versa. The following are some of the salient differences. First, unlike dual coding, the SI model does not draw a major distinction between verbal and nonverbal content categories or processes. It turns out, however, that most of the SI tests that use verbal materials and processing define factors that fall under symbolic and semantic content categories, whereas most of the nonverbal tests fall into the figural categories. Some of Guilford's tests are also mixtures in that the material may be nonverbal but the task requires verbal processing or vice versa. In the dual coding framework, such tasks initially depend on referential processing, followed perhaps by additional cognitive processing by one representational system or the other.

The two approaches also differ in the way they define the terms symbolic and semantic. Guilford (1967) defines symbolic information as being "in the form of signs, materials, the elements having no significance in and of themselves, such as letters, numbers, musical notations, and other 'code' elements" (p. 227). In dual coding theory, however, symbols do have significance in that they correspond to cognitive representations and they "stand for" something else in the sense that they can activate other representations. Moreover, pictures and images are viewed as having a symbolic function along with the more verbal symbolic elements listed by Guilford. Guilford's treatment of semantic information is appropriately complex (1967, pp. 227–236) and generally similar to the present approach, including recognition of the possibility that semantic information can be nonverbal or figural. Nonetheless, there is much less emphasis in his approach on the nonverbal than on the verbal side, and the SI semantic information tests are generally verbal in content and processing requirements. This verbal emphasis is unlike the emphasis on verbal-nonverbal referential relations and imaginal processing in the dual coding approach to semantics.

The product and operation categories of SI generally have comparable conceptual distinctions in dual coding theory, but here, too, there are differences that appear to stem from a relatively greater emphasis on processing in the present approach. The emphasis shows up specifically in the distinction between representational, referential, and associative levels of processing, which has no direct counterpart in the SI model. The latter includes only a partial parallel in that the convergent and divergent production categories correspond primarily to the associative level in dual coding. The differential emphasis also appears in the product categories, which are essentially structural concepts in SI (e.g., relations and transformations viewed as the end product of operations) whereas dual coding explicitly accommodates both the structural and processing aspects of such concepts (e.g., transformations are dynamic processes, which generate a transformed representation). Nevertheless, the difference is mainly one of conceptual emphasis, as will be seen from the fact that many of the SI factor-defining tests provide evidence for dual coding processing distinctions.

Other correlational and factor-analytic approaches are generally more restricted in scope than Guilford's, but they are equally relevant to aspects of the dual coding approach. The more prominent ones include Carroll's (e.g., 1976) analysis of cognitive dimensions, the work of E. B. Hunt and his collaborators (e.g., Hunt, Frost, & Lunneborg, 1973) on memory and language processes, and the work of Das, Kirby, and Jarman (1975) on simultaneous and successive modes of processing. Some of these and other specific contributions will be reviewed in appropriate contexts in the following sections.

Symbolic habits versus abilities

Symbolic habits refer to the person's characteristic or preferred modes of thinking, or cognitive styles. These are to be distinguished from cognitive abilities, which refer to the efficiency of performance on cognitive tasks. Thus, one might be a habitual "imager," for example, without necessarily being proficient in a cognitive task that depends on the use of imagery, or a verbal thinker without scoring high on tests of language ability.

The distinction was operationally incorporated into the dual coding approach in the form of an individual difference questionnaire (IDQ) that was intended to measure verbal and nonverbal (imaginal) thinking habits (Paivio, 1971, pp. 495–497). The IDQ consists of a series of true-false statements that indicate a tendency or preference for an imaginal mode of thinking (e.g., I often use mental pictures to solve problems) or a verbal mode (e.g., Most of my thinking is verbal, as though talking to myself) in a variety of situations. A detailed factor-analysis of the items (Paivio & Harshman, 1983), based on two separate samples of more than 300 respondents each, revealed a highly stable factor structure. The interesting points for present purposes are the following: First, a two-factor solution provided a reasonable description of the factor structure, one factor being defined by items that refer to a preference for imagery and the other defined by items referring to verbal thinking. Each factor correlated more than .9, with the respective total imagery and verbal scores based on all of the original items, thereby validating the intuitive construction of items based on dual coding theory. The habit-ability distinction emerged from a six-factor solution (the maximum justified number of reliable factors), which confirmed the presence of relatively general imagery and verbal factors, and also revealed more specific imagery and verbal factors defined by small subsets of items. The relevant point is that the general imagery factor was defined primarily by items referring to imagery preference, and one other factor, defined by only two items, could be viewed as reflecting imagery ability. The verbal factors, in contrast, were defined primarily by items referring to proficiency in the use of language. Thus, the IDQ seems to reflect a mixture of symbolic habits and abilities.

The analysis suggests that the IDQ could be revised with a view toward a more balanced selection of ability and habit items for both verbal processes and imagery. The present version has served to reveal that distinction and confirm the multidimensional nature of individual differences in imaginal and verbal processes that has also emerged in other research to be reviewed below.

Verbal versus nonverbal processes

The dual coding emphasis on distinct verbal and nonverbal symbolic systems is supported by data showing that scores on tests that are presumed to depend on verbal processes fall under factors orthogonal to those that depend on nonverbal processes, including consciously reported imagery. Guilford's (1967) research provides the most comprehensive and systematic data. As already mentioned, his symbolic and semantic content factors are generally defined by such verbal ability tests as verbal-associative fluency to words or pairs of words, vocabulary, and so on. The relevant nonverbal tests fall under the content category of figural information, which Guilford defined as being in concrete form, as perceived or as recalled in the form of images (his recent replacement of this category by separate visual and auditory content categories has no consequences for the present discussion). The tests include various spatial and cognitive ability tests that define different figural ability factors. Examples are Thurstone's Space Relations, Minnesota Paper Form Board (MPFB), and Cube Visualization.

We noted earlier that Guilford's approach has been criticized on methodological grounds. It is important, therefore, to point out that the separation of verbal from nonverbal spatial abilities does not depend on his use of orthogonal rotations and the subjective nature of the SI model. All general factor-analytic studies have identified spatial factors that are distinct from other general and specific factors including verbal ones (see references cited by Pellegrino & Goldman, 1983, p. 163). Carroll (1983), one of Guilford's critics, summarized the characteristics of two separate dimensions, which he identified as Verbal knowledge and Speed of mental comparisons. The latter is defined largely (though not entirely) by nonverbal cognitive tasks that require such rapid processing that they probably preclude verbal mediation. It is important to note, too, that the distinction appears early in life. For example, T. L. Kelley (1928, cited in Guilford, 1967, p. 415) obtained factors identifiable as verbal, memory, and two spatial abilities in children three to six years of age. Other studies cited by Guilford have revealed separate factors for perceptual speed, verbal, and figural reasoning among normal and mentally deficient populations with a mental age as low as two years. The general conclusion is that separate verbal and nonverbal factors emerge from virtually all factor-analytic studies that have included relevant tests, with each class dividing further into different specific factors, as would be expected from the assumption that the two systems perform a variety of different functions.

Finally, the factorial separation has been demonstrated using tests specifically targeted to measure some aspect of imagery as distinguished from verbal processes. Thus, Di Vesta, Ingersoll, and Sunshine (1971), and Paivio and Rogers (described in Paivio, 1971, pp. 495–497) identified separate imagery factors as defined by objective figural ability tests and subjective questionnaire tests, which in turn were independent of one or more factors defined by verbal ability tests. Similar results have been obtained with children in early school grades (Forisha, 1975; Paivio & Cohen, 1979).

In summary, the results of general factor-analytic studies of human abilities, as well as more specific studies using selected verbal and spatial tests, are consistent with the basic postulate of dual coding theory in that they reveal separate factors related to a variety of verbal skills on the one hand and nonverbal abilities on the other.

Symbolic versus sensory modalities

The research that followed Galton's (1883) questionnaire approach to imagery vividness attempted to distinguish between sensory modalities of imagery. The early studies (e.g., Betts, 1909) and more recent ones (e.g., Sheehan, 1967) showed that rated vividness of imagery was highly correlated across modalities, providing no evidence for types as defined by sensory modality. This negative finding may reflect problems with the concept and measurement of vividness, to be discussed in more detail in a later section, since other evidence points to modality-specific distinctions in abilities.

Guilford's SI model draws a factorial distinction along sensory lines (independent of symbolic and other nonsensory categories) as indicated especially by his recent terminological change from figural content to visual and auditory content (e.g., Guilford, 1982). A separate kinesthetic ability category has also been identified. Some evidence comes from Fleishman, Roberts, and Friedman (1958), who reported a factor that appears to qualify as an auditory figural ability in Guilford's scheme, as defined by rhythm and melody discrimination tests. Fleishman and Rich (1963) also found that visual-spatial and kinesthetic abilities were independent. Consistent with these factor-analytic results, O'Connor and Hermelin (1978; Hermelin &

O'Connor, 1982, p. 43), using sighted and congenitally blind children, obtained experimental evidence that space was organized differently by visual and kinesthetic sensory systems.

Our own research has also provided some relevant information on nonverbal sensory-specific abilities. One series of studies (Paivio, 1982a, pp. 184–186) investigated the relation between modality-specific abilities and performance on symbolic comparison tasks. The predictors were tests of visual spatial ability and kinesthetic ability. The symbolic comparisons involved "real-life" size and weight comparisons with words or pictures as items. For example, subjects indicated which is larger, a *toaster* or a *cat*, or which is heavier, a *tennis ball* or an *apple* when the pairs were presented as printed words or as drawings of the objects equated in physical size. Kinesthetic ability turned out to be the best predictor of individual differences in symbolic weight-comparison time. Another (unreported) experiment showed that individual differences in average reaction times for symbolic weight comparisons were only slightly correlated with symbolic size-comparison time. Thus, the results suggest that the ability to process information about the sizes of objects using visual memory knowledge is largely independent of the ability to process information about the relative weights of objects using kinesthetic memory.

The literature also contains some evidence of verbal factors that are distinguished by sensory modality. In Guilford's model, these fall under factors called cognition of symbolic units (Guilford, 1967, pp. 73–75). The visual factor is defined primarily by tests that require identification of words from incomplete information or in interfering contexts. Examples are Thurstone's Mutilated Words test, Disenvoweled words (the vowels are blanked out), anagrams, and four letter words embedded in a line of letters without breaks. Examples of the auditory tests are Haphazard Speech (the words to be recognized are spoken with unusual inflections), Illogical Grouping (words or phrases spoken out of order), and words heard in singing. Carroll (1962) has also identified a specific phonetic-coding ability factor among his predictor tests of foreign language learning ability.

In summary, the available factor-analytic data are consistent with the dual coding distinction between symbolic (verbal-nonverbal) and sensory modalities, but a clear factorial separation along both dimensions remains to be demonstrated within a single study.

Structural and processing levels

The aim of this section is to identify individual differences related to the theoretical distinction between representational, referential, and associative structures and processes. Individuals presumably differ in the availability and accessibility of mental representations corresponding to verbal and nonverbal units, referential interconnections between them, and associative interconnections between units within each system. These differences must be inferred from ability tests that require the subject to access representational information in different ways, so processes and structures generally will not be distinguished. Again, we must rely on scattered findings because we lack systematic evidence from comparisons of the three levels using comparable types of tests.

Representational processing

Representational processing can be measured by tests that tap the individual's ability to recognize objects and words varying in familiarity. Thresholds and reaction times for perceptual recognition are appropriate candidates. Production measures such as reading latency would do only as approximations because they involve a modality crossover from visual representations to speech production systems for words, rather than simple access of representations that correspond to the stimulus itself. In brief, even at this level we run into all of the complications that motivated Morton (1979) to elaborate his logogen model so as to include visual and auditory input logogens as well as output logogens common to each. Reading measures also raise the further problem of finding a comparable measure on the nonverbal side. Picture naming will not do because it clearly shifts to the referential coding level as specified by the theory. Thus, we are left ideally with measures that require only identification of a stimulus by recognition or matching tests of some kind. That idealization, however, will have to be relaxed in the present review.

The relevant factors in Guilford's model fall under cognition of figural and symbolic units. We have already considered tests that require recognition of words under impoverished conditions (e.g., Mutilated Words). All have the problem that they require a spoken or written naming response to stimuli. This problem is especially serious in the case of figure completion or closure tests that require verbal identification of mutilated pictures of objects because this confounds representational and referential encoding. The fact that the nonverbal completion tests load significantly (though modestly) on the same factor (cognition of figural units) as comparable tests involving words (Guilford & Hoepfner, 1971, p. 74) could mean that the different tests are tapping a general ability to deal with representational units on which referential ability is dependent. Be that as it may, the general factor-analytic studies have not included a sufficient number of appropriate tests to permit "pure" verbal and nonverbal representational abilities to emerge as factors even if such a distinction exists.

Ernest (1980) obtained results consistent with the view that Mutilated Words and Closure Speed (with nonverbal stimuli) both implicate nonverbal processing related to the imagery system: Scores on both tests correlated significantly with imagery ability as measured by spatial manipulation tests. Mutilated Words also correlated slightly ($r = .20$) with a measure of verbal-associative fluency and the verbal scale of the IDQ in one of two studies.

Otherwise, both figural completion tests were unrelated to verbal ability. The results could mean that the completion tests tap a representational processing skill that also contributes to spatial manipulation test performance or, conversely, that completion test performance depends to some extent on spatial ability. Interpretations are complicated by the fact that the completion tests and spatial ability have their main loadings on separate figural abilities in Guilford's studies, presumably because the factors are defined by other tests as well, and because orthogonal solutions are imposed on the factor structure.

This review illustrates the ideal requirements for the identification of representational encoding abilities and the complexities associated with existing studies that approximate but do not fully satisfy those requirements. The conceptual and empirical picture is somewhat clearer in the case of processing at the referential level.

Referential processing

This type of processing is measured by tests that require a crossover from verbal to nonverbal representations or vice versa. Picture-naming and word-imaging tasks are obvious candidates. Factor-analytic studies of cognitive abilities have sometimes included naming reactions to nonverbal stimuli but not parallel tests of imaginal referential reactions. Theoretically, the relation between these reverse referential reactions could vary, depending on the precise nature of referential experience. For example, Begg (1976) was able to demonstrate different effects in memory tasks depending on whether the target items (nonsense words) had served as responses to picturable stimuli or as stimuli for imagery reactions in a prior phase of the experiment. Naturally occurring referential experiences are likely to be bidirectional, however, so some correlation would be expected.

The factors that most closely implicate referential reactions in Guilford's approach are those requiring convergent production of verbal units to nonverbal stimuli (e.g., Guilford, 1967, pp. 172–173). For example, Picture-Group Naming should qualify as a measure of verbal referential responding to classes of objects. However, the factor also loads on Word-Group Naming, Verbal-Relations Naming, and other tests that are conceptually more appropriate to the associative level of processing in the dual coding approach. Guilford (1967, p. 173) was uncertain about the factorial status of simpler naming tests such as Color Naming and Form Naming, although he suggested that they might turn out to be factorially separate from convergent production of semantic units because colors and forms are concrete whereas classes and relations are abstract. That suggestion is certainly consistent with the approach taken here but definitive information is unfortunately lacking at this time.

The results of research summarized by Perfetti (1983, p. 70) also suggest that referential ability may be independent of verbal representational coding and other verbal abilities. The research was generally concerned with iden-

tifying specific abilities that differentiate high-ability and low-ability r
Name retrieval to different kinds of stimuli was investigated as one p
correlate. Subjects with high reading ability were significantly faster than
low-ability subjects when naming printed words, but not when naming
colors, pictures, or digits. Taking color and picture naming as defining verbal referential processing speed, the results suggest that this processing skill
is distinct from other verbal abilities associated with word naming and reading ability generally.

We turn next to studies more specifically concerned with the concept of
referential processing ability. Bucci and Freedman (1978) were the first to
study this kind of ability, which they called Referential Activity (RA). They
measured RA in terms of naming speed for familiar nonverbal stimuli, especially colors, corrected for word-reading time. The subject first reads 100
color words (red, green, yellow, blue, repeated in random order) and then
names the corresponding colors in the same format. The RA score is the
difference in total times between the color-naming and word-reading task.
Thus, it is a "pure" measure of verbal referential coding.

Bucci (1984) also found that this simple measure correlated in theoretically interesting ways with more complex verbal behaviors. Persons with
high RA scores characteristically used metaphorical expressions to distinguish closely related colors, for example, lime green, burnt orange, flesh, for-
est green, mahogany, clay, mud, and so on. Low RA subjects more often
used combinations of the basic color term and adjectival modifiers to characterize the same colors: dull green, reddish brown, reddish orange, greenish
yellow. Thus, the high RA subjects apparently made more use of images of
concrete entities to categorize the colors whereas low RA subjects relied
more on verbal connections between color terms. In a descriptive narrative
task, high RA subjects produced relatively concrete, specific, and definite
descriptions suggestive of imagery as a mediator, whereas low RA subjects
tended to be more abstract and vague, again suggesting that they relied relatively more on word-to-word links.

It is notable, too, that RA scores did not correlate significantly with the
vocabulary and similarity measures of verbal abilities in the Wechsler Adult
Intelligence Scale nor with an associational fluency test from Guilford. The
independence was expected because these ability tests seem primarily to
reflect abstract or logical connections within the verbal system. However,
RA did correlate significantly ($r = .42$) with the comprehension score from
the WAIS. This also was expected because the comprehension test includes
items that refer to concrete situations and actions (e.g., what to do if one
sees smoke and fire while in a movie theatre), so that imagery can be used
as an aid to answering the questions.

In summary, Bucci's research has isolated a referential ability that seems
to be separate from at least one measure of verbal representational ability,
as well as independent of other verbal abilities that may be based primarily
on connections within the verbal system. The approach has been innova-

tive, predictive, and heuristic. It should lead to further interesting inquiries. A question that arises in the present context is the relation between verbal and nonverbal referential ability. The basic RA test is a measure of the ability to respond verbally to nonverbal stimuli, rather than of nonverbal (imaginal) responses to verbal stimuli. Bucci's research indicates that RA is related to the use of imagery in such verbal tasks as narration and comprehension, but such tasks presumably include both imaginal referential reactions to linguistic stimuli (e.g., the cues for narratives and WAIS items) and verbal referential reactions to the mediating images (the narrations and solutions to verbal test items). The research was not designed to distinguish the two directions of referential activity.

We have begun to investigate the problem as part of a larger program of research on individual differences from the dual coding perspective. An initial study (Paivio, Clark, & Digdon, unpublished) involved line drawings of over 200 familiar objects and their labels as stimuli. We have used these materials in experimental studies of memory and other cognitive tasks over the years, and so normative information was available on naming responses and their average latencies. Accordingly, we chose the most common labels as word stimuli in the present study. Subjects were individually presented the words and pictures one at a time in separate sessions, counterbalancing order so that some subjects began with the words and others, with the pictures. They were instructed to generate a name covertly to each picture and an image to each word as quickly as possible, indicating when they had the name or image by pressing a key. Following the key press, they wrote down the label or sketched their image without any time constraint. The data were analyzed in various ways to determine effects of different attributes (e.g., normative familiarity, uncertainty, etc.), order in which the two tasks were presented, and so on. The relevant point for present purposes is that, however the data are analyzed, mean-naming latency and image latency correlated substantially over subjects. For example, averaging over all items and the two orders of presentation (imaging first versus naming first), the correlation was .71. These data indicate that verbal and imaginal referential processing times are significantly but not perfectly correlated, as expected from the hypothesis that referential experiences are often but not always bidirectional.

We now plan to refine the measurement of the two classes of referential reactions and investigate their relations to other levels of processing and performance on different cognitive tasks. Earlier research (e.g., Ernest & Paivio, 1971) had differentiated imaginal referential reaction time experimentally from verbal associative reactions and revealed correlations between both of these and other measures of individual differences in imagery. However, those studies were not designed with the present aims in mind and they serve mainly as additional guides for the more systematic and analytic research that this complex problem demands.

Associative processing

At the associative level, we again find more relevant evidence on the verbal side than on the nonverbal side. Verbal-associative ability has been measured most often by production tasks which, in Guilford's framework, are divided into divergent and convergent production. An example of the former is associative fluency, in which the subject is required to write as many word associates as possible in a given time to some stimulus such as a first letter or a word. Convergent production tasks require a unique response to a simple or compound stimulus. An operationally clear example would be giving a common associate to two or more stimulus words, although Guilford reports that such tests divide their variance into divergent and convergent production. As mentioned earlier, another problem is that some of Guilford's tests implicate a mixture of referential and associative processing, so we need to be selective in the examples we draw from his research.

The SI tests that are most relevant to verbal-associative processing ability fall under factors involving symbolic and semantic content. Tests of symbolic and semantic divergent production abilities that seem to be highly verbal are Word Fluency (writing words containing a specified letter), Associational Fluency (writing synonyms to word stimuli), and Expressional Fluency (writing different four-word sentences given a set of initial letters for each word). Examples of convergent production ability tests that appear to be highly verbal are: Word Group-Naming (described earlier), Association III (writing a word similar in meaning to two given words), and Missing Links (producing three words to complete a chain of associations between two words).

The mixed verbal-nonverbal character of some of Guilford's factors was illustrated earlier by the Picture-Group Naming test, which loads on a symbolic convergent production factor along with verbal association and verbal relation tests. Another less obvious example is Object Naming, in which the stimuli are general class labels, such as minerals. Here, the associations may be mediated by imagery, as indicated by our own factor-analytic finding (Paivio, 1971, p. 496) that Object Naming loaded on an imagery factor rather than one of several verbal factors. The latter were defined by more "purely" verbal tests, including verbal fluency as measured by the number of associations to four concrete and four abstract words. In Guilford's research, too, symbolic and semantic factors have their strongest loadings on verbal tests. These observations suggest that a common set of verbal-associative abilities can be isolated, though nonverbal factors sometimes contribute to the verbal-associative responding through referential interconnections.

We turn now to the even more difficult problem of identifying individual differences in nonverbal-associative processing. One of the guiding assumptions is that nonverbal visual information is organized synchronously (in parallel) into higher-order structures, and that processing is governed by such organizational constraints. Thus, relevant abilities would have to do with the richness of visual-spatial information in long-term memory, speed of accessing such information, speed and accuracy of generating spatial compounds, and so on. Appropriate categories in Guilford's model include figural systems and figural implications, given the definition of systems as "organized or structured aggregates of items of information; complexes of interrelated or interacting parts" and of implications as "Circumstantial connections between items of information, as by virtue of contiguity, or any condition that promotes 'belongingness'" (Guilford & Hoepfner, 1971, p. 21).

Processing at this level could be measured by requiring subjects to generate associated images to objects or their pictures, provided that the objective indicator of imagery minimizes verbal mediation. Drawing and object construction tasks are possible candidates among the tests used by Guilford. For example, Figural Production requires the respondent to add lines to given lines to produce meaningful objects. The test seems to tap both representational and associative levels of processing because its factor variance is shared between divergent production of figural units and divergent production of figural systems (as well as figural implications). A test called Sketches similarly requires production of recognizable objects from simple figures and it loads on the same factors as Figural Production. A construction test called Making Objects is also a close candidate because it requires the subject to combine figures in various ways to form named objects, but the inclusion of names reduces its nonverbal purity. Nonetheless, it loads on the same three figural abilities as the other tests just mentioned. It is theoretically important, too, that these figural tests do not load on the same factors as the more verbal-associative tests in Guilford's studies.

To summarize, general factor-analytic studies and more specific correlational studies provide evidence of abilities related to representational, referential, and associative structures and processes. The degree to which the three levels of processing are factorially distinct remains unclear, however, as does the conceptual distinction between the two directions of referential processes, that is, nonverbal-to-verbal and the reverse. Moreover, the distinction between verbal and nonverbal processing receives clearer support at the associative than at the representational level. We obviously need more evidence using tests that have been systematically designed to measure the different kinds of processing in comparable ways. One heuristic value of the dual coding perspective is that it permits us to identify such empirical gaps and to broaden our understanding of cognitive abilities by trying to fill them in.

Organizational and transformational abilities

The emphasis in this section is on individual differences in the manner and efficiency with which cognitive information is organized and transformed.

The guiding theoretical assumption is the synchronous-sequential processing distinction between nonverbal and verbal systems, which in this case would be supported by corresponding ability patterns. We should be able to identify abilities related to sequential organization and transformation of verbal information on the one hand and synchronous organization and transformation of nonverbal spatial and sensory information on the other.

Organization and transformation are discussed together because they are related functions and because little is available on "pure" organizational abilities that do not also involve transformations. As we have already seen (chap. 4), a conceptual distinction is nonetheless possible: Organization entails encoding activity in which input information is simply reorganized during encoding. For example, constructing an interactive image from separate pictures of two objects requires some cognitive reorganization of the initial relation between the objects. However, the resulting spatial configuration need not be transformed further. Transformations, on the other hand, require manipulation of mental representations. Image rotation is currently a familiar nonverbal example and is a component of a variety of spatial ability tests. On the verbal side, organizational processing is implicated whenever verbal or nonverbal input in a particular format is reorganized verbally in some way during encoding. For example, a matrix of printed words or pictures could be encoded into any number of possible verbal sequences, with uniform or variable temporal spacing of items (rhythmical patterning), or pitch variation (tonality), and so on. Transformations would involve further mental manipulation of the encoded verbal-sequential representation.

It should be remembered, too, that organizational and transformational processing is always preceded by and perhaps intermixed with encoding activity. For example, in addition to the initial sequential encoding required in all tasks, instructions to construct an interactive image from the names of two objects requires verbal-imaginal referential encoding as well as image organization. The picture matrix example mentioned above would similarly require verbal referential encoding as part of the sequential organization itself. However, the factorial separation of organizational and transformational tests from those that measure encoding abilities distinguishes operationally between those components.

A few of Guilford's tests seem to be relatively pure measures of organizational processing. For example, combining figures to make nameable objects (the Making Objects test already mentioned above) and Forming Alternative Faces from movable tops and bottoms of faces clearly require the ability to organize figural components into a coherent (synchronous) entity. It is uncertain, however, whether the organizational processes at that level are precisely the same as those implicated in mentally organizing different objects in some systematic way. On the verbal side, sentence synthesis and sequential association require rearrangement of a given series of words into a more meaningful sequence. These examples also illustrate the relation between organizational processing and associative structures in that patterns resulting from organizational processing would depend on existing associations.

Transformation is one of the basic product categories in Guilford's model and it is accordingly tapped by a variety of tests. Transformations are defined in that context as "changes of various kinds (redefinitions, shifts, transitions, or modifications) in existing information" (Guilford & Hoepfner, 1971, p. 21). The definition encompasses more than is intended in the present context. In particular, redefinitions imply complex processes that may include elaborate associative processing as well as some transformation of the initial mental representations that are evoked by a specified (defined) situation. For example, a key test of redefinition is Gestalt Transformation in which the items require shifts of function. Thus, one question asks the respondent to indicate which one of five named objects could be used to start a fire. The correct item is "pocket watch," the face cover of which could be removed and used as a condensing lens. The solution clearly depends on transformation of the watch as well as a restructuring of the situation in the Gestalt sense. However, it also requires generation of an image or verbal label of the sun, presumably as a convergent associative reaction to images evoked by such key words as "fire" and "watch" in the question. Accordingly, the term transformation will be used here in a less complex way to refer to those structural modifications of test-elicited mental representations that are required if the items are to be answered correctly.

The most familiar transformation tests are those that require spatial manipulations. These include Thurstone's Space Relations, Flags, the MPFB, and a series of tests that define Guilford's cognition of Figural Transformations factor (e.g., Guilford & Hoepfner, 1971, p. 75). Examples from Guilford are Block Rotation, Aptitude-Spatial, Paper Folding, and Block Visualization. Recall that the last of these consists of items in which a colored block of wood is verbally described and the subject is required to answer questions about the parts that result when the block is cut up into smaller cubes. The interesting aspect is that Block Visualization, though verbal in content, shares common variance with other spatial manipulation tests in which nonverbal visual forms are used as items to be transformed. Thus, the source of the common variance appears to be mental transformations applied to nonverbal visual representations generated either directly from perceptual stimuli (representational encoding) or indirectly from verbal descriptions (referential encoding). Moreover, in some of these tests the transformational operation is itself primed by verbal components of test questions that essentially ask the respondent to visualize the outcome of a transformation.

Despite the shared variance, the correlations among different spatial manipulation tests are variable and generally modest. The variability could reflect differences in (a) the stimulus objects that are to be transformed (e.g., block diagrams *versus* clocks), (b) the precise nature of the transformations (e.g., rotation on a two-dimensional plane versus cube slicing), or (c) some subtle differences in verbal instructions (e.g., asking the subject to visualize the outcome of a transformation versus instructions simply to indicate which of a set of alternative objects is the same as a given target item). Whatever its source, the partial independence of the tests suggests that they are tapping somewhat different specific abilities or component skills within a general ability domain, the nature of which is yet to be determined.

The existing figural transformation tests also do not exhaust the kinds of transformations that can be imposed on nonverbal representations. Introspective reports suggest that object images can be altered in shape, size, color, movement, and so on. Gordon (1949) devised an imagery-control questionnaire in which the items refer to such transformations. Respondents are asked if they can see (image) a car, see its color, see it in a different color, turned upside down and righted again, running down a hill, and the like. The responses to individual items are scored and summed so as to yield a general imagery-control score. However, individuals may differ in the component transformations, which could be investigated by more objective ability tests yet to be devised. The challenge applies as well to transformations of nonverbal representational information in other sensory modalities, such as changes imposed on rythmical or tonal patterns and tactile or haptic qualities of objects. Moreover, given the sequential nature of musical patterns and motor activity, sequential transformations could be investigated in the nonverbal symbolic domain as well. Dual coding theory needs to be fleshed out through comprehensive studies along those lines, but the empirical gaps are there regardless of one's theoretical perspective.

The major characteristic of verbal transformations is that they involve changes imposed on a sequential structure. The clearest examples in Guilford's test battery are those that relate to cognition of symbolic transformations. Thus, Finding Letter Transformations, Seeing Letter Changes, Reading Backwards, and Reading Confused words (Guilford & Hoepfner, 1971, p. 78) all require some kind of transformational processing of the structure of verbal material. However, the transformations could be done on the basis of the linear-spatial frame of the print rather than requiring sequential transformations in the strict (temporal) sense. A pure test of the latter would be one that can only be carried out by sequential mental transformations. This could be achieved, for example, by presenting verbal material auditorily and requiring respondents to transpose the acoustic elements mentally in order to answer an item. Nonetheless, it is likely that the printed materials in Guilford's tests do engage the verbal system and tap sequential (verbal) transformational ability to some degree.

Guilford's tests also include transformations in semantic and behavioral content categories and in several operational categories. Some of these would be appropriate here, but many are complex and appear to correspond to a mixture of categories in the present theoretical system. In any case, the above examples serve to illustrate the implications of the approach in regard to transformational abilities.

The dual coding approach just discussed links synchronous and sequential processing functions to nonverbal and verbal systems. Das, Kirby, and Jarman (1975) proposed an alternative model of cognitive abilities in which the analogous distinction between simultaneous and successive synthesis was not tied to the nonverbal-verbal one. Their model was based on Luria's (1973) neuropsychological distinction between a brain process that synthesizes information into simultaneous, quasi-spatial groups and one that integrates information into successive, temporal series. Kirby and Das (1976) were specifically critical of the dual coding linkage of such a processing distinction to imagery and verbal systems. However, my reexamination (Paivio, 1976a) of the factor-analytic data that Das et al. (1975) used as evidence for their model revealed that almost all of the tests that consistently loaded highly on their simultaneous-synthesis factor implicated nonverbal visual-spatial processing. Conversely, successive processing was consistently defined by serial-verbal recall of short tests of words presented auditorily. For example, one study used 8 tests that I asked two independent judges to categorize in terms of the degree to which they require imaginal or verbal processing. The results were clear for 7 of the tests: All those that loaded on the simultaneous factor in Das et al. (1975) were rated as predominating in image processing, whereas the successive tests were rated as predominantly verbal. One test in the simultaneous factor was rated as verbal but here the judges noted that some of the test items may predominate in imagery and others in verbal processing. The controversy entails other issues as well, but the main point for present purposes is that Das et al. (1975) generally did not distinguish their amodal simultaneous-successive processing ability model from the dual coding one. This does not preclude the possibility of finding nonverbal motor skills that include sequential components, and verbal processing skills with synchronous aspects (see Paivio, 1976a pp. 70–71), but this remains to be demonstrated.

Evaluative processing abilities

Recall from chapter 4 that the evaluative functions of the representational systems refer to their use in the analysis and evaluation of the properties, elements, or dimension of linguistic and nonlinguistic objects and events. These can be characterized as *reflexive functions* of the symbolic systems in that verbal and nonverbal processing activities are applied to information in verbal and nonverbal representations; that is, the symbolic systems reflect on themselves. Hockett (1963) had proposed reflexiveness in this sense as one of the design features of language. The idea is extended here to verbal and nonverbal symbolic systems, with reference specifically to individual differences in relevant abilities.

Evaluative abilities could be tested by any task that requires the individual to make judgments about nonverbal or verbal information stored in semantic or episodic memory. A clear example of the former is the symbolic comparison task that requires one to decide which of two symbolically presented items has more or less of some property, such as size (which is larger, a *lamp* or a *zebra*?), weight (which is heavier, an *apple* or a *baseball*?), value (which costs more, a *shirt* or a *toaster*?), and so on. Reaction time experiments of this kind are discussed in chapter 9. Individual differences were studied in many of these experiments, and one correlational study has been reported (Paivio, 1980, pp. 142–152). The latter used paper-and-pencil tests of symbolic comparisons of size and shape (angularity roundness) of pairs of named objects, and comparisons of the angular separation of pairs of clock times (in which of the following times are the minute hand and hour hand farther apart, 9:20 or 7:50?). Performance as measured by the number of items correctly answered in a fixed time period was correlated with a variety of other cognitive tests. A multiple regression analysis showed that Space Relations and a verbal Inference test were significant predictors of size and clock comparisons, with Inference being best in the case of size and Space Relations in the case of clock comparisons. These results are relevant here because they show clearly that verbal and spatial abilities are components of the reflexive evaluative activity involved in symbolic comparisons, and that the contributions of each class of ability differs, depending on the exact nature of the information that is being analyzed and compared. A further general point of interest is that the correlations between comparison task performance and the other cognitive tests, though sometimes significant, were modest (range .01 to .43) indicating that the comparison tasks require processing abilities that are partly independent of those used in the other tasks.

The above tasks presumably require evaluative processing of nonverbal representational information generated to verbal cues. A simple example of a comparable verbal evaluative task is comparisons of the relative pronounceability of pairs of printed words or the names of items presented as pictures. The task has been investigated experimentally (see chap. 9) but not systematically from the perspective of individual differences.

Evaluative abilities are also tapped by tests that require one to "compute over" mental representations, that is, to determine the quantitative value of some structural aspect of representational information. Counting the windows of one's house from memory is a commonsense example. A comparable task in which the structural information would be the same for different respondents is counting the corners of an imagined block letter. The latter task has been studied experimentally (see chap. 9) and it could be used to study individual differences, although this has not been done. Note that the quantitative target information in such tasks presumably is not directly represented in long-term memory, although the structural information from which it can be computed is directly available. The tasks are complex in that they entail mental scanning or other kinds of internal processing of the representational information, thereby implicating component skills on which individuals could differ.

The above examples illustrate the kinds of tasks that could be used to measure evaluative abilities that depend on representational information. We now turn to relevant factors and tests from Guilford's research. These fall primarily under the evaluation category of operations, which is defined as "Comparison of items of information in terms of variables and making judgments concerning criterion satisfaction (correctness, identity, consistency, etc.)" (Guilford & Hoepfner, 1971, p. 20). The nonverbal tests in this category are grouped under the figural evaluation factors, and most consist of items that require perceptual judgments rather than ones based on figural information in long-term memory. For example, the test with the highest factor loading on evaluation of figural units is Perceptual Speed, which requires the respondent to find, from a set of alternatives, a pictured object that is identical to a given one. From the present perspective, such tests clearly implicate nonverbal and verbal evaluative processing, but the processes generally do not operate on internal representations. The defining tests for evaluation of figural transformations are exceptions in that they implicate mental rotation or rearrangement of given figures, suggesting that the figures must first be imaged.

The verbal evaluation tests generally fall under the symbolic and semantic content cagetories. For example, evaluation of symbolic classes has been defined most consistently by Sound Grouping, which requires one to find a word that does not belong to a set of printed words because it sounds different. The judgment must be based on an analysis of the acoustic structure of words, perhaps requiring covert pronunciation. Other potentially relevant tests can be found under evaluation of symbolic relations, systems, transformations, and implications. The interesting point in the present context is that virtually all of the symbolic evaluation tests are verbal in content and in the analytic processing they demand.

The tests for evaluation of different kinds of semantic content (units, classes, etc.) also consist of verbal items, but many require mental comparisons that could be based on either verbal or nonverbal knowledge. For example, Word Checking requires the respondent to choose one of four words that fits a specified criterion, such as that a named object must be manmade. The test called Best Word Class similarly requires selection of one of four classes to which a given object best belongs (e.g., *palm* best belongs to the class *tree*), which could be based on associations in either the nonverbal or the verbal system. Other tests implicate interactive processing based on both verbal and nonverbal information. For example, Verbal Analogies III consist of such items as Traffic is to Signal as River is to (bank, dam, canal, sandbags). The correct choice presumably depends on images of situations that include the relevant objects and on verbal evaluation of a functional relation between them (e.g., that signals and dams both stop something). As a final example, Punch-Line Comparisons require the respondent to choose punch lines that are more clever or unexpected for a given cartoon. This dual verbal-nonverbal processing requirement seems to be generally characteristic of the semantic evaluation tests, perhaps reflecting a similar duality in everyday evaluative processing.

Mnemonic abilities

The emphasis here is on abilities related to performance in episodic memory tasks, particularly with reference to meaningful stimulus items that are processed in some way by verbal or imaginal systems during encoding. The mnemonic functional category is directly related to Guilford's operational category of memory abilities, which he defines as "Fixation of newly gained information in storage" (Guilford & Hoepfner, 1971, p. 20). Memory abilities should be further divided into encoding, storage, and retrieval components, but this breakdown does not appear in Guilford's research nor in the ability literature in general, and so we are restricted in what can be said about such refinements.

Let us first consider the SI memory factors and then the gaps they leave according to the present perspective. The verbal-nonverbal distinction is especially clear in this case in that the vast majority of tests with significant loadings in the figural memory category use nonverbal forms or pictures of objects as target items, whereas those in the symbolic and semantic content categories use words or numbers (Guilford & Hoepfner, 1971, pp. 238–241). The exceptions are generally ambiguous in that their variance is shared between different factors and some clearly require dual (referential) processing during encoding or retrieval. Thus, Books and Authors and Number-Letter Association are designated as figural implications memory tests, but they turn out to have even higher loadings on the corresponding semantic and symbolic (verbal) memory factors. Conversely, two tests consisting of nonverbal items load primarily on the symbolic or semantic content categories, but they also load on corresponding figural factors. Two others with nonverbal items load significantly only on the semantic units and semantic classes factors, but both implicate verbal processes: Picture Memory requires the respondent to recall the names of studied pictures, and Picture Class Memory is a recognition memory test in which the items to be studied and the correct test pictures are different objects from the same object class, so that mediation by a class label is likely to be the most efficient strategy. It can be concluded, accordingly, that all of Guilford's most relevant memory tests and factors can be consistently classified in dual coding terms as implicating either verbal or nonverbal processing or a referential crossover between systems.

Other relevant points for our purposes are that memory for items (units) is relatively distinct factorially from associative memory (implications), and each of these from order memory tests (generally grouped under memory for either symbolic or semantic systems). As expected from a dual coding perspective, the order memory tests also fall into different factors than those that require memory for spatial information, although the SI model does not draw a distinction along those lines.

The following are the most notable empirical gaps when the factor-analytic research is viewed from the present perspective. First, the memory research described above did not make any provision for measuring individual differences in sensory modalities of memory. All of the tests listed by Guilford and Hoepfner (1971) use visual stimulus materials. Kelley (1964) did include both auditory and visual tests in his study, but found no factorial separation by modality. Other attributes (e.g., memory for hues, kinesthetic memory) have been individually investigated in different studies, but apparently not in the context of broad factor-analytic studies of memory abilities. Individual differences in some of these isolated sensory-memory tests will be mentioned in later chapters.

A second important gap is the virtual absence of systematic information on individual differences in the ability to apply mnemonic strategies to memory tasks. The problem has been investigated developmentally and it is now well-established that children acquire increasingly efficient strategies for learning and remembering, with a significant leap occurring sometime after the 7–8 year age period (e.g., see Pressley, 1982). However, at any given age individuals presumably differ in such abilities, and perhaps distinctively so in regard to imagery-mnemonic strategies as compared to verbally based ones. It would be especially interesting, for example, to compare individual differences in memory performance under instructions to generate integrated or interactive images to pairs of items, with comparable verbal-mediational instructions, and each of these with rote memory. Such studies appear not to have been done, although each has received some individual attention. J. Richardson (1978) conducted a paired-associate study of that kind, in which individual differences were measured by the number of pairs for which a subject reported using imaginal mediators. This measure correlated very highly ($r = +.80$) with recall performance, indicating that the experiment revealed an ability to make successful use of imagery mediators in a memory task.

Note that the emphasis here is on the overall ability to use imaginal or verbal representations and processes for the purpose of remembering presented items. However, the use of mnemonics includes such component processes as referential or associative encoding, organization or transformation of representations (e.g., generating interactive images), and retrieval based on referential processing of the remembered mediators (e.g., verbal decoding of a mediating image). Any or all of these components may contribute to the overall success in using a given strategy.

Such component abilities have not been systematically investigated in the context of the target-memory tasks themselves, although numerous studies have investigated the relation between memory and conceptually relevant abilities as measured by separate tests. For example, spatial manipulation tests may tap the organizational and transformational abilities used in generating interactive images to items in a memory task. The relations observed in such studies have been extremely variable (e.g., Ernest, 1977; Paivio, 1971, chap. 14), perhaps because the memory and ability tests used in them differ too much on irrelevant but effective variables. Such results will be described in subsequent chapters.

Imagery-vividness

I have left imagery-vividness to the last because it does not fit neatly into the dual coding framework despite its historical prominence and general conceptual relevance to the theory.

The study of individual differences in the functional attributes of imagery began with vividness. This debut is understandable in light of the emphasis on consciousness in early structuralist and functionalist schools of psychology: Images are conscious experiences that can vary in their vividness or clarity, and performance on any task that depends on such images should be predictable from individual differences in vividness. Galton (1883) initiated the study of this attribute using a questionnaire that asked respondents to think of some definite objects, such as their breakfast table, and then answer questions concerning the brightness, definition, coloring, and so on, of the image. Betts (1909) developed a quantifiable expansion of the questionnaire in which subjects rated their images of various objects and experiences on a 7-point scale ranging from "Perfectly clear and as vivid as the actual experience" to "No image present at all, you only *knowing* that you are thinking of the object." The items referred to different sensory modalities of imagery and, as we noted earlier, Betts found a positive correlation between the reported vividness for the different modalities, without any evidence of different imagery types as defined by modality. This observation was confirmed in a later factor-analytic study by Sheehan (1967) using a shortened version of the Betts questionnaire. Other modifications of Galton's method have also been developed (e.g., Marks, 1972).

We have also seen that self-report measures of imagery tend to be uncorrelated with objective performance tests, and this generalization holds particularly for the vividness questionnaires (see Ernest, 1977, p. 184). The vividness measures do show moderate correlations with other self-report measures, including the imagery scale of the IDQ, but the correlation coefficients are variable and often nonsignificant. Such results are disappointing from the classical viewpoint that the functional usefulness of imagery is linked to consciousness and, accordingly, to vividness as a prominent dimension of conscious experience. The early research using the Galton and Betts questionnaires failed to show the expected relations with performance on objective performance tests in which vividness should have been important (e.g., Fernald, 1912). Similar failures have been common in more recent studies as well, indicating that the effective use of imagery does not always depend on its reported vividness or clarity.

A specific problem is that imagery-vividness is inherently a subjective experience that cannot be directly linked to an objective correlate in the same way as reported perceptual experiences can be matched against perceptual objects. Comparisons of vividness ratings accordingly depend entirely on the assumption that raters are using the same criteria when they respond to the scale. In fact, vividness scales are known to be subject to response bias, particularly among males (Ernest, 1977, p. 185). Such research has been sparse, however, and it deserves to be pursued more extensively using a variety of techniques. For example, measures of other subjective attributes should be included so that any general response set could be partialled out to yield purer measures of vividness.

Despite the empirical and logical problems associated with the vividness tests, there is some encouraging recent evidence that the test scores sometimes can successfully predict memory performance (i.e., Marks, 1973; see Ernest, 1977, for a review) as well as performance on other tasks presumed to require the use of imagery (e.g., Finke, 1980; Finke & Shepard, in press; Wallace, 1984). Further confirmation of such observations using improved tests would buttress the case for the classical idea that imagery-vividness has real functional significance.

Eidetic imagery is relevant in the present context because it refers to a particularly vivid form of visual imagery in which the image seems to be projected onto a surface, rather like a perceptual afterimage. The phenomenon received considerable research attention in the early decades of this century, and again more recently when interest in it was revived by Haber and Haber (1964). They introduced a measurement procedure that was subsequently adopted by others. Their subjects were shown a standard set of picture slides one at a time for a fixed period. After each slide, the subject continued to look at the screen where the picture had been exposed and answered a series of questions designed to reveal the presence of eidetic imagery. The suggested criteria for such imagery included the experience of an image "out there," which endured at least 40 seconds, and which the subject described in the present tense. Accuracy of memory had previously been considered a key criterion, but the evidence that the Habers obtained in different studies turned out to be inconsistent on that point (see Paivio, 1971, chap. 14).

Cohen and I (Paivio & Cohen, 1979) investigated eidetic imagery as a psychometric problem by assigning scores to each of the component tests and then correlating and factor analyzing these along with scores from a battery of other cognitive tests. We confirmed the presence of an eidetic factor as defined by the items that refer to the subjective experience of an externalized image. However, we found no evidence of a bimodal distribution but obtained instead a continuous distribution of scores. Other observations were that the memory performance items defined a factor that was relatively independent of the subjective eidetic factor, and that spatial abilities and imagery-vividness tests loaded on different factors, which also were separate from eidetic imagery. These results confirm various distinctions already discussed in earlier sections. The relevant point here is that they also raise doubts concerning the phenomenon of eidetic imagery as traditionally interpreted. While a subjective eidetic factor can be identified, it seems to be unrelated to a variety of other cognitive abilities, and only slightly and inconsistently related to memory performance. Haber (1979), too, has recently taken a skeptical position in regard to this over dramatized but seductive phenomenon.

We have now concluded the analysis of individual differences in mental representations and processes. The empirical findings show a reasonable consistency with the general framework provided by dual coding theory, although the gaps in relevant information are striking in all of the areas covered. I have entirely omitted any discussion of individual differences in motivational and affective characteristics from the dual coding viewpoint because direct evidence is lacking. An interpretive analysis would be quite straightforward because such traits are often measured symbolically by questionnaires, rating scales, and other verbal response techniques that sometimes implicate imagery as well. The subjects' responses reflect the strength of their verbal-associative and referential habits in the content areas defined by the test items—for example questionnaire or projective tests of needs, motives, emotions, and so on. I have used a variety of such techniques in my research on individual differences in emotional reactions to audiences (summarized in Paivio, 1965b) and the implications of dual coding theory could be explored in such problem areas. In the meantime, the cognitive aspects of individual differences will be considered again in the subsequent chapters in the context of research evidence on the various functional implications of dual coding and other representational theories.

7
Meaning and Semantic Memory

The aim of this chapter is to apply dual coding theory to problems of meaning and semantic memory. The application is quite direct because the theory is largely about the structure and functions of semantic memory representations. It will be useful to begin by rephrasing the theoretical assumptions in order to appreciate their implications for the empirical studies of meaning and semantic memory that follow.

MEANING

The dual coding approach to meaning adheres to the general empiricist perspective on which the theory is based. The psychological meaning of a stimulus pattern is defined by the total set of reactions typically evoked by it. The reactions may be verbal or nonverbal, so that the potential meaning reactions to a word would include word associations, referent images, nonverbal motor reactions, and affective reactions. Nonverbal objects are similarly meaningful by virtue of the referent (descriptive) labels, motor and emotional reactions, and associated images that they can arouse. The reaction potential is, of course, a characteristic of the responding individual and not of the stimulus, and the precise nature of that potential depends on the experiential history of the person. Common experiences account for shared meanings within a community. That is what is meant by the above reference to typicality of reactions as a defining characteristic of meaning.

The actual pattern of reactions that is aroused by a stimulus in a particular situation depends on contextual factors as well as the person's particular semantic response repertoire. Thus, activated meaning is probabilistic and variable over situations and people. Of course, some reactions are highly probable within individuals and groups, which accounts for the relative stability of the meanings of such conventional stimuli as words.

The theory shares general and specific features with a variety of other empirically based theories of meaning, but it is distinguished from any given one by the total set of assumptions and the special emphasis placed on some of those assumptions. The recognition that meaning is variable and contextually determined is shared with contextual theories at least as old as Titchener's (see Allport, 1955) and as recent as Olson's (1970). The identification of meaning with reaction patterns is in agreement with associative and behavioral approaches to meaning, such as those proposed by Deese (1965) and Osgood (1953). The principle differences are as follows. Although Deese recognized that nonverbal reactions, including images, are aspects of associative meaning, he emphasized verbal associations because of their accessibility to empirical study. Conversely, he used the subjectivity of imagery (along with other arguments) to justify the minimal attention given to it in empirical studies of meaning. The dual coding position accepts the verbal-associative emphasis but at the same time gives imagery equal status in the theory on grounds that are no less empirical than those that justify verbal and other reactions as aspects of meaning.

Dual coding differs from Osgood's theory most generally in not adopting an abstract componential base for meaning. That is, Osgood identifies meaning with a pattern of fractional (covert) responses abstracted from behaviors to things, and which become conditioned to words and other signs. By contrast, dual coding theory emphasizes such holistic reactions as verbal responses and images as the basis of psychological meaning. The images can be parts of a larger structure (feather, wing, bird), but they are nonetheless holistic entities rather than abstract components, except in the sense that a concrete component (including a simple contour) can be abstracted out of the whole. Conversely, we know from experience how to compose larger entities from the concrete components. Thus, dual coding can be grouped with classical field theories of meaning whereas Osgood's theory is an empiricist member of the class of atomic or feature-based theories. Here, too, dual coding is distinguished by its special emphasis on imagery as a dominant class of meaning-reaction to certain types of stimuli. This emphasis was absent in early field theories and in Osgood's approach, although the importance of imagery as an aspect of meaning has been recognized by other behaviorists (e.g., Mowrer, 1960; Sheffield, 1961; Staats, 1961, 1968).

Finally, dual coding is characterized by its emphasis on different levels or kinds of meaning-reactions, which fall out as a corollary of the general structural and processing assumptions of the theory. Recall that the structural description entails representations corresponding to verbal and nonverbal stimulus events, referential interconnections between the two, and associative interconnections between representational units within each class. In the present context, this is a description of the structure of semantic memory according to dual coding theory. Activation of representations via different pathways as previously described is a statement of the semantic processing assumptions of the theory. The following are the important points to note.

SEMANTIC MEMORY

First, the availability of verbal and imaginal representations is itself an essential part of semantic memory, and the activation of such representations constitutes the first level of effective meaning. It suffices as a basis for stimulus recognition and for judgments of familiarity or frequency. Second, the referential interconnections correspond to traditional views of meaning as reference, with the addition that the relationship is assumed to be bidirectional (though not necessarily symmetrical). Moreover, the connections in each direction are one-to-many and their activation is probabilistic and dependent on the experiential history of the individual with such relations. Finally, associative interconnections between verbal representations corresponds to classical word-association approaches to meaning, with the difference that it is explicitly stated that the associations are between cognitive representations of words (cf. Hayes-Roth & Hayes-Roth, 1977; Kiss, 1973). The verbal-associative component of dual coding theory also corresponds in principle to network models of the organization of the subjective lexicon. However, the associative structure of the nonverbal system has no direct parallel in current network approaches to semantic memory. The closest parallel is with the idea of concept nodes, which are distinguished from lexical representations in theories such as that of Collins and Loftus (1975). The sharp difference is that such theories assume that the conceptual entities are discrete and amodal at all levels of a conceptual hierarchy, whereas dual coding theory assumes that they are modality specific and holistic. This point was explicated in chapter 4 in the discussion of the analogue nature of imagens, which correspond to entities of different sizes—parts of objects, whole objects, objects as part of larger ensembles (scenes) and events, which are based on prior perceptual experiences and imagery reactions. Units are hierarchical in the sense of perceptual nested sets, and what portion of a hierarchy is activated to generate imagery or to affect task performance depends on contextual cues and target stimuli.

The model nonetheless accommodates the problems to which traditional and contemporary semantic memory concepts are addressed. Associative meaning has already been mentioned. The differences between specific and general terms is conceptualized in terms of the organizational structure of both systems. Within the verbal system, a given general term must share associations with a range of specific members of the general class, and the associations vary in probability or strength. These can be viewed as vertical associations within a hierarchy. In addition, there are direct (horizontal) associations among specific members of the class. These associative relations can be inferred *partly* from category-instance norms (Battig & Montague, 1969) and from free-association norms (e.g., Palermo & Jenkins, 1964)—partly, because the data may also reflect the influence of nonverbal representations activated through referential interconnections. For example, *table* as a verbal response to *furniture* may be mediated by an image of a table for some subjects some of the time, but not necessarily for all subjects nor under all circumstances. The determining factors would be individual difference variables and contextual cues. The same reasoning applies to horizontal associations.

It can be seen that this is essentially an exemplar theory of the meaning of general concepts in that a term such as furniture has a high probability of evoking a particular imaginal and verbal response. Of course, it remains an exemplar theory even if furniture evokes images of general settings, such as a kitchen or a living room, so that a number of exemplars are more or less accessible from the image. It is not enough, however, to say that it is an exemplar theory because that fails to capture the idea of a pattern of potential reactions, both verbal and nonverbal, that are subject to contextual influences and are probabilistic in nature. Thus, the approach is rather like a combination of exemplar and probabilistic views of concept representation (Smith & Medin, 1981).

The theory is especially suited to handle the difference between concrete and abstract (high and low imagery) verbal material. In fact, the theory evolved from analyses of specific effects of word concreteness in various tasks. The major postulated difference between concrete and abstract words (the same argument applies to larger linguistic structures) is that concrete word logogens have more direct connections with referent imagens than do abstract words. This is an inference from a variety of simple observations, including especially the fact that concrete words exceed abstract words in their rated capacity to evoke images and in reaction time measures of imagery arousal to them. Both classes of words have interconnections with the representations of other words in the verbal system. The specific nature and structure of the verbal-associative networks for concrete and abstract words presumably differ in systematic ways that reflect differences in the contexts in which they have been acquired and used, but in general it can be said that concrete and abstract words are semantically differentiated by the degree of availability of referential interconnections. Concrete words have both referential and verbal-associative meaning, whereas abstract words depend relatively more on verbal-associative interconnections for their meaning. Since the activation of meaningful reactions depends partly on contextual cues, the analysis implies further that the activated meaning of abstract words would depend particularly on the verbal context itself.

The theory is also designed to handle differences between pictures and words in semantic memory as well as episodic memory tasks. Such effects are predictable from differences in the structural and functional properties of imagens and logogens that are directly evoked by pictures and words, and differences in the nature and probabilistic distribution of referential and associative reactions to the two classes of stimuli. Referential reactions are highly probable to both pictures and words. On the average, however, naming may be a more likely response to familiar pictures than imaging is to the words in the absence of specific instructional sets or task demands (Paivio, 1971, chap. 6). Specific implications of this aspect of the model will be described later in this chapter, as well as in subsequent ones.

A final point concerns the dual coding conceptualization of verbs, adjectives, and such relational terms as prepositions. Such terms pose no special problem at the representational and verbal-associative level of meaning, but they do raise a classical problem at the referential level.

The problem arose in connection with imagery theories of meaning. Huey (1908) expressed it in his analysis of reading for meaning, which he interpreted as involving the arousal of images and feelings by sentences. Along with Titchener and others, however, he was unable to resolve the apparent impasse created for the theory by the difficulty of imaging to relational words like *under* and *upon*. Bugelski (1971b) suggested that there is no problem here if one recognizes that such words cannot be imaged alone, but that one can imagine relationships between objects brought together by such terms. In brief, Bugelski emphasized the arousal of images by phrases or sentences rather than by individual words.

The present position is in agreement with Bugelski's analysis as far as it goes. The analysis can be extended as well to verbs and adjectives in that these can be concretized and reacted to imaginally only as properties of objects. Normally the object is specified in a phrase or sentence. However, the present view is that images can be generated to verbs, adjectives, and prepositions even when these are presented alone. Such image generation would usually depend on prior activation of a noun associate via interconnections in the verbal system. For example, *in* might evoke the associate, *house*, and the two together would activate some appropriate image. It is also possible, theoretically, that *in* might directly evoke an image of an appropriate object that can function as a container, given certain antecedent experiences and contextual cues that encourage activation of the image system. The same analysis can be applied to verbs and adjectives, as well as to abstract nouns. The precise nature of the possible reactions is an empirical question.

The above problem arises only in connection with the comprehension of relational and other terms. It does not arise in the same form in the case of the production of such terms in response to situations or even pictures. The objects, along with interrelations and activities, are directly present in actual situations, and the descriptive terms can be activated relatively directly. Thus, verbs, adjectives, and prepositions function essentially as referential responses to actual situations and, with somewhat more uncertainty, to static pictures as well.

The discussion thus far has been based entirely on an exemplar approach to representations, but other possibilities can also be envisaged within an imagery-based approach to meaning. For example, Strømnes (1973) proposed that the meanings of relational terms such as prepositions or comparable morphemic operators rely on abstract geometric representational systems, which may differ across languages. He tested this approach using a pictorial approach in which abstract line drawings were constructed to convey the meanings of various Finnish case endings and Swedish prepositions.

Strømnes's approach can be interpreted as a kind of visual schema or geometric prototype theory of the meaning of relational terms.

Processing assumptions

Semantic memory models include special assumptions concerning processes that operate over representational structures to permit semantic decisions to be made about relations between concepts at different levels of generality. The most widely adopted assumption is that of spreading activation over the pathways of the network (e.g., J. R. Anderson, 1983; Collins & Loftus, 1975). An alternative view is that concepts are related to each other in terms of shared features, and that semantic decisions are based on feature matching, that is, computation of feature overlap (e.g, Smith, Shoben, & Rips, 1974). It has been shown that the two approaches are structurally isomorphic (Collins & Loftus, 1975; Hollan, 1975), but they assume different processing mechanisms, with network models emphasizing retrieval of pathways between concepts, and feature models emphasizing comparison of semantic elements (Smith et al., 1974). Ratcliff and McKoon (1981) failed to confirm predictions from spreading activation models using a priming task involving episodic memory for paragraphs. However, their data may not be relevant to semantic memory tasks and in any case evidence from other recent studies (e.g., de Groot, 1983; Seidenberg, Waters, Sanders, & Langer, 1984) suggests that activation spreads automatically to close associates.

The present theory incorporates variants of both classes of processing assumptions. Functionally, spreading activation is assumed with respect to referential and associative processing, where one representation activates another via connecting pathways. A matching process is assumed in the case of perceptual recognition, where a perceptual pattern activates and is somehow compared with memory representations. Verbally evoked images can also be compared with perceptual stimuli or with each other in tasks requiring similarity judgments. However, the comparison process in dual coding theory is not based on totally abstract, amodal semantic features. It is assumed instead that a comparison can be based either on the global shape of perceptual or semantic memory representations, or on particular perceptual components or dimensions of those patterns, depending on task demands or contextual cues.Thus, judgments of the similarity of the shape of American states (Shepard & Chipman, 1970) and of colors (Fillenbaum & Rapoport, 1971) given only their names as cues may be achieved by a global comparison, whereas symbolic comparisons of objects on such attributes as size (e.g., Moyer, 1973; Paivio, 1975d) are based on a single dimension. The conceptualization is essentially the same as Garner's (1974) distinction between integral and dimensional processing. It may be, too, that integral processing generally precedes dimensional processing (Lockhead, 1972), although the temporal sequence might depend on task demands.

EMPIRICAL IMPLICATIONS AND EVIDENCE

This section reviews illustrative studies that bear directly on dual coding predictions concerning meaning and semantic memory processes and structures. Additional relevant studies are considered in other contexts in subsequent chapters. The review emphasizes the distinction between representational, referential, and associative levels of meaning as well as implications of the overall structural-processing model involving all three processing levels.

Perceptual recognition

Paivio and O'Neill (1970) reasoned that perceptual identification should depend primarily on the availability of representations corresponding to the target stimuli rather than on further processes or associated representations evoked by them. The problem is related to phenomena associated with the concepts of perceptual sensitization, perceptual defence, and subception, which imply that affective and other semantic properties of stimuli can affect stimulus recognition, or that the properties can be identified at thresholds below the recognition thresholds for the stimuli. The issues are controversial and different analyses have been proposed (e.g., Erdelyi, 1974; Zajonc, 1980). A full discussion is unnecessary here and it suffices to say that O'Neill and I assumed that *cognitive* representations that are associatively related to a stimulus cannot be evoked unless the stimulus is first identified, so they cannot affect the identification process.

We accordingly predicted that word attributes related to representational availability will affect perception, whereas referential and associative meaning attributes will not. Word frequency and familiarity presumably reflect representational availability, so they should correlate positively with ease of identification. Word-imagery value is a measure of the availability of referent images, and verbal-associative meaningfulness (m) is a measure of the availability of verbal associates. Neither should affect word identification. These predictions were generally confirmed in a tachistoscopic recognition experiment: Word frequency showed its usual positive relation to ease of identification, word-imagery had no effect when familiarity and m were controlled, and m showed a small but significant relation so that high m words were identified somewhat more easily than low m words. These findings were replicated in binaural and dichotic auditory recognition experiments (O'Neill, 1971), with the difference that the effect of m was further reduced when words were controlled on both frequency and rated familiarity. Thus, except for a small residual effect of *m*, the results were consistent with predictions from dual coding theory.

The absence of any effect of imagery value on perceptual recognition is particularly noteworthy because it contrasts so sharply with the strong positive effect of the variable in a variety of episodic memory tasks. Those effects will be reviewed in the next chapter. Here, it is relevant to mention that the contrasting effects were obtained within a single experiment by Winnick and Kressel (1965). They found no difference in visual duration thresholds for concrete and abstract words but a subsequent free recall test for the same words, administered without any further exposure to them, showed better recall for the concrete (high imagery) words.

The above findings for imagery value appear to be contradicted by some studies in which high imagery concrete words were reported to be identified more easily than abstract words when presented to the left visual hemifield (presumably implicating the right hemisphere) though not when presented to the right field (left hemisphere). However, such an interaction can be interpreted without reference to imaginal representations or processes simply by assuming that concrete words are represented in the right hemisphere as well as the left, whereas abstract words are more likely to be represented predominantly in the left hemisphere. The empirical justification and theoretical rationale for that suggestion are considered in chapter 12. Let it be noted, however, that the findings from different studies are inconsistent and that one of the most extensive studies (Boles, 1983) found no interaction between concreteness and visual field. At the same time, Boles strongly confirmed the Paivio and O'Neill findings with respect to representational and referential processing in that word familiarity was significantly related to overall recognition whereas imagery and concreteness values were not (see also Gernsbacher, 1984).

Referential and associative tasks with word stimuli

Different results are predicted in semantic memory tasks that require referential or associative processing. Familiarity and frequency should still be relevant because they affect representational access, which is necessary for the subsequent activation of other representations. The facts generally conform to that expectation. For example, it is well known that the frequency and latency with which words occur as associative responses in association norms correlates highly with their frequencies in ordinary language usage. This result shows that frequency affects the availability of the response in an associative task, just as it does in perceptual recognition. The response locus of the effect was directly revealed in a synonym production task (J. Clark & Paivio, 1984). Synonym pairs were selected from available norms so that the members of the pairs differed in their general frequency of usage. Subjects were shown one member of a pair and asked to respond with a synonym. The results showed that the low frequency synonym elicited the high frequency member of the pair 80% more often than the high frequency synonym elicited its low frequency partner. Moreover, the asymmetry occurred with both concrete and abstract pairs, indicating that the frequency effect is independent of referential meaning. Name frequency also has a powerful effect on the time it takes to name a picture (e.g., Oldfield, 1966), and frequency effects appear in picture- and word-priming studies (e.g., Huttenlocher & Kubicek, 1983; Kroll & Potter, 1984) independent of other variables to be discussed in a later section.

The above examples serve to illustrate frequency and familiarity effects that are pervasive in semantic memory tasks requiring associative processing of one kind or another. We turn now to such associative tasks without further discussion of the contributions of representational processing as reflected in frequency effects, except to note that the effects of the variables to be considered are independent of frequency.

In contrast with the negative results for representational processing, the imagery-concreteness level of words is a potent variable in semantic memory tasks. Moreover, it interacts in theoretically relevant ways with other variables. One kind of interaction reflects the distinction between referential and verbal-associative processing. For example, Paivio (1966) showed that reaction time for image arousal is faster for concrete than abstract nouns, as expected from the idea that the former have more direct functional connections with the image system than do abstract nouns. However, reaction time to generate a verbal associate differed much less for concrete and abstract words, suggesting that verbal-associative interconnections are more comparable for the two word types than are referential interactions. Janssen (1976) demonstrated the differential effect on imagery and verbal reaction time with rated imagery-value varied over a 7-point scale. Yuille and Paivio (1969) extended the task to pairs of nouns differing in imagery-concreteness level. Participants were asked to generate an image or a verbal mediator to connect the members of each pair. Again, imagery latency varied with word-imagery level but verbal-mediational latency did not. Completely consistent with dual coding theory, these simple interactions are not readily explainable in terms of common coding theories without post hoc assumptions.

J. Clark (1978; 1983) tested predictions from dual coding theory in an associative task using concrete and abstract words, and explicitly contrasted those predictions with ones suggested by verbal-associative and conceptual-representational (e.g., propositional) models. The task required participants to generate discrete free associations to synonyms distributed with various interword lags in a list. The crucial variable was the concreteness level of the synonyms, so that half were concrete and high in imagery (e.g., *revolver-pistol*) whereas others were abstract (e.g., *liberty-freedom*). The predictions were based on the three models as shown in Figure 7–1.

Note that the verbal model shows that synonymous words are represented separately in semantic memory and that they are related only through their associations with each other and the associations they share with other word

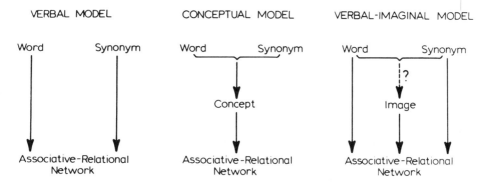

Figure 7-1. The structure of semantic similarity for three models of semantic memory according to J. Clark (1978).

representations. The conceptual model is based on the assumption that synonyms share a common semantic representation (e.g., see J. Anderson & Bower, 1973, pp. 207–208). The important point to note is that neither the verbal nor the conceptual model differentiates between concrete and abstract words: Concrete synonyms such as *revolver-pistol* and abstract ones such as *liberty-freedom* are represented and related to other units in exactly the same general way.

The dual coding model combines the verbal and conceptual models. Concrete and abstract synonyms alike have separate verbal representations that are connected only via the associative-relational network. In addition, however, concrete synonyms converge on a common referential representation, or image. Accordingly, the dual coding model is like the verbal model for abstract synonyms and like the conceptual model for concrete ones. Dual coding also differs from the conceptual model in assuming that the postulated common meaning for concrete synonyms is modality specific (imaginal) rather than abstract and amodal, but that distinction has no predictive consequences for the association task, although it does for others.

The models suggest different predictions in regard to the degree of overlap between associations to synonyms. The verbal and associative models are similar in that they predict no systematic differences between concrete and abstract synonyms, since the same mechanisms apply to each class of words. They differ in that the conceptual model predicts a relatively high degree of associative overlap because synonyms have a common conceptual representation that enters into associative relations with other concepts, whereas the verbal model predicts a relatively low level of associative overlap because synonyms have separate verbal representations and each will enter into its own relationships with other representations. The dual coding model shares predictions with the other two models. It predicts a relatively high degree of associative overlap for concrete synonyms because they share an imaginal representation, and lower associative overlap for abstract synonyms because they do not converge on a common image.

The results were most consistent with the dual coding model in that associative overlap scores were significantly higher for concrete than abstract synonyms. The proportion of related associative responses were .35 for concrete synonyms and .23 for abstract synonyms, when different subjects associated to each member of a synonym pair, and .45 and .32, respectively, when the same subjects associated to both members of a synonym pair at different times. Other interpretations are always possible but for our purposes the study serves to illustrate the kinds of predictions that dual coding theory suggests in regard to a semantic memory task—predictions that differ from and were better supported empirically than predictions arising from two other general classes of models.

It is relevant also to consider effects attributable to properties of the image system and of individual imaginal representations on performance in referential processing tasks. One implication of dual coding theory is that the speed with which images can be evoked by words should depend partly on the probability distribution (uncertainty) of referent imagens. We tested this prediction in the referential processing study by Paivio, Clark, and Digdon (unpublished), which was described in chapter 6 from the individual difference perspective. Our measure of image uncertainty was the number of different objects that subjects drew to illustrate their mental images after they had pressed the reaction-time key. These uncertainty scores correlated significantly ($r = .29$) with mean image latency scores for a set of 255 items, confirming the prediction and paralleling the effects of response uncertainty in naming and verbal associative tasks (see further below).

Such characteristics as size and complexity of the imaged objects could also affect reaction times, depending on task demands. The synchronous-organization hypothesis of dual coding theory (see chap. 4) implies that imagens corresponding to integrated objects are available as holistic entities. Thus, referential access time to such imagens should not vary with complexity or size, although any post-access processing of component information could take additional time that would be affected by these attributes.

The variable results that have been obtained in different studies are generally consistent with the above analysis. Hoffmann et al. (1983) found no correlation between image latency to words and complexity of the imaged concepts as measured by estimates of the number of figurative features for the concepts. In the unpublished study described above, we found no correlation between image latency and rated size of the imaged objects but we did find a low but significant correlation of .23 between latency and rated complexity of the imaged objects. A possible interpretation is that some subjects delayed pressing the reaction-time key until they were sure that they could draw a reasonable facsimile of the image, which would result in longer delays for more complex images. Such post-access influences presumably were absent in the Hoffmann et al. (1983) study. Kosslyn (1980) and his colleagues (e.g., Farah & Kosslyn, 1981) have usually found that image generation time increased with the complexity of the imaged objects and the size of the generated image. Kosslyn predicted such effects from his computational model, but they could be alternatively interpreted in terms of the kinds of post-access processes discussed here. For example, Kosslyn's imagery instructions typically emphasize the importance of forming "clear and accurate" images, which could reinforce attention to details. The use of episodic memory tasks (e.g., Farah & Kosslyn, 1981), in which subjects study displayed objects until they think they can form accurate images of them, could also affect response time because episodic retrieval becomes more difficult as amount of detail increases, or because subjects spend more time deciding about the "accuracy" of their generated images as complexity increases. These and other possibilities require further study before different models can be appropriately evaluated.

Picture-word comparisons in semantic memory tasks

Comparisons of pictures and words have been used more often to test different models. A simple observation is that it takes longer to name a picture than to read the printed name of the picture (Fraisse, 1960; Potter & Faulconer, 1975). The dual coding interpretation is that reading a word is mediated relatively directly by activation of a visual logogen, whereas picture naming requires an additional "crossover" from the imagery system to the verbal system. The verbal model would explain the same finding simply in terms of greater variability in appropriate verbal responses to pictures than to printed words. In fact, it has been shown that naming latency increases with labeling uncertainty (Lachman, 1973), just as word-association latency increases with associative variety. However, reading latency remains faster than naming latency even when uncertainty is minimized, so it is unlikely to be the sole factor responsible for the effect. A combination of crossover time and response uncertainty provides a more complete explanation and is consistent with dual coding theory.

The difference between reading and naming speed is not consistent with simple versions of the conceptual model, which assume that naming and reading are mediated by a common semantic representation. However, more sophisticated versions can explain the difference on the basis of the assumption that word reading may be mediated directly by lexical representations, whereas picture naming first requires one to access a semantic representation. This assumption renders the conceptual model indistinguishable from dual coding with respect to the naming-reading comparison. Nonetheless, the observation itself provides a useful baseline for other tasks that have been used to test predictions from the three models.

A possible inference from dual coding theory is that category decisions should be faster with words than pictures because, according to the theory, the verbal system is specialized for processing abstract information. Accordingly, the fact that category decisions are faster with pictures than words has been taken as evidence against dual coding (e.g., Potter & Faulconer, 1975).

However, the inference is not necessarily correct for all tasks. General terms such as *furniture* and *insect* are rated high on concreteness and imagery value (Paivio, Yuille, & Madigan, 1968). Moreover, there are at least two ways in which general information could be represented in images. One is by a grouping of category instances so that, for example, a general category such as fruit might be imaged as a basket containing different kinds of fruit (cf. Paivio, 1971, chap. 3). The other is a representation of general information by imaged exemplars (cf. Anderson & McGaw, 1973), which serve as category prototypes in Rosch's (1975b) sense.

Dual coding theory actually suggests that decisions about general information might be made on the basis of either general terms or concrete (imaginal or perceptual) representations, depending on task demands. If verbal processing is emphasized by contextual cues or instructions, participants may rely primarily on associative relations within the verbal system, such as the association between *sparrow* and *bird*. If perceptual characteristics and imagery are made salient, performance might be based on imaginal structures and associations, or on referential relations between representations in the two systems. The following studies illustrate some of the possibilities.

Friedman and Bourne (1976) presented subjects with pictures or verbal labels of object pairs that were either the same or different in their category memberships (e.g., both animals or not) or in physical size (e.g., both either large or small, as compared to one large and one small). They found that both category and size judgments were faster with pictures than words. They interpreted this finding to be inconsistent with dual coding theory because they assumed that the theory predicts that category judgments should be faster with words than pictures. They accordingly attributed the picture-word difference to a picture advantage in perceptual discrimination. Pellegrino, Rosinski, Chiesi, and Siegal (1977) obtained a similar result with a task requiring size or category judgments of single stimuli in relation to a predefined reference point. They suggested that the picture superiority is due simply to the extra acoustic-phonemic decoding step that is required before words can be processed at the semantic level. The semantic decisions themselves are mediated by a memory system common to both pictures and words.

The above results are also quite consistent with dual coding theory, for reasons presented earlier. Indeed, the Pellegrino et al. (1977) hypothesis is formally equivalent to a dual coding interpretation of performance in tasks that depend on nonverbal information for their execution. Like Friedman and Bourne, however, Pellegrino et al. (1977) assumed that the common semantic memory representations are conceptual and abstract, rather than being imaginal and modality specific. Their studies did not permit one to distinguish between the alternative interpretations.

Te Linde (1982) attempted to tease the alternatives apart using the Friedman and Bourne (1976) procedure, and asking participants to make judgments about relative size or associative-relatedness. The two nondual coding hypotheses specified above predict that both kinds of judgments would be faster with pictures than words, either because pictures are relatively more discriminable or because words require an extra phonemic decoding step. However, te Linde reasoned that dual coding predicts picture superiority only in the case of size judgments. Associative-relatedness judgments might be equally fast with pictures and words because associations between such items as table and chair arise from experiential contiguities between the referent objects as well as their names, and the associations are accordingly represented in the associative structures of both the verbal and imagery systems (Paivio, 1971, chap. 3). Alternatively, associative decisions might be faster with words because the association norms used for choosing pairs are themselves based on verbal responses, so verbal-associative structure might be favored as a determinant of the judgmental decisions.

The results showed the usual picture advantage for size judgments but not associative judgments, which is consistent with the first dual coding alternative. However, one of te Linde's experiments yielded results that are also troublesome for dual coding theory. In addition to picture pairs and word pairs, te Linde used mixed picture-word pairs in the two judgmental tasks. He reasoned that decision latencies for the mixed condition should be intermediate to the other two conditions in the case of size judgments, which is what occurred. However, decisions should be slowest in the mixed condition with association judgments because one concept would have to be encoded in the format of the other (either picture-to-name or name-to-image) before the judgment could be made. The unexpected result was that associative decision speed did not differ significantly for the mixed picture-word pairs and the homogeneous pairs. That finding seems more consistent with the conceptual coding model than with dual coding as it presently stands.

The above finding may have limited theoretical generality although it is yet to be fully explained. The limitation is indicated by an extension of the experiment in which te Linde and I confirmed a simple prediction from dual coding theory. The associative judgment task was again used with the addition of referentially related picture-word pairs (e.g., a pictured hammer together with its printed name), as well as associatively related mixed pairs (pictured hammer and the word *nail*). Dual coding theory predicts that referential judgments would be faster than associative judgments with mixed pairs because an associative judgment ordinarily would require a referential crossover before an associative judgment can be made on the basis of structural relations in either system. This prediction was clearly confirmed. In addition, we found that associative judgments tended to be slower with mixed pairs than with homogeneous picture-picture or word-word pairs—a nonsignificant trend also observed by te Linde (1982) and which is at least consistent in direction with dual coding theory.

The results reviewed up to this point illustrate confirmed predictions from dual coding. I turn now to some findings that appear to be more consistent with single code (propositional, conceptual) models, as well as relevant findings that have not yet been used to evaluate the different theories.

Potter, Valian, and Faulconer (1977) asked their participants to decide whether a picture or a word probe was related in meaning to an immediately preceding sentence. They found no difference in response times to the two kinds of probes. The times tended to be faster to drawings than to words in the case of high imagery sentences and faster for words than pictures in the case of low imagery sentences, as expected from dual coding theory, but the tantalizing interaction did not approach significance.

Guenther (1980) similarly required his participants to decide whether picture or sentence probes were true or false of previously studied picture and prose episodes. True probes described or depicted events that were either explicitly or only implicitly part of one of the episodes. The response times to explicit probes were faster when they were in the same modality (picture or prose) as their episodes than when they were in the opposite modality, but response times to implicit probes did not differ for same and opposite conditions. Guenther interpreted these results to mean that conceptual memory is identical for pictorial and prose episodes and, moreover, that the conceptual memory is represented in an abstract form. However, other explanations are also possible. Guenther's sentences, like his pictures, depicted concrete episodes. This suggests that subjects could easily image the events in the prose episodes and may have been prompted to do so by the use of mixed presentation conditions in which picture episodes and prose episodes alternated. Thus, conceptual memory may have been the same for all episodes, but imaginal rather than abstract in form. Alternatively, the mixed presentation may have encouraged subjects to verbalize to pictures and image to sentences, thereby resulting in dual coding of episodes. Either interpretation could account for the equivalence of pictures and sentence probes under the implicit condition. The imagery interpretation is somewhat favored by the observation that response times were generally faster to picture than to sentence probes, but the more conservative conclusion is simply that Guenther's findings do not rule out an interpretation based on dual coding theory.

Other potentially relevant studies have used a priming interference paradigm similar to the Stroop (1935) color-name interference task. Participants are shown line drawings of familiar objects with printed words superimposed on them. The words are either related in some way to the pictures (e.g., they refer to members of the same category) or they are unrelated. The subject is required to name the pictures. A general finding is that the reaction time for picture naming is longer with the superimposed word than when the pictures are presented alone. In addition, Rosinski (1977) found that words in the same semantic category as the picture (e.g., "pig" on a picture of a dog) result in more interference than words from other categories. Rosinski interpreted his findings as support for a common (abstract) semantic memory system that is accessed by both pictures and words, as opposed to dual coding. However, Lupker (1979) pointed out that a dual memory system would be quite compatible with the data, since the interference effects seem to be attributable primarily to competition between verbal responses accessed relatively directly from words and more indirectly from pictures. Lupker also found that picture naming was retarded more by high imagery words than by low imagery words. The effect is consistent with either of two dual coding interpretations: Subjects tended to image to high imagery words, especially since they occurred in the context of pictures, thereby delaying the naming responses; or, high imagery words are in a verbal-associative system that is somewhat distinct from the representational system for low imagery words, so the latter interfered relatively less with picture naming. A variety of other factors can also contribute to the interference effect (cf. Lupker & Katz, 1981, 1982) but these are not specifically relevant here because they do not distinguish between dual coding and other theories.

Irwin and Lupker (1983) studied semantic priming in several experiments using pictures and words both as primes and as targets. Participants were instructed to categorize, name, or report the color of the prime, and to either name or categorize the target. Priming effects were observed for all combinations of prime and target modality, but their magnitude varied with processing instructions. For example, presentation of a prime facilitated categorization of a target from the same category but did not facilitate naming of the target, and both words and pictures could be named faster than they could be categorized. The latter finding is most relevant here because Irwin and Lupker interpreted it to be contrary to the assumption that pictures provide access to a semantic code prior to a name code. It seemed instead that pictures, like printed words, allow access to their names before their category labels.

The Irwin and Lupker findings are difficult to interpret in dual coding terms because their subjects were required to respond verbally to the prime as well as the target stimuli, thereby ensuring a verbal set that would tend to obscure whatever nonverbal semantic processing also occurred to pictures. Nonetheless, the faster naming than categorization of pictures is easily explained in terms of multiple referential connections between imaginal and verbal representation, with activation of particular connections being probabilistic and subject to contextual influences. Thus, "furniture" and "chair" can be viewed as alternative referential responses to a picture of a chair, with chair being more probable and, hence, faster than furniture. Alternatively, the categorical response might be mediated some of the time by prior specific verbal referential encoding, accounting for the generally faster naming than category-coding times. Thus, the seemingly anomylous finding in the Irwin and Lupker study is actually quite consistent with dual coding theory.

The remainder of this chapter reviews studies specifically designed to test common coding and dual coding interpretations of picture-word priming effects. Carr, McCauley, Sperber, and Parmelee (1982) investigated naming reaction times for word and picture targets as a function of a number of variables, the most relevant of which, for present purposes, is whether a preceding prime was a word or a picture. The pattern of results suggested that the meaning of pictures and words was represented by a common semantic code. However, the representation appeared to be more easily activated by picture primes than by word primes, and picture naming benefited more than word naming from semantic activation, suggesting that "perceptual information extracted from the stimulus is more similar to the content of conceptual representations in memory when pictures are being processed than when words are being processed" (p. 771). In brief, the semantic representation is not completely amodal but functionally more like pictures than words. This conclusion is partly in agreement with dual coding theory—partly, in that the theory suggests that verbal processes also play an important role in semantic decisions.

Another series of (simultaneously published) studies used priming and other paradigms to test the two theoretical approaches in picture-word and bilingual processing tasks, with ambiguous results. The bilingual studies are reviewed in chapter 11 and here we deal only with the monolingual picture-word experiments. Kroll and Potter (1984) reported five experiments in which they compared reaction times for lexical and object decisions. The lexical task required the subject to state whether a printed letter string is a word or a nonword. The object task required the subject to decide whether a picture is a real object or a nonobject with an object-like appearance. Decision times were measured under a variety of conditions, including priming by semantically related or unrelated words or pictures (the subject decided whether both pictures or both words were "real"). The results of three experiments in which separate groups received words and pictures showed that lexical and object decisions were affected similarly by the different manipulations, which is consistent with the common-coding hypothesis. Two further experiments used both words and pictures in what Kroll and Potter described as a mixed reality decision task in which subjects decided whether a word or picture represented a real thing regardless of the form of presentation. Here, the reaction times were much longer than those in the pure lexical or object decision task, and there was little conceptual transfer across repetition of different surface forms, although there was facilitation when the same surface form (picture or word) was repeated. The authors conclude that the results of the five experiments suggest that the major component involved in lexical or object decision is a form-specific representation of the word or visual object. In brief, the results were more consistent with a dual coding than a common coding interpretation.

Vanderwart (1984) arrived at the opposite conclusion from the results of a study in which words were primed either by printed objects or by object names in a lexical decision task. In one experiment, the primes were conceptually identical, associatively related, or unrelated to the target words. In another, the target words were related to the primes in different ways: category labels (e.g., bear-*animal* as the prime-target pair), verbs (e.g., broom-*sweep*), adjective (needle-*sharp*), members of a compound (e.g., telephone-*call*), or a general term (e.g., dress-*fashion*, clock-*time*). The critical result was that, in all of these conditions, related pictures (as compared to unrelated ones) primed the word targets at least as effectively as word primes. Vanderwart's interpretation was that the results are consistent with a single system of semantic representation rather than form-specific systems.

It is particularly important to evaluate carefully the basis for the negative conclusion regarding form-specific systems because it was directed explicitly at dual coding theory and serves as a paradigm case for such criticisms. Thus, Vanderwart stated that the picture-priming results "are clearly not consistent with Paivio's (1971) dual-coding theory which maintained that time-consuming intersystem translation would cause cross-form priming to be less than within-form priming, particularly for abstract targets" (1984, p. 79). She then added (p. 80, footnote 3) that her data refuted even the more recent formulation of the theory according to which abstract attributes that pertain to qualities of objects can be processed by the image system. If this were true, she argued, then an interaction effect should have occurred in which targets that more directly represent dimensions of objects (e.g., adjectives) show more evidence of image processing (i.e., a relative picture-priming advantage) than other dimensions. That interaction was absent.

Vanderwart's conclusion is not an inappropriate inference from the earlier versions of dual coding theory. I had suggested (1971, chap. 3) that imaging to abstract nouns, adjectives, prepositions, etc., requires concretization which might usually occur via verbal-associative processing. For example, one images to "religion" by first thinking of the verbal associate "church." If we assume that this interpretation applies to picture-word relations, Vanderwart's conclusion is correct. However, the 1971 analysis also allowed for the development of more direct associations between images and abstract terms that are frequently used in association with concrete referents, e.g., "liberty" and the Statue of Liberty for Americans. Though not explicitly stated at that time, the analysis was obviously intended to encompass any word class. Still, my guess at that time was that such direct activation of images by abstract terms is less likely than mediated activation by more concrete associates, which could turn out to be wrong.

It was also recognized explicitly in the 1971 formulation that objects have different referential labels varying in strength or probability of occurrence in a manner similar to verbal-associative hierarchies. The precise nature and range of such referential hierarchies was left for future research to determine, although picture-naming studies already provided considerable information. What is especially lacking is information on contextual modification of the probabilities with which different referential reactions occur, as well as conceptually more remote associative reactions, both in generation and in judgmental tasks. Relatedness judgments and the priming task are relevant paradigms that have provided suggestive evidence. For example, comparisons of relatedness judgments for referentially and associatively related picture-word pairs, described earlier, indicated that picture-name (e.g., boy picture-boy name) judgments are made more quickly than picture-indirect verbal associate (boy picture-girl name) judgments. This implies that specific referential relations are functionally more direct (more probable) than associative ones. Vanderwart's priming results, like te Linde's (1982) results for relatedness judgments, suggest that within-system (e.g., word-word) versus between-system (e.g., picture-word) associative relations may be *relatively* comparable in their functional closeness. Both appear to be less direct (or more uncertain), however, than specific picture-word referential relations, at least when the most common label is used as the picture name.

With those observations as background, the current dual coding analysis of Vanderwart's results is as follows. First, the different types of associative relations she used could all derive from experiences with objects and words as well as intraverbal contexts. That is, we say or hear the words *animal*, *sweep*, *sharp*, *call*, and *time* not only in association with the words bear, broom, needle, telephone, and clock, but also in association with the referent objects bear, broom, and so on. Indeed, the meanings of the relatively abstract target words (animal, sweep, etc.) that are relevant to concrete objects are likely to be learned initially in the context of the objects. No wonder, then, that the pictured objects were effective primes for the words used by Vanderwart. Second, any differential priming effectiveness of different types of relations would depend on relative differences in word-object and word-word associative experiences, not simply on whether the target word is an adjective as compared to some other word class.

Dual coding accordingly predicts that priming effects will vary systematically with relational and item attributes that cut across linguistic form classes and relations. For example, the imagery value of the target items should be an effective variable in the context of concrete primes. In general, the theory would predict the pattern of picture-word results from a combination of representational, referential, and associative measures along with such task variables as the temporal relation between prime and target. The theory would be evaluated in terms of its success in predicting different patterns of results, such as Vanderwart's as compared to those reported by Kroll and Potter, given that information on the theoretically relevant variables is available. The unique strength of the theory is precisely that it has predicted different patterns of effects for the same variables under different specified conditions. It remains to be seen how it fares in relation to priming and other current semantic memory paradigms when the crucial variables are systematically manipulated. In the meantime, results such as Vanderwart's are consistent in principle with the current version of the theory.

The empirical ambiguities in the above studies (as well as the bilingual processing studies reviewed in chap. 11) were noted by several commentators in the same journal issue (Glucksberg, 1984; Kolers & Brison, 1984; Snodgrass, 1984). Among these, Snodgrass proposed a resolution in terms of a three-level model in which the first two levels correspond essentially to the general features of dual coding theory and the third is an abstract, amodal representational system that can be accessed from either of the two modality-specific systems. The general processing assumption is that subjects are flexible in their processing strategies, so that they can use the second or third level according to task demands. Thus, results such as those of Kroll and Potter (1984) would be explained in terms of level-two processing and one's like Vanderwart's (1984) in terms of level-three processing. The main problem with this approach is that it presently lacks independent means for specifying when the different processing levels will be used. Without such specification, the theory has unlimited power and is essentially untestable because any outcome can be accommodated post hoc by resorting to one or the other level of processing. Dual coding theory also is flexible but it is based on principled assumptions and operational processes that permit it to be tested, not always with positive outcomes, as we shall see later.

This completes the review of dual coding theory as an approach to problems of meaning and semantic memory. It differs from other contemporary approaches primarily in its emphasis on modality-specific, symbolic information about objects, events, and reactions to them as the psychological basis of meaning and semantic decisions. The theory accounts for general and abstract meanings in such terms without resorting to such amodal conceptual entities as abstract semantic features and more complex propositional representations. This is not to deny the usefulness of features, propositions, and the like as concepts that *describe* the information that is assumed to be psychologically coded as perceptual, motor, affective, and verbal memories. Such abstract entities simply play no explanatory role in the theory. The issues will be considered further along with more evidence in subsequent chapters, including the following one, which focuses on episodic memory.

8

Episodic Memory

Episodic memory refers in general to memory for specific events that occurred at a particular time and place (Tulving, 1972), such as the word lists that are presented to subjects in the typical laboratory experiment. Thus, episodic memory is distinguished operationally from the semantic memory tasks that were considered in the previous chapter. Whether there are any structural or functional differences between episodic and semantic memory is still an open theoretical question (for a review, see Tulving, 1983) on which I take a particular stand without attempting to resolve the contentious issues. The classification of memory phenomena is a complex problem in its own right and various taxonomies have been suggested, ranging from a tripartite division into episodic, semantic, and procedural memory (e.g., Tulving, 1983) to a scheme consisting of six different types of memory (Brewer & Pani, 1984).

The present position is implicit in the description of dual coding theory presented in chapter 4, and entails acceptance of the episodic-semantic memory distinction in two senses. The first is that there are always two sources of information that contribute to performance in any memory task, one external and one internal. The external source is the memory material presented to a subject. The internal source consists of the long-term memory representations and processes that are activated by the presented material and the context in which it occurs. The second sense of the distinction is that the internal source "contains" (can make available) two types of representational information, one being information that cannot be attributed to a particular external episodic source and the other, information that can be attributed to such a source. This aspect of the distinction is most closely related to the defining characteristics of semantic and episodic memory as originally proposed by Tulving. Our general knowledge of the world and of language is semantic in the sense that, for the most part, we do not attribute that knowledge to specific learning episodes. The internal information that can be attributed to specific external sources is by definition episodic memory information whether the event occurred recently or long ago. Such information can influence memory performance if an episodic memory task reminds us of the earlier episode and the activated memory itself becomes part of the current memory trace. The implication is that an episodic memory trace is a mixture of information derived from external and internal sources, which is a common general assumption that has been expressed in various ways by different researchers. The idea will be rephrased below in terms of dual coding concepts.

The balance of the chapter expands on the theoretical sketch that was introduced in chapter 4, and then reviews evidence bearing on the different theoretical assumptions, along with findings that have been presented as problematic for aspects of the theory. The theoretical approach includes general assumptions concerning memory structures and processes along with specific assumptions related to memory for verbal and nonverbal events that vary in sensory modality. We begin with a discussion of the structural and functional properties of the memory trace, ignoring the difficulty of distinguishing these conceptually and empirically from the encoding and retrieval processes (e.g., see Murdock, 1974) that we consider next.

MODALITY AND STRUCTURE OF THE MEMORY TRACE

The most general structural assumption is that the memory trace is a conglomerate of modality-specific, verbal and nonverbal information derived directly from perceptual events (the external source) as well as information associatively generated by those events (the internal source). The source is predominantly external when we remember specific characteristics of nonverbal or verbal stimuli, such as pictures or sentences, and it is predominantly internal when we recall dreams and daydreams or the words that we said to ourselves as we observed some external event in the past. Thus, like the external events, the internally generated events are themselves specific episodes that we can remember although it is difficult to assess the accuracy of such recollections in the absence of an objective criterion against which to compare them.

Other theories (e.g., Bower, 1967; Flexser & Tulving, 1978; Underwood, 1969; Wickens, 1970) also assume that the memory trace consists of a pattern of attributes, features, or components that can affect memory performance jointly or separately, depending on specific task requirements. The precise nature of the attributes and the composite trace that results from their combination varies across models, but they are generally interpreted as being rather abstract in character. Recent holographic-associative memory models (Eich, 1982; Murdock, 1982) assume that the features of two associated items are convoluted into a composite trace that does not directly resemble the representation of the two contributing items. Specifically, the "meaning of the features in the association is not the same as the meaning of the features in the items" (Eich, 1982, p. 631). This view differs from the dual coding assumption of modality specificity, although it will be seen that dual coding also allows for an important element of novelty in composite traces resulting from associative tasks.

Dual coding also differs from schema theories, which assume that the memory trace is amodal, propositional, or script-like. Nonetheless, the present approach incorporates the idea that the trace is schematic, in the sense that it is both incomplete and systematically altered; incomplete, because of inherent structural limitations on how much information can be encoded and stored, and because encoding processes are necessarily selective; altered, because representational information generated from long-term memory is added to the composite trace. The changes are systematic in ways that are yet to be fully understood.

The present theory also includes specific assumptions concerning the organization of nonverbal and verbal information in episodic storage. These assumptions derive directly from the general assumption that the nonverbal (image) system is specialized for processing spatial and synchronous information whereas the verbal system is specialized for sequential processing. With respect to the episodic trace, the nonverbal, visual trace information about a unitary object or an organized scene, whether derived from external objects or imagery-encoding activity, is characterized by its spatial organization and synchronous (simultaneous) availability. The corollary is that order information about a series of objects or pictures should be poorly retained unless encoding activity adds information from which the sequential order can be reconstructed. Verbal labeling of the objects is one way of achieving this, but other possibilities are discussed below as well.

In contrast, the information in a verbal trace is assumed to be organized sequentially, so that the presented order of a list of words is relatively well-retained. The sequential organization is attributable to the auditory-motor (phonemic) nature of verbal memory representations and the processes that operate on them, which implies that printed words must be phonemically coded if list order is to be well-retained. A general implication is that sequential memory effects should be dependent on how directly the phonemic code can be accessed from the stimuli.

Other storage issues concern the mnemonic efficiency and durability of the memory trace. A strong implication of the independence hypothesis of imaginal and verbal codes is that dually-coded items will be remembered better than unitarily coded items. This implication is a simple quantitative consequence of additivity of independent components of a memory trace. We shall also see that the nonverbal trace component, at least if it is visual, leads to better memory performance than the verbal component, both individually and in their additive combination when items are encoded dually. However, dual coding theory contains no primitive assumptions that would suggest that imaginal and verbal episodic traces differ in rate of forgetting, and no simple empirical generalization is possible because relevant studies have produced different patterns of results (e.g., Begg & Robertson, 1973; Deffenbacher, Carr, & Leu, 1981; Hasher, Riebman, & Wren, 1976; M. J. Peterson, 1975; Postman & Burns, 1973, 1974).

ENCODING ASSUMPTIONS

All memory theories assume that the memory trace is a product of encoding activity. In dual coding theory, the encoding possibilities follow the structural and processing assumptions of the general model. Thus, a target item can be encoded to representational, referential, or associative levels. Representational encoding implies that a given item generates a perceptual memory trace that preserves the structural attributes of the input item. For example, printed words and pictures set up visual traces, and auditory words and environmental sounds set up auditory traces. The encoding can be quite elaborate even at this stage because the presented item generates a specific new trace and also activates a "similar" mental representation from semantic memory. The "new" trace corresponds to what is traditionally meant by iconic or sensory memory as well as short-term memory because it is assumed that the trace retains sensory information for a longer period than is usually attributed to iconic memory (cf. Paivio & Bleasdale, 1974). If the input item is completely novel, as in early learning by the infant or as approximated if adults are presented unfamiliar stimulus patterns, the trace is correspondingly new and relatively unelaborated. Its effective duration is also relatively brief, although aspects of the trace may persist for some time to constitute the beginning of a stable mental representation. The issue here parallels Hebb's distinction between a short-term activity trace and a long-term structural trace, a distinction that he later questioned (Hebb, 1961) because of his own evidence that novel sequential patterns set up a memory trace that is not disrupted by subsequent items to the degree that he expected if the trace consisted only of temporary (reverberatory) activity. We need not take a strong stand on the issue here, although it remains important for memory theories in general.

A further complication is that printed words are ordinarily coded promptly into an auditory-motor (phonemic) form in a manner analogous to imaginal-verbal referential encoding. Whether such recoding is automatic or not is an open question in reading research, but in any event it is clear that reading is commonly associated with articulatory and auditory activity. The occurrence of such activity is generally important theoretically because it points to the sensory modality-specific nature of the mental representations that result from the recoding activity. The evidence is somewhat problematic for amodal representational (e.g., propositional) theories, but it is not decisive with respect to the contrast between processing theories and dual coding because both predict that phonemic verbal coding of printed words is less effective than "deeper" semantic coding, at least in some tasks.

The preceding analysis also applies in principle to the relation between different nonverbal sensory modalities. For example, familiar environmental sounds presumably activate nonverbal auditory representations relatively directly and might also activate visual images of the corresponding objects: The ring of a telephone and the sound of laughter are recognized and are memorable to some degree as distinctive sounds, but they also tend to evoke visual images of a telephone and a laughing person. It may be more appropriate theoretically to view such sensory elaboration within symbolic modalities as a special type of associative processing rather than representational processing, but the conceptual distinction is unimportant as long as it is recognized that such processing activity is relevant to episodic memory performance in some tasks.

Referential encoding

Referential encoding activity produces referentially related verbal and nonverbal memory trace components. Such a dual trace can arise, for example, if an object or picture is presented together with its name, or if the subject names a presented picture or generates a referential image to a word. The subject-generated memory representations are assumed to be functionally equivalent to representations that are directly elicited by presented items in the sense that an image of an object generated to its name has the same mnemonic properties as the image evoked by the object itself, and likewise for generated and presented verbal labels. The parallel refers to the nature of the information that can be retrieved from verbal and nonverbal traces (see further below) and the relative mnemonic value of the two types of codes. For example, visual images that are elicited by pictures (representational coding) or generated to their names (referential encoding), are perceptual memory representations that contain information about the spatial properties and appearance of the remembered objects, whereas a verbal episodic memory trace, however generated, does not contain such information directly.

Associative encoding

Associative encoding entails elaborative processing within either symbolic modality, so that the resulting memory trace includes information about more than one verbal or nonverbal item. Associative encoding occurs to some extent in all list-learning tasks, but paired-associate learning is the paradigm case and serves as the principal example in the present discussion. Organizational effects, elaborative encoding at the word or sentence level, schemas, and so on, are also accounted for at the associative level of encoding.

Like referential encoding, associative encoding can be based directly on representations corresponding to the input items, or a combination of these together with representations generated from semantic memory. Thus, direct (new) associations begin to develop between verbal traces evoked by a pair of contiguously presented words, or between nonverbal traces evoked by pictured objects, even if the pair members are not associated through prior experience. If they are associated, the contiguous presentation alone may suffice to activate the relational information from semantic memory or long-term episodic memory, thereby facilitating associative retrieval (cf. Kammann, 1968; Murray, 1982). Associative relational effects based on semantic memory are even more apparent at the sentence level in the facilitative effects of semantic integration (defined by sequential associative dependencies; e.g., Rosenberg, 1969) and semantically congruent or precise elaborations (e.g., Stein & Bransford, 1979; for an overview, see also Bransford, Stein, Vye, Franks, Auble, Mezynski, & Perfetto, 1982) on memory for sentences or words in sentences.

The nature of the encoding activity and resulting associative relation can be effectively controlled by encoding instructions. For example, subjects may be told to associate a pair of words by mentally generating a phrase or sentence containing the pair, or to associate a pair of pictured objects by imagining them to be interacting in some way. The latter requires organizational and transformational processing of the input items based on semantic memory information. The task involves a combination of referential and associative encoding if subjects learn word pairs by generating mental images of their referents. The external events are entirely verbal and the subjectively generated ones are presumed to be mainly nonverbal. The reverse combination of external and internal modalities is achieved if subjects are asked to generate verbal mediators to connect a pair of objects or their pictures. We shall see that memory performance in such tasks varies with the precise nature of the recall task in interaction with the type of relation specified by the encoding instructions.

The most general implication of the encoding assumptions is that memory performance depends on the type of code (e.g., verbal or nonverbal), number of codes or trace components that result from the different kinds of encoding activity, and the relations between trace components rather than on the amount of processing involved in generating the coded trace. In contrast, some other contemporary approaches emphasize processing rather than trace structure as the determining variable. The most influential of these is the depth of processing approach originally proposed by Craik and Lockhart (1972) and later modified in various ways (e.g., Craik & Tulving, 1975). The original version assumed that processing is a continuum that varies in level or depth from a relatively superficial sensory level (e.g., acoustic processing) to deeper semantic levels. Later versions have relied more on the concept of elaboration than on levels or depth, but the attention remained on some kind of processing continuum on which items can be located as a function of encoding tasks. These concepts have been subject to various criticisms (e.g., Baddeley, 1978; Triesman, 1979), such as the circularity of the concept of processing depth as an explanation of memory performance. Nonetheless, we shall see that it has been possible to contrast predictions from the level or elaborative processing model with those from dual coding by manipulating empirical variables that have been accepted as defining operations for the crucial theoretical variables in the two approaches.

RETRIEVAL PROCESSES

A basic assumption in the dual coding approach to retrieval is that trace contact in both cued recall and recognition is based on a similarity match between the pattern of information evoked by the retrieval cue and the information in the memory trace. In its general form, this assumption is shared with distributed memory models (e.g., Eich, 1982; Murdock, 1982; Pike, 1984) and other contemporary theories of memory (e.g., Gillund & Shiffrin, 1984; Lockhart, Craik, & Jacoby, 1976; G. Mandler, 1980; Ratcliff, 1978), which rely at least partly on similarity matching along with such concepts as stimulus familiarity value (cf. the familiarity-increment hypothesis, Paivio, 1971, pp. 194–196) to explain retrieval. However, the present assumption rests on a specific interpretation of the information that gets compared in the matching process. The distributed memory models in particular describe similarity matching as a feature comparison, with recognition depending on feature overlap between test items and items stored in memory. One problem with this approach is the difficulty of defining features and feature patterns. They could be interpreted as abstract, amodal entities, holistic parts of larger wholes, or global-dimensional attributes of such wholes. Only the two holistic interpretations are consistent with the present approach. I assume, therefore, that matching is based on modality-specific (verbal or nonverbal), holistic attributes of the test stimulus and any information it generates from semantic memory or long-term memory, which can be compared with the information stored in the to-be-remembered episodic memory trace. Given such a definition of features, it remains appropriate to describe the degree of similarity between the perceptual-motor patterns and memory traces in terms of feature overlap.

The analysis implies that, in cued recall, there is some probability that the retrieval cue will access and activate that part of the trace that contains identical or similar information. Retrieval of the target response then depends on the probability that the activated part of the trace will reinstitute or redintegrate a portion of the remainder sufficient to mediate the correct response. This interpretation is an essential part of the conceptual-peg hypothesis of dual coding theory, as described further below. The analysis also implies that an episodic memory trace ordinarily contains more information than is required to produce a response that meets the criterion of correctness in a given test situation, and that access to the relevant part is probabilistic.

As an illustration, consider subjects who are asked to learn word pairs by means of imagery. The episodic events include the general experimental context, instructions, target word pairs, and images generated to the pairs.

Retrieval is prompted by presenting one member of each pair as a retrieval cue, which initiates the following processing sequence: First, each stimulus word is encoded to the representational level (a logogen is activated) in a manner similar to the original encoding that occurred to that word during pair presentation on the study trial. A successful match between study-test encodings means that the stimulus is recognized. The activated logogen then activates a referent image, which also is likely to be similar to the image that was generated during the study trial because the image was a highly probable reaction to begin with and its occurrence would increase the probability that it would be activated again by the retrieval cue. Next, the imaginal component of the trace is likely to redintegrate the remainder of the pair image, which in turn has some probability of being decoded into a verbal representation that matches the verbal response component of the episodic trace, thereby permitting the correct response to be generated.

Memory for episodic events with nonverbal objects can be similarly analyzed, with the difference that the encoded trace and encoded retrieval cue need not include a verbal component. For example, pairs of pictured objects may be stored in an imaginal form and subsequent presentation of one member of the pair would serve to redintegrate an image of the pair with some probability. The image presumably could mediate an identifying verbal response even if verbal labeling had not occurred during encoding.

A variant of the above situation is where a nonverbal event evokes recall of a similar past event, both of which can be subsequently recalled and described verbally. Such recollections are interesting theoretically because the two episodes have not been associated in experience, and yet one can effectively redintegrate the other, presumably through a similarity-matching process. Rarely studied in the laboratory, recollective experiences of this kind are common enough in real life. For example, my adult son recently told me of an incident in which he saw a large dog excitedly harassing a little boy. The scene triggered a memory of a similar event that occurred to him and his sisters when they were children—an incident that I also remember because I became involved in it as I restrained the dog. Several aspects of the experience are relevant. First, my son's recollection of the earlier incident was immediate and spontaneous. Second, that recollection was embedded in the memory of the more recent event that elicited the recall of the earlier one. Finally, the entire pattern of multiple recollections was itself cued by our conversation. The anecdote serves mainly to illustrate the embedded nature of many complex memories and to raise questions about such matters as the interpretation of similarity and speed of memory access in such cases (see Tulving, 1983, for a fuller discussion of recollective experiences).

Variation in degree of similarity between trace and test encodings is crucial in all memory tasks, but it is particularly amenable to study in recognition tests. Recognition performance is known to depend on the number of distractors used and on their similarity to the target items (e.g., see Paivio

& Bleasdale, 1974). Thus, recognition accuracy remains high over a longer test interval if the distractors are dissimilar to the target than if they are similar. Confusion errors are a function of both physical similarity and functional or conceptual similarity (e.g., Anisfeld & Knapp, 1968; Frost, 1972; Nelson, 1981; Underwood, 1965). In terms of the present analysis, the conceptual similarity effects are based on verbal or nonverbal encoding reactions that are stored as part of the trace.

Finally, retrieval effects are assumed to be an interactive function of the structure of the stored trace and the demands of the retrieval task. For example, the degree of trace integration is crucial to redintegration of the entire compound trace by a retrieval cue, as indicated by the positive effect of interactive pictures or interactive imagery instructions on cued recall. The degree of integration is relatively ineffective in noncued item recall or recognition tasks, and integration may even hinder performance in tasks requiring discrimination between different items (Begg, 1982). This analysis is particularly relevant to dual coding theory because its organizational assumptions suggest differences in the nature and degree of integration that is possible within verbal and nonverbal memory structures, differences that lead to predictions of interactive effects of theoretically relevant empirical variables and task demands.

Let us summarize the principal theoretical assumptions before turning to the empirical evidence. According to dual coding theory, the episodic memory trace is a conglomerate of modality-specific information (rather than amodal or propositional information) based on internal and external sources. The trace is generated through some combination of representational, referential, and associative process activity. Retrieval of target information is influenced by the similarity relation between the trace components evoked by the retrieval cue and the encoding pattern resulting from all factors operating during the original episodic experience, as well as by associative factors. A number of more specific assumptions are related to the special status attributed to the distinction between verbal and nonverbal events and the memory systems that are specialized for dealing with the two kinds of information, along with the sensory distinction. These include: (a) distinctiveness (modality specificity) of verbal and nonverbal memory codes, (b) independence and additivity of their joint effects in some tasks, (c) differences in the way that complex verbal and nonverbal information is organized in storage, and (d) retrieval differences associated with the organizational distinctions and task demands.

EMPIRICAL EVIDENCE

Predictions and interpretations based on the above assumptions will now be evaluated using the operational procedures associated with the dual coding approach, with emphasis on the effects of relevant stimulus attributes and various experimental manipulations (for a review of effects associated with individual difference variables, see Ernest, 1977). The procedures are used systematically to affect the probability that imaginal and verbal processes will be implicated in a given episodic memory task. Inferences based on the experimental effects are occasionally supplemented by subjects' reports of the nature of their consciously experienced memories and their mnemonic strategies.

The review will show that dual coding theory accounts for a wide range of episodic memory data, which cannot be handled easily by propositional-computational approaches except by the addition of post hoc assumptions with each new turn in the data. The following are some of the important general features to note: (a) a relatively small set of theoretical assumptions suffices to account for diverse independent phenomena; (b) these assumptions predict specific changes and even reversals of effects as a function of task conditions; and (c) different classes of empirical variables often produce parallel effects, presumably because they converge on the same underlying processes. Criticisms and negative evidence will also be considered. The first three sections deal with the more general assumptions and the remainder with the specific structural and functional assumptions of the theory.

Modality specificity of the memory trace

The general empiricist assumption of dual coding theory leads to the view that the episodic memory trace must be a modality-specific and relatively detailed representation of experienced events rather than being amodal and abstract in the sense suggested by schema and propositional theories of memory. Evidence directly relevant to the issue has been conveniently reviewed by Alba and Hasher (1983) in an article on a prototypical schema theory of memory. They concluded that the evidence suggests that the memory representation is far richer and more detailed than would be expected on the basis of schema theory. The most relevant facts, for present purposes, include: (a) above chance memory for the sensory, lexical, and syntactic detail of verbal passages, and (b) storage of separate integrated units of a stimulus complex, rather than an integrated schematic representation in which the details are lost. Such facts are entirely consistent with dual coding theory.

External and internal source components of the memory trace

A variety of memory phenomena suggests that the episodic memory trace combines information derived from external (perceptual) sources and from internal (semantic memory) sources. A particularly relevant example is the positive effect of imagery variables on word recall, which can be interpreted to mean that internally generated mnemonic information (the image) supplements the information provided more directly by the presented word.

Other dual-source phenomena include memory for words as compared to memory for their sensory attributes, recall of generated as compared to presented words, and reality monitoring (the process of distinguishing between external and internal source information). The two sources combine in different ways—independently, interactively, one or the other dominating, and so on—depending on experimental demands. The various possibilities will be reviewed briefly, along with some salient theoretical positions related to them.

The positive memory effects of word-imagery value and imagery-mnemonic instructions suggest that the mnemonic contributions of external and internal sources are at least partly independent and additive. This interpretation is uncertain, however, because the dual-source variable is confounded with verbal-nonverbal dual coding, that is, the external code is verbal and the internal-source code is presumably nonverbal. Stronger evidence for additive contributions of the two codes will be reviewed in a subsequent section, in which we also try to disentangle dual coding and dual-source effects. Another kind of evidence comes from independent effects of physical attributes, such as visual or phonemic similarity, and semantic attributes on memory (e.g., Frost, 1972; Runquist & Blackmore, 1973). A final example of independence is differential forgetting of external and internal information sources, as in memory for exact wording or surface-structure syntax as compared to semantic information in sentences (e.g., Begg, 1971).

Interaction of external and internal sources is suggested by the finding that instructions to attend to such visual attributes as case and color of printed words increases retention of the input mode but depresses recognition memory for the words (e.g., Light & Berger, 1974; Light, Berger & Bardales, 1975). Such studies actually contrast two types of external information, namely, printed word forms and variation in some specific visual attribute of the print. However, Light and her colleagues interpret the effects as a trade-off between memory for visual (external) and semantic (internal) attributes of words, depending on attentional deployment. A further example of external-internal source interaction is the finding by Light et al. (1975) that visual attributes of high imagery words were retained better than visual attributes of low imagery words when subjects were instructed to attend to case and color as well as word meaning, but not when they were only instructed to attend to word meaning. The authors suggested that, in the former condition, subjects may have incorporated the physical attributes into some image or verbal phrase that also conveyed the semantic aspects of the item. The interpretation implies that the interaction resulted from greater ease of internal recoding of the physical attributes of concrete than abstract words.

The so-called generation effect, that is, superior recall for subject-generated words than for presented words (e.g., Jacoby, 1978; McFarland, Frey, & Rhodes, 1980; Slamecka & Graf, 1978), suggests that internal source information is sometimes more memorable than external source information (see also Dosher & Russo, 1976). However, the reverse effect has also been observed. Data from dual coding research incidentally revealed that verbal recall was higher for pictures or words (picture labels) that had been explicitly repeated (picture-picture, picture-word, word-word) than for once-presented pictures or words that subjects repeated by generating imaginal or verbal codes to them, even when the images and verbal codes were externalized as drawings and written words (e.g., Paivio, 1975a, Fig. 1, p. 191). Thus, an additional experimenter-provided item contributed more to recall than did equivalent subject-generated (internal source) information. A related observation comes from unpublished studies done in collaboration with Wallace Lambert and James Clark. Subjects in these studies were required to generate translation equivalents (French or English) or synonyms to stimulus words and then recall either the elaborated-on stimulus or the generated response. Recall in all cases was at least as high and usually higher for the stimulus than the response. The reasons for the different patterns of effects are not yet clear, but for present purposes they illustrate that external and internal sources of information can contribute differentially to recall.

The above experiments indicate that subjects are able somehow to distinguish between external and internal sources of information. How this is done has been the focus of research by Marcia Johnson and her colleagues (e.g., Johnson, 1983; Johnson, Kahan, & Raye, 1984; Johnson & Raye, 1981; see also R. E. Anderson, 1984) on what they call "reality monitoring," which refers to processes that people use to decide whether remembered information had an external or internal source. Some of the differences that play a role in the decisions are that external memories include more contextual, sensory, and semantic details, whereas internal memories include more information about cognitive operations. Such differences can lead to memory traces that preserve source information very well, but confusion is increased by semantic and sensory similarity between memories from the two sources. This kind of confusion is particularly relevant here because it suggests that the two sources of trace information are functionally equivalent, that is, they can contain similar (confusible) information, including modality-specific sensory information. A related phenomenon, modality-specific interference, will be discussed in more detail shortly.

In addition to the above effects, the two sources of information may combine in ways that suggest some kind of fusion or modification of source components in the memory trace. Tulving (1983) presents a systematic analysis of this idea in terms of the process of ecphory, which he defines as a constructive activity that combines the episodic information from the engram (memory trace) and the semantic memory information from the retrieval cue. In Tulving's theory, ecphory plays a central role in retrieval along with the process by which the ecphoric information is converted into a recollective experience or overt memory performance. He describes similar ideas by others and cites indirect or suggestive evidence for ecphory, such as changes in memory for a perceptual episode after subjects have been presented misleading verbal information relevant to some aspect of the episode (Loftus & Loftus, 1980).

In a later section, I present more direct evidence for the present version of the dual-source hypothesis, showing that internal and external source information can be functionally equivalent and that they can combine in their effect on performance.

The role of similarity

We have already touched on the role of similarity in retrieval. Here we focus attention on the potency of similarity, both as a perceptual (external source) variable and as a semantic (internal source) variable. Frost (1972) studied the effects of visual and semantic similarity on organization in free recall. Visual similarity was varied among drawn objects by portraying them in four different orientations: vertical, horizontal, slanted to the left, or slanted to the right. Semantic similarity was defined by common category membership of subsets of items, so that equal numbers consisted of animals, articles of clothing, vehicles, and furniture. Memory was tested by recognition of pictures or recall or recognition of their names, with the subjects expecting one type of test or the other. Interest centered on clustering of items in recall. The results showed clustering on the basis of visual similarity, common category membership, or both, depending on which type of test was expected. Visual and conceptual similarity can also be sources of confusion among picture stimuli and hence interfere with recall in a paired associates task (D. L. Nelson, Reed, & Walling, 1976). The important point in the present context is that episodic memory performance is affected by visual similarity of presented pictures as well as by their internal relatedness at an associative level of meaning.

D. L. Nelson and his colleagues (see Nelson, 1981) also demonstrated effects of sensory-representational similarity and taxonomic or associative relatedness in cued-recall tasks using words as stimuli. Similarity was defined by association norms in which subjects produced either rhyming associates (e.g., *salt, halt, malt*) or meaningfully related associates (e.g., *salt, pepper, sugar*) to stimulus items. Facilitative effects of similarity on cued recall showed up as complex interactions among the type of cue-target relation (rhyming or taxonomic), its normative strength, the number of alternative targets in the set from which a given response item was drawn, and whether the cues had been present or absent during the study trial. The relevant conclusion here is that sensory-representational similarity (external source) and associative relatedness (internal source) can independently affect cued recall of words.

Runquist (1971) found that physical similarity between the stimulus members of a verbal-paired associates lists, in which similarity was measured by the number of common letters, interfered with paired-associate learning. The effect occurred even when the stimuli were highly meaningful words that were conceptually distinct, suggesting that the physical similarity effect was largely automatic. It is as though the subjects could not turn off a physical analogue (shape) processor operating at the verbal stimulus and representational level, despite the distinctiveness of the items in terms of referential and associative meaning.

The following studies are especially relevant to dual coding theory because they demonstrated positive or negative similarity effects that were presumably based on imagery and verbal encodings. Groninger and Groninger (1982) required their subjects to encode a series of concrete and abstract nouns by spelling, defining, or generating images (which they then described). Three weeks later, the subjects tried to recognize the words using encoding sets that were either congruent or incongruent with those used during initial encoding. The results showed significant (facilitative) congruence effects for imagery encodings with concrete words and for definitional encoding with abstract words. Moreover, in the case of imagery, recognition was improved more for words having the same specific image during both encoding and retrieval than for ones having different image representations. Groninger and Groninger interpreted the results in terms of a combination of dual coding and the Lockhart et al. (1976) view of encoding-retrieval similarity matching in recognition memory tests. Moreover, a subsequent replication and extension enabled Groninger and Groninger (1984) to conclude that it is the congruent *content* (e.g., images) rather than congruent processing operations (e.g., Kolers, 1973) or similarity of gist that best accounts for the facilitating effect of congruent encoding sets.

Conceptually similar results were obtained by Slack (1983) using sentences. Subjects heard sentences in the context of either a comprehension task or an image-generation task, and then tried to recognize the sentences in a forced-choice recognition test in which the distractors were similar to the targets in different ways. Image-generation instructions enhanced later recognition, but only for semantically similar test items and only for high imagery sentences containing concrete noun concepts. Slack argued that the effect could not be accounted for by an alternative (semantic) model of test-item recognition and interpreted the results to mean that subjects discriminated the semantically similar items by elaborating the sentence encodings through image processing. He did not directly test for imagery during the recognition test, but the implication is that rather precisely encoded imagery was reinstated as part of the retrieval context for target sentences, permitting them to be discriminated from the semantically similar distractors.

The following experiments revealed contrasting positive and negative effects of common imaginal encoding to different words. Recall from the previous chapter that concrete synonyms presumably can be represented by common referential images whereas abstract synonyms generally lack such common representations. From this assumption, J. Clark (1984) predicted and confirmed that repetitions of synonyms in a list would produce a greater increment in the recall of concrete than abstract words because the concrete synonyms would benefit from the repeated arousal of a common image. On the other hand, despite higher overall accuracy of recall for concrete materials, more synonym confusions would be expected in memory tasks involving concrete than abstract synonyms, and this, too, has been confirmed in a number of experiments (Anderson & Hidde, 1971; Begg & Paivio, 1969; Kuiper & Paivio, 1977; but see also Brewer, 1975).

The above findings indicate that sensory similarity (spatial orientation), representational-structural similarity (rhyming or visual shape), and similarity of imaginal or verbal referential encodings can affect episodic memory retrieval of either verbal or nonverbal items. The effects can be either positive or negative, depending on the nature of the memory task. It is unlikely that all of these effects can be attributed to a correlation between sensory similarity and associative contiguity in past experience, and, to the extent that they cannot, the similarity effects violate the terminal meta-postulate as discussed in chapter 3.

We turn now to evidence relevant to the more specific assumptions of dual coding theory. First we deal with various implications of the assumption that verbal and nonverbal memory systems are structurally distinct and functionally independent, and second, with the implications of the organizational assumptions of the theory.

Structural distinctions and functional independence of verbal and nonverbal memory systems

The available evidence provides support for weaker and stronger versions of this assumption. The weaker versions imply that the memorizer correctly remembers qualitative distinctions in the symbolic reactions to that information. Stronger versions imply that the mnemonic contributions of the two codes are independent and additive in a quantitative sense. Our coverage moves from weaker to stronger implications. The relevant evidence comes from subjective reports, modality-specific interference studies, memory performance of individuals with sensory defects (revealing something about the sensory modality of images), and statistical independent and additive effects of the two codes.

Evidence from subjective reports

Postexperimental subjective reports of learning strategies have consistently supported the functional distinction between imagery and verbal representational-mediational processes in episodic memory tasks. Paivio (1971) described the earlier evidence in detail and J. Richardson (1980) updated the picture, so a brief summary will suffice. First, subjects typically report using imagery mediators to learn pairs of high imagery nouns, whereas they report verbal or rote strategies with abstract pairs. These item-specific strategies showed up even in the reports of subjects who were given instructions to use particular associative strategies (Paivio & Yuille, 1969): Those questioned after one learning trial generally reported following a given strategy, whereas those who were questioned after the second or third trial shifted progressively away from apparently inappropriate or inefficient instructional strategies (e.g., imagery with abstract pairs, verbal mediators with concrete pairs) and toward the pattern predicted from dual coding theory. Second, the frequency of reported use of imagery correlates highly with recall scores for concrete pairs but not abstract pairs. Third, reports indicating correct recall of a mediating image are associated with correct response recall under imagery instructions (Yuille, 1973), and verbally reported recall of the image can precede recall of the target response (May & Clayton, 1973).

Subjective reports are open to the criticism that they may not accurately reflect the cognitive processes actually used in task performance. They may instead be epiphenomenal correlates without any causal role, or they may simply reflect the subjects' conformity with what they believe to be the expected responses. Such arguments are familiar from other areas of psychology (e.g., Nisbett & Wilson, 1977), and they have reappeared in the context of other imagery tasks (to be considered in the next chapter) in the guise of the use of tacit knowledge to simulate operations on images (Pylyshyn, 1981). Similar interpretations of this kind had already been considered and rejected in regard to subjective reports of mediation strategies (Paivio, 1971). For example, if subjects used knowledge about their memory performance as a basis for their reported strategies, performance and reports would be expected to correlate. However, this account would not explain why the frequency of reported use of *imagery* correlated with learning performance, whereas *verbal* mediation reports did not, nor why the imagery-performance correlation only occurred with concrete, high imagery noun pairs (see also J. Richardson, 1978). A strong case could thus be made that subjects' reports actually tell us something about representational processes that play a causal role in episodic memory. A weaker conclusion is that subjective reports are not decisive in themselves but, when considered together with the experimental data, they provide compelling evidence for dual coding effects in episodic memory. Of course, the verbal reports themselves require explanation in terms of the experiential history of the individual and the current task, as well as analysis in terms of the cognitive mechanisms employed (cf. Ericsson & Simon, 1984). The dual coding analysis would emphasize verbal-referential and associative responding to the episodic memories themselves and to the contextual cues in the postexperimental questionnaire.

Modality-specific interference

When a perceptual task selectively disrupts performance on a concurrent mental task (involving episodic or semantic memory processes) or vice versa, it is generally assumed that common processing systems are invoked.

Dual coding is specifically indicated by double-selective interference between verbal-perceptual and mental tasks on the one hand, and nonverbal-perceptual and mental tasks on the other. Such effects were demonstrated in the now-classic studies by Brooks (1967, 1968), and other investigators have subsequently explored different variants of the basic procedure. However, the interpretation of the crucial effects has been disputed. J. Richardson (1980) noted that the findings are inconsistent in regard to interference between spatial tasks and memory tasks that are presumed to require visual imagery. For example, Baddeley, Grant, Wight, and Thomson (1974) showed that a visual-tracking task selectively interfered with memory performance under imagery instructions but not with memory for concrete (as compared to abstract) items. Warren (1977) similarly found no selective effect of recall-concurrent tracking on recall of concrete words, although he did find that such tracking interfered selectively with picture recall. Thus, the effects for imagery-mnemonic instructions and pictures are consistent with dual coding theory, but the absence of an effect in the case of concrete words is not.

Other results (summarized in J. Richardson, 1980, p. 57) suggest that, in the case of the Brooks-type task, the disruption implicates a spatial-processing system rather than a visual-sensory one. This argument is not damaging to dual coding theory, however, because visual imagery is assumed to include spatial information as an essential component. In any event, the component of spatial information that is independent of the visual modality is not necessarily amodal but can be conceptualized instead in terms of haptic or other specific perceptual modalities. Brooks's findings accordingly qualify as reliable examples of modality-specific interference.

Other findings appear not to be subject even to the above criticisms. An experiment by den Heyer and Barrett (1971) required subjects to recall both the location and identity of a set of letters that had been presented in different positions in a grid. A visual- or verbal-interpolated task (or no task) was required between presentation and recall. The results showed a striking interaction so that the position-recall score was disrupted much more by the visual than by the verbal-interpolated task, and the reverse occurred in the case of identity recall.

Several investigators have similarly found that verbal and visual-nonverbal distracting tasks selectively interfered with memory for pictures and words in a manner consistent with dual coding theory (e.g., Colpo, Cornoldi, & De Beni, 1977; Pellegrino, Siegal, & Dhawan, 1975; Warren, 1977). As already mentioned, the effectiveness of different mnemonic techniques is similarly disrupted by appropriate perceptual-motor tasks. Saltz and Nolan (1981) reported one of the most informative studies of that kind in that it systematically compared the effects of visual, motoric, and verbal competition tasks on memory for sentences learned with the aid of visual imagery, motoric enactment, or verbal-only instructions. The results clearly showed that sentence recall was disrupted when the competition task and mnemonic technique matched (e.g., motoric competition and motoric imagery), but not when they differed. Thus, the study supports the distinction between imaginal and verbal representational codes in episodic memory and distinguishes as well between visual and motoric components of imagery (for a further, kinematic-motor distinction, see Zimmer & Engelkamp, 1985).

Finally, some researchers have even succeeded in obtaining theoretically appropriate selective-interference effects using concrete and abstract verbal materials. Janssen (1976) demonstrated such effects in recall of word lists. Klee and Eysenck (1973) showed that a concurrent visual-spatial memory task selectively disrupted the comprehension of high imagery (concrete) sentences, whereas a verbal memory task was relatively more disruptive in the case of abstract sentences (for a critique, see Holmes & Langford, 1976). Glass, Eddy, and Schwanenflugel (1980) showed a converse effect in which memory for visual patterns was selectively disrupted by a verification task with high imagery sentences. Given the negative findings described earlier, the precise limiting conditions for such effects remain to be determined, but the evidence as a whole favors continuity between perceptual and memory modalities, as well as the distinction between verbal and nonverbal codes.

Sensory defects and the modality specificity of imagery

At issue here is the sensory modality of images evoked by concrete words for individuals with sensory defects. Words such as *thunder* are high in auditory imagery but low in visual imagery, whereas ones like *rainbow* are high in visual but low in auditory imagery. The implications of the contrast were investigated (Paivio & Okovita, 1971) using congenitally blind people as subjects. The relevant finding was that the blind showed better memory for words of high auditory imagery than words that are low on such imagery, but they did not similarly benefit from visual imagery-value. Conversely, the memory performance of sighted people was more affected by variation in visual imagery than auditory imagery of words. We suggested that this was strong evidence that language-evoked imagery is modality-specific.

Zimler and Keenan (1983) reported similar experiments which showed that the recall performances of blind subjects "were remarkably similar to the sighted." In one experiment, both groups recalled more high visual than auditory imagery words, and in another, both performed in a comparable way in recalling words that referred to red or round objects. Zimler and Keenan concluded that these "results challenge Paivio's [modality-specific imagery] theory and suggest either (a) that the visual imagery used by sighted is no more facilitating than the abstract semantic representations used by the blind or (b) that the sighted are not using visual imagery" (p. 269). A third experiment used a concealed imagery task (cf. Neisser & Kerr, 1973) and showed that the blind, like the sighted, recalled more "pictorial" (visible) than concealed targets.

The results obtained by Zimler and Keenan are interesting but they are less damaging to dual coding theory than the authors suggest. First, they observed that sighted subjects were consistently inferior to the blind on recall of words with auditory referents and, in their Experiment 1, the blind were inferior to sighted subjects on pairs with visual referents. These observations are consistent with the modality-specificity hypothesis, as Zimler and Keenan acknowledge. The most problematic finding was the generally high performance of blind subjects with high visual imagery words, especially words referring to red objects. However, Zimler's and Keenan's high visual imagery lists included many words with referents that could be experienced by active touch, either as real objects (e.g., flag, mirror, snake, diamond) or as toys (e.g., tower, hill, roof, star). Even their "red" words referred to concrete objects (apple, blood, catsup, etc.), and thus could easily generate motor, tactile, or olfactory imagery that could mediate memory performance in the blind. Okovita and I had explicitly tried to avoid using such words in one experiment (Paivio & Okovita, 1971, Exp. II), though not with complete success.

The haptic (or other sensory) imagery hypothesis is in agreement with one of Zimler's and Keenan's proposals. The disagreement arises only because they assumed that "Paivio's (1971) modality-specific imagery hypothesis" refers only to visual imagery. That is not the case generally, nor is it true specifically in regard to blind subjects, since I have alluded to their reliance on other sense modalities, including a general spatial sense based on behavioral exploration of the environment and the possibility of concretization of purely "visual" words like *shadow* through association with other modalities, such as temperature changes when one moves into the shade (Paivio, 1971, pp. 519–520). The same comment is applicable in principle to Hampson's and Duffy's (1984) more recent finding of similar verbal and spatial selective-interference effects with congenitally blind, sighted, and blindfolded-sighted subjects.

We have used similar reasoning in the analysis of signability of words and its effect on associative memory among the deaf (Conlin & Paivio, 1975). In general, therefore, we have always assumed that the concrete meaning of words and any mediating imagery they evoke in memory tasks are based on whatever sensory modalities are available to a person.

Independence and additivity of nonverbal and verbal memory codes

The strongest implication of the independence assumption is that the mnemonic effects of imaginal and verbal codes are statistically independent and additive. Code independence can be inferred from procedures that do not reveal the joint contributions of verbal and nonverbal codes to performance (e.g., Bahrick & Bahrick, 1971; Nelson & Brooks, 1973). Here, I present evidence for additive increases in memory when we have reason to believe that both codes (i.e., referentially related trace components) have been encoded and stored and the same target memory can be retrieved from either code, as compared to the case in which only one of the codes has been stored.

Free-recall experiments have provided the most direct quantitative support, but the results of associative tasks have also been consistent with code additivity. The probability of imaginal and verbal coding has been manipulated by varying item attributes (high versus low imagery words, or pictures versus words), encoding instructions, or both. We begin with the effects of the imagery-concreteness level of verbal materials.

Effects of word imagery and concreteness. It has been repeatedly shown that words or larger linguistic units that are rated high in their image-evoking value or concreteness (or both) are generally remembered better than low imagery, abstract materials in item-memory tasks (for comprehensive reviews, see Cornoldi & Paivio, 1982; Denis, 1979; Paivio, 1969, 1971, 1972; J. Richardson, 1980). These findings are consistent with the dual coding idea that high imagery items readily evoke nonverbal imagery and that the imaginal representations serve as a supplementary memory code for item retrieval along with the verbal code elicited directly by the words.

I was concerned from the outset (Paivio, 1963, 1965a, 1968) with the possibility that the effects could be explained in terms of processes related to some other confounding attribute. By 1971, more than 20 alternatives had been empirically ruled out, but additional possibilities continued to be proposed from time to time. For example, Anderson and Bower (1973) suggested that concreteness effects could be due to abstract words having more dictionary meanings or greater lexical complexity than concrete words, since either difference would result in greater uncertainty and confusion and, hence, poorer recall for abstract words. It turned out, however, that abstract words do not have more dictionary meanings than concrete words (Begg, Upfold, & Wilton, 1978), and neither variable could account for concreteness affects on memory (Peterson & McGee, 1974; J. Richardson, 1975). The general conclusion is that no other attribute has yet been identified that can explain the positive effects of word imagery although, not surprisingly, some show independent correlations with memory scores for items (Cornoldi & Paivio, 1982). Despite the high correlation between the two attributes (e.g., .83 in the Paivio et al., 1968, norms), imagery even surpasses concreteness as a predictor of recall (e.g., Christian, Bickley, Tarka, & Clayton, 1978; Paivio, 1968; Rubin, 1980). It was once thought that concreteness might itself have some independent predictive value, but the chief proponent of this view (J. Richardson, 1980) has concluded that the conventional imagery interpretation is probably correct in the case of memory tasks. Thus, imagery-value continues to stand out as a predictor of memorability of items within the range of meaningful verbal material. In the case of free recall and item-recognition memory, the effect can be explained most readily as an additive contribution of imaginal and verbal codes to performance, with the probability of spontaneous or strategic imaginal coding being higher in the case of concrete than abstract words. Organizational processes could contribute as well (e.g., compound images), but such processes are more prominently implicated in associative recall tasks, as we shall see in a later section.

Picture-word comparisons. Turning next to picture-word comparisons, we expected that pictures of common objects would be remembered even better than concrete words on the assumption that subjects are more likely to label the pictures spontaneously than they are to image to concrete words. Thus, the probability of dual coding, hence, recall, would be higher for pictures than concrete words (Paivio, 1971, pp. 179–180). Note that the recall prediction applied specifically to item-memory tasks such as free recall and recognition memory, as well as paired-associate learning. The prediction has been repeatedly confirmed. The picture advantage was not expected in tasks requiring immediate memory for item order for reasons related to the organizational assumptions to be discussed later on. We shall now consider more direct evidence that dual coding contributes to the picture superiority effect although it is not the whole story.

The dual coding independence hypothesis was directly supported by the predicted finding that repeating a picture and its printed label in a list of items has an additive effect on free verbal recall, relative to recall levels obtained for once-presented pictures and words (Paivio, 1974b, 1975a). It is theoretically important that the additive effect occurred even under massed repetition conditions, that is, when a picture and its label followed each other immediately in the list, because massed repetitions normally produce less than additive effects when the repeated items are identical words (see Crowder, 1976, chap. 9) or, as demonstrated in our experiments, identical pictures. The results also indicated, however, that pictures and words contribute unequally to their additive effect, with the picture contribution being about twice that of words. Moreover, the two-fold picture advantage over words occurred even for once-presented items under incidental recall conditions designed to minimize the probability of dual coding. These results clearly support code additivity and suggest, in addition, that the image code is mnemonically superior to the verbal code for reasons that are yet to be fully understood.

Madigan (1983, p. 81) suggested that the code-additivity hypothesis might not apply to recognition memory because he found substantially higher recognition scores for pictures than words even when the pictures had been presented along with unrelated spoken words. Nonetheless, picture recognition was somewhat higher when the pictures had been accompanied by their names and the general pattern of his picture-word results (Fig. 3–3, p. 69) suggests additivity of codes along with picture superiority, much as in the free-recall studies described above. If encoding activity is not experimentally controlled, however, dual coding might play a smaller role in the picture superiority effect in recognition than in recall because pictures are less likely to activate a verbal code when subjects expect a recognition test than when they expect a recall test (Babbit, 1982). In addition, recognition may be relatively less dependent on elaborative processing (Paivio, 1976b) although augmented by it (Wiseman, MacLeod, & Lootsteen, 1985).

Effects of encoding instructions. The differential effects of picture and words on free recall are matched by a series of conceptually related, though once again operationally distinct, effects of imagery and verbal instructions. In the most relevant of these (Paivio, 1975a; Paivio & Csapo, 1973), subjects were briefly shown each of a series of concrete nouns with instructions either to image to a given word or to pronounce it, rating the difficulty of imaging or pronouncing during a 5-second interitem interval. Following list presentation, the participants were unexpectedly asked to recall the items. The following are some of the theoretically interesting observations: (a) recall probability for imaged items was twice as high as for pronounced items; (b) imagery encoding raised the level of word recall to the same high level as picture recall under comparable encoding conditions; (c) massed repetitions of items that subjects encoded dually by generating an image to them on one occurrence and pronouncing them on the other resulted in an additive effect on their recall relative to recall levels calculated for once-presented items that had been imaged or pronounced. In contrast, massed repetitions produced less than additive recall increments when a repeated word was encoded in the same way on each presentation, that is, imaged on each or pronounced on each. The remarkable parallel between the patterns of results for these subjective encoding conditions and the picture-word results described above can be seen in Figure 8–1, where the two sets of data are plotted together. The only difference is that recall was generally higher in the picture-word experiment, perhaps partly because external source information was more memorable than internal source information and partly because recall was intentional in the picture-word experiment, whereas it was incidental in the encoding experiment. It should be emphasized that the predictions and results just discussed for repeated items refer specifically to massed repetition conditions and not spaced repetitions. The latter generally have additive and, occasionally, superadditive effects even with items that have been identically encoded on each presentation. The spacing effects are not yet fully understood and further discussion of them is unnecessary for our purposes.

Evidence from memory for movement patterns. Dual coding has also been extended to the analysis of memory for movement patterns. Hall (1980) selected 18 movement patterns according to criteria of uniqueness and simplicity. These were presented to blindfolded subjects as passive movements; that is, the experimenter traced a pattern which the subject experienced by holding a handle that reproduced the pattern. The subjects rated each pattern on the ease with which it could be imaged visually, following essentially the procedure used by Paivio et al., (1968) for scaling words for imagery. Six high imagery and six low imagery patterns were then presented to another group of blindfolded subjects, who were asked to form a visual image of each pattern as it was presented. They were then given a recognition test

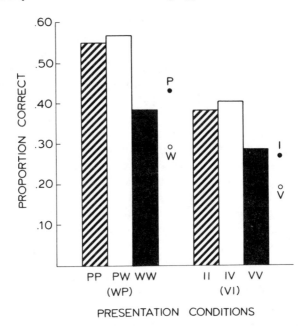

Figure 8-1. Correct recall proportions for pictures (P) and words (W) encoded by drawing (Dr) or writing (Wr), and repeated and once-presented words encoded imaginally (I) or verbally (V) on each presentation. Adapted from Paivio (1975a, Figure 1).

using a subset of the studied patterns along with new distractors. Recognition performance was significantly better for the high imagery than for the low imagery patterns. A subsequent experiment (Hall & Buckolz, 1983) showed similarly that reproductive free-recall performance varied directly with the imagery value of a pattern. Moreover, the effect was the same whether or not subjects had been instructed to image the patterns. The majority of subjects in each condition in fact reported both imaging and verbally labelling the patterns. The dual coding interpretation of these results is that visual imagery facilitated memory for movement patterns by adding to a kinesthetic memory baseline. Verbal coding could have contributed as well, either by facilitating image coding or by directly mediating retrieval of the movement pattern.

The additive effect of imaginal and verbal coding was more directly supported in an experiment by Chevalier-Girard and Wilberg (1980). Their subjects were presented geometric movement patterns under a no-strategy control condition, visual imagery instructions, and imagery-plus-labelling instructions. Free recall of the movement patterns increased dramatically with number of codes for both immediate and delayed tests. For example, the immediate recall probabilities (estimated from Fig. 2, p. 113 of the article) were .48, .68, and .83 for the control, imagery, and imagery-plus-labelling conditions, respectively. The authors suggested that the coding instructions added to a motor memory baseline, with labelling perhaps contributing by making a visual image more accessible. They also suggested a conceptual or semantic coding interpretation of the effects. That class of interpretation has not been directly evaluated in the area of movement memory, but presently we shall consider its general plausibility with reference to encoding effects associated with memory for pictorial and verbal material.

Critique and further evidence on additivity

All of the above results are problematic for conceptual coding theories that assume that nonverbal (pictorial, imaginal, kinesthetic) and verbal information alike are stored in an amodal propositional form in memory. Perhaps the results could be explained, however, by levels of processing or some other elaborative processing model that does not attach crucial importance to the imaginal-verbal distinction. For example, J. R. Anderson (1978) suggested that theoretical reliance on picture-word differences is fading because pictures are not necessarily better remembered if words are "deeply encoded." Note that this conclusion is consistent with our finding that *imagery* encoding of words sometimes wiped out the picture-word differences (cf. Durso & Johnson, 1980). The problem then is to distinguish between the modality-specific code (imagery) interpretation and the semantic depth interpretation. Leaving aside such logical arguments as the circularity of the latter, let us consider a direct test of the two approaches in which rule-of-thumb defining operations for depth were accepted at face value.

D'Agostino, O'Neill, and Paivio (1977) compared predictions from the two approaches using materials employed in tests of dual coding along with encoding operations that are typically used to define levels of processing. The materials consisted of lists of pictures, concrete words, and abstract words. The encoding operations consisted of visual-structural, phonemic, and semantic decisions concerning each item, the last requiring a judgment of whether an item (in the case of pictures, its name) would fit into a sentence frame. These operations demand increasingly deep (or elaborate) processing, according to Craik and Tulving (1975). Since the levels approach does not suggest any qualifications attributable to differences in materials per se, it generates the prediction that recall would increase with depth for all three types of items.

Dual coding predicts similarily that recall of concrete words will increase uniformly with "depth" because the semantic (sentence) processing task is most likely to arouse imagery as well as verbal-associative processing. In the case of pictures and abstract words, however, phonemic and semantic processing should result in equivalent recall. Equivalence is predicted for pictures because phonemic coding of their names ensures dual encoding, as does the semantic coding task. For abstract words, the phonemic and semantic tasks would ensure only representational encoding. The semantic task might increase abstract word recall to some extent through verbal-associative elaboration, but the effect should be minimal because of the low probability of image arousal to abstract words. The results were completely consistent with the dual coding predictions: For concrete words, recall increased significantly from structural to phonemic to semantic conditions; for pictures and abstract words, phonemic and semantic processing produced equivalent recall, with both exceeding the structural condition.

Further specific evidence favoring dual coding over levels of processing has been obtained in bilingual-episodic memory tasks involving different encoding conditions. These are reviewed in chapter 11.

To summarize up to this point, functionally equivalent patterns of results have been obtained in numerous experiments using variation in word-imagery level, picture-word comparisons, and imaginal versus verbal encoding instructions. The comparable patterns were generally predicted from the dual coding hypothesis that verbal and nonverbal episodic memory representations are functionally independent and additive even when they correspond to the same concept. Moreover, the mnemonic contribution of the nonverbal (visual-imaginal) trace component consistently turned out to be greater than that of the verbal component. This differential effectiveness continues to defy explanation in terms of confounding item attributes and list-level variables such as interitem organization and distinctiveness (see the discussion by Paivio & Csapo, 1973), although, as we have already noted earlier, memory for either words or pictures can be modified by experimental manipulation of such variables (see also Intraub & Nicklos, 1985). Dual coding theory was originally neutral in regard to the relative mnemonic value of the two codes, but the observation contributes to the theory because it reveals an additional functional distinction between the two representational systems, albeit one that requires more detailed understanding.

The results as a whole seem not to be directly explainable in terms of current propositional, levels of processing or other theories that do not take account of qualitative and quantitative differences in the mnemonic properties of nonverbal imaginal and verbal information. Such approaches lack assumptions that would be necessary to account for the potency of item imagery and imagery instructions in the above tasks, as well as the differential effectiveness of integrative versus separate imagery instructions and a variety of other findings to which we now turn.

Synchronous versus sequential organization

This section deals with the implications of the organizational assumptions of dual coding theory for episodic memory performance. In general the assumed specialization of the imagery system for synchronous organization leads us to look for evidence that multiple units of nonverbal (visual) information, whether from external or internal sources, can be relatively easily organized so that the components are functionally integrated and simultaneously available without losing their separate identity. In addition, spatial information can be retrieved from the trace. Conversely, the sequential organizational capacity of the verbal system implies that multiple verbal units are organized in episodic memory so that their sequential input order, or subjectively generated order, is relatively well-preserved in the trace. These hypotheses lead to predictions of performance differences in associative, item memory, and sequential memory tasks as a function of differences in item attributes and processing strategies. Retrieval demands also take on special importance.

Synchronous organization and the imagery system

Here we consider the effects of variables that operationalize the degree to which the information in subject-generated or perceptually (pictorially) presented compound images is spatially organized and functionally integrated in memory. The emphasis is on visual-spatial structures in particular, although other modalities will be mentioned as well. The British associationists referred to such mental structures as synchronic or simultaneous associations. They also implied that redintegration of the whole by a component (e.g., when one thinks of the sun, one simultaneously has the idea of the sky) is a functional characteristic of such associations. Modern researchers have directly operationalized structural integration by presenting pictures in which two or more objects are shown in some kind of meaningful or interactive relation to each other, as compared to a functionally separated relationship; or by presenting verbal descriptions or sets of words and instructing subjects to generate compound mental images in which the referents of the words are integrated or separate. The functional criteria for synchronous organization include memory for spatial relations, simultaneous availability of component information as evidenced by chunking and freedom from sequential constraints during retrieval, and redintegration effects. Redintegration has been inferred from the attributes of items that render them effective as retrieval cues during test trials, and from comparisons of performance in cued and noncued memory tasks. We shall review evidence relevant to each of these functional properties but with emphasis especially on redintegration.

Memory effects of spatial organization in complex pictures has been studied by comparing real-life scenes with pictures in which the objects are jumbled or disconnected. Such studies have shown, for example, that organized presentation facilitates immediate memory identification of objects from the pictures (e.g., Biederman, Rabinowitz, Glass, & Stacey, 1974), memory for spatial location of objects, especially on the vertical dimension (J. M. Mandler & Parker, 1976), and new learning based on prefamiliarization with the pictorial information (J. H. Reynolds, 1968). Such results suggest that organized pictures produce memory representations that facilitate retrieval of certain kinds of information, but they do not permit strong inferences to be made concerning specific functional properties that might account for the organizational effects.

An experiment by L. R. Peterson, Holsten, and Spevak (1975) provides a direct bridge to our subsequent discussions of the redintegrative properties of subject-generated mental images because it shows that such images are functionally integrated even when generated piecemeal from sequential input. Specifically, their subjects generate visual images of letters given only sequences of binary-auditory signals (dots and dashes) as input. Subjects in one experiment accurately recognized the letters in these imaginary arrays in both upright and rotated orientations. Subjects in another experiment were instructed to use spatial imagery of this kind to reproduce the sequences of dots and dashes. They reproduced much longer sequences than control subjects, indicating that the imagery had effectively integrated the input information into chunks from which the sequences could be retrieved.

We turn now to associative memory phenomena that implicate the redintegrative properties of compound mental images. Effects that might be attributable to the organizational structure of compound images and the redintegrative properties of retrieval cues were extensively investigated in the 1960s and early seventies. This early research has been reviewed elsewhere in detail (e.g., Denis, 1979; Paivio, 1969; 1971; J. Richardson, 1980), so we need only summarize the most relevant general findings. First, it was demonstrated that associative learning of picture pairs is better when the pair members are shown as meaningful units (e.g., a hand inside a bowl) than when they are shown as separate units (e.g., a hand beside a bowl) (Epstein, Rock, & Zuckerman, 1960). Subsequently, Bower (1970) demonstrated an analogous effect using imagery instructions. It had already been clearly established that instructions to generate compound images to link two words facilitate associative learning. Bower showed that the organizational structure of the inferred images is important by asking his participants to form images in which the referents of the words are either interacting or separated. Cued recall was significantly higher under the interactive condition. This effect is not attributable to other confounding variables such as image bizarreness (see Wollen, Weber, & Lowry, 1972). Associated information can also be retrieved more quickly from conceptually integrated pictorial structures than from unintegrated pictures (Klix & Metzler, 1982).

Next we consider the attributes of effective retrieval cues. Bower and Glass (1976) demonstrated that fragments that comprise significant parts of a drawn figure are especially effective retrieval cues for redintegrating memory for the entire pattern. This observation has obvious implications for the analysis of the effective components of imaginal mediators in paired-associate memory tasks, but such implications have not been explored empirically. Instead, the attention has been on the properties of the items that serve as retrieval cues.

As in the case of other item memory tasks, the imagery value or concreteness of items is the best predictor of performance. The theoretically important point is that the effect is stronger when imagery is varied on the stimulus side of pairs than when it is varied on the response side of pairs in the standard paired-associate procedure. More generally, the imagery value of the item that serves as the retrieval cue for its associate is particularly important. Systematic comparisons established that the stimulus effect of word imagery could not be explained in terms of verbal factors, such as frequency of usage or associative meaningfulness, nor a variety of other semantic attributes of words. The possibility that the effect may be due to stimulus discrimination rather than associative and retrieval mechanisms was also considered from the outset (Paivio, 1965a). The results of numerous studies (see Paivio, 1971, pp. 289–291; Tatum, 1976; Wicker, Thorelli, & Saddler, 1978) permit us to reject the discrimination hypothesis and to conclude instead that the stimulus-imagery effect is attributable to associative and retrieval mechanisms. It should be noted at the same time that stimulus imagery also facilitates item discrimination, as in verbal discrimination learning (e.g., Paivio & Rowe, 1970; Rowe & Paivio, 1971). In fact, it has been shown (Paivio & Rowe, 1971) that imagery can have simultaneous but distinct effects on discrimination and incidental associative learning.

Let us put the stimulus-imagery effect into an explicit theoretical context. The effect was originally predicted from an early version of the imagery organization-redintegration idea, the so-called conceptual-peg hypothesis, which I summarized as follows:

> The argument is that the stimulus member of a pair serves as a "conceptual peg" (a term first introduced, without reference to imagery, by Lambert & Paivio, 1956) to which its associate is hooked during learning trials when stimulus and response members are presented together, and from which the response member can be retrieved on recall trials when the stimulus member is presented alone. On the assumption that imagery can serve a mediating function, as the imagery-memory technique suggests, it follows that the ease of learning the stimulus-response association will depend partly on the image-arousing capacity of the individual nouns and on the stimulus member in particular. The imagery value of both stimulus and response would contribute to the formation of a compound image, consisting of images evoked by the individual items when the two are presented together, thereby affecting the formation of mediated association. On recall trials, however, when the stimulus is presented alone, its image-arousing value would be particularly important, for the stimulus member must serve as the cue that reinstitutes the compound image from which the response component can be retrieved and recoded as a word. The hypothesis leads to the prediction that a positive effect of noun imagery will be greater on the stimulus side than on the response side of pairs. (Paivio, 1969, p. 244)

The quotation refers specifically to the learning of noun-noun pairs, but the hypothesis and the confirmatory results extend to larger verbal structures as well as to picture-word comparisons. An example of the former is an experiment by R. C. Anderson, Goetz, Pickert, and Halff (1977), in which they found that concreteness of subject-noun phrases of sentences enhanced phrase recognition as well as the probability of recalling the predicate, given recognition. The authors suggested that "a concrete phrase makes a good conceptual peg because it is likely to be given a specific, stable coding and because it tends to redintegrate the whole sentence" (1977, p. 142). Picture-word studies have similarly demonstrated quite consistently that pictures are superior to their concrete-noun labels as stimulus terms, although not necessarily as response terms in paired-associate learning (Dilley & Paivio, 1968; Paivio & Yarmey, 1966; Yarmey, 1974). The conceptual-peg interpretation was strongly supported recently by a stages-of-learning analysis of the associative effects (Brainerd, Desrochers, & Howe, 1981), which located the picture-superiority effect at the retrieval stage.

Considered together, the effects of integration variables and stimulus imagery are clearly consistent with the hypothesis that the imagery system is specialized for synchronous organization of separate meaningful units in episodic memory. The interpretation was strengthened and its implications systematically extended in a series of experiments by Ian Begg. These capitalized on comparisons of performance in cued and noncued memory tasks. Begg (1972) compared free and cued recall of individual words from concrete phrases, such as *white horse*, and abstract phrases, such as *basic truth*. He found that cuing by one member of the pair incremented recall relative to the free-recall condition for the concrete phrases but not for abstract phrases. Following a line of reasoning previously proposed by Horowitz and Prytulak (1969), Begg concluded that the differential cuing effects can be interpreted in terms of integrated imaginal memory traces that are redintegrated by high imagery words. Subsequently, Begg (1973) found that a recall increment from free to cued recall for concrete noun pairs was greater under integrated than separate imagery instructions. Thus, interactions of task with item-imagery value and with integrative-imagery instructions converged on the organization-redintegration hypothesis.

Begg (1982) further extended the theoretical reasoning to include cases in which integrative imagery might actually have a negative effect. This effect would be expected in item recognition and verbal discrimination learning, which require discrimination in memory between a correct target item and one or more incorrect alternatives. Embedding the target item and the incorrect alternatives into integrated traces should make it more difficult to achieve such discrimination. Begg (1982) obtained the predicted negative effects in a number of experiments.

In summary, a wide variety of findings are consistent with the hypothesis that the imagery system is specialized for synchronous organization of multiple units of information in memory. The relevant classes of observations are that: (a) paired-associate learning is easier if the pair members are shown or are encoded imaginally in an interactive relation as compared to a conjunctive (separated) relation; (b) learning is positively related to the concreteness or image-arousing value of the items, particularly the items that serve as retrieval cues for their associates, and this differential effect has been identified as a redintegration effect; (c) a recall increment from free to cued recall is greater with concrete, high imagery words than with abstract ones, and under interactive imagery than under separated imagery instructions, supporting the integrative and redintegrative capacity of imagery; (d) these effects have been obtained with different types of materials (noun pairs, adjective-noun pairs, pictures and picture-word pairs, sentences), indicating that synchronous organization is a very general capacity of the nonverbal imagery system.

Empirical and theoretical challenges to imagery organization

Some important qualifications must also be recognized. Most of the research to date has used pairs of items and we need more information on how many and what kinds of units can be effectively integrated in episodic memory. Howe's (1985) test of a mathematical model of associative memory suggested that three concrete words could be effectively integrated, and Baker and Santa (1977) found that instructions to form interactive images to groups of four successively presented words in a list of 24 concrete words substantially increased recall relative to a standard control condition. A number of other studies have similarly used sets of three or more items (e.g., Begg, 1978; Begg & Sikich, 1984; Morris & Stevens, 1974). The problem needs to be more systematically explored in such extensions. A second qualification is that the theoretical conclusions are essentially restricted to visual imagery. That is, we know little about synchronous organization in other modalities or across sensory modalities. One exception, suggested particularly by the ability of blind subjects to profit from spatially integrative imagery instructions (Jonides, Kahn, & Rozin, 1975; Kerr, 1983) is that nonvisual (e.g., motor or haptic) information apparently can be integrated in the memory trace. Finally, we have assumed that the integration-redintegration effects in episodic memory are not attributable to verbal traces. This assumption was justified by absence of evidence for integrative memory with abstract verbal material. There are, however, some discordant findings that warrant close attention.

Day and Bellezza (1983) questioned the integrated visual imagery interpretation of the effects of concreteness in associative learning. Their critique was based on experiments in which subjects were asked to form composite images to pairs of concrete or abstract nouns, rate the clarity and vividness of each image, and then recall the second member of each pair given the first one as a cue. In addition, the pair members were either highly related or unrelated according to ratings by independent judges. The critical results were that the subjects in the recall experiment rated their composite images to related abstract pairs (e.g., democracy-liberty) as being more vivid than their images to unrelated concrete pairs (e.g., cheese-fur), but they nonetheless recalled more concrete than abstract response words. Day and Bellezza took this as evidence against dual coding theory and the visual imagery hypothesis, and proposed instead that the results are best explained by a concreteness hypothesis according to which learning "is based on general knowledge of how classes of concrete objects interact in the physical world" (1983, p. 252).

The results are interesting in their own right but I disagree that they are inconsistent with dual coding theory. Day and Bellezza stated that, in "dual coding theory, abstract nouns are represented only in the linguistic-verbal system, whereas concrete nouns are represented both in the verbal-linguistic and in the pictorial-imagery system" (p. 256). Moreover, "the emphasis in dual coding theory is on the nature of the representation of individual nouns, and the theory can account for neither the imagery nor the recall performance found here" (p. 256). These assertions are unjustified for the following reasons: (a) Abstract nouns are not assumed to be represented *only* by the verbal system if this is intended to mean that they cannot arouse images. The correct statement is that they are less likely to arouse images or do so with greater difficulty than concrete pairs because of less direct access to the imagery system. In fact, all of our imagery-latency studies have indicated that subjects can form images to abstract pairs, given enough time. (b) As already emphasized earlier, the imagery aroused by concrete nouns is not restricted to visual or "pictorial" imagery. (c) The emphasis in many experiments has been on individual nouns, but the theory does not deny verbal contextual effects on image arousal (e.g., see Paivio, 1971, p. 268). Such contextual effects on imagery and correlated shifts in recall performance were in fact experimentally demonstrated by Begg and Clark (1975). Finally, (d) Day and Belleza ignored the important theoretical role of stimulus-noun imagery (the conceptual-peg hypothesis) in associative retrieval from integrated images.

Some of the above factors and others not mentioned by Day and Belleza can be used to explain their finding that imagery ratings were higher but recall lower for abstract related pairs than concrete unrelated pairs. Conjoint presentation of a pair of abstract nouns presumably served to prime the arousal of relevant situational images, particularly given that subjects had unlimited time to view and rate each pair. In the recall task, however, the mediating image would have to be redintegrated by one member of the pair and the response member retrieved from that image. Abstract nouns would be at a disadvantage on both counts because they generally lack direct referential interconnections with imagens. Thus, they may not easily evoke the same image as the pairs did during encoding, and even if they did, image-decoding errors would be likely because of high uncertainty in the relations between the content of the images and abstract response terms. On the other hand, unrelated concrete pairs would evoke compound images whose components are highly probable referents of each word. During retrieval, the stimulus term would be highly likely to redintegrate the same image because of the strong referential relation to one component, and decoding errors would be relatively unlikely because of a similar relation in the case of the other (response) component. This analysis is simply a restatement of the conceptual-peg hypothesis of dual coding theory. In addition, it is known that semantic or associative overlap is generally higher among abstract than among concrete words (e.g., Paivio & Begg, 1971), so intralist interference would be greater in the abstract case. All of these possibilities are consistent with dual coding theory and prior empirical research related to it. Whether they in fact account for the Day and Bellezza results remains to be determined.

The next set of data are more troublesome for the imagery-integration hypothesis. Marschark and Paivio (1977) investigated integrative recall of concrete and abstract sentences using several designs previously used by others with concrete sentences only (J. R. Anderson & Bower, 1973; R. C. Anderson & Ortony, 1975; Foss & Harwood, 1975). We found that recall was generally higher for concrete than abstract sentences, but recall was equally integrative or holistic ("the whole greater than the sum of the parts") for both types of sentences. This finding is problematic because dual coding theory suggests that integrative recall should be higher for concrete than abstract sentences because imagery provides an integrating mechanism for the former. Moreover, this expectation was supported by Begg's (1972) finding of integrative recall of concrete but not abstract phrases at least as defined by a recall increment from free to cued recall. Marschark and I were unable to account for our apparently discrepant finding in any satisfactory way consistent with dual coding and we suggested that the addition of a third, common coding system would solve the problem. My preference, however, is to seek alternatives that would be consistent with dual coding. One possibility is that the materials used in our experiment were particularly conducive to verbal-associative encoding that would mediate apparently integrated or holistic sentence recall even in the abstract case. Until such possibilities are experimentally confirmed, if they are, the Marschark and Paivio finding remains more of an embarrassment for dual coding theory than other negative observations reported in the literature.

Sequential organization and the verbal system

We turn now to the contrasting hypothesis that the verbal system is specialized for sequential organization of information in memory, whereas the nonverbal system is not. The reference again is to the organization of multiple discrete units, verbal or nonverbal, in episodic memory tasks. The strong implication is that verbal items, or verbally-encoded items, should be recalled better than nonverbal items or encodings in sequential memory tasks but not in item-memory tasks.

The first systematic test of this hypothesis (Paivio & Csapo, 1969) compared memory for pictures, concrete nouns, and abstract nouns in the two kinds of tasks under fast and slow rates of presentation. The fast rate (5.3 items/sec) was designed to preclude covert naming of pictures and imaging to words during the interitem interval, but permit the items to be recognized (in theoretical terms, representational coding was possible, whereas referential coding was not). The slower rate (2 items/sec) was intended to permit naming reactions. The crucial findings for present purposes were that, at the fast rate, pictures were inferior to words in the sequential memory tasks (memory span and serial learning) but not in item-memory tasks (free recall and recognition); at the slow rate, conversely, pictures were not significantly inferior to words in the sequential tasks and they were superior to words in the item-memory tasks. The inferiority of pictures in fast-rate sequential tasks is attributable to the inaccessibility of the verbal code, and their superiority in slow-rate item-memory tasks is consistent with the additivity hypothesis of dual coding theory, as discussed earlier.

We confirmed the sequential memory results using discrimination of recency and serial reconstruction tasks, which do not require verbal responding (Paivio, 1971, p. 237). The results have also been extended to auditory verbal and nonverbal stimuli (Paivio, Philipchalk, & Rowe, 1975; Philipchalk & Rowe, 1971; Rowe & Cake, 1977). Specifically, we found that environmental sounds (of a telephone, train, clock, etc.) were inferior to words in serial recall but not in free recall tasks. Confirmatory results were also obtained by del Castillo and Gumenik (1972) using forms that varied in familiarity and nameability.

A number of studies have also provided evidence relevant to both the synchronous and sequential organizational hypotheses of dual coding theory. Smythe (1970; summarized in Paivio, 1971, p. 284) followed unidirectional paired-associate learning of pairs of pictures, concrete nouns, or abstact nouns with both forward and backward cued-recall tests. Reaction times for correct recall showed associative symmetry for pictures and concrete words, but faster forward than backward recall for abstract pairs. Thus, recall was free from sequential constraints (e.g., synchronous) when the image code was available but not when only the verbal code was readily available.

Snodgrass, Burns, and Pirone (1978) referred to the differential organization hypothesis of dual coding theory as the interaction hypothesis which "states that pictorial memory codes are specialized for spatial structures and verbal memory codes are specialized for temporal structures" (p. 206). They tested the hypothesis using a pair-order recognition paradigm in which subjects were shown picture pairs and word pairs in a spatial (side by side) order or a temporal (successive) order, and were then required to recognize whether test pairs were in the same or reverse order. In addition, pairs were studied under either imagery or verbal coding instructions. Snodgrass et al. (1978) developed several versions of a mathematical model that permitted them to evaluate both item and order recognition independently. The results of several experiments were consistent with the interaction hypothesis. Moreover, the data were predicted better by two versions of the dual coding model (deterministic and probabilistic dual coding) than by a single-code (levels of processing) model.

Santa (1977) used a reaction-time procedure to investigate the contrasting organizational properties of imaginal and verbal representations in short-term memory performance. Subjects were shown a composite stimulus consisting of three simple geometric forms or their verbal labels (e.g., triangle, circle, square), followed by a comparison display, and were required to indicate whether target and comparison stimuli contained the same elements, ignoring transformations of position. For example, in Santa's Experiment 3, the elements in the target were positioned inside a square frame so that the display was an integrated ("good") figure, which resembled a human face when the elements were geometric forms. The comparison test consisted of a similar configuration or a horizontal, linear array of the elements. Santa hypothesized that the form displays would be represented in memory as spatial images and comparisons therefore should be faster when the test display is a good figure identical to the target. However, he expected word targets to be recoded from left to right and top to bottom into a sequential verbal representation. If so, comparisons should actually be faster with horizontal test arrays whose linear order matches the sequential verbal representation of the target than with the good figure test displays physically identical to the target. The predictions were generally confirmed.These and other results from three experiments permitted Santa to conclude that verbal representations are sequentially constrained but are not bound by the spatial properties of the stimulus, whereas representations of geometric forms preserve spatial relations among the components and are less constrained by sequential ordering.

M. J. Peterson (1975) compared memory for the contents of 4 × 4 spatial matrices under perceptual, imagery, or verbal coding conditions. Students in the perceptual conditions saw a matrix containing letters in 12 cells for an inspection period. Students in the imagery and verbal conditions listened to auditory messages that described the matrices, and the imagery subjects were instructed to imagine the matrix being described, whereas those who were in the verbal condition did not receive imagery instructions. Recall was tested by a probe procedure in which the subjects were required to fill in four empty squares in a test matrix. It is relevant to note incidentally that recall was best in the perceptual condition, intermediate in the imagery condition, and poorest in the verbal condition; moreover, forgetting over a 10-sec interval occurred only in the verbal condition. More directly relevant in the present context, recall was best for the corner cells of seen and imagined matrices, suggesting that the memory representation was spatial in nature, whereas the verbal condition did not show this effect. Instead, when recall was scored as a function of input order, the verbal condition showed a serial position effect that is characteristic for verbal materials, namely, better recall for primacy and recency than for middle positions. Thus, in present terms, the recall results showed the contrasting patterns that would be expected from the synchronous *versus* sequential organization hypothesis of dual coding theory.

A variety of other experiments (e.g., R. E. Anderson, 1976; Healy, 1975, 1977; O'Connor & Hermelin, 1972) have also yielded results that are at least partly consistent with the differential organization hypothesis of dual coding theory. However, further studies are needed to determine why the contrasting effects are sometimes subtle.

Critique and further evidence on sequential memory

The hypothesis that sequential information is not efficiently stored in the imagery system was questioned by Bugelski (1974) on the grounds that certain imagery-mnemonic techniques permit one to retrieve a long list of items in their input order. Such results are not at all inconsistent with the dual coding hypothesis, however, because they entail reconstruction of input order from either verbal-sequential or nonverbal-spatial structures in long-term memory. For example, the one-bun, two-shoe rhyming mnemonic permits the memorizer to retrieve order information because each item is associated with a number corresponding to its input order, but there is no evidence that the discrete images themselves contain the order information. On the other hand, order information can be derived from spatially organized imagery of the kind associated with the version of the ancient method of loci in which target items are imagined as objects deposited in specific "places" encountered during an imaginary walk in a familiar environment. The sequential order is not directly represented in the imagery but is instead reconstructed from the spatial order of locations in the imaginally experienced cognitive map. It could be argued as well that the motor component of the imaginary walk provides a sequential thread to the mnemonic activity (Paivio, 1971), although the spatial layout probably is a sufficient basis for reconstructing the input order of a particular set of items. In any case, successful serial reconstruction using an imagery mnemonic does not necessarily mean that any direct sequential learning has taken place. The results of verbal learning experiments by Young, Overbey, and Powell (1976) in fact suggested that interactive images used in learning do not "contain" sequential information, but the issue merits further investigation using the method of loci and other imagery mnemonics.

We encounter a somewhat different analytic problem in the case of memory for the temporal order of continuously changing visual events that have not been associated with motor activity or correlated sequences of ordered locations. Consider a fireworks display that consists of continuous visual-spatial transformations and discrete changes in color. It could be argued that the sequence of the spatial transformations can be retained and reexperienced in imaging because the visual system is specialized for spatial processing. However, random sequences of discrete colors may not be well remembered because continuous transformations cannot be imposed on them unless the sequence happens to correspond to the color circle. An experiment by Kolers and von Grünau (1976) provided some evidence relevant to the functional distinction, although not memory. They found that when two different forms, such as a square and a triangle, are presented in separate locations at an interstimulus interval that induces apparent motion, the observer simultaneously perceives one shape continuously changing into the other. In the case of color, however, the change is discrete and sudden rather than gradual. The two types of change could be induced at the same time, so that perceived motion of a red square and a blue triangle is accompanied by a gradual change in shape and a sudden change in color, with the color always appearing to fill the contours of the changing shape. Since the physical change in shape was also sudden, the perceived continuous change in form must reflect a transformational capacity of the visual system that is absent in the case of color processing. The implications of the functional contrast remain to be directly investigated in memory tasks.

Certain findings from auditory perceptual research are relevant to the visual problem just discussed as well as the specific functional properties that underlie the sequential processing capacities of the verbal system. Warren, Obusek, Farmer, and Warren (1969) found that subjects were unable to report the order of four nonverbal sounds (hiss, buzz, high tone, low tone) presented rapidly in a repetitive cycle, although they had no difficulty recognizing the individual sounds. Conversely, they were able to judge the order of similarly presented spoken digits. These findings are obviously consistent with the dual coding hypothesis concerning sequential memory. Subsequently, Bregman and Campbell (1971) showed that subjects could judge the order of tones if they were perceived as a unitary stream. Such apparent streaming was determined by tonal similarity (membership in a common high or low frequency range). It was also affected by the nature of the transition, so that tonal sequences were more likely to be perceived as unitary when the frequency transitions from tone to tone, though fast, were gradual rather than sudden. Rhythm has also been found to contribute, along with similarity, to stream organization and sequence identification.

Bregman and Campbell (1971, pp. 248–249) also suggested that temporal judgments are relatively easy with speech units because vocal sounds form similarity groupings and because transitions in speech are not instantaneous. Accordingly, a sequence of speech sounds constitutes a unitary stream for the speech system. To this we can add the earlier suggestion that the sequential processing capacity of the verbal system is related to its articulatory motor properties. The specific hypothesis, then, is that the verbal system is specialized for sequential (including sequential memory) processing because of its simultaneous capacity for dealing with rapid articulatory transformations and acoustic (tonal and rhythmic) transitions. If nonverbal auditory sequences (e.g., music) contain similar transitions or can be similarly processed (e.g., by humming), they can be effectively remembered as well. The same generalization may be applicable to visual sequences.

SUMMARY

The evidence considered in this chapter provides a systematic, comprehensive, and coherent case for the dual coding approach as well as for the constructive-empiricist philosophy of science that the approach represents. Dual coding theory and the convergent operational approach associated with it have been applied to a wide range of memory and learning tasks using different materials. The tasks include associative memory, item memory, sequential memory, and discrimination learning with materials ranging from pictures, to concrete and abstract words or larger units. The tasks have been done under standard (free strategy) conditions as well as under instructional sets to use imagery or other theoretically relevant strategies. The theoretically based predictions have included complex interactions between the type of memory task (e.g., sequential versus item memory, free recall versus cued recall), item attributes (e.g., pictures versus words, or concrete versus abstract words), and instructionally induced or reported mnemonic strategies (e.g., imaginal versus verbal). The results have generally conformed to theoretical expectations, with remarkable agreement in the patterns of effects produced by empirically distinct though theoretically related operations (e.g., picture-word, concrete-abstract word, and imaginal-verbal mnemonics). Some important inconsistencies remain to be resolved, especially ones that arose in connection with sentence memory, along with substantial empirical gaps to be closed in. All in all, however, the results to date provide strong support for the dual coding approach to aspects of episodic memory, and they strain the explanatory capacity of current propositional or other single-code, representational-processing theories unless they are modified by post-hoc assumptions that essentially represent rephrasing of the core assumptions of dual coding theory.

9
Manipulation and Use
of Representational Information

Many cognitive tasks require the performer to analyze, evaluate, and manipulate the properties of mental representations in order to respond appropriately. Typical examples include comparisons of perceived and imaged objects, symbolic comparisons, mental transformations, and computations based on representational structures. Such phenomena have been at the center of recent debates concerning the nature of mental representations, and some (e.g., mental transformations) have a long prior history in which they figured prominently in the study of individual differences in mental imagery. Here, the relevant findings are analyzed and interpreted in terms of dual coding theory, again in contrast to propositional and tacit-knowledge interpretations. Problem solving and other complex tasks that implicate different combinations of the basic process are also discussed.

Collectively, the reviewed studies bring into focus the functional similarities between perceptual-motor and imaginal structures and processes. We have already seen that dual coding shares with other imagery-based theories the assumption that mental representations and processes are analogous to perceptual-motor processes in the sense that the information in mental representations and the operations that can be performed on them are related in a nonarbitrary and continuous fashion to their perceptual-motor counterparts. The parallel cannot be exact, however, because the internal events in question are not directly controlled by external stimuli as are perceptual events. Thus, visual imagery is usually an impoverished (inaccurate) or distorted analogue of visual perception, and the operations that can be performed on images do not precisely parallel the operations that can be performed on perceptual objects. What the evidence suggests, however, is that mental and perceptual representations contain similar structural information and that it can be used and manipulated in similar ways.

STRUCTURAL AND FUNCTIONAL SIMILARITIES
BETWEEN PERCEPTION AND IMAGERY

A variety of procedures have been used to determine the degree of similarity in the information that can be derived from perceived and imaged objects and the uses to which that information can be put. Some procedures demand reactions to single stimuli under perceptual and imagery conditions, and others, comparisons of pairs of perceived or imagined objects. A selective and brief summary follows because the evidence has been comprehensively reviewed and interpreted by others (e.g., Finke, 1980, 1985; Finke & Shepard, in press).

One approach capitalizes on the fact that perceptual responses can be primed. For example, prior exposure to particular printed words will selectively reduce tachistoscopic thresholds for the same words. The relevant studies in the present context are ones that have used imagery to prime perception. Leeper (1935) and Steinfeld (1967) showed that relevant verbal information (e.g., a story about the sinking of a liner, which presumably evoked imagery) facilitated recognition of fragmented objects (e.g., a fragmented figure of a ship). More recently, Shepard and his colleagues (e.g., Shepard & Metzler, 1971; Cooper, 1975) have used a similar paradigm in which they measured the reaction time to a test stimulus when the subject has or has not formed a preparatory visual image of the stimulus. The typical result is that the discriminative response (for example, indicating whether a numeral is correctly oriented or a mirror image) is fast and accurate when the preparatory image is appropriate, but considerably slower when no image or an inappropriate image has been formed. Such results are generally accepted as evidence that the mental representation aroused by the priming condition is structurally similar to the analogous perceptual representation.

Podgorny and Shepard (1978) provided more direct evidence for the comparability of imagery and perception using spatially localized probes. A subject is shown a grid with a figure, such as a block letter F, or simply imagines such a figure on a blank grid. One or more small colored dots are presented and the subject indicates whether or not at least one dot falls on the portion of the grid defined as figure. The following were some of the crucial results. Reaction time was only slightly slower (50 msec on the average) under the imagery than the perceptual condition; error rates in both conditions were low; reaction times showed no consistent dependence on the position of the probe within the grid; and off-figure responses in both cases decreased in reaction time with the distance of the probed square from the figural portion of the grid. These and other findings (e.g., Attneave & Pierce, 1978; Farah, 1985; M. J. Peterson & Graham, 1974) are all consistent with the idea that common representational structures underlie imagery and perception.

Psychophysical studies by Kerst and Howard (1978) and Moyer, Bradley, Sorensen, Whiting, and Mansfield (1978) also provided information on the quantitative similarity of perceptual and memory (presumably imaginal) representations. Their participants were required to estimate the sizes or lengths of stimulus objects or patterns that were presented perceptually or only named. The functions observed under the two conditions were similar, except that the exponent of the power function was smaller for remembered than perceived size. The interpretation favored by the investigators was that memory judgments involve "re-perception" of the stimuli. Results obtained more recently by Algom, Wolf, and Bergman (in press) using a variety of procedures also are generally consistent with the re-perception hypothesis. An alternative interpretation, suggested by a study of individual differences in size estimates (McKennell, 1960), is that perceptual-size judgments of familiar objects are themselves determined primarily by remembered size. The relevant point for present purposes, however, is the general similarity in the quantitative information that is available from imaginal representations and perceptual ones.

Perceptual-imaginal similarities have also been revealed by studies that require comparisons of perceived or imaginal stimuli. Shepard (1978) used the concept of second-order isomorphism to describe the similarity observed in the functional relations among objects when they are perceived as compared to when they are imagined in response to names. The conclusions were based on analyses of similarity-rating data for pairs of stimuli. The general finding was that the similarity data were statistically indistinguishable between the perceptual and imagery conditions for such objects as two-dimensional shapes (e.g., of the states of the United States), spectral colors, familiar faces, and musical sounds. Multidimensional analyses indicated further that, in both conditions, subjects based their judgments on physical properties of the objects—irregularity and other dimensions for shape, hue for colors, and so on.

Kosslyn and his collaborators (e.g., see Kosslyn, 1981; Kosslyn, Pinker, Smith, & Schwartz, 1979) have also provided evidence for perceptual-like functional properties of visual imagery. The following observations illustrate different functions: (a) more time is required to "see" properties of smaller than of larger images; (b) image-scanning time varies directly with the distance between points in a spatial image; (c) larger objects "overflow" sooner than smaller ones when the subject is asked to imagine the object approaching the viewer; and (d) the acuity of visual imagery decreases toward the periphery of the visual field, much as in visual perception. Also relevant in this context is a study by Lockhead and Evans (1979), which showed that the apparent size of a mentally imaged object decreased monotonically with increases in the distance of a blank screen that was provided as a viewing surface.

Finke's (1980) general review included evidence from his own research showing that the functional similarity between perception and imagery in the kinds of tasks we have been considering is clearer for vivid imagers than for nonvivid imagers as defined by a vividness questionnaire. Recently, Wallace (1984) reported particularly striking vividness effects on the ability to use visual imagery to produce visual illusions. Subjects in the imagery conditions were asked to imagine lines that were missing from illusion-inducing figures. The results of three experiments showed that vivid imagers consistently reported image-produced illusions, which were equal in magnitude to perceptual illusions. In contrast, nonvivid imagers reported an illusion only when lines were physically present. These results provide strong evidence for the functional equivalence of perception and imagery, especially because experimental manipulations and individual differences converged on the same conclusion.

SYMBOLIC COMPARISONS

The symbolic comparison task, a variant of the similarity comparison paradigm, has produced a number of findings that bear directly on the perceptual analogue nature of mental representations and some of the principal assumptions of dual coding theory. The task had been introduced earlier but Moyer (1973) was the first to see its significance for the study of mental representations. Moyer asked his participants to indicate by a key press which of two named animals is larger in real life. He found that it takes less time to make the comparison as the size difference increased. For example, the decision was faster for *mouse-dog* than for *cat-dog*. The overall pattern was a logarithmic function similar to what is observed with perceptual stimuli that differ in physical size. The same general function has been observed with other symbolic dimensions as well, although its specific shape sometimes differs from that observed under perceptual conditions (e.g., Baum & Jonides, 1979). The continuous nature of this *symbolic distance effect* (Moyer & Bayer, 1976) suggests that subjects base their decisions on analogue representations in long-term memory. Thus, the results are generally consistent with dual coding and other theories that assume that cognitive representations are perceptual-memory analogues of the objects they represent. The symbolic distance effect is, however, inconclusive in itself because it can also be predicted from some verbal-associative and propositional models.

A number of other results provide additional support for the analogue interpretation and dual coding theory in particular. Paivio (1975d) showed that the symbolic distance effect emerged with size comparisons even when the influence of potential verbal-associative factors was minimized by constructing pairs so that the item that was larger (or smaller) in a particular pair became the smaller (or larger) item in another pair. Another experiment revealed that size-comparison times are no faster for within-category (animal-animal) comparisons than they are for between-category (animal-object or object-object) comparisons. This finding is consistent with the idea that subjects' comparisons are based on analogue representations generated to names rather than on lists, semantic networks, or propositional trees in which object representations are grouped by category and attribute values are represented by ordered labels. Note that the argument applies specifically to taxonomic categories, since comparison times have been found to differ when the symbolic distances to be compared fall within or between labeled regions of a spatial structure (Baum & Jonides, 1979) or a perceptual continuum (te Linde & Paivio, 1979).

Picture-word comparisons provide a more general set of critical findings. Dual coding theory clearly predicts that symbolic comparisons of concrete attributes of objects will be faster with pictures than with words because the relevant nonverbal representations (imagens) are accessed (or activated) more quickly when pictures serve as stimuli. Conversely, verbal attributes will be accessed relatively more quickly from printed words. Paivio (1975d) confirmed both predictions with object-size and name-pronounceability comparisons. The former used pictured objects that did not differ in perceived size but did differ systematically in symbolic (real-life) size. The size comparisons were faster for pictures than words and both classes of stimuli yielded the typical (and similar) symbolic distance effect (for comparable effects with children, see McGonigle & Chalmers, 1984). In contrast, the pronounceability comparisons were faster with printed words than pictures—an unsurprising result, given the known difference in naming reaction time favoring printed words (e.g., Fraisse, 1968), but nonetheless theoretically relevant because it is a direct reversal of the result for symbolic size comparisons.

In an unpublished experiment, we systematically varied the difference in rated pronounceability between the members of pairs of abstract words, concrete words, and pictures. Figure 9–1 shows the results from the symbolic comparison task. Note that the comparisons were slower for pictures than words, and that pictures and concrete words yielded the usual symbolic distance effect. The absence of a distance effect and the generally faster comparison times for concrete words than for abstract words were unexpected and lack any obvious explanation at this time. Otherwise, the results are consistent with the modality-specificity assumption of dual coding theory. That is, the logogens on which the pronounceability comparisons are based must contain the necessary articulatory information for the decision, or they at least generate covert pronunciation responses that can be evaluated and compared on their articulatory properties.

Another unpublished experiment (summarized in Paivio, 1978c) required subjects to decide which of two object labels was the more familiar (used more frequently). The decisions were faster when the items were presented as printed words than when they were presented as pictures of the referent objects. This task differs from pronounceability comparisons in that familiarity is not directly represented in the articulatory pattern of a word. Nonetheless, the information necessary for familiarity judgments must be stored in some way in the verbal-representational system, either as a strength attribute or perhaps as multiple representations correlated with frequency (cf. the data and theory on the memory effects of episodic frequency, e.g., Hintzman & Block, 1971). In any case, the finding that comparison time for name familiarity is faster with printed words than with pictures as stimuli accords with dual coding theory.

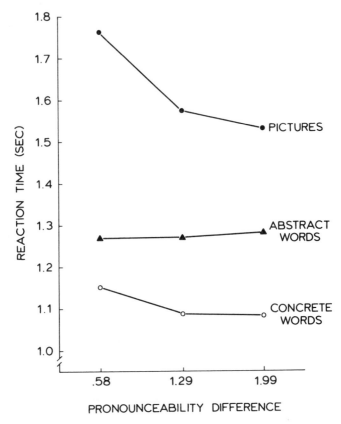

Figure 9-1. Mean reaction time for pronounceability comparisons for (the names of) pictures and concrete and abstract words as a function of the difference in rated pronounceability.

A Stroop-like conflict effect and a reversal of it under appropriate conditions (Paivio, 1975d) provided further support for the assumption that knowledge about the sizes of objects is represented in a perceptual-analogue form. Subjects were shown pairs of pictures or printed words in which the physical size of pair members was the same, or in which one member of the pair was physically larger than the other. In the latter case, the size difference was either congruent with the real life-size difference (a zebra depicted as larger than a lamp) or incongruent with it (a zebra depicted as smaller than a lamp). Subjects in one series of experiments were asked to decide which member of each pair was larger in real life. The results showed the Stroop-like conflict with picture pairs, so that decision time was slower for incongruent than for congruent pairs. No evidence of conflict was observed with printed words as stimuli. These results were predicted from dual coding theory according to the reasoning that knowledge about size is represented in modality-specific imagens that are perceptual memory analogues of the perceived objects, and that memory size-perceptual size incongruency resulted in a response conflict. The conflict was expected to be absent or at least reduced in the case of printed words because they must first activate relevant logogens which in turn activate representations in the image system. Accordingly, relative physical size of the printed words would be irrelevant.

Another group was asked simply to decide which member of each pictured pair looked farther away. A reversal of the size conflict was expected because objects known to be relatively large appear to be farther away when they are depicted as smaller than objects known to be relatively small. Conversely, the decision would be difficult when pictured size differences are congruent with real life-size differences. The strong confirmatory results along with the contrasting effect for size comparisons are shown in Figure 9–2. The important theoretical point is that performance on both tasks depends equally on the same representational information, namely, knowledge about real life size. Thus, the same representations mediate contrasting reaction time patterns when the task is changed. This is especially strong support for the modality-specific, perceptual-analogue nature of the long-term memory representation of objects differing in size.

A variant of the size-comparison task produced further evidence consistent with dual coding theory. Paivio (1978a) presented subjects with pairs of digital clock times (e.g., 8:45 and 3:25) and asked them to press a key to indicate in which time the hour and minute hands of corresponding analogue clocks form the larger (acute) angle. The answer for the example would be 3:25. The task is interesting partly because the angular size differences can be precisely quantified, and it yields a particularly smooth symbolic distance effect. More interesting is the fact that it permits one to combine per-

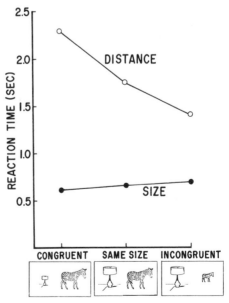

Figure 9–2. Mean reaction time for symbolic size and apparent distance comparisons for pictured pairs in which the pictured size differences are congruent or incongruent with real life-size differences. From "Perceptual Comparisons through the mind's eye" by A. Paivio, 1975, *Memory & Cognition, 2,* p. 644. Reprinted by permission.

ceptual and symbolic information in different ways. Both times can be presented digitally, or both as drawings of analogue clocks, or one digitally and the other analogue. A simple prediction from dual coding theory is that comparison times should be faster for the mixed condition than for the digital-digital condition because only the one digital time need be converted into an imagined analogue clock in the former case. The prediction is not trivial because precisely the reverse prediction can be derived from propositional-type theories, namely, that the digital-digital condition should be faster than the mixed condition. Banks (1977) in fact made a conceptually equivalent prediction in connection with size comparisons of perceptual forms that varied in size and nonsense names that had been repeatedly associated with the forms. The results of the Paivio (1978a) experiment confirmed the dual coding prediction in that comparison times were faster for the mixed digital-analogue than for the digital-digital condition. Of course, the comparisons were fastest for the perceptual (analogue-analogue) condition.

The generality of the additivity of perceptual and symbolic information was confirmed in another study (summarized in Paivio, 1980) using angularity-roundness comparisons of objects presented as pictures, words, or picture-word pairs. Subjects saw pairs of items (e.g., *tomato-goblet, penny-newspaper*) that differed in roundness according to normative ratings, and they were asked to indicate which member of each pair was the rounder or more angular. The results were that the comparison times were reliably slowest for word-word pairs, intermediate for the mixed word-picture pairs, and fastest for picture-picture pairs, again as expected from dual coding theory.

The theory also suggests that the difference between purely symbolic and mixed conditions should reverse if subjects could be induced to do the comparison task verbally or computationally. This can be achieved in the case of clock comparisons in which subjects are required to compare the angular separation of the hands on two clocks. A computational algorithm can be used to arrive at the correct answer because minutes are related to hours by multiples of 5, and this ratio is faithfully reflected in the relative positions of the two hands of a clock. If such a strategy were used, the comparisons should be faster for a digital-digital than for a digital-analogue condition.

The problem was investigated in an unpublished experiment in which subjects were instructed on the computational procedure and then were required to apply it to comparisons of digital-digital or digital-analogue clock times. Other subjects were asked to use imagery in the same task. Figure 9-3 shows an interaction that strongly confirmed the crucial prediction in that comparisons were much faster for the pure digital than for the mixed condition under computational instructions but the difference was in the opposite direction under imagery instructions. The latter aspect differs from the Paivio (1978a) experiment in that the mean reaction time for digital-analogue comparisons was considerably slower under imagery instructions than without such instructions. This could be because subjects who were

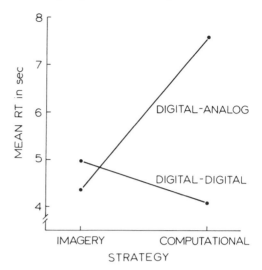

Figure 9-3. Mean reaction time for comparisons of digital-digital (DD) and digital-analogue (DA) clock times on what would be the difference in the angular separation of the hour and minute hands if both clocks were analogue, for groups instructed to use an imagery strategy or a computational strategy.

instructed to use images thought about them as well as using them (cf. Holyoak, 1977, p. 48), whereas the uninstructed subjects in the earlier experiment simply used them. The results in any case demonstrate sharply contrasting effects when subjects do the same task using a computational (verbal) procedure as compared to imagery.

Conceptually similar contrast effects were reported by W. J. Friedman (1983) using comparison tasks and other procedures that required reasoning about the months of the year. For example, two experiments required subjects to decide which of two months would come next going either forward or backward from a reference month. Friedman reasoned that this task would most likely involve image processing. The contrasting (verbal) tasks required subjects to recite month names covertly in order to determine a particular temporal distance. The results showed relatively faster responses on the former task and greater effects of temporal distance and direction on the latter task, which Friedman interpreted as supporting the distinction between image and verbal-list processing. Other results in the study were also consistent with that interpretation.

Cognitive abilities and symbolic comparisons

This section is concerned with the role of individual differences in imaginal and verbal abilities in symbolic comparisons. We routinely administered several key tests to subjects who had participated in different symbolic comparison tasks. The imagery-ability tests included: Space Relations, the Minnesota Paper Form Board, and Cube Visualization (see chap. 6). These tests were usually combined into a single imagery-ability score (e.g., Paivio,

1978a). Verbal ability was generally measured by a test of verbal-association fluency from Guilford (1967). Other tests will be identified in the context of the relevant studies.

A dual coding analysis suggests that both imaginal and verbal abilities might be relevant whenever the comparison is based on a concrete perceptual attribute and the items are presented as verbal stimuli. Imagery abilities are implicated because the comparisons presumably depend on the availability of representations in the imagery system. Verbal abilities are implicated because the imaginal representations must be accessed (encoded) via the verbal system. The relative contribution of each class of ability presumably would depend on the extent of verbal processing required during the encoding stage.

The results of a number of experiments in which word pairs or picture pairs were compared on concrete dimensions have consistently shown that scores on the imagery-test battery correlated with comparison time, whereas the verbal scores did not. The relations were not always significant, but high imagery subjects generally had faster reaction times than low imagery subjects. The results were particularly clear in the case of clock comparisons (Paivio, 1978a), where the Pearsonian correlation between imagery ability and reaction time, averaged over four different experimental groups, was a highly significant $-.40$. The corresponding pooled correlation with verbal fluency was zero. The correlation with imagery ability is not surprising, inasmuch as the imagery tests and the clock-comparison task require the subject to use spatial information. Nonetheless, the ability tests and the clocks task are quite different in their procedural details, so the imagery tests must be tapping an imagery-processing system with considerable functional generality. This conclusion is reinforced by the finding that comparison times are faster for high-imagery than for low-imagery subjects in the case of symbolic size and shape (angularity-roundness) comparisons (Paivio, 1980).

It is important to note, too, that imagery ability did not correlate with comparison time on verbal attributes (name familiarity and pronounceability) in the relevant studies mentioned earlier. Thus, imagery ability plays a role in comparison tasks that presumably depend on imaginal processes but not in ones that depend instead on verbal processes. Verbal-associational fluency would be expected to fare better as a predictor in comparisons based on verbal attributes, and the correlations with familiarity and pronounceability comparisons were in the appropriate direction, though generally not significant. The clock-comparison study in which imaginal and computational strategies were contrasted permitted simultaneous evaluation of the contribution of imaginal and verbal abilities to performance under conditions in which they should be differentially relevant. Consistent with what would be expected, verbal-associative ability correlated significantly with comparison time under the computational instructions ($r = -.32$) but not imagery instructions ($r = .09$), whereas imagery ability correlated more highly with comparison time under imagery instructions ($r = -.34$) than computational instructions ($r = -.04$). Such results invite further studies in which imaginal and verbal abilities are systematically compared using a variety of mental comparison tasks and a larger battery of ability tests selected according to the theoretical considerations presented in chapter 6.

The above summary refers to the separate contributions of nonverbal and verbal abilities to performance on symbolic comparison tasks. We have also obtained some evidence for a joint contribution of the two classes of abilities to performance. An extensive correlational study done in collaboration with Richard Harshman used tests that sampled verbal and figural abilities. The former included a measure of abstract verbal reasoning (the Inference Test), as well as word fluency and expressional fluency tests from Guilford's (1967) battery of tests. The nonverbal tests included: Space Relations, the MPFB, and a perceptual closure test. Paper and pencil versions of the size comparison and clock-comparison tasks (using word and digital pairs) were also included to permit group testing (see Paivio, 1980, pp. 149–151).

The data were subjected to simple correlational and stepwise-regression analyses. The results showed that two verbal and two spatial tests correlated significantly with performance scores on the size-comparison test, but only two of these contributed significantly to the multiple correlation. The best predictor was the Inference test (simple $r = .43$), followed by space relations ($r = .35$). The novel contribution of these results is that they implicate verbal abilities in symbolic size comparisons more clearly than did the earlier studies, although, as mentioned above, it was always assumed on theoretical grounds that the verbal system plays an essential role in such tasks, at least when words serve as stimuli.

The pattern of results was different for clock comparisons in that Space Relations was the best predictor of comparison scores ($r = .35$), followed by the Inference test ($r = .29$, $p < .05$). No other test contributed significantly to the prediction. The results are consistent with those observed in the comparison reaction time experiments described above in that the imagery system seems to dominate in the clock-comparison task. The additional contribution from verbal reasoning is also appropriate, especially since words and digits served as stimuli. The verbal contribution might be reduced if picture pairs were used for size comparisons and mixed analogue-digital pairs for clock comparisons.

The results that have been reviewed thus far bear on the general functional distinction between nonverbal imagery and verbal processing systems. The idea that the cognitive representations in the two symbolic systems also vary in their sensory modality suggests that performance in symbolic comparison tasks could be predicted from even more specific abilities. Toward that end, Alain Desrochers and I (reported in Paivio, 1982a) attempted to predict individual differences in reaction time for symbolic weight comparisons from performance on a relevant perceptual task. The symbolic comparison task required subjects to indicate which of a pictured or named pair of objects is heavier (or lighter) in real life. For example, which is heavier, an *apple* or a *tennis ball*? Thus, the participants literally "weighed things in their minds." The task yielded the typical symbolic distance effect and faster responding to pictures than words.

The individual-difference measures included spatial and verbal ability tests, as in previous experiments. The novel test was a weight-comparison task patterned after the psychophysical task originally introduced by Weber to study sensory thresholds. We adapted it to measure individual differences in kinesthetic or proprioceptive sensitivity. First, as Fleishman and Rich (1963) had done earlier, we tried to determine difference thresholds for individuals. This turned out to be noisy and impractical, so we shifted to a simple accuracy score based on a series of comparison trials. We also changed from successive comparison, used in the first experiment, to simultaneous comparison done with one weight in each hand. The subjects picked up both weights simultaneously then lowered the heavier one as soon as they had made their decision. The weights were on reaction keys, so that a clock started when the weights were picked up and stopped when one weight was lowered onto a key. We could thereby correlate the subjects' average weight-comparison times with their times in the symbolic comparison task.

The general pattern of results over three experiments was that the psychophysical test of kinesthetic ability was the most consistent predictor of symbolic weight-comparison time. Averaged over the first two experiments, the weight comparison accuracy score correlated significantly ($r = -.33$) with symbolic comparison times when pictures served as items but not when words were used. That is, the subjects who were more accurate in weight discrimination were also relatively fast in symbolic weight comparisons with pictures. The spatial imagery-ability and verbal fluency tests did not correlate significantly with symbolic comparisons. The absence of a correlation with imagery ability seems puzzling, given the dual coding argument that weight is a concrete attribute of objects. More about that below.

The third experiment showed that the reaction time measure of kinesthetic ability was an even better predictor of symbolic weight-comparison time, the correlations being .43 and .46 for the picture and word conditions, respectively. As a control test, we included a perceptual discrimination test that did not depend on kinesthetic ability, namely, comparisons of lines that differed in length. It turned out that comparison times on that task also correlated significantly with symbolic weight comparisons, suggesting that the two perceptual comparison tasks and the symbolic weight-comparison tasks implicate a common general ability related to reaction time. Nonetheless, partial correlational analyses showed that the correlation between perceptual weight-discrimination time and symbolic weight-comparison time remained significant when line-length discrimination time was partialled out, whereas line discrimination was not a significant predictor when weight discrimination was similarly controlled. Up to this point, then, it could be concluded that kinesthetic ability was the best predictor of symbolic weight-comparisons in our experiments.

The results are consistent with the view that the representations used in symbolic comparisons include a modality-specific component that is shared with or similar to the perceptual processes involved in discriminating objects on various sensory dimensions. Thus, the individual-difference data converge on the perceptual interpretation of processing in experimental studies of imagery reviewed earlier. The conclusion from the present data remain tentative, however, in view of the fact that we failed to confirm it in a subsequent experiment. A clear implication of the modality-specific hypothesis is that we should be able to demonstrate modality-specific correlations between perceptual and symbolic comparison tasks whatever the modality involved. For example, reaction time for perceptual-size comparisons should be the best predictor of symbolic-size comparisons, just as weight comparisons were the best predictor of symbolic weight-comparison time. We tested this in a factorial experiment using both size and weight dimensions. The results were entirely negative in that none of the critical correlations was significant, including those involving weight comparisons. The failure to replicate the pattern obtained in the three previous experiments on weight comparisons is particularly puzzling. It may reflect subtle procedural changes but, if so, the modality-specific correlations are less robust than the initial positive results led us to believe. The inconsistency can only be resolved by further experiments. In the meantime, the positive results remain encouraging, but tentative, in regard to the strong modality-specific hypothesis.

Other effects in symbolic comparison experiments

Several other theoretically interesting effects are associated with symbolic comparisons. The most frequently studied are lexical marking and congruity effects. The former refers to observation that comparisons on such bipolar dimensions as larger-smaller are generally faster when subjects are asked to choose the member of the pair that corresponds to the lexically unmarked comparative (the one that can serve as the label for the dimension as a whole) rather than the marked comparative, in this case the *larger* as opposed to the smaller member. The congruity effect is that reaction times are generally faster when the comparative is congruent with the value range of the stimuli than when it is incongruent. For example, comparisons are faster when subjects choose the smaller member of two relatively small, named objects or the larger of two large ones than when they choose the smaller of two large objects or the larger of two small ones.

The two phenomena have been interpreted in terms of analogue (Moyer & Dumais, 1978), abstract semantic (Banks, 1977), and expectancy-priming (Marschark & Paivio, 1979) processes operating during information retrieval or the comparison stage. At the moment, the last interpretation seems to have most support from the data. A series of experiments by Marschark (1983; Marschark & Paivio, 1979,) showed that (a) lexical marking and congruity effects are mutually exclusive except under special conditions; (b) the congruity effect is limited to the procedure in which subjects are first given the comparative (e.g., "choose the larger") and then the stimulus pair, rather than the reverse (stimulus-comparative) order, again except under special procedural conditions that are predictable from the priming hypothesis; and (c) the congruity effect occurs only with symbolic comparisons and not perceptual comparisons.

The priming hypothesis that accounts for these findings is essentially an information-retrieval hypothesis which states that a word such as *larger* (or smaller) sets up an expectancy that biases semantic memory access in favor of a set of items that are congruent with the cue. In other words, the cue primes retrieval of congruent items from semantic memory.

The priming hypothesis and the results it has generated are relevant here because they reflect an empiricist view. That is, the subjects' expectancies and the resultant priming of semantic memory are a consequence of their prior experiences with such stimuli as the word "large" and the set of objects that correspond to that term. The effect in the symbolic comparison task is on the speed of accessing or activating the relevant set of symbolic representations and their attribute values. The comparison process itself is independent of and subsequent to that priming effect, and is based on the representational information that has been activated.

A related phenomenon was independently observed in an unpublished experiment that Albert Katz and I conducted, and in a published study by Holyoak, Dumais, and Moyer (1979). The question was whether symbolic comparisons would be faster for associatively or semantically related pairs than for unrelated ones. As mentioned above, Paivio (1975d) found no differences in size comparisons as a function of category membership (animal-animal versus mixed object pairs). However, the study did not test for more direct within-pair relations. Katz and I used ratings of the frequency with which named referent objects have been experienced together to establish high and low related pairs. The critical result was that symbolic comparisons were faster with the related pairs. Holyoak et al. (1979) obtained similar results with several different measures of associative or semantic relatedness. They considered alternative models based on scanning (search) and comparison processes. The present view is that the relatedness effect is mainly a retrieval phenomenon: Related pairs are "located" more quickly than unrelated ones. Comparisons are then performed on the representational information that has been accessed or generated. This analysis is essentially the same as the one applied above to the priming interpretation of congruity effects.

This completes the review of symbolic comparison effects that are consistent with a strong version of dual coding theory. The relevant findings include: the symbolic distance effect, faster comparison times with pictures than words on attributes of concrete objects and the reverse on attributes of linguistic representations, correlations between relevant individual-difference variables and symbolic comparisons, and positive effects of associative-(experiential) relatedness between pair members or between the search cues (e.g., the comparative term) and the representations to be compared. A modified set of conclusions will be presented following a consideration of criticisms, additional puzzling findings, and alternative interpretations of the various symbolic comparison phenomena.

Theoretical challenges and further evidence on symbolic comparisons

The first critique concerns the Stroop-like conflict effect that I reported (Paivio, 1975d) for symbolic size comparisons when perceptual size differences of pictured objects were incongruent with real life-size differences. The effect did not occur with words as stimuli. Foltz, Poltrock, and Potts (1984) argued that my results were an artifact of my design. I had used a repeated stimulus-set design in which the same pairs were repeated a number of times in different size-congruity arrangements. Thus, episodic memory for previous judgments could affect comparison speed. Such episodic memory effects would be controlled by an infinite set procedure in which each item is presented only once. Foltz et al. (1984) repeated my experiment using only words as stimuli and varying the design. In agreement with my results, they found no congruity effect when word pairs were repeated. However, they did obtain a congruity effect with the infinite set design.

The results obtained by Foltz et al. (1984) modify my conclusions, but they did not rule out picture-word differences in the size-congruity effect and thereby demonstrate that the general prediction from dual coding theory is wrong. Their study included no direct comparisons of pictures and words. They did include Arabic digits along with digit names and object names in a second experiment because Besner and Coltheart (1979) had previously obtained the size incongruity effect with digits. Foltz et al. (1984) found that stimulus type interacted with symbolic distance and congruity *versus* incongruity, which are theoretically interesting and would not be predicted by dual coding theory. However, they do not rule out a dual coding interpretation of the original picture-word difference in congruity effects, for the following reasons.

First, anticipating the finite set argument, I showed that the congruity-incongruity effect was much larger for pictures than words even on the first trial, before items had been repeated. Foltz et al. (1984) acknowledged that result but argued that it was based on too few observations to be considered reliable. Nonetheless, they did not go on to test their concern directly. Second, my repeated-pairs design did not eliminate the size-congruity effect for pictures as it did for words in the Foltz et al. (1984) experiment and my original one. Foltz and his collaborators recognized this anomaly and proposed what seems to me to be a modified dual coding interpretation based on differences in speed of accessing different kinds of information: "In the word condition, responses would be made more quickly by retrieving previous responses, whereas in the picture condition, responses would be made more quickly by comparing the size of the objects on each trial. Thus, a size-congruity effect would be observed for pictures but not words" (p. 244). Third, my 1975 prediction was that the congruity (conflict) effect should be absent or reduced in the case of words, that is, at least smaller than the effect for pictures. Foltz et al. (1984) counter this by pointing out that the congruity effect (incongruent RT minus congruent RT) in their infinite-set design using words (115 ms) was larger than the effect in my picture condition (89 ms). However, these differences are based on very different mean RTs in the two experiments—more than twice as long in the Foltz et al. (1984) experiment than in mine. The proportionate (to baseline) difference was actually greater in my experiment than in theirs, e.g., the incongruent/congruent ratio was 1.15 for my pictures and 1.08 for their words. Fourth, in comparison with same-size pairs, Foltz et al. (1984) observed only a congruity effect and not an incongruity effect for object names, whereas I obtained both in the case of pictures, with the effect in each case being approximately the same magnitude as the Foltz et al. (1984) congruity effect. This difference, too, is left unexplained. Finally, they do not comment on my finding, crucial to dual coding theory, that my size-congruity effect with pictures was reversed when subjects were asked to judge the relative apparent distance of the two pictured objects.

The above analysis shows that the dual coding interpretation of picture-word differences in the size-congruity effect remains plausible. However, the Foltz et al. (1984) study also revealed a general effect of perceptual-size differences that modified symbolic comparisons regardless of the content of the physical stimuli. I would not have predicted that general effect from dual coding theory and some theoretical modification may be required to accommodate the effect after we know more about its limiting conditions through further research.

A second general finding that seems problematic for dual coding theory is that the symbolic distance effect occurs even when the comparisons are made on such abstract dimensions as pleasantness and monetary value of objects (Paivio, 1978d), intelligence and ferocity of animals (Banks & Flora, 1977; Kerst & Howard, 1977), and the goodness or pleasantness values of abstract words (A. Friedman, 1978; Paivio, 1978d). Since imagery and analogue theories assume that the distance effect is mediated by representations that somehow represent values on continuous dimensions, the question arises as to the nature of such analogues when the information is abstract rather than perceptually concrete. The problem appears to be compounded for dual coding theory by the further observation that comparison times on pleasantness and value of objects in the Paivio (1978d) studies were faster with pictures than words.

The following is a suggested resolution (Paivio, 1978d) that is in keeping with the general assumptions of dual coding theory. Such attributes as pleasantness and value, though relatively abstract in the sense that they are not correlated with simple perceptual dimensions, are nonetheless characteristic of things rather than words or are based on learned reactions to things. Thus, roses are pleasant and diamonds are expensive because of their intrinsic sensory properties and the events and behaviors that have been associated with them. Those characteristics are part of our semantic memories of the objects and events, and participants in a comparison task must access those memories before they can make the required decisions. Words and pictures alike provide access to the memory representations, but pictures do so more directly.

The symbolic distance effect with abstract attributes could be explained by the further assumption that the abstract properties are represented in a continuously variable (or finely graded) form in appropriate sensory-motor systems. For example, pleasantness might be based on interoceptive and motor systems that mediate affective reactions. Originally learned in response to things, such reactions become associated with perceptual representations (imagens) corresponding to the visual shapes of the objects. This analysis is in keeping with the dual coding assumption that verbal and nonverbal representational systems are orthogonal to sensory modalities (see chap. 4) within the limits imposed by contingencies in experience. Thus, in the present case, the imagens that are activated by concrete words or pictures are closely accompanied by motor and affective components that enable comparisons to be made on attributes based on such information. The symbolic distance effect obtained with comparisons of abstract words on goodness or pleasantness can be similarly explained if we assume further that the affective components have become conditioned directly to such words. In addition, as already mentioned earlier in connection with symbolic-size comparisons, differences in the strength of verbal associations between the comparative term and the comparison stimuli could contribute to the symbolic distance effect at least in the case of words.

Individual-difference data are consistent with the above analysis. Subjects with high scores on imagery-ability tests had faster comparison times than those with low ability in the case of both pleasantness and value comparisons (Paivio, 1978d). Verbal fluency showed no relation to comparison time, except in interaction with imagery in the case of pleasantness, so that subjects who scored high on both abilities were faster than those who were low on one or both types of ability tests. The dual coding interpretation is that the nonverbal representations closely associated with pleasantness and value information are more quickly accessed by subjects with high ability in dealing cognitively with nonverbal objects than by those with lower ability. High verbal ability may also contribute to speed of access when words serve as stimuli, or comparison speed in the associative manner described above.

The converse of the above problem occurred in the case of symbolic comparisons based on memory for color information. Paivio and te Linde (1980) found that the reaction time to compare objects mentally on either brightness or hue did not differ for pictures (uncolored line drawings) and words. This finding was unexpected from a dual coding perspective because color, being a perceptual attribute of things, should be more closely associated with imaginal than verbal representations. This apparent anomaly was reinforced by the finding that imagery-ability scores did not correlate with the comparison times. We were able to rationalize the findings because other behavioral and neuropsychological data have independently shown that color is a puzzling attribute. For example, De Renzie and Spinnler (1967) found that aphasics with normal color perception showed disturbances in their memory for object color even when the color-memory task did not require color naming. This observation, along with others reviewed by Paivio and te Linde (1980), implicates verbal mechanisms in the processing of long-term memory information about object color more closely than in the processing of other dimensions. The precise nature of the verbal contribution and other possible sources of the anomaly remain to be determined. Pending such clarification, we conclude from the observations that color information is associated as closely with verbal representations as with object representations in long-term memory.

At first sight the color-comparison results seem consistent with abstract representational theories, the argument being that knowledge about object color is amodal and conceptual in nature, and equally accessible from either pictures or words. Such an explanation would conflict with other post-hoc propositional interpretations regarding picture superiority effects in comparison tasks and other semantic memory tasks. The typical claims from the propositional perspective are that semantic memory representations are more quickly accessed from pictures than words, or that pictures have some perceptual-processing advantage over words. Such an account offers no principled solution to the variable results. We have seen that dual coding theory runs into the same problem, but it fares better than the abstract conceptual approaches in that it predicts picture-word reversals on tasks that involve verbal as compared to nonverbal attributes. The color-comparison data are anomalous and challenging for any current theory of mental representations. As such, they are clear evidence that dual coding predictions can be disconfirmed, and that modifications or additions are required.

Another troublesome observation concerns the effect of transferring from pictures to words or vice versa in comparison tasks. Paivio and Marschark (1980) obtained asymmetrical transfer effects with animal intelligence and object pleasantness comparisons when subjects first completed a block of trials with one kind of material and then switched to comparisons of the same concept pairs with the other type of material. Switching from pictures to words appeared to have a negative effect, whereas switching from words to pictures appeared to have a positive effect. We proposed a tentative interpretation that would be consistent with the general assumptions of dual coding theory, but our attempt turned out to be inadequate to account for results that we obtained in subsequent experiments. Marschark, te Linde, and I explored the generality of the apparent transfer effect using the attributes of size and brightness. These attributes are interesting because both are concrete and yet they differ in terms of the initial picture-word difference in comparison time. That is, symbolic-size comparisons are faster with pictures, whereas brightness-comparison times do not differ for pictures and words. To our surprise, we found essentially no concept-specific transfer with either attribute. When materials were switched but concepts remained the same, it was as though the subjects were starting the task from scratch. Their reaction time pattern was indistinguishable from that of subjects who were given new concept pairs along with the switch in materials.

These results seem puzzling from the viewpoint of dual coding as well as conceptual coding models because both suggest that some positive transfer should occur when materials are switched because subjects would continue to use the same imaginal or propositional representations for the comparative judgments. The repeated activation of those representations would be expected to facilitate comparisons even if new encoding processes are required by the switch in materials.

We explored the problem further by repeating the study with the more abstract dimension of intelligence and pleasantness. As in the original experiments by Paivio and Marschark (1980), we found some evidence of concept-specific transfer, revealed in this case by faster reaction times for conditions in which only materials were switched than for conditions in which both concepts and materials were switched. Moreover, the differential effect was clearest when switching from words to pictures, at least in the case of intelligence. Assuming that the encoding problems after the switch are equivalent for experimental and control groups, it appears that the transfer effect is attributable to comparison processes.

The two results to be explained are the absence of transfer effects in the case of concrete attributes, and evidence of some asymmetrical transfer in the case of abstract attributes. The absence of transfer can be readily explainable by a joint consideration of episodic and semantic memory processes. First, repeated comparison trials with the same concept pairs and materials results in progressively faster reaction times. This obviously is a learning effect, which is dependent on episodic memory. That is, reaction times decrease to the extent that subjects remember that particular word or picture pairs had occurred before and they had made a particular response to them (cf. the earlier discussion of the effects of repeated-pair designs in the context of the Stroop-like size-congruity effect). Semantic memory processes are also activated repeatedly, but their activation is not thereby facilitated to any marked extent because they are a product of long-term learning experience and reaction times based on them are relatively asymptotic.

If the above analysis is correct, why did we observe different transfer effects for concrete and abstract attributes? A possible answer is that semantic memory is particularly stable for concrete attributes such as size and color because those attributes are perceptually apparent and well learned as a result of experience with the referent objects. Such stability is less likely in the case of animal intelligence because most people have not repeatedly made intelligence judgments about animals and the process is more inferential than it is in the case of concrete attributes. Consequently, the experimental task does produce some change in semantic memory—having decided, say, that a mouse is smarter than a frog, one's knowledge of that difference is augmented. The knowledge is associated with the mental representations of frogs and mice and would facilitate subsequent comparisons to some degree, even if the stimuli that activate those representations are changed. The asymmetrical transfer favoring the word-picture sequence is consistent with the dual coding interpretation that the image system has priority in that task. Finally, the less reliable transfer effect with pleasantness comparisons may mean that pleasantness is a better learned and discriminated (though complex) perceptual attribute and, hence, more stable in semantic memory than is animal intelligence.

The above interpretations are speculative but they help to make sense out of some unexpected observations without requiring any major changes in the assumptions of dual coding theory, or other representational theories for that matter. The rethinking is instead at a more general level, based on a consideration of the relative modifiability of episodic and semantic memories as a function of episodic experience.

This completes the summary and analysis of evidence from studies using the symbolic comparison paradigm. I deal next with a task that requires transformations of internal representations.

MENTAL ROTATIONS

Mental rotation studies have been cited most often as support for analogue models of mental representations. However, J. R. Anderson (1978) and others (e.g., Yuille, 1983) have argued that propositional-computational models could also account for the findings. That argument is plausible in the case of mental rotation of perceptual stimuli, such as the block diagrams originally used by Shepard and Metzler (1971). A propositional account is more dubious in the case of the rotation function obtained when subjects compare an imaged and a perceptual stimulus, as in one experiment by Cooper and Shepard (1973). They asked subjects to image a letter or number and then rotate the image through a series of 45-degree angles to the verbal cues "up," "tip," "down," and so on, prior to the presentation of a variably oriented perceptual-test stimulus that was to be identified as a normal or backward version of the target character. The major result was that the reaction time for the decision increased progressively as the difference between the expected (imaged) orientation and the actually presented orientation increased.

Analysis of the quantitative details of the rotation function and other observations led Cooper and Shepard to propose that subjects were rotating an internal representation, that the rotation is an analogue process bearing a one-to-one relation to the corresponding physical rotation, and that the rotating internal representation is abstractly isomorphic to the corresponding visual stimulus—that is, it is a visual image. Other observations are also consistent with that interpretation. One is that, up to a certain point at least, the speed of mental rotation appears to be independent of stimulus complexity (e.g., Cooper 1975; for some qualifications, see Pylyshyn, 1979b; Yuille & Steiger, 1982). Another is the experimental demonstration of an illusion of apparent movement in rotating images (Robins & Shepard, 1977; Shepard & Judd, 1976), which suggests among other things that the mental image moves through locations in space (for a general discussion of apparent rotational motion and its theoretical significance, see Shepard, 1984). A final supportive example is that the slope of the rotation function was found to correlate highly with preference for imaginal thinking as measured by the Paivio and Harshman Individual Difference Questionnaire (see chap. 6), at least for male subjects (Tapley & Bryden, 1977). Complex relations have also been found between aspects of rotation performance and scores on spatial and questionnaire tests of imagery ability (Hatakeyama, 1981).

It seems puzzling, however, that mental rotation effects have also been obtained with early- and late-blind participants (Marmor & Zaback, 1976), which suggests that the rotated representation need not be a visual image. At the same time, it does not mean that the representational process is amodal. The blind recognize objects by active touch and it is reasonable to suppose that their internal representations incorporate the structures resulting from this haptic experience. It follows that their mental rotations may be based on kinesthetic and motor processes (cf. the comparable argument in chapter 8 regarding their episodic memory performance). Indeed, this may also be the case among sighted subjects, as suggested by the analysis of eye-fixation patterns associated with the mental rotation task (Just & Carpenter, 1976). Cooper and Shepard (1973, p. 162) recognized the possibility that, for some subjects, a rotating visual image included kinesthetic concomitants.

We can conclude from the above findings that mental rotations are based on both visual and haptic representational systems. Internal representations of perceptual patterns include both components for the sighted, whereas the visual component is absent for the congenitally blind. Mental rotation may be based largely on the activity of the haptic component for both types of subjects. It should be noted, in addition, that verbal processes play an important role in that the internal representations and the rotational activity (whatever its precise nature) are partly controlled by verbal cues from the experimenter as well as the subject. The control is most obvious in the Cooper and Shepard task described above, in which subjects were asked to image an alphanumeric character and then rotate the image to verbal cues. Thus, the task promotes referential coding and the activation of transformational processes that operate on the generated representation. The representations and processes alike are modality-specific derivations of perceptual-motor experiences with the same types of objects.

SEQUENTIAL CONSTRAINTS ON PROCESSING

The dual coding distinction between synchronous and sequential representational structures and processes implicates task differences in sequential constraints. Information in synchronous structures can be processed with relative freedom from sequential constraints. For example, most people can describe the appearance and contents of their living rooms with apparent ease from any perspective and in any order from memory. This informal observation suggests that the mental representation of the living room is simultaneously *available* for processing, and that portions of the representation become accessible as visual images, the contents of which can be described in different orders. A verbal structure such as the alphabet is also represented as a whole, but the processing of component information is sequentially constrained: The alphabet can be recited easily in the forward direction but not backward.

We explored the implications of the above analysis experimentally using tasks that required timed processing of synchronous and sequential structures. The synchronous structures were two-dimensional upper-case block letters that were selected to differ systematically in the number of inner and outer corners (e.g., L , F , E). The subjects were presented such letters or they were asked to image them. They were then required to count the number of inner and outer corners beginning at a specific point and proceeding in either a clockwise or a counterclockwise direction. In addition, the letters were sometimes presented in normal orientation and sometimes backwards (a left-to-right reversal), or subjects were asked to image the letters in either orientation. The expectation was that processing time would be little affected by letter orientation or counting direction in either the perceptual or image condition, although the perceptual task would be generally faster.

The sequential structures were printed words differing in number of letters (e.g., mother, university, conversation) presented in a typed form or similarly imaged. The left-to-right letter sequence was either normal or backward in each case. Thus, in the image condition, subjects were presented a spoken word and asked to visualize it, either normally oriented or as a word spelled backward. The processing task in all cases was to read off the letters of the visually presented or imaged word either forward (left-to-right) or backwards (right-to-left). The prediction here was that processing speed would be affected more by orientation and processing direction under the image than under the perceptual condition. In particular, backward spelling would be much slower than forward spelling in the image condition because the internal structure of mental representations for words is sequentially organized and processing is constrained by that structure.

The results are shown in Figure 9–4. As expected, processing time was little affected by the experimental manipulations in the perceptual condition. The image condition, however, produced a striking contrast: Corner counting was only slightly affected by orientation and counting direction, whereas word spelling was much slower in the backward direction than forward regardless of whether the imaged array was normal or left-right reversed. These results clearly support the hypothesis that different processing constraints are associated with synchronous and sequential representational structures.

The task and the interpretation are open to several criticisms. One is that the dual coding distinction between nonverbal and verbal representations was not strictly maintained because individual block letters are visual-verbal symbols, as are printed words. However, a block letter is an elementary verbal symbol with no lower-order verbal components, whereas a printed word has letters as components. Accordingly, analysis of the visual structure of a block letter is less directly linked to the properties of the verbal system

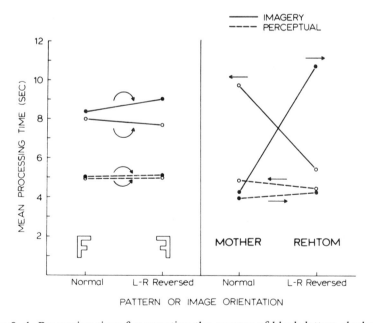

Figure 9–4. Processing time for counting the corners of block letters clockwise or counterclockwise and spelling words left-to-right and right-to-left under perceptual and imagery conditions.

than is analysis of the letter-unit structure of a printed word. Counting corners is a verbal task but there is no intrinsic correspondence between particular corners of, say the pattern F and particular numbers. Counting is constrained by the geometric structure only in the sense that it is easier to proceed systematically in a clockwise or counterclockwise direction than to count corners randomly. There is, however, a one-to-one correspondence between the linear order of letters in a printed word and their names, and the naming sequence in turn corresponds to the sequence of phonemes in the spoken word. It is the sequential phonemic structure of words that ultimately constrains processing in the spelling task.

A second possible criticism is that a block letter is visually less complex than a printed word and that it is therefore easier to generate an integrated visual image of a letter. Consistent with this view, Weber and Harnish (1974) found that imaged words could be processed equally quickly in either direction only if they contained no more than 3 letters. Thus, there is a limit to the "perceptual span" of visual word images, which was exceeded in the present study. The essential point could be made, however, without requiring subjects to visualize printed words. They could be asked instead to spell words forward or backward, and the former would surely be faster than the latter. The word-visualization task was used in an attempt to make it qualitatively equivalent to block-letter visualization, but this control was at the cost of visual complexity differences in the two types of stimuli.

A related argument is that letter units are simply more integrated than words. It is difficult to support such a claim on the basis of the usual criteria for functional integration. Familiar words are generally assumed to be integrated verbal units on the grounds that they can be recognized at a glance during reading, quickly named, and quickly written or spelled. The striking difference is in the type of integration: Letter units are synchronous-spatial structures, whereas words are sequential structures, and this intrinsic difference is what constrains computational or other processing of the component information.

A final point concerns the structure-process distinction itself. The task of counting the corners of an imaged letter is compatible with that distinction in than an image is apparently generated and can be reversed independent of the computational task. The counterargument is that structure and process are not distinct and that the task of counting the corners of an imaged letter is better characterized as counting the steps of a generation procedure at the same time as the letter pattern is generated. The procedural argument is even more compelling in the case of words as representations, namely, that the representational structure *is* the procedure used in spelling or writing a word. Such arguments are essentially equivalent to the behavioristic view that representations are learned behavioral patterns. The problem with both views is that the procedural or behavioral pattern must be represented in some permanent way if one is to know what is to be generated. The representation of that knowledge is structural by definition, and behavioral evidence tells us something about the nature of different kinds of structures and the functions that they serve.

PROBLEM-SOLVING AND OTHER COMPLEX TASKS

Up to this point we have considered relatively simple tasks that require the performer to evaluate or manipulate internal representations. We now touch on the implications of dual coding theory for performance on more complex tasks traditionally described under such headings as problem solving, concept attainment, and creativity. The role of representational processes in motor skills will also be discussed.

The application of dual coding theory to problem-solving tasks is straightforward: Performance is mediated by the joint activity of verbal and nonverbal systems, with the relative contribution of each system depending on characteristics of the task and cognitive abilities and habits of the performer. The more concrete and nonverbal the task, the greater the contribution of the imagery system; the more abstract and verbal the task, the greater the contribution of the verbal system. Individuals differ in the extent, manner, and efficiency of employment of each of the systems according to their verbal and nonverbal habits and skills. The demands of the task and individual-difference variables will determine the degree to which the various dual coding processes (referential, associative, transformational, evaluative, organizational) are brought into play. The mnemonic properties of the two systems also take on special importance in some tasks.

The functional distinctions suggest qualitative and quantitative differences in the nature of imaginal and verbal contributions. Recall that the imagery system is characterized by its capacity for organizing multiple units of unrelated information quickly into synchronously-organized compounds, which can be efficiently redintegrated by a cue that gives access to a component. The retrieved information is simultaneously available in that it can be scanned and evaluated with relative freedom from sequential constraints, and it can be reorganized or transformed in various ways. Taken together, these characteristics imply that imagery contributes richness of content and flexibility in the processing of that content, so that diverse bits of information can be quickly retrieved, compared, evaluated, transformed, and so on. I have suggested (Paivio, 1971, 1975b, 1983c) that the imaginal attributes may underlie the intuitive leaps of imagination that often characterize creative thinking (cf. Rugg, 1963) and they may explain why concrete visual models play such an important role in the process of discovery (cf. Arnheim, 1969). Language and the verbal system, on the other hand, provide precise means (conceptual pegs) for retrieving imaginal memories and guiding the processing of the retrieved information. Its capacity for sequential organization in particular suggests that the verbal system contributes logical order to ideation that would not be possible on the basis of imagery alone. That logical potential implies, too, that verbal processes may predominate in the later stages of the task sequences, e.g., the so-called verification stage of discovery, whereas imagery may predominate at earlier stages, at least in some tasks.

Kaufmann (1980) presented a theory of problem solving that has much in common with the present approach, particularly in that he emphasizes similar functional distinctions between imagery and linguistic representations, although he also disagrees with some specific points in dual coding theory. The agreements are that the imagery system brings together previously unrelated pieces of information that can be examined together in a unified image (p. 124) and subjected to transformational activity (p. 155), whereas linguistic representations are more precise, superior in sequential organization (p. 125), and subject to processing constraints (pp. 138–139). Kaufmann also agrees that visual imagery is crucial during the discovery phase of problem-solving, which he deduces from his general theory in which the functional usefulness of the two systems is related to the novelty of the task. Thus, he views linguistic representations as more appropriate when the task is familiar, whereas imagery becomes increasingly appropriate and adaptive as the novelty of the task increases (p. 167).

The disagreements may be more apparent than real, resulting from differences in interpretation and emphasis. For example, Kaufmann argues (pp. 44–45) that, in contrast to my view (Paivio, 1971; p. 388), it is language rather than imagery that lends speed to thinking. This particular claim is difficult to evaluate because Kaufmann provides little direct evidence on processing speed, but I can comment on the general problem. My statement in 1971 referred essentially to transformational thinking, and I still maintain theoretically that transformations of spatial and visual information cannot be done rapidly by means of language alone, although some transformational problems can be solved indirectly and slowly using verbal or computational reasoning if one knows the algorithm. I would now add the qualification that the verbal system would be superior in problems requiring transformations of sequential information and that the imagery system could only mimic such transformations by encoding sequentially organized information into a linear-spatial analogue and then reorganizing the spatial order of elements. Finally, any theoretical perspective needs to accommodate different components and stages of complex tasks, some of which may be handled more quickly and efficiently by the verbal system and others by imagery. For example, Kaufmann and I would agree that imagery is likely to be more efficient ("swifter") than language in encoding multiple bits of concrete information into an integrated whole, whereas the reverse would be expected when abstract information must be encoded and organized into logical or grammatical sequences. These comments are also relevant to other objections raised by Kaufmann—for example, that I have "pressed the case for imagery too hard at the expense of language" (p. 45)—but I will forgo a detailed examination of the contentious points and turn instead to some illustrative research findings. Interested readers will find a more comprehensive review of relevant studies in Kaufmann (1980).

Spatial problem-solving and cognitive maps

Spatial problem-solving using cognitive maps is a classical example of tasks that are analyzable in terms of the functional properties of synchronous mental representations and imagery. Tolman (1948) introduced the concept of the cognitive map to explain spatial maze learning in rats. The observation that rats could choose appropriate new routes if a change was introduced in the environment suggested that they used a field-like cognitive map to solve a new spatial problem (for a review of more recent evidence on such map-like representations in animal spatial memory, see Roberts, 1984). Geographers applied the concept and related ones, including mental imagery, to the analysis of how people view their environment (e.g., see the volume edited by Downs & Stea, 1973). Psychologists have studied the properties of cognitive maps experimentally, and a few examples from that literature will serve our purposes.

A particularly relevant general finding is that, even when subjects learn a route map entirely by sequential exploration, they behave as though they have acquired a picture-like, cognitive map or synchronous representation in which locations and routes are simultaneously available. Levine, Jankovic, and Palij (1982) referred to this property as the principle of equiavailability and supported it by showing that subjects who had learned simple four- or five-point maps by moving over the successive locations could subsequently take a shortcut to get from one point to another. Note especially that equiavailability is revealed in this case by freedom from sequential constraints in using representational information in a novel way. It has also been shown (e.g., Hanley & Levine, 1983; Moar & Carleton, 1982) that, under certain conditions, subjects can integrate separately learned path sequences into a single cognitive map in which paths or locations are simultaneously available both within and between paths.

Other studies have been concerned with the accuracy and consistency of spatial location information in cognitive maps, when "viewed" from different perspectives. For example, does my cognitive map of my living room provide geometrically consistent information about the locations of objects in it when I imagine the room from two different doorways? The answer suggested by research is that it does not. Moar and Bower (1983) investigated the question in one experiment by requiring subjects to judge the direction between pairs of American cites (e.g., New York and Chicago) in both directions. The judged directions were found to be consistently non-reversible. This and other results from the study suggested that cognitive maps contain internally inconsistent spatial information, contrary to the properties of Euclidian geometry. Moar and Bower nonetheless concluded that the findings are not necessarily at odds with an analogue interpretation of visual images (which subjects reported using) because the spatial inconsistency may result from retrieval or inference processes operating on spatially consistent representations, or from the use of separate visual images, each of which may individually contain spatially consistent properties.

The results of a series of experiments by Hintzman, O'Dell, and Arndt (1981) are more difficult to reconcile with any simple analogue interpretation of cognitive maps. Hintzman et al. (1981) required their subjects to indicate surrounding environmental target locations while imagining themselves in a particular spot facing in various directions. Interest centered on the possible use of mental rotation to achieve the orientation shifts and on the relative accessibility of locations in the cognitive map. Reaction time and error data suggested that mental rotations were used when the spatial information was visually presented but not when subjects relied on a memorized cognitive map. In regard to the accessibility question, the response data showed a striking M-shaped pattern, so that targets were located most quickly when they were adjacent to or directly opposite the imagined orientation, and slowest when they were in intermediate positions. Hintzman et al. (1981) interpreted this pattern to mean that the locations were not equally accessible, as a parallel access hypothesis would predict. These and other results, such as practice effects for particular orientation-target pairs, led Hintzman et al. (1981) to suggest generally that "cognitive maps are not strictly holistic, but consist of orientation-specific representations, and—at least in part—of relational propositions specific to object pairs" (p. 149). The authors also cite other studies in which the investigators favored a propositional-representation hypothesis because it accounts for biases in spatial judgments that are difficult to explain in terms of analogue maps.

Let us examine the cognitive-mapping problem from a dual coding perspective. The most general point to emphasize at the outset is that dual coding does not imply that synchronous cognitive maps are completely veridical (Euclidian) analogue representations of a spatial environment, nor that performance on cognitive-mapping problems depends solely on nonverbal representations, whatever their form. Distortions and inconsistencies occur even in perception as a function of contextual factors, as evidenced most clearly by visual illusions, so there is no reason to expect that cognitive maps would be any more Euclidian in their functional properties. Verbal processes would also be expected to play a role in cognitive-mapping because we learn to express spatial locations, distances, and relations in linguistic terms. Some of these become strong habits that serve as cardinal reference points (e.g., right, left, front, back; north, south, east, west) that guide and sometimes bias our spatial responding, as do other heuristic devices (cf. Lederman, Klatzky, & Barber, 1985; B. Tversky, 1981). The linguistic and behavioral spatial habits can be described in propositional terms, but such rephrasing adds nothing to the explanation.

As in the case of other tasks, the relative contributions of nonverbal and verbal processes to performance in cognitive-mapping tasks would depend on experimental conditions, along with individual-difference variables (e.g., spatial-orientation ability) that will not be discussed here. The Hintzman et al. (1981) experiments probably encouraged verbal processing because cognitive maps were learned using pictures of familiar objects that were accompanied by their printed labels or (in one experiment) familiar cities presented as names. Moreover, the stimuli were located at regular spatial intervals in a circular pattern as were the locations on the response board, which would encourage sequential and relational verbal processing during acquisition and test trials, and lend particular salience to the cardinal points: front, back, left and right. Thus, subjects presumably acquired a synchronously organized spatial representation in which the information is simultaneously available (although not simultaneously accessible) along with verbal and motor habits that biased scanning processes as well as direct access to salient information in the manner indicated by the M-shaped response pattern. Given the repeated test trials, episodic memory for previous responses to orientation-location pairs would also have an effect, as in the finite stimulus-set design used in some of the mental comparison experiments described earlier. This speculative analysis is in general agreement with the explanation proposed by Hintzman et al. (1981), except that the dual coding analysis includes no recourse to propositional representations. By way of comparison, experiments in which subjects learn irregular cognitive maps, in which locations are not named (e.g., Levine et al., 1982), would be less likely to engage the verbal system.

Cube visualization

The cube visualization task described in chapter 6 is another classical example of a problem that apparently requires use of the imagery system. Performers who are asked how they solved the problem invariably report using visual imagery and it is difficult to see how it could be done otherwise, except by laborious verbal computations. Nonetheless, the task as a whole also requires use of the verbal system in that the performer must respond appropriately to the verbal instructions to think of a cube of a particular color, to slice it in certain ways, and to count the number of cubes with the properties indicated by the question. Thus, the task demands elaborate referential, transformational, and evaluative processing involving both systems in specifiable ways.

Syllogistic reasoning

Three-term series problems also reveal the contributions of both symbolic systems. Subjects are given a problem such as *Tom is taller than Sam. John is shorter than Sam. Who is tallest?* This task was the focus of a debate in which some theorists (e.g., DeSoto, London, & Handel, 1965; Huttenlocher, 1968) proposed an image-based explanation even in the case of abstract problems, whereas others (e.g., Carpenter & Just, 1975; H. Clark, 1969) have favored a more abstract, linguistic analysis. The upshot of the debate seems to be that both positions are partly correct. Johnson-Laird (1972) suggested the subject may change strategies with increasing experience with the task. The individual may first use an image-based procedure, supplemented perhaps by some principle of "natural order," and later switch to a procedure more consistent with a linguistic model. Such a change would be consistent with Kaufmann's novelty hypothesis concerning the usefulness of imagery and linguistic representations. The effective use of different strategies can also be modified by experimental manipulations. For example, Shaver, Pierson, and Lang (1974) showed that performance on three-term series problems improved when subjects were instructed to use imagery. Finally, as we have already seen (chap. 6), individuals differ in their preferred strategies and abilities, so that some individuals may rely on spatial imagery to solve such problems, whereas others use a linguistic strategy (e.g., MacLeod, Hunt, & Mathews, 1978; Sternberg, 1980; Sternberg & Weil, 1980). Such observations are completely consistent with dual coding theory.

Concept learning and identification

Concept-formation tasks have also provided relevant evidence. Imagery processes and such related variables as concreteness-abstractness of concepts were emphasized in classical discussions of concept learning and, after a period of neglect, they have reemerged in some current approaches (see the references in Katz & Paivio, 1975). Heidbreder (1946) demonstrated that concrete concepts are easier to learn than abstract concepts. Katz and Denny (1977) showed that the difference could be accounted for, at least in part, by imagery and differential memory for instances. Under conditions of high memory load in which subjects had to remember past instances, concepts represented by high-imagery noun instances were learned faster than concepts represented by low-imagery nouns. When the memory requirement was removed, however, both classes of concepts were learned at about the same rate. The suggested explanation was that imagery facilitated memory for the instances.

Katz and Paivio (1975) subsequently investigated the role of imagery in a concept-identification task using imagery instructions and concepts rated as either high or low in imagery value. The instances representing the two classes of concepts were equally concrete, permitting them to be presented either as pictures or words. Concepts rated as easy to image were attained more readily than concepts rated difficult to image, and learning of the former was especially facilitated when subjects were instructed to image (cf. Dyer & Meyer, 1976). These findings were as predicted from dual coding theory. Unexpectedly, learning was not affected by the picture-word mode of the instances, and we were unable to provide a satisfactory explanation for that negative finding.

Albert Katz has presented a variety of other empirical and theoretical observations that are relevant here. In a study of concept dominance (Katz, 1978), he identified four independent components that correlated with the probability that a dominant sensory feature would be elicited by a word (e.g., "round" as a response to "pearl"). These components seem to represent different aspects and degrees of imaginal and verbal reactions to names. For example, one of the components was indexed by a measure of the perceptual saliency of one's image to other objects. A series of experiments showed that each of these component dimensions predicted the ease of categorizing exemplars according to a common conceptual (sensory) feature. Later, Katz (1983) presented an informative discussion of individual differences in imaginal and verbal strategies as measured by the IDQ (see chap. 6) and their relations to self-concepts, creativity, and other measures. For example, he found that the verbal scale of the IDQ correlated significantly with self-reports of creativity, whereas the imagery scale correlated marginally with performance on a figural test of creativity. Katz views such results in terms of an interactionist model in which the functional role of individual differences is modified by environmental conditions in predictable ways.

It would be interesting and relevant to extend the dual coding analysis to specific examples of scientific thought. Anecdotal descriptions of the role of imagery in creative discoveries are common in the literature and I have offered brief interpretations in dual coding terms (Paivio, 1971, chap. 15; 1983c). Space limitations exclude any systematic treatment of the problem in the present book and I conclude this section by referring the reader to two sources of relevant data and analysis. One deals with imagery in technological problem-solving and creativity (Krueger, 1981). The other is a remarkable new treatise on imagery in scientific thought (A. Miller, 1984), which focuses especially on twentieth-century physics and the work of Einstein, Poincaré, Boltzmann, and Heisenberg.

Mental practice effects on motor skills

The final topic to be considered here is the use of imaginal and verbal processes in mental practice of motor skills. Many successful athletes have reported using imagery rehearsal to improve or maintain their performance levels (e.g., see Suinn, 1983). The problem has also been studied experimentally for more than 20 years (for a review of the early research, see A. Richardson, 1969). The research has been analyzed recently by Feltz and Landers (1983) using meta-analytic procedures to determine effect sizes for 60 studies in the literature. Their analysis indicated that mental practice influences performance more than no practice. The effect sizes were larger on the average for studies that used cognitive tasks, such as finger-maze learning, than for ones that used motor or strength tasks, but even the latter showed positive effects overall. No study has shown that mental practice is better than equivalent physical practice, but the gain in comparison with no practice is theoretically and practically interesting. The problem is to determine when and why mental rehearsal techniques are effective.

Feltz and Landers doubted that mental practice enhances specific skills through "low-gain innervation of muscles that will be used during actual performance," and they suggested instead that the effects might be due to a general preparatory effect, including the priming of an optimal tension level. Others have considered such factors as the effect of language on action, the functional equivalence of imagery and movement, the internal or external perspective of imagery, and the modifying effects of individual differences in imagery and other abilities on imagery-rehearsal effects (see Annett, 1982; Denis, in press; Hall, in press; P. Johnson, 1982; Suinn, 1983).

I have proposed an analytic framework (Paivio, in press) based on dual coding mechanisms as outlined in chapter 4. The emphasis is on motivational and cognitive functions of imaginal and verbal processes operating at general and specific levels. The general motivational level refers to physiological arousal and affect, and the specific level refers to goal-oriented behavior. On the cognitive side, the distinction is between general behavioral strategies and specific responses involved in motor skills. The imagery system provides the medium for experiencing and manipulating these reactions vicariously. Language permits access to and control of the relevant imaginal experiences that are to be rehearsed.

The motivational functions depend on our capacity to imagine goal objects and situations that we like or dislike, activities in those situations, and the consequences that follow the imagined activities. Maladaptive levels of tension arise from imagining negative consequences in sports situations. Some coaches and sports psychologists have tried to help athletes deal with the problem by teaching them how to reduce anxiety and tension using imagery rehearsal. This translates specifically into elimination of negative (covert or overt) verbalization that results in images of failure, and substitution of positive verbalization designed to arouse images of success and reduce tension. Some positive results have been reported from the application of such techniques (Suinn, 1983) but the problem calls for much more controlled study before the facts and their interpretations are clear.

Imagining positive outcomes in sports situations can also serve a specific motivational function in maintaining practice and other goal-related activities at high levels during periods when objective incentives are absent. Anecdotal and research evidence (Singer & Antrobus, 1972) suggest that such achievement imagery is quite common in daydreams, and some athletes have claimed that imagining themselves winning and receiving awards has helped maintain their motivation to practice (Paivio, in press). The implication is that the achievement imagery is part of a causal chain that results in improved motor skills and competitive successes, but we lack direct scientific evidence on the nature, frequency, and consequences of such imagery.

The usefulness of imagery as a means for rehearsing behavioral strategies and skills hinges on its functional properties. Memory is especially crucial because any effects of mental practice would depend on how accurately performance situations and behaviors can be represented in imagery, and how well the critical components of such imagery can be remembered and transferred to actual performance. Accuracy of imagery would depend in turn on perceptual-motor experiences that include optimal performance. Apart from actual practice under the guidance of a coach, what kinds of procedures could be used to augment the richness of the experiential base for imagery and maximize the efficiency with which the relevant information can be retrieved? One possibility is a film-plus-imagery technique in which the performer first watches a skilled performance and then tries to image the performance from memory. He or she then watches the film again while noting any inaccuracies in the imagery, and then images the performance again while striving to update its accuracy. Verbal processes become salient at this point because language provides the retrieval cues for memories expressed as images. Sports psychologists recognize the important role played by language and accordingly have tried to develop systematic and precise instructions for imagery rehearsal. However, researchers also need to develop ways of assessing and augmenting the accuracy of the performer's imaginal responses to such instructions.

This completes our review of the manipulation and use of internal representations in a variety of simple and complex tasks. We turn finally to a general critique and an alternative class of explanation.

TACIT KNOWLEDGE AND RELATED THEORETICAL ALTERNATIVES

Propositional approaches of one kind or another have been considered throughout the chapter as theoretical alternatives to imagery-based theories in general and dual coding theory in particular. Here we consider related accounts that emphasize tacit knowledge, tacit cues, and experimenters' expectations as sufficient explanations of certain effects.

Pylyshyn (1981) criticized such findings as Kosslyn's image-zooming data on the grounds that subjects have tacit knowledge of what happens to perceptual stimuli under conditions analogous to those described in the imagery instructions, and that they adjust their responses accordingly. Tacit knowledge is a plausible interpretation of some findings, but experimental support for it was generally lacking at that time and Kosslyn (1981) was able to provide convincing counterarguments. More recently, however, Intons-Peterson (1983) provided experimental evidence that the results in imagery paradigms can be affected by the experimenters' expectations, presumably via cues that they unintentionally produced while instructing subjects. The tasks that showed such effects included comparisons of perceptual and imaginal acuity and map scanning, and identification of rotated hands after perceptual or imaginal priming. In each case, perceptual-imaginal reaction time differences varied with the experimenters' beliefs. Analysis of taped transcriptions of instructions given by experimenters showed that those who expected imagery to yield faster reactions than perceptual conditions took more time to read the imaginal-prime portion than the perceptual-prime portion in the hand-rotation task; and conversely for the experimenters who expected imagery to be slower than perception.

Intons-Peterson (1983) was careful to point out that her results did not suggest that imagery was not used in such tasks nor that previous imagery research should be dismissed as biased. In fact, her own experiments yielded distance functions in imaginal as well as perceptual map-scanning, and mental rotation effects in the hand-rotation task, both of which are consistent with imagery interpretations. She emphasized instead that her results argue for the inclusion of safeguards against experimenter expectancy and demand effects, especially in the more ambiguous and vulnerable paradigms that are used to study imagery. Finally, she recommended that imagery researchers use tasks that typically require mental manipulations that are difficult to achieve without using imagery, such as comparisons of imagined figures.

Other recent studies have shown directly that the tacit knowledge hypothesis is plausible in the case of imagery effects but not others. Denis and Carfantan (1985) gave adult subjects a questionnaire in which they were asked to predict the typical outcomes of various imagery experiments that were described. The subjects generally predicted correctly that imagery would have positive effects in verbal memory, spatial reasoning, and deductive reasoning. However, they were generally unable to predict the typical outcomes of experiments on mental rotation, mental scanning, verification times for properties of objects in small *versus* large images, and the effects of imagery rehearsal on motor performance. Reed, Hock, and Lockhead (1983) had people estimate lengths and mentally scan diagonal lines, spirals, and mazes. They obtained large differences in the rate of scanning the three configurations, regardless of whether people scanned percepts or images. These differences could not be accounted for by differences in length estimates or by the subjects' tacit knowledge of their scanning rates. The authors concluded that their results are most consistent with the hypothesis that people actually scan in the mental scanning task.

The above studies demonstrate that the tacit knowledge hypothesis can be tested empirically and that the kinds of tasks that we have reviewed in this chapter are not readily explained by it. It is also relevant to note that the dual coding approach provides a more general and strategic defense against the tacit cues and knowledge argument. The defense is that the theory predicts different and sometimes contrasting effects under specified experimental manipulations, effects that are difficult to explain in terms of the experimenters' and subjects' beliefs. Examples are: the reversal of picture-word differences in symbolic comparison time with verbal and nonverbal attributes, the Stroop-like conflict effect for size comparisons with pictures but not printed words, the reversal of the conflict effect when subjects' judged the relative distance of pictured objects, and the reversal of clock-comparison times for symbolic and mixed perceptual-symbolic conditions when subjects used a computational strategy as compared to an imagery strategy. Such systematic and predicted variations in effects are comparable in principle to the different effects and relations observed in episodic memory tasks under conditions that differentially implicate verbal and imaginal coding during task performance (see chap. 8).

Somewhat paradoxically, the above counterargument is reinforced by negative evidence in that the experimenters' or subjects' expectations could hardly account for our *failure* to obtain certain effects that we initially predicted on the basis of a dual coding analysis. We have seen that those effects are challenging to the theory, but they require a response other than the tacit knowledge interpretation just considered.

It is important to note, finally, that dual coding theory is not compromised by evidence that the subjects' beliefs or tacit knowledge influence their performance in some cognitive tasks. Such factors are easily interpreted in dual coding terms as nonverbal and verbal information about objects and events and their behavioral affordances, information that is represented in the two symbolic systems and used when it is adaptive to do so. The activation and use of such information implicates the same dual coding processes as other representational phenomena that we have discussed, that is, representational, referential, and associative processing, evaluative and mnemonic functions, and so on, as described in chapter 4. Often the effective "belief" is simply a verbal description that is evoked by the experimental conditions and that operates reflexively to modify performance on the task. If that occurs, we could say that the task is "cognitively penetrable" but that would not add to the explanation.

CONCLUDING COMMENTS

This chapter has reviewed some of the principle findings from studies concerned with performance in tasks that require manipulation of mental representations, or evaluation and computation of information associated with such representations. As in the case of episodic and other semantic memory studies reviewed in previous chapters, the findings are more consistent with the empiricist idea that mental representations consist of modality-specific structures, which include or can be operated on by modality-specific processes, than they are with propositional-computational or other abstract conceptual approaches. More specifically, they are generally consistent with the general assumption of the updated dual coding theory proposed in chapter 4. The theory also encountered some troublesome findings that were unpredictable from its assumptions and in one instance (symbolic color comparisons) were simply inconsistent with it. Such observations need to be empirically and theoretically resolved, with whatever consequences may be necessary for the theory. The inconsistencies and predictive failures are far more numerous, however, in the case of the abstract propositional theories and their proponents have had to resort repeatedly to post hoc assumptions to account for such findings. More generally, such theories do not include any primitive assumptions that would predict a variety of modality-specific effects that are consistent in principle with the empiricist assumptions of dual coding theory. I conclude once again that the findings in the areas of research reviewed in this chapter justify a preference for dual coding theory over abstract propositional theories in terms of the constructive-empiricist criterion of empirical adequacy—dual coding theory "saves the phenomena" better than the other class of theories, and it does so with a minimum of assumptions.

10
Language Comprehension and Production

We have already dealt with many aspects of language in the context of such topics as memory for words or phrases, meaning and semantic memory, and language-evoked imagery. This chapter treats language as a problem in its own right, with emphasis on more extended behavioral segments than words or phrases, and with particular attention to comprehension and production of such segments. We begin with a theoretical orientation to the topic and then turn to applications of the theory to the basic phenomena of comprehension and production, as well as special problems associated with figurative language. Bilingualism, also a special and complex topic, is treated separately in the next chapter.

THEORETICAL ORIENTATION

Chapter 2 pointed out the complex relations between language and the concept of representation. Language is itself a representational system that symbolizes the perceptual and behavioral world, and plays an important role in mediating our interactions with it. It is also used reflexively to symbolize language itself. These representational and mediational functions of language are enormously complex in their own right. The complexity is multiplied because representational theorists have found it necessary, or at least compelling, to postulate mental representations for language. These mental representations preserve the properties of language stimuli and reponses in verbal-associative approaches to the topic. Largely because of the creative nature of language behavior and the related logical argument against the so-called terminal meta-postulate of classical associationism, the mental representations for language became more abstract, tied in particular to the idea of internalized generative rules. The prototype of this approach was Chomsky's (1965) transformational generative grammar which retained its basic features in subsequent revisions, including his most recent theory of government and binding (Chomsky, 1982). Other linguistic approaches in the 1960s and seventies differed from Chomsky's mainly in their emphasis on the semantic nature of the elements and rules of the representational system (e.g., Fillmore, 1968; Lakoff, 1971). The general characteristics of these linguistic approaches, modified by developments in artificial intelligence and by psychological evidence, were carried over into various propositional approaches to cognition and language (e.g., Anderson & Bower, 1973; Kintsch, 1974; Norman & Rumelhart, 1975).

A common feature of the above classes of theories is their unimodal character: The representations for language are assumed to consist of entities and rule-like processes of a single type, with specific variations defined by assigning different labels to them. Thus, the mental representations (the deep structures for language) are themselves language-like though abstract. The recent emphasis on modularity of representations (Chomsky, 1982; Fodor, 1983) seems to be a departure from this unimodal approach, but on close examination it turns out not to be so for the modularity is in the functions of different subsystems of language. The postulated representational system, though functionally differentiated, is still of a uniform, propositional type.

What is missing from such theories? It is the possibility that language is profoundly influenced by a separate, nonlinguistic representational system consisting of knowledge structures and processes that differ fundamentally from linguistic (or propositional) representations and processes. This is the dual coding view that is to be developed further in this chapter. Somewhat comparable approaches have been proposed recently by some linguists. Fillmore (1977), for example, modified his case-grammar theory by putting special emphasis on the perceptual (or imagined) scenes to which linguistic terms are related. Meanings, he says, are relativized to scenes in the sense that the viewers perspective can differ, depending on the saliency of such aspects as agent, instrument, or object. These differences in perspective are implied by the cases and grammatical structures of language. Similarly, in a paper entitled, "Linguistic gestalts," Lakoff (1977) emphasized the role of concrete situations and related actions in semantic and grammatical distinctions. The linguistic elements and structures are not only related to such perceptual-motor experiences but derive from them and are dependent on them for their meaning. Chafe (1975) has proposed similar ideas. A variety of psychological approaches are also compatible with dual coding in that they assume that sensorimotor experience and semantic factors derived from them are primary in language development and use (e.g., Hebb, Lambert, & Tucker, 1971; Macnamara, 1972).

The following is a brief review of language-relevant dual coding assumptions already discussed earlier, together with more detailed analysis of the problem of syntax, including syntactic creativity.

According to dual coding theory, meaning consists of the relations between external stimuli and the verbal and nonverbal representational activity they initiate in the individual. Three levels or types of relations are assumed: representational, referring to the relation between familiar linguistic or nonlinguistic units and the corresponding verbal or nonverbal representations that the stimuli activate; referential, referring to relations between verbal and nonverbal representations corresponding to the conventional relation between nonlinguistic events (objects, properties, actions) and their names; and associative, the relations among different verbal representations on the one hand and among different nonverbal representational units on the other. No other entities such as abstract conceptual representations are assumed. Concepts are defined entirely in terms of the representational units and relations specified by the theory. Control processes are assumed in the theory but these, too, are defined in terms of the same classes of representations and relations. Referential activity, as in naming an object or imaging to a name, is a probabilistic reaction influenced by the verbal and nonverbal context, including such highly constraining events as verbal instructions to name or image; and similarly for associative activity.

All semantic or meaningful processes in language comprehension and behavior are assumed to consist of the three types of relational activity, in varying proportions. The application includes such higher-order cognitive contributions to or expressions of language processing as inference and linguistic reasoning. It also applies directly to abstraction in language in that abstract language is assumed to be relatively more dependent on intraverbal associative relations and the linguistic context than is concrete language. Some of the empirical implications of the analysis were reviewed earlier (e.g., chap. 7), and others are considered below.

Earlier discussions also included aspects relevant to syntax. Specifically, syntactic behavior includes a substantial component based simply on associative habits. Habitual phrases and idiomatic expressions are obvious examples. Another is the positive relation between associative frequency as defined by association norms and frequency of usage of the response term in natural language (see chap. 7). Such assertions presumably are not controversial, since all linguists and psycholinguists could agree that language performance is influenced by associative experience. Many, however, have denied that associative principles have anything to do with syntactic productivity, which, they would claim, is the hallmark of linguistic competence. But even here there are aspects that can be theoretically analyzed in terms of associative principles coupled with assumptions about general cognitive processes, such as the ability to generalize by analogy from specific exemplars to new ones.

Verbal behavior that can be described in terms of grammatical classes is a crucial example—crucial because all linguistic theories of syntax make use of such descriptive abstractions, and some linguists (e.g., Chomsky) assume that the speaker-listener has mental representations corresponding to such abstractions. It was already pointed out in chapter 4 that such an assumption is justified in a very special and direct sense in literate societies, where children explicitly learn grammatical analysis. Thus, they learn names for the parts of speech—noun, verb, adjective, and so on—as well as names for larger structural and functional units such as phrases, sentences, and the subject-predicate distinction. Such labels become part of the speaker's verbal repertoire, represented mentally in his or her verbal-associative structures. Such grammatical-verbal representations would be expected to play a role in mediating aspects of grammatical behavior: For example, they enable a speaker to generate nouns, or to parse a sentence into subject and predicate if asked to do so.

Of course, young children and people in nonliterate cultures speak grammatically though they may not have learned the meta-language necessary for grammatical analysis. Such speakers use rules in the sense that an observer with a grammatical theory can assign a grammatical description to their speech. The generative-linguistic claim is that their mental competence system must include abstract entities corresponding to grammatical classes. But is it necessary to make this assumption? Could it be the case instead that children first learn a small set of two-word utterances and then begin to generalize by analogy to other similar constructions using already-learned words? Associative mechanisms for such learning have been proposed in the form of contextual generalization (Braine, 1963) and mediational learning (Jenkins & Palermo, 1964). These were rejected by transformational theorists and eventually by the proponents themselves as being insufficient to account for recursions and transformations in language. Nonetheless, even the critics acknowledged that such learning may play a role in some aspects of grammatical behavior, including productivity.

The traditional associative approaches are also unsatisfactory from a dual coding perspective because they assume the associative factors in grammatical skills are entirely intraverbal. In dual coding theory, intraverbal associations, whether direct or mediated, are only part of the syntactic story. The other part has to do with the role of nonverbal factors operating in conjunction with verbal ones. The nonverbal factors include experience with nonverbal objects and events during language acquisition, and situational contexts and imagery processes during language use. These can be interpreted as semantic and pragmatic factors that operate at all levels of language, from the word level to the creative production and understanding of discourse. A child learns the names of things, qualities, actions, and relations in situational contexts to which they are relevant. Parts of speech thus have a clear nonlinguistic experiential base. Larger units, such as nominal phrases, are extensions of one-word names designed to identify specific referents and to distinguish them from perceived or imagined alternatives (cf. Olson, 1970).

According to such an approach, sentences, such as *The boy with the red hair won the race*, need not be interpreted as embedded constructions in which the qualifier, "with the red hair," is derived via transformation from an underlying sentence of the form *the boy has red hair*. Instead, from the speaker's viewpoint, "The boy with the red hair," or its stylistic variant, "The red-haired boy," is simply an extended nominal, the use of which is pragmatically determined by the communicative need to specify a particular person. The controlling variables are situational, not linguistic. A formal system that includes only linguistic elements may require recursive rules to generate such sentences, but a human speaker may not. Expressions of that type have been learned and, given the basic descriptive vocabulary and a set of prepositions and other relational terms, they can be generated productively in any new situation because that situation contains the stimuli for eliciting such responses.

The same general analysis can be applied to more extended linguistic constructions. Children in literate societies learn to categorize sentences as affirmatives, negatives, interrogatives, and so on, because they have been taught to do so. They have also learned to generate such sentences to verbal instructions or transform one sentence type into another. In brief, they can behave like transformational-generative grammarians. Again, however, the cues for generating the different types of constructions in communicational contexts are found in the situational and linguistic context. Younger children and people in preliterate societies use various grammatical constructions as well because they have learned to do so in such contexts when the need arises, without necessarily knowing how to generate the different types to instructions nor how to transform one type into another. Of course, a transformational theory of grammar does not require the latter type of understanding but the point here is the reverse, that productive use of different sentence types in the absence of intraverbal transformational skills does not demand explanation in terms of a more abstract system of grammatical competence. Bowerman (1973) argued similarly that it is gratuitous to interpret the language of young children as reflecting understanding of such concepts as deep structure subject when the evidence does not justify such interpretations.

Syntactic creativity can thus be explained partly by reference to changing situational contexts together with changes in the attentional focus and behavior of the speaker in those contexts. The explanatory potential of such an approach is greatly enhanced by adding imaginal contexts to situational ones. That is, imagery provides a private situational context for both the creative production and understanding of concrete language in particular. The apparent linguistic creativity in communicational situations arises from a continuously shifting interplay of situational focus (where this is relevant), intraverbal context, and imagery. The nonlinguistic perceptual and imaginal factors free language from the finite-state limitations of associative models precisely because we are not dealing here with fixed intraverbal associative probabilities, but with contextual variables that can have their own independent influence at any point during the flow of discourse.

The analysis of more abstract discourse depends on two general qualifications of the above. First, given initial learning of some syntactic constructions in situational contexts, the syntactic learning can be extended to other vocabulary even without the situational and imaginal support (for the details of the argument and supporting evidence, see chap. 5). Second, the creative productivity and understanding of abstract discourse depends relatively more on intraverbal contextual factors (as compared to nonverbal ones) than does concrete discourse (Paivio & Begg, 1971).

In summary, the representational substrate and dynamic processes assumed in dual coding theory provide the basis for an analysis of natural-language behavior as it occurs, for example, in connected discourse. For the most part, only the broad principles and hypotheses derived from the theory can be specified at this time because relevant evidence is sparse. Some of that evidence, both positive and negative, is reviewed below along with more detailed dual coding analyses (for additional relevant studies of imagery effects in particular, see Denis, 1984).

LANGUAGE COMPREHENSION

We begin with the problem of comprehension, noting at the outset that we are not dealing with an all-or-none phenomenon as implied by the "click of comprehension" metaphor. Instead, comprehension can vary in kind and in the level of processing involved (cf. Mistler-Lachman, 1975). The criterion for what constitutes understanding an utterance varies with the circumstances in which it is uttered and the characteristics of the listener. A statement that contains a passing reference to Einstein's equation $E = mc^2$ can be understood well enough by a layman to permit conversational exchange without a full understanding of the implications of the equation. A conversation between physicists may require a deeper understanding.

In the present context, depth of understanding is assumed to vary according to the different levels of processing specified by dual coding theory. Sometimes a felt sense of familiarity, based mainly on activation of verbal representations, may be all that is experienced and it might even be sufficient. More generally, however, understanding would entail additional processing at referential and verbal associative levels. Thus, $E = mc^2$ might evoke an image of Einstein, or the mushroom cloud of an atomic explosion, or it might evoke verbal associates that include the name Einstein, theory of relativity, and so on. A major implication is that referential and associative imagery reactions are more likely to be part of the comprehension of concrete than abstract material. Verbal-associative reactions could predominate in the case of abstract materials but could also constitute all or part of the comprehension of concrete materials, depending on the context.

Sentence and text concreteness effects as evidence

We turn now to evidence that bears on crucial aspects of the above analysis, beginning with the role of imagery and verbal processing in the comprehension of concrete and abstract sentences or passages. In one of the first experiments of this kind, Paivio and Begg (1971) showed university students concrete and abstract sentences and required them to press a key either when they had understood a given sentence or when they had generated an image to it. The main findings were, first, that imagery reaction times were significantly faster to concrete than abstract sentences although comprehension time did not differ significantly; and second, comprehension and imagery reaction times were more highly correlated for concrete sentences (.71) than for abstract sentences (.60).

We interpreted these results to mean that comprehension is more dependent on imagery in the case of concrete than abstract sentences. However, no unidirectional *causal* dependency is assumed in the present analysis, so the more appropriate phrasing is that imagery is more likely to be part of the comprehension process, or that imagery and comprehension are relatively more closely associated, in the concrete than the abstract case. The temporal relations between the criterion responses for comprehension and imagery can vary according to task demands, as evidenced by the finding that, in one of our experiments, comprehension reaction times were generally faster than imagery reaction times even to concrete sentences, but imagery was faster than comprehension in a second experiment that used more complex concrete sentences. The different results in the two experiments might simply reflect differences in the criterion for responding. We suggested, for example, that subjects under the imagery set may have responded to the complex sentences in the second experiment before reading the entire sentence, whereas those under the comprehension set did not respond until they had read the whole sentence. Concrete sentence processing may have involved imagery under both instructions.

The relation between imagery value and comprehension speed has also varied across experiments. Whereas we found no significant difference in comprehension reaction time for concrete and abstract sentences, many experiments have shown that concrete sentences are evaluated for truth or meaningfulness faster than abstract sentences (Holmes & Langford, 1976; Jorgenson & Kintsch, 1973; Klee & Eysenck, 1973). The concrete sentence advantage has been found both when the verification task involved explicit (paraphrase) semantic relations between stimulus sentences and verification sentences and when it involved implicit (inference) relations (Belmore, Yates, Bellack, Jones, & Rosenquist, 1982). On the other hand, Glass, Eddy, and Schwanenflugel (1980) found no difference in verification latency for sentences containing concrete and abstract words, and the decisions actually took longer for high-imagery than for low-imagery sentences when imagery value was defined by whether or not imagery was required to verify a statement. Eddy and Glass (1981) later showed that the negative effect of sentence imagery occurred only when sentences were presented visually, presumably because visual presentation interfered with imagery. The latter observation bears on the modality-specificity of processing in comprehension tasks, to which we return below. The relevant point here is that the effect of imagery value in comprehension tasks can vary from positive to negative, depending on task variables and how imagery is defined.

Denis (1982a) used individual differences in imagery as well as variation in concreteness to demonstrate that imagery slows up meaningful processing of written material under some circumstances. The subjects were selected to be high imagers or low imagers according to an imagery-vividness questionnaire. Their task was to read a passage with the expectation that they would later have to answer questions about the content of the text. The results were that reading times were longer for high imagers than low imagers when the text consisted of imageable (descriptive) material, but times did not differ for the two groups when the text content was abstract and nonimageable. That imagery actually played a role in text processing was supported by the additional findings that (a) high imagers spent relatively more time elaborating images while they read imageable text, (b) low imagers were able to engage in imagery activity during reading when instructed to do so, and (c) imagery facilitated memory for the text.

The results of the studies considered thus far suggest that imagery plays an important role in the comprehension of concrete sentences and passages, with effects on performance varying as a function of task variables and individual difference in imagery. The studies were not designed, however, to examine simultaneously the role of verbal and imagery processes as viewed from the dual coding perspective. In the study described earlier (Paivio & Begg, 1971), we suggested that comprehension of abstract sentences is relatively more likely to be dependent upon the verbal context and verbal-associative reactions than upon imagery, but we did not directly manipulate such verbal factors. The other studies reviewed above generally did not consider how abstract sentences might be comprehended.

Schwanenflugel and Shoben (1983) obtained some direct evidence that the comprehension of abstract sentences is dependent on contextual factors, so that, with sufficient prior contextual cues, their abstract sentences were just as comprehensible as their concrete ones but not so in the absence of contexts. The authors take this as evidence against a dual coding model which assumes that comprehension is dependent solely on the contributions of verbal and imaginal codes aroused by the target sentences. However, that is their own interpretation of dual coding theory, not the theory under discussion here, which clearly takes account of contextual factors in the analysis of concreteness effects on comprehension.

The dual coding analysis is further supported by a study by O'Neill and Paivio (1978) in which, among other things, subjects provided ratings of imagery, comprehensibility, and sensibleness for normal concrete and abstract sentences, as well as anomolous sentences that were constructed by arbitrarily substituting content words from one sentence to another. The relevant finding was that the substitutions produced rating decrements for both concrete and abstract sentences, but the effect was greater for the concrete ones. This difference was especially marked in comprehensibility and sensibleness, which were higher for concrete than abstract normal sentences, but the difference was completely *reversed* when the sentences were highly anomalous. Such a reversal did not occur in the case of imagery ratings, which remained higher for concrete than abstract sentences even when they were anomalous. The dual coding interpretation is that the comprehension of concrete sentences was affected by changes in the sensibleness of the imaginal context aroused by sentence wording as well as by the wording changes themselves, whereas comprehension of abstract sentences was affected only by the changes in wording. Imagery ratings were less affected by anomaly because the concrete content words could still evoke imagery, albeit of a bizarre (nonsensible) kind. In brief, image bizarreness could account for both the drastic reduction in sensibility and the relatively high image-arousing value of anomalous concrete sentences.

An experiment by Marschark (1978, 1979) yielded another kind of evidence for dual coding effects. Marschark presented passages auditorily in such a way that the subjects could control the rate at which they heard each word, and so that this word-by-word processing rate could be measured. The passages consisted of high-imagery and low-imagery paragraphs that were carefully matched on a variety of other attributes. The relevant result in the present context was that, under instructions to comprehend the passages, the processing time patterns were strikingly different for the different passages: Subjects spent relatively more time on the major content words of high-imagery passages, and more time on syntactic aspects of low-imagery passages. These results together with the results of a strategy questionnaire completed by subjects after the experiment suggested that high-imagery language was understood largely by visualizing its semantic content, whereas low-imagery language was understood largely in terms of its intraverbal patterning.

The inferences concerning imaginal and verbal processes in comprehension in the above studies were based on manipulation of the imagery value of language materials and reported processing strategies. More direct evidence for modality-specific differences in processing emerged from an experiment by Klee and Eysenck (1973). Their participants listened to concrete or abstract sentences presented concurrently with a visual- or verbal-interfering task. The sentences were meaningful or anomalous, and the subjects indicated which was which by pressing a key. The interesting result was a significant interaction that was consistent with the dual coding hypothesis. The comprehension latencies were longer with visual than verbal interference for concrete sentences, and conversely, longer with verbal than visual interference for abstract sentences. These were the results that Klee and Eysenck expected from the hypothesis that visual imagery is used in comprehending concrete sentences and that image formation was disrupted by the visual-interfering task, whereas verbal processing (e.g., arousal of verbal associations) predominates in the case of abstract sentence comprehension and this processing was disrupted by the verbal-interpolated task.

The Klee and Eysenck experiment has been criticized on methodological grounds (Holmes & Langford, 1976) but without any direct demonstration that the general pattern of results and conclusions are wrong. In fact, Eddy and Glass (1981) and Glass, Millen, Beck, and Eddy (1985) obtained results indicative of modality-specific (visual or visuospatial) interference effects on the processing of sentences judged to require imagery for their verification, thus supporting at least the image half of the Klee and Eysenck conclusions. Sadoski (1983) also found evidence of modality-specific interference during oral reading of parts of stories that evoked most imagery, namely, the story climaxes (see further below).

The above experiments suffice to illustrate the dual coding approach to comprehension. Imagery plays an essential role in the comprehension of concrete, high imagery verbal material when comprehension depends on knowledge about the concrete properties of objects, their actions, or their spatial arrangements, knowledge that is directly represented only in the imagery system. The contribution of imagery is supplemented by effects that are attributable to verbal processes, including associative dependencies among the words of an utterance and any further verbal associations aroused by the wording. The effects of imagery and verbal processes are additive, in both a positive and negative sense. Their combined effects are positive to the extent that the verbal patterns correspond to high-probability associative relations in the verbal-representational system and the evoked imagery corresponds to sensible real-world scenes. The effects are negative when the verbal patterns are anomalous and the aroused imagery is bizarre. Such imagery processes are less probable in the case of abstract sentences, so their comprehension depends *relatively* more on verbal processes alone. In addition, comprehension of both types of material is affected by the general verbal and nonverbal situational contexts in which they occur because the target material and the context affect the pattern of verbal- and nonverbal-representational activity. Finally, individual differences in imagery and verbal abilities and strategy preferences affect the nature of processing during comprehension.

Evidence from sentence-picture comparisons

The studies considered thus far used only language material to study imagery and verbal processing in comprehension tasks. Other studies have tested imagery-based and propositional models using comparison tasks in which subjects must decide as quickly as possible whether a presented sentence or description is true or false (informationally same or different) with respect to a referent picture. Models of verification generally assume that the target and referent must be encoded into some common format so that the information in each can be compared. Propositional models (e.g., Carpenter & Just, 1975; Chase & Clark, 1972) assume that the common code is propositional in form, so that a sentence and a referent picture would both be transformed into logical propositions and the true-false decision is based on the match or mismatch between propositions. Verification time is assumed to depend on the complexity of the comparison process (the number of constituent comparisons required), which in turn is a function of sentence complexity. Other single-code alternatives are that such comparison tasks are based essentially on image encoding of the comparison stimuli or on verbal encoding of both (Rosenfeld, 1967).

The dual coding interpretation is that the comparisons could be based on either imaginal or verbal processing or both, depending on the nature of the target stimuli, experimental instructions, and contextual cues that influence the subject's expectancies, and individual differences in imaginal and verbal habits and skills. Imaginal encoding would be favored when the target sentences are concrete, when pictures are used and *expected* as comparison stimuli, and when the subject is predisposed to use imagery. Verbal coding would be more likely when the sentences are abstract, other sentences are expected as referents, and the subject is predisposed to use verbal strategies. Rosenfeld's (1967) results were consistent with a strong imagery interpretation in a same-different comparison task that used all possible pairings of picture and descriptions as targets and comparison stimuli. When the procedure included an interstimulus delay that permitted the first stimulus to be encoded before the second appeared, comparisons were fastest with pictures as comparison stimuli (cf. Seymour, 1973). Other studies (e.g., Paivio, & Begg, 1974; B. Tversky, 1969) showed that the comparison could be based on either a verbal or nonverbal code, depending on what the subject expected as the comparison stimulus. J. Glucksburg, Trabasso, and Wald (1973) generally adhered to a propositional interpretation of the results from a complex verification study with pictures and sentences; however, they also suggested that, under some conditions, the pictorial information need not be propositionalized and that imagery processes might play some (unspecified) role. The present view is that their results can be interpreted completely in terms of dual coding simply by substituting "verbal code" in most instances in which their analysis relied on a propositional code.

The most direct inferential evidence for different processing strategies, one imaginal and the other linguistic, comes from a study by MacLeod et al. (1978). Their analysis of verification times of individual subjects in a sentence-picture comprehension task revealed two groups of subjects. The larger group showed a pattern of results that was well fit by Carpenter's and Just's (1975) linguistic-comparison model. The smaller group was poorly fit by the model, and the results suggested instead that this group used a pictorial-spatial strategy. Psychometric tests showed in addition that the two groups differed in spatial ability but not in verbal ability. A subsequent experiment by Mathews, Hunt, and MacLeod (1980) confirmed and extended these findings by demonstrating that some subjects normally used a pictorial strategy and others a linguistic strategy, and that the strategies could be modified by training on one or the other. The results were interpreted in terms of Hunt's (1978) theoretical analysis of flexibility in information processing. That analysis and the results are also generally compatible with dual coding assumptions.

Schema research and dual coding

Next we review certain studies that were done to test schema theories of text comprehension. We shall see how the results can be alternatively interpreted in dual coding terms. In essence, the common aim of these studies was to induce subjects to construct different schemata from narrative scripts by presenting instructions or other cues that biased them to read the scripts from different viewpoints (other schema studies have relied on the cultural experiences of the readers). R.C. Anderson and Pichert (1978) asked their subjects to read a story that described a home from the viewpoint of a prospective home buyer or a burglar. The results suggested that the different perspectives affected how the story was encoded (understood) and remembered by directing attention to items that are significant in light of the schema; e.g., a fireplace and a leaky roof in the case of the home buyer, silverware and a coin collection in the case of the burglar. The dual coding interpretation is that the verbal instructions and the story together activated different patterns of verbal and imaginal encoding. Prior experiences with descriptions or movies of burglaries, for example, would affect encoding so that the instructional cue, burglar, is more likely to prime coin collection than leaky roof as verbal associates, and conversely for the verbal cue, home buyer. The different patterns of verbal activation in turn induce different patterns of imagery, in which different items are salient. This explanation can be viewed as a paraphrase of the schema interpretation, but it is nonetheless significant because the postulated mechanisms are more explicit in the dual coding view and the vague concept of schema has no necessary explanatory role. The effects are due simply to verbal-contextual cues, the text itself, and the patterns of verbal and imaginal activity induced by context and text.

Dual coding processes are even more directly implicated in a series of studies by Bower and his colleagues. Owens, Dafoe, and Bower (1977) induced their subjects to identify with either the water skier or the driver of a boat in a water-skiing story. The procedure resulted in different patterns of recognition errors and other data consistent with the different perspectives. Moreover, when asked to describe the mental images they experienced while reading the story, the subjects' descriptions revealed different spatial perspectives that corresponded to the viewpoint of the different characters. Thus, subjects who identified with the skier visualized the scene as though it were through his eyes and the skier's actions as if they themselves were performing them. Conversely, they were outside observers of the driver's actions. The authors concluded that the differences in visualized perspectives could account for the actor-observer effects on memory and other tests. The present interpretation is that the differences were initiated entirely by verbal-contextual and story cues, which induced different patterns of activity in the verbal system and eventually in the referential imagery aroused by that system.

Another study, by Black, Turner, and Bower (1979) is particularly important because it revealed the effects of subtle linguistic variables on imagined perspectives and on comprehension. The experiment contrasted verbs such as come and go in compound sentences. The first half of each sentence introduced a main character and his or her location, and the second half described an event from either the same or a different vantage point. For example, "Terry finished working in the yard" was followed by either "and *went* into the house" or "and *came* into the house." The former has a consistent vantage point in that the "viewer" stays in the imagined setting and watches the actor move away from it. The "came into the house" sentence requires one to change one's viewpoint. The researchers accordingly reasoned that it should take longer to understand the phrase with the changed vantage point than the unchanged one. This prediction was confirmed by reading-time data. Moreover, in a second experiment, the changed sentences were rated relatively harder to understand.

The results of the Black et al. (1979) study suggest that it is reasonable to interpret the effects of other lexical and grammatical variables in terms of subtle differences in the nature of the imagined scenes that they induce. Active-passive differences, for example, should be reflected in predictable differences in imagined focus and perspective. Fillmore's (1977) interpretation of the meanings of case categories and relations in terms of different perspectives on imagined scenes similarly becomes more plausible (cf. mental models in text comprehension, e.g., Johnson-Laird, 1983; Morrow, 1985).

Dual coding theory also provides an alternative to various specific propositional schema models of text comprehension (e.g., Kintsch & van Dijk, 1978; Rumelhart & Ortony, 1977; Thorndyke, 1977). The Kintsch-van Dijk model will suffice as an example because it has been worked out in considerable detail and has influenced other investigators of text processing. The model has recently been extended and elaborated by van Dijk and Kintsch (1983) in ways that make it more compatible with dual coding theory, but we shall see later that it still differs from the latter in its basic representational assumptions.

It is assumed in the Kintsch-van Dijk model that discourse is interpreted as a set of propositions ordered by various semantic relations among the propositions. The resulting semantic structure is characterized at microstructure and macrostructure levels, the former refering to the structure of the individual propositions and their relations, and the latter, to the global nature of the entire discourse. The microstructure is characterized as a hierarchical sequence of propositions which have some degree of *referential coherence*, which corresponds notationally to argument overlap (repetition) among propositions. If the text is found to be referentially coherent, it is accepted for further processing; if not, inference processes are initiated to close the gaps. The propositions must also be organized globally at the macrostructure level, that is, they must be connected to the topic or theme of the discourse or some portion of it, such as an episode. These macrostructures, too, are described in terms of abstract, connected propositions, and their function in the model is to reduce the information in the text base (the microstructure level) through deletion and different types of inferences based on the gist of the text. The two structural levels are related by a set of semantic-mapping rules called macrorules, which are applied under the control of a general schema. The latter is the formal representation of the reader's goals in reading, the clarity of which depend on such factors as the degree to which the text is conventionalized and the degree to which the reader reads with a special purpose in mind.

The investigations of the model have shown that highly conventionalized story texts have well-defined, coherent structures when transformed into the propositional descriptions. More important, the model has had considerable success in predicting text comprehension as measured by tests of readability and memorability (see Kintsch & van Dijk, 1978, for a summary). Such an approach has also been used to construct structurally equivalent stories and movies (Baggett, 1979), which were processed in similar ways by subjects in a recall task.

The up-dated model proposed by van Dijk and Kintsch (1983) elaborates on the above in various specific and general ways. A relevant specific change is that coherence is now defined more generally in terms of semantic-propositional relations that take account of world knowledge. Such specific changes are a consequence of a general elaboration of the model, which distinguishes three levels of text representation in memory, including verbatim surface representation, a propositional textbase much as described above, and a situational model. The last of these is "not part of the text representation proper but a model that the hearer or reader constructs about the situation denoted by the text" (p. 337). The authors argue that situation models are required to account for such linguistic and psychological phenomena as reference, coreference, coherence, situational parameters, and perspective.

The addition of the situational model to the general theory obviously renders it more similar to dual coding theory, which also includes situational representations that can be experienced as imagery. There is a fundamental difference, however: It turns out that van Dijk's and Kintsch's proposed representational structure for situational models also has a propositional format (pp. 344–346). Thus, with reference to the representation of an accident, we have "at the top a predicate, filled with information about 'having an accident,' and followed by a list of participants, for example, in such a way that the agent role can be filled by the person him- or herself. . . . The event is then localized in place, time, and conditions" (p. 345). The context of their discussion makes it clear that the reference is to the format of the situational model as *constructed and used by the reader or hearer,* and not simply to the theorists' descriptive format for the model (see my earlier discussion of the distinction in chap. 3). As we have repeatedly asserted, no common representational format of this kind is assumed in dual coding theory.

I believe that the van Dijk-Kintsch model and other propositional discourse models provide a useful descriptive approach to discourse structure in terms of a common, abstract language, and to predictions when the structural description is combined with processing assumptions. The central question here is whether they adequately describe the actual coding and processing mechanisms involved, and whether their predictions are better than what might be achieved by other approaches. The dual coding approach would begin with an examination of the verbal-contextual and associative structure of a text. Thus, the parallel to an analysis of argument repetition or propositional (semantic) repetition would be the analysis of literal repetitions and associative relations between content words in the text. The associative relations would presumably vary in remoteness. The overall verbal cohesiveness of the text could then be indexed by some measure of verbal-associative overlap (cf. Deese, 1965). A parallel to a hierarchical description might emerge from analysis of the referential generality of words in the text. The text analysis could be supplemented by associative data obtained from readers at different points of the text. The text and the activated associates might even include discourse-descriptive associates such as theme, plot, episode, and the like, depending on the subjects' prior experiences with text analysis. This approach has a close linguistic precedent in the work of Halliday and Hasan (1976), who described text cohesion in terms of connections or ties between words in different sentences. Anaphoric prepositions, repetitions, synonyms, and superordinate-subordinate relations, among others, contribute to cohesiveness in their analysis.

The dual coding analysis of discourse processing would go beyond the verbal level to include the imagery aroused by text material. Thus, the linguistic bases for cohesion in the analyses by Kintsch and van Dijk or Halliday and Hasan would now have nonlinguistic parallels in such reactions as common referential images evoked by coreferential terms, synonyms, and the like. Episodes would be reflected in the imaginal contexts or situations that are continuously or repeatedly evoked by associatively and contextually related (cohesive) wording. The overall theme or schema might be represented partly by a relatively specific image that recurs in some form throughout the text to recurrent verbal cues. In short, both verbal and imaginal contexts and associations contribute to the reader's psychological organization of text including its overall integration or cohesiveness.

I have shown elsewhere (Paivio, 1983c) how this general approach and specific hypotheses and assumptions of dual coding theory can be applied to aspects of literary analysis. The precedents were analyses in which the concept of imagery played a prominent role. For example, in her study of Shakespeare's imagery, Caroline Spurgeon (1935) drew special attention to what she described as dominating images, or "iterative imagery which runs not only through a passage but all through a play and which may represent the 'leading motives' of the plays": swift and soaring movement as manifested particularly in the flights of birds in *Henry V*; the sense of sound throughout *The Tempest*; the dominating image of light—of the sun, moon, stars, and reflected light of beauty and love—in *Romeo and Juliet*; and so on. Other writers have proposed similar analyses of other works, such as the thematic symbolic role of the shooting of the albatross in Coleridge's *The Rime of the Ancient Mariner*, and of the white whale in Melville's *Moby Dick*.

The dual coding reinterpretation of such literary analyses emphasizes the independent and additive contributions of imaginal and verbal processes to the organization, access, and retrieval of information in the literary works. The special thematic and symbolic functions of images are analysed in terms of the role of specific imaginal exemplars as the prototypical representations of general categories and ideas, and as conceptual pegs for storage and retrieval of other related information in the poem or story. Thus, just as Rosch (1975a) showed that prototypical category exemplars can serve as reference points or standards against which other relevant information can be evaluated, so too might the albatross symbol serve as the fabric or orienting theme of the *Ancient Mariner*. The literary interpretation that the symbol "carried in its train the ground plan of the poem" and served to release "thronging images" (Lowes, 1927, p. 228) illustrates the function of a specific image as a retrieval cue (conceptual peg) for other images that gave rise to the poem as a whole.

The research approach would be to apply similar analyses to discourse processing in laboratory studies in which verbal content is varied in ways designed to reveal the thematic and other contributions of imaginal and verbal representations and processes. Experimental studies of this kind are yet to be done, but a correlational study by Sadoski (1983) yielded results that are consistent with aspects of the dual coding analysis. Fifth-grade elementary school students were required to read (aloud) a story that contained several illustrations. Following the reading, the students completed a number of story comprehension and recall tasks, including a general question regarding imagery ("Do you have any pictures or scenes in your mind that you remember from this story?"). Analysis of the retrospective reports of imagery revealed two groups of subjects: Those who reported an image of the story's climax and those who did not. The climax was not illustrated in the text, so the reported imagery presumably occurred spontaneously during reading. A more interesting finding was that reporting a climax-image correlated with several comprehension and recall measures. In addition, a factor analysis revealed a series of factors which Sadoski interpreted as successive levels of comprehension, with deeper levels characterized by a general verbal factor and a key imagery factor. The imagery factor received significant loadings from reported story-climax imagery as well as recall scores for the theme, events, and plot of the story, suggesting to Sadoski that it is a thema factor that represents the essential meaning of the story. The results and interpretation are consistent with the above analysis of the thematic, symbolic, and retrieval (conceptual peg) functions of images in literary works. Sadoski in fact concluded that the results are particularly supportive of the conceptual-peg hypothesis and dual coding theory in general. The generality of the results and conclusions were confirmed in a replication study (Sadoski, in press) that included several design modifications, including use of an unillustrated text.

Sadoski's studies nicely illustrate how imagery and dual coding concepts can serve as an alternative to propositional schema (or script) approaches to text comprehension and memory. It would be easy to extend the research in various ways designed to provide more specific tests of dual coding. For example, measures of imaginal-referential ability, as defined in chapter 6, might predict story climax imagery and other responses specified by Sadoski. Such extensions would not be trivial because it could turn out that there is something special about text-elicited imagery reactions that is not tapped by tests that use lists of words or pictures as stimuli. The same argument applies as well to other extensions of dual coding operational procedures to the text level.

LANGUAGE PRODUCTION

The emphasis in this section is on creative production rather than on reproduction based on episodic memory, although a sharp distinction is not always possible. The constructive novelty of speech and writing has always been a central problem for theories of language, although Chomsky drew special attention to it as the *raison d'être* for generative grammars. The propositional schema theories discussed in the preceding section, though most often studied in relation to comprehension and memory, are applicable at least in principle to production (e.g., see Kintsch & van Dijk, 1978). In addition, processing stage models have been designed specifically to handle production. For example, Garrett (1975) proposed that speakers first decide on a message, then a syntactic outline, then content words (nouns, etc.), then function words and affixes, and finally produce speech. The sequence of stages is an inference based especially on the analysis of different kinds of speech errors (for a review see Paivio & Begg, 1981, chap. 9). Others (e.g., Dell & Reich, 1981; McNeill, 1979) favor a more flexible approach in which processing activity is assumed to go on at many levels at once.

The dual coding approach is of the flexible variety, since it assumes in general that speech production is controlled by parallel processing and sequential processing mechanisms operating at different levels and in different degrees, depending on the nature of the speech task, the context, and speaker characteristics. As already mentioned earlier in this chapter, the most general assumption is that production is cognitively controlled by the cooperative activity of the nonverbal representational system and the verbal system. The activity would always include the representational level, and different mixes of referential and associative processing. Referential processing would be maximized in descriptive tasks, such as describing a scene, in which the nonverbal system is directly activated by perceptual stimuli and it in turn initiates verbal-referential activity; or describing one's living room from memory, where the nonverbal system is indirectly activated by verbal cues (e.g., a request to describe the room). Of course, verbal-associative processing also must be used in describing, but such activity would predominate when the speech task is an abstract one, such as a discussion about religious beliefs. In every case, the lexical and syntactic selection would be influenced by ever-changing verbal and nonverbal contextual cues (instructions, questions, listener's expressions, ongoing events), as well as the context provided by what the speaker has already said. Creative productivity is an inevitable consequence of such contextual shifts, including the syntactic creativity that results in production of embedded sentences and other complex constructions—creative, because the contextual changes are not fully predictable; inevitable, because language must accommodate itself continually to such contextual changes if it is to serve a communicational function efficiently.

Studies that have examined the effects of nonverbal-perceptual stimuli, imagery variables, and associative variables on lexical and syntactic choices and on productive fluency provide relevant evidence. The evidence is spotty rather than systematic, but it serves to illustrate the approach and the research possibilities. We begin with effects on selection of wording and syntax.

Olson (1970) proposed a referential-contextual approach to meaning in which he argued that semantic decisions, such as the choice of a word, are determined by the speaker's knowledge of the intended referent rather than by syntactic or semantic selection restrictions. The decisions are made so as to differentiate the intended referent from some perceived or inferred set of alternatives. Thus, precisely how one designates or describes an object depends on its context. The point was illustrated by an experiment in which a child saw a gold star placed under a small wooden block and was required to tell a second child, who didn't see the event, where the gold star is. The star was always placed under the same block but the alternatives varied in size, shape, color, and number; or there was no alternative. The crucial result was that what the speaker said varied in the way predicted by the theory, e.g., "It's under the white one," or "It's under the round one," or "It's under the round, white one," and so on, depending on the alternatives. In general, the descriptive labels were sufficient to distinguish the intended referent from the perceived or inferred alternatives, with some redundancy added. In information-theoretic terms, the statements were phrased so as to reduce uncertainty.

The above accords with the dual coding assumption that referential interconnections are one to many, in both directions, so that an object can activate different descriptive logogens; or a name, different imagens. The alternatives vary in probability of activation depending on the situational context and on the individual's prior experiences using the alternatives. Olson's analysis lends precision to the approach and his results are consistent with the predictive implications of the theory for lexical decisions in verbal descriptions.

Osgood (1971) extended the analysis to encompass perceptual events over time and effects on syntactic as well as lexical choices. His subjects were shown a series of demonstrations using such objects as balls of different size and color, plates, tubes, and poker chips. The content and sequence of the demonstrations were designed to induce certain presuppositions, to provide for contrasts over time and space, and so on. The subjects were told to describe the perceptual event or events in a single sentence as though it were told to a young child who could not see the events.

A number of predictions concerning the effects of temporal and spatial contexts on descriptions were confirmed. Determiners shifted abruptly from the indefinite *a* to definite *the* when there was an immediate reappearance of an object and tended to shift back toward *a* when the reappearance was delayed over demonstrations. Shifts from the use of object names to pronouns occurred when the object entered into more than one action or relation within the same demonstration. Still other demonstrations influenced the richness of adjectival qualification in noun phrases and other aspects of description.

Other hypotheses were not confirmed. For example, demonstrations designed to induce the use of passive constructions or center embeddings did not have significant effects, perhaps because such constructions are rare in ordinary descriptive speech. It remains to be seen whether perceptual or imagery tasks can be devised so as to have the intended effects. Some encouragement toward that end comes from a study by James, Thompson, and Baldwin (1973), in which subjects were more likely to shift from active to passive in sentence recall when the grammatical object was higher in imagery value than was the grammatical subject.

The important general conclusion from Osgood's study is that lexical choices with grammatical functions cannot be predicted entirely from syntactic theories. Instead, certain constructions are strongly influenced by the temporal sequence of events and the spatial relations among objects in the situation in which descriptive speech occurs. In dual coding terms, the productive choices are determined jointly by nonverbal factors, including perceptual objects and events as well as episodic images of them (which permit comparison over time), and verbal factors that include the temporal context of successive descriptions and the speaker's acquired verbal descriptive habits.

We turn next to studies in which variables directly relevant to dual coding theory were manipulated. Begg, Upfold, and Wilton (1978) investigated the role of imagery in verbal communication by varying the concreteness of words that served as target items for communication between pairs of people. In the first of a series of experiments, one person was shown a word and required to produce a sequence of one-word clues that the other person used to try to guess the target word. Thus, the experiment required productive lexical choice on the part of the speaker and inferential understanding on the part of the listener. The main finding was that concrete words were guessed with significantly fewer clues than abstract words, as Begg et al. (1978) expected on the basis of their imagery hypothesis. The results and conclusions were confirmed in four other experiments in which procedural variations were used to rule out alternative explanations and to specify the locus of the concreteness effect. The authors concluded that concrete words are communicated more effectively than abstract words because the former enable people to make use of perceptual knowledge to specify the referents of the words. Concrete words are thereby distinguished easily from each other and interpreted similarly by speaker and listener. Abstract words lack perceptual referents and are defined instead by their relations with other words. Accordingly, they are relatively confusible with each other and liable to different interpretations by speaker and listener.

The above studies provided evidence for the effects of perceptual and imaginal processes on lexical and syntactic choices on language production and communication. Some studies (e.g., Prentice, 1968; Rosenberg, 1967) have also demonstrated effects of verbal associations on lexical selection and syntactic arrangement, but such effects remain to be more systematically investigated, as do the joint effects of imaginal and verbal processes. Both classes of variables have been included in some studies of the fluency of speech production as measured by rate, pause patterns, and speech errors, to which we now turn.

Goldman-Eisler (1961, 1968) introduced an experimental procedure in which individuals were shown humorous *New Yorker* cartoons. When the subject had "got the point" of a cartoon, he or she described the contents of the story it depicted and then formulated the general point, meaning, or moral of the story. Thus, the descriptive part of the task was relatively concrete, whereas the interpretive part was more general or abstract. The major finding was that more pauses occurred during the generalizations than during the descriptions. In other words, concrete descriptive speech was less hesitant and more fluent than abstract speech. Lay and Paivio (1969) confirmed Goldman-Eisler's results using three levels of task abstraction and difficulty.

Reynolds and Paivio (1968) investigated the effects of variables more directly relevant to dual coding theory. Their stimuli were concrete and abstract nouns equated for familiarity, which subjects defined orally. Analysis of the definitions showed that the concrete words, relative to the abstract ones, elicited longer definitions, with faster initiation of the definitions, fewer silent pauses, and fewer nonfluencies of other types. In brief, concrete words were generally easier to define (cf. O'Neill, 1972) and generated more fluent speech than the abstract words.

Reynolds and Paivio also obtained information on the role of verbal-associative processes in the definitions task. The speakers were identified as high or low on a prior verbal-associative productivity test in which they wrote associations to stimulus words. The experiment showed that the definitions of the high-associative productivity participants contained more words, had faster starting latencies, and were more fluent than those of the low-productivity subjects. The definitions given by the high-productivity subjects were also judged to be better definitions of the concepts. These differences are particularly noteworthy because the two groups were originally distinguished on the basis of a written association test, whereas the experimental task required oral production of natural, grammatical speech. Thus, the results apparently reflected the influence of individual differences in rather general verbal-productive skills.

The dual coding interpretation of the above findings is straightforward. The concrete descriptive tasks require a high degree of referential exchange between the verbal and imagery systems. Cartoons activate the image system directly and concrete words do so indirectly. In either case, the descriptions or definitions are based on perceptual or perceptual-memory information, which activates relevant descriptive representations in the verbal system. The relatively fluent speech presumably results from the simultaneous availability of complex images, appropriate to the task, combined with verbal-associative processes. The fluency of more abstract interpretations and definitions presumably depends more exclusively on such properties of the verbal system as availability and length of sequentially organized verbal-representational chunks as measured, for example, by associative-fluency tests.

The plausibility of the dual coding analysis was enhanced by a further set of results. Segal (1976, described in Paivio, 1975b) presented subjects with groups of two, three, or four unrelated abstract words, concrete words, or object pictures with instructions to make up sentences using a given set of items. For example, the subject might see the words *house, apple,* and *pencil,* or pictures of their referents. The relevant result here concerns the latency of sentence generation as measured by a key press when subjects "had the sentence in mind" (which was followed by their writing the sentence). The latencies were faster for concrete words than abstract words and still faster for pictures than concrete words. The latter finding was a counterintuitive prediction from dual coding theory because commonsense considerations, as well as any theory that emphasizes linguistic processes, would lead one to expect faster sentence construction when the words to be used are actually given. The results suggest instead that pictures have the advantage because they can be encoded relatively directly and quickly by the imagery system into an organized scene, which can then be described via the referential interconnections.

This completes the analysis of language comprehension and production, as applied to language in general. The next section puts the emphasis on figurative language in particular.

REPRESENTATIONAL PROCESSES IN FIGURATIVE LANGUAGE

Metaphors and idioms of various kinds pose a special problem for theories of language because they are commonly used and understood despite the fact that they are literally anomalous. Proverbs are also problematic because they are used in an extended, figurative sense, although many of them could also be used literally—for example, it is literally true that "all that glitters is not gold" but it is unlikely that it would be used in that literal sense except in a discussion of "fool's gold." Of course, frozen idioms and familiar metaphors and proverbs may not present any special analytic difficulty because their metaphorical meaning has been overlearned. The theoretical problems arise when one considers novel figurative expressions, as we do here. We begin with a general analysis of psychological issues and approaches, and then move to the dual coding approach, emphasizing its implication for comprehension, but with some attention as well to memory and production.

Students of metaphor have generally identified similarity, relation, and integration as core concepts in the analysis of metaphor processing. The topic and vehicle (the subject and predicate) of a metaphor share something in common. The relation between these similar or shared elements as well as the ones that are not shared contribute somehow to the appreciation for and interpretation of the metaphor. Finally, the cognitive end-product of the interpretation is some kind of novel, integrated representation. Theories of metaphor processing differ in the way they conceptualize the representational elements, structures, and processes that are presumed to be the basis of similarity, relational, and integrative reactions to a metaphor.

Three general classes of theoretical approaches to the problem can be identified: (a) emphasizing perception and imagery, (b) verbal-mediating processes, and (c) abstract representations and processes. The dual coding approach combines the first two along with a set of specific assumptions and hypotheses.

The perception-imagery approaches generally assume that topic-vehicle similarity is perceptually based, entailing, for example, a transfer of sensory experiences as in synesthetic metaphors (cf. Asch, 1958; R. Brown, 1958; Osgood, 1963); or they assume that the resulting holistic meaning of metaphors is based on some kind of "abstractive seeing" as represented in imagery (Langer, 1948). Imagery was also given a prominent role in G. Miller's (1979) analysis of metaphor. Verbal-mediational approaches (e.g., Koen, 1965) assume that similarity and relational reactions are essentially based on verbal-associative overlap between topic and vehicle. The abstract representational approaches analyze similarity of topic-vehicle relations in terms of semantic component or feature overlap (e.g., Malgady & Johnson, 1976; Ortony, 1979; Osgood, 1963). Their analyses of topic-vehicle relations also take account of dissimilarities in semantic representations, including asymmetry in the position of common features in the defining feature sets of the two terms (e.g., Ortony, 1979). Finally, some of these theorists have proposed that the integrated representation that emerges during metaphor comprehension *is* the overlapping feature representation that is evoked by the topic and vehicle (Malgady & Johnson, 1976), or some kind of common abstract representation that is more than the sum of the attributes of each constituent (Honeck, Riechmann, & Hoffman, 1975; Verbrugge & McCarrell, 1977). Models of metaphor processing based on such ideas also include other assumptions that need not be reviewed here.

The dual coding approach is based on the general assumption that the representational processes that mediate figurative language behavior are modality-specific (verbal and nonverbal) cognitive reactions that are associatively evoked by the metaphor and the context in which it is used. Thus, it combines features of the imagery and verbal-associative approaches cited above (a similar dual process approach has been proposed recently by Harnad, 1982). Earlier (Paivio, 1979), I suggested five specific ways in which imaginal and verbal processes could jointly contribute to metaphor comprehension and production: (a) dual coding enhances the probability of finding a common ground, that is, a connection between topic and vehicle, in long-term memory; (b) the synchronous or integrated nature of imagery enables large amounts of potentially relevant information to become available quickly, if at least one term in the metaphor is high in image-arousing value; (c) imagery ensures processing flexibility because it is relatively free from sequential constraints; (d) topic and vehicle are retrieval cues for relevant information; and (e) verbal processes, because of their sequential nature, keep search and retrieval on track; that is, the metaphorical terms themselves and the verbal associations they arouse constrain the search and retrieval process more than imagery does, precisely because imagery is relatively free from sequential constraints and, therefore, is more likely to lead to irrelevant flights of fantasy.

These points were elaborated on in the original context (Paivio, 1979) and here I will comment only on two issues related to them, one arising from the research literature on metaphor and the other from a test of a hypothesis associated with the proposed retrieval function of metaphorical terms.

The first issue concerns the role of imagery in the processing of figurative language. Honeck et al. (1975) found that memory for proverbs was better when cued by related interpretations than by unrelated ones when the proverbs were high in imagery value but not when they were low in imagery. Despite that observation, the authors preferred an abstract conceptual-base interpretation of comprehension and recall of proverbs, partly because another experiment showed that subjects recognized interpretations of proverbs better after instructions to encode them for their intended meaning than after instructions to visualize their literal meanings. The present analysis of the issue simply follows the argument already presented in the section on language comprehension. Comprehension is a complex and multilevel process, generally, and it must be especially so in the case of novel figurative expressions. Imagery is likely to play a role in comprehension, especially when the language includes concrete terms that readily evoke imagery, and its arousal might facilitate performance in a criterion test of comprehension but it need not always do so. The dissociation was demonstrated in the experiment by O'Neill and Paivio (1978) described earlier, in which anomaly had effects on comprehensibility and imagery ratings: Interchanging content words from different meaningful sentences reduced the sensibleness of concrete strings more than of abstract strings, but imagery ratings were less disrupted by anomaly. The interpretation was that concrete terms could still evoke imagery even in anomalous contexts, but that the pattern of imagery may be bizarre or otherwise unconducive to a meaningful interpretation.

The parallel argument in the case of figurative expressions is that imagery could interfere with a metaphorical interpretation because the imagery is irrelevant or inappropriate. The possibility is illustrated by a study by Billow (1975) in which the presentation of pictures along with metaphors sometimes interfered with metaphor interpretation by children, perhaps because the pictures added irrelevant detail. Imagery could be similarly misleading because it biases a literal interpretation rather than a figurative one. Such an effect would be especially likely in the case of proverbs like *All that glitters is not gold*, which can be interpreted literally as well as figuratively, but such garden-path imagery is possible with any figurative expression. Consider the following example: As a young child, one of our daughters was chattering away in a charming manner and her mother said, "Won't Grandpa get a kick out of that mouth!" Whereupon the girl began to sob and imploringly said, "I don't want Grandpa to kick me in the mouth!" Imagery apparently facilitated comprehension, but not of the intended idiomatic message.

Concerning the retrieval function of topic and vehicle, the dual coding proposition is that high imagery value of both terms facilitates retrieval of imaginal and (indirectly) verbal-referential associations from long-term memory, either of which could provide a common ground for interpretation. In effect, the topic and vehicle can be viewed as conceptual pegs for semantic memory information. I suggested further that the imagery value of the metaphorical vehicle (predicate) would be especially important on the assumption that processing begins and is guided by the vehicle because its meaning determines the metaphorical interpretation of the topic (cf. M. Black, 1962; Verbrugge & McCarrell, 1977).

The hypothesis received some support from subjective reports by individuals who were asked to interpret a novel metaphor and to describe what thought processes had preceded the interpretation (Paivio, 1979, pp. 169–170). Most respondents said they started with the vehicle and that they had imaged its referent. A metaphor rating study (Marschark, Katz, & Paivio, 1983) also showed that the imagery value of the topic and vehicle predicted metaphor goodness and interpretability even when a number of other variables were statistically controlled. Moreover, vehicle imagery was the better predictor (for related memory effects, see Marschark & Hunt, in press).

Subsequently, however, Jim Clark and I (unpublished) obtained experimental results that disconfirmed a particular aspect of the above hypothesis while confirming the importance of imagery. The conceptual-peg hypothesis was tested by orthogonally varying the imagery value of topic and vehicle of metaphors. Subjects were asked to press a key when they had interpreted a metaphor and then to write a paraphrase indicating their understanding. This aspect of the results showed that interpretation reaction time was facilitated only when both metaphorical terms were high in rated imagery and the metaphor as a whole had been previously rated as relatively easy to understand. A second feature of the experiment provided more striking results. Some subjects were primed with either the topic noun or the vehicle noun prior to presentation of the entire metaphor. The prediction from the conceptual-peg analysis was that priming with the vehicle would be more helpful than priming with the topic noun. The results were precisely the opposite: Topic-priming speeded up metaphor interpretation relative to the no-prime condition, whereas vehicle priming retarded interpretation time.

The unexpected results call for a revised hypothesis concerning the retrieval functions of topic and vehicle. The vehicle could still dominate in metaphor processing because its meaning determines the interpretation of the topic, but the topic must be known before one can begin to consider what aspects of the meaning of the vehicle are relevant. In brief, the topic constrains the associative reactions evoked by the vehicle, so the topic is processed first. That is why topic-priming facilitated metaphor interpretation in the experiment just described. The analysis also explains why vehicle-priming had a negative effect: Presentation of the vehicle in isolation presumably evoked associations that were irrelevant to the interpretation of the topic in metaphorical terms—either verbal associations or imagery or both. Isolated presentation of the vehicle is precisely the kind of condition that would encourage unconstrained flights of fantasy. When the topic is known, however, the associative search process may stay by the vehicle, so that more time is spent processing the vehicle than the topic.

The revised hypothesis permits us to reinterpret the subjective report data mentioned earlier. The participants were asked to interpret the "metametaphor," *To the student of language, a metaphor is a solar eclipse.* The participants generally said that they first thought about (imaged) an eclipse and then thought about what it might have to do with metaphor. But their introspective analysis is misleading because the metaphor was presented orally, so they would have heard and presumably understood the topic before hearing the vehicle. Their semantic *search* process may have begun with the vehicle, but only in light of its relation to the topic.

The analysis can be extended to metaphor comprehension and production in natural communicational situations. When a speaker uses a metaphor, it is always in a specific situational and verbal context. That context constrains the choice of a familiar metaphor or the production of a novel one so that it will be relevant to the topic of conversation. Similarly, the listener's interpretation is constrained by the same context. The ongoing process in both parties is associative, including the associative pattern of the conversational content as a whole, and the associations it selectively arouses in the speaker. However novel, the generated metaphor is probabilistically determined by the context and the speaker's verbal- and nonverbal-associative habits. The listener's interpretation is constrained by the context, the metaphor itself, and his or her associative habits.

The communicational situation contrasts with most experimental studies of metaphor comprehension and memory, in which metaphors are typically presented in isolation, except for the context of other metaphors. The interpretation of each metaphor is unconstrained by a relevant communicational context. This may be why there is so much variability in the interpretation of metaphors by subjects in psychological studies. Such variability would not be conducive to the communicational function that Ortony (1975) emphasized in his analysis of metaphor but, fortunately, it is likely that the variability would be reduced by the communicational context itself. It is clear in any case that context contributes to the understanding of novel metaphors (Gildea & Glucksberg, 1983).

This concludes our selective analysis of representational processes in relation to language comprehension and production. We turn next to an extension of the dual coding approach to bilingualism.

11

Bilingual Cognitive Representation

The bilingual mind presents some unique problems for students of cognition. Persons who have mastered two (or more) languages must have two distinct representational subsystems of some kind, since they are able to deal separately and meaningfully with different acoustic and response patterns. (Actually, they must have more than two subsystems if they also read and write in both languages, but I will simplify the present discussions by ignoring the further analytic complexities that would arise if we were to deal fully with the different sensorimotor components of bilingual language skills as outlined in chapter 4.) Moreover, bilinguals must have some way of switching efficiently from one linguistic code to the other in bilingual contexts. This means that bilingualism entails productive representational systems corresponding to the units and structures of each language, and functional interconnections between them. That much is relatively uncontroversial among cognitive theorists interested in bilingualism. What is controversial is the interpretation of the cognitive processes implicated in bilingualism: Does the ability to speak and understand two languages mean that one has two ways of remembering, knowing, and thinking? Or are the two language systems functionally connected to a common cognitive or conceptual system?

The contrasting positions, as defined originally by Kolers (1963), have been described variously as independence versus interdependence, language dependent versus language independent, and separate versus shared-memory and cognitive systems. The independence-interdependence contrast will do for our purposes. The independence position implies that the bilingual has two functionally independent cognitive subsystems (including memory stores) associated with the two languages. The interdependence position is that the separate linguistic systems are functionally connected to a common conceptual system, including a shared-memory store. The latter view, it should be noted, is entirely consistent with common coding or propositional approaches to cognition in general (e.g., see Rosenberg & Simon, 1977).

The contrasting views and their empirical implications have been discussed in detail elsewhere (e.g., Kolers, 1963; Kolers & Gonzales, 1980; McCormack, 1977; Paivio & Begg, 1981, chap. 13; Paivio & Desrochers, 1980; Paradis, 1980). Here, I simply list some of the major research findings that have been interpreted as support for one position or the other, and then

239

describe a dual coding model of bilingual memory and cognition and show how it deals with such findings and other issues in bilingualism.

The independence position is supported by the following observations: (a) the bilingual's word associations to translation-equivalent words in the two languages differ more than would be expected from the interdependence or common conceptual view; (b) language switching takes time in production tasks and some comprehension tasks; (c) bilinguals are able to remember the language in which a word was presented in a mixed language list more accurately than would be expected on the basis of chance; (d) changing the language of a set of words produces a release from proactive inhibition in a Brown-Peterson short-term memory task; (e) additive memory effects consistent with the idea of independent memory codes have been obtained in free recall tasks using bilingual repetitions or bilingual encoding of items, and (f) priming effects sometimes do not transfer from one language to the other.

The following results have been interpreted as more consistent with an interdependence or shared-system position: (a) similar associations are given to stimulus words in a bilingual's two languages too often to support an absolute independence position; (b) positive transfer effects occur in a variety of verbal learning tasks when the word lists are switched from one language to another for bilinguals; (c) free recall of bilingual lists by bilinguals shows clustering of items by conceptual category but not language; and (d) translation and picture-naming reaction times are comparable, suggesting that both are mediated by the same amodal conceptual system.

The most relevant of the issues and contrasting findings will be discussed in more detail following a review of the present theoretical approach.

A BILINGUAL DUAL CODING MODEL

The bilingual dual coding model (Paivio & Desrochers, 1980) is in one sense a specific version of the independence approach to bilingual cognition, but it also includes a common representational system that provides a basis for interpreting some findings that appear to support the interdependence hypothesis. Overall, the model provides a comprehensive account of both sets of findings summarized above and has unique implications that go beyond those that arise from the independence or interdependence positions separately considered. The theory includes all of the general assumptions presented in chapter 4 and adds specific ones concerning the relations between verbal representational systems corresponding to the two languages and of each of those to the nonverbal system. The theory is schematically modeled in Figure 11–1.

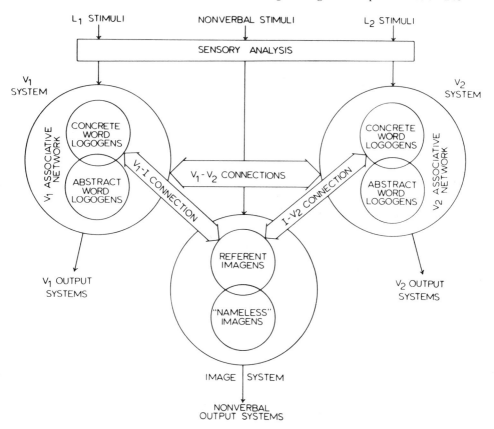

Figure 11-1. Schematic representation of the bilingual dual coding model showing for languages L_1 and L_2 the corresponding verbal systems (V_1 and V_2) and their connections with each other and with the imagery (I) system. From "A dual coding approach to bilingual memory" by A. Paivio and A. Desrochers, 1980, *Canadian Journal of Psychology, 34,* p. 391. Copyright © 1980 by Canadian Psychological Association, Reprinted by permission.

Relations between nonverbal and verbal systems

The basic independence assumption of dual coding theory is extended in the bilingual version so that the nonverbal imagery system is assumed to be functionally independent of both verbal systems. Simply stated, the assumption implies that bilinguals can perceive, remember, and think about nonverbal objects and events without the intervention of either language system and, conversely, that they can behave or think verbally without constant input from the nonverbal system. The systems are at the same time functionally interconnected at the referential level, so that verbal activity in either language system can be influenced by the imagery system and vice versa. It is assumed further that the two verbal systems (V_1 and V_2) corresponding to the bilingual's two languages (L_1 and L_2) have referential inter-connections to the image system (V_1-I and V_2-I in Figure 11–1) that are partly shared and partly independent. That is, the verbal translation equiv-alents in L_1 and L_2 may or may not activate the same nonverbal represen-tational information, depending on the way the two languages have been acquired. This assumption translated into the familiar idea that translation equivalents do not necessarily have identical referential meanings.

We shall see presently that the assumptions have unique implications for some basic issues in the psychology of bilingualism. One issue that is rele-vant at this point concerns the translation process. The implication is that the image system provides an indirect access route from one language to the other. Under some circumstances and for some words, translation can be mediated in that a logogen in V_1 activates referential imagens which in turn activate referential logogens in V_2. In other cases, translation might occur more directly, as suggested by the following set of assumptions.

Relations between the two verbal systems

In a manner paralleling the relations between image and verbal systems, the bilingual's two verbal systems are also assumed to be functionally indepen-dent but partly interconnected. The independence is limited in the sense that it cannot include the possibility of concurrent activity of both systems, at least on the response side (one cannot speak two languages at the same time). It does imply that one language system can be used in comprehen-sion, memory, or production without necessarily being dependent on or influenced by the other. A language switch can occur with a change in the input language or such nonverbal contextual cues as the nature of the audi-ence. Once the switch has occurred, activity goes on within a system accord-ing to the representational units, structures, and associative or grammatical processes specific to the language in question. The idea of partial intercon-nectedness implies that the switch can occur directly between language sytems, but only via specific access routes. The nature of those access routes (points of contact, associative connections) can be understood by consider-ing the relation *between* V_1 and V_2 and how these compare or contrast with the relations among verbal units *within* each system.

The relations between V_1 and V_2 are assumed to be such that the access occurs primarily between logogens corresponding to translation equivalents in the two languages. Thus, a switch or translation is more probable between translation equivalents than between nonequivalents in the two languages. A French-English bilingual, for example, will switch from *boy* to *garçon* or from *girl* to *fille* rather than from *boy* to *fille* despite the strong associative connections that normally exist between the two concepts (boy-girl, garçon-fille) in either language. Within-language connections are also assumed to be more varied than between-language connections, so that the conditional transition probabilities are high between translation equivalents and relatively low between nonequivalent terms in the two languages. In contrast, the transition probabilities within languages have more diverse and flatter hierarchies in that, although a given connection may have a relatively high activation probability (for example, *boy-girl*), there are also an indefinite number of lower-probability links (for example, *boy-lad*, *man*, and so on). Thus, the functional connections between V_1 and V_2 logogens approximate one-to-one relations, whereas the interconnections within each system are many-to-many and variable in their strength.

It must be emphasized that the postulated between-within difference in interconnections is a relative one. Anyone who has tried to translate from one language to another knows that it is often difficult to come up with the most appropriate translation for a given term in one language because of polysemy and differences in the nuances of even the most closely related terms. Such observations imply that the relations between translation equivalents can be many-to-many, as are the associative relations within a language. Nonetheless, the between-language relations are assumed to be "tighter," more constrained, than those within a language.

A further qualifying assumption is that the connections between translation equivalents can vary in number and strength over language units and individuals. Individuals who have acquired their two languages in bilingual settings that require frequent translation or in study programs that emphasize translation practice are likely to have stronger direct interconnections among more translation-equivalent terms than persons who have learned the two languages independently in different settings with a minimum of translation experience. The skilled simultaneous translator represents one extreme in frequency of translation practice and, presumably, consequent richness and strength of direct V_1-V_2 interconnections. We can at least conceive of individuals at the other extreme who have acquired two languages entirely independently, without translation experience, and therefore find it difficult to translate directly from one language to the other. Most bilinguals presumably fall somewhere in between, directly translating many words and expressions with relative ease and having difficulty finding the appropriate translation equivalents in other cases. All bilinguals would have the alternative possibility of indirect translation mediated by the imagery system, as suggested earlier.

The theory also includes functional assumptions regarding conditions that determine the arousal or activation of representations either directly or via their interconnections. Again, these are simply extensions of the dual coding assumptions described in chapter 4. Activation is assumed to be determined by the current stimulus situation in interaction with individual differences in the verbal- and nonverbal-representational structures and abilities of the bilingual individual. Relevant stimulus conditions include the properties of linguistic stimuli (which of the bilingual's languages is involved, its concreteness or image-arousing value, and so on) as well as nonlinguistic objects and events. Either class of stimuli could be the focus of attention as speech to be understood and responded to, or objects to be described; or they could be contextual stimuli, such as instructions to translate speech, describe scenes, image to words or descriptions, or any number of experimental procedures that may or may not prime translation. The individual differences that are specifically relevant to the bilingual situation are those that result from the individual's unique history of acquisition and use of the two languages, including the situational contexts in which they were used. Such experiences would determine the nature of the representational content of V_1 and V_2 as well as of the nonverbal image system, and the functional interconnections between systems. Some of the possibilities were already introduced above in regard to variability in direct V_1-V_2 interconnections and the degree to which V_1 and V_2 are associated with shared as compared to distinct nonverbal imagens.

All of the functional assumptions can be rephrased in terms of processing mechanisms, as in chapter 4, with the most unique addition being a translation processor, or set of processors, which would include the conceptual equivalent of the code-switching mechanism postulated by some students of bilingualism. The present conception is more elaborate because it includes both direct and image-mediated switching mechanisms, described in terms of cross-language activation via direct or indirect functional interconnections. In keeping with the general empirical nature of the theory, such mechanisms are assumed to be experientially determined and modality-specific. They consist of associative processes that are activated by specific cues and affect the probability that the bilingual's other verbal system will be brought into play. The observational consequences are that individual differences in bilingual cognitive structures and processes interact with stimulus variables to affect the probability of different kinds of linguistic or nonlinguistic reactions.

IMPLICATIONS AND EVIDENCE

We turn now to a review of the implications of the theory for some current issues in the psychology of bilingualism. The review includes reinterpretations of research findings in terms of the theory, and presentation of some new evidence stemming from research specifically designed to test its implications. The issues and phenomena are separated for convenience into those that predominantly implicate semantic memory structures and processes and those that mainly implicate episodic memory.

Semantic memory implication

Considerable attention has been given to the implications of a distinction originally suggested by Weinreich (1953), who classified bilinguals into compound, coordinate, and subordinate types according to specified relations between the bilingual's linguistic systems and their conceptual systems. Psycholinguistic researchers (e.g., Lambert, Havelka, & Crosby, 1958; Osgood & Ervin, 1954) subsequently emphasized the compound-coordinate dichotomy. Compound bilinguals were presumed to have good control of their two languages but these are connected to a single, fused conceptual system. The English word *bread* and the French word *pain*, for example, would have identical meanings. Coordinate bilinguals, on the other hand, were assumed to function like unilinguals in each of their languages, since the two conceptual systems that are acquired through each language are clearly differentiated. Thus, for the French-English coordinate bilingual, the words *bread* and *pain* would have somewhat different meanings, stemming from distinct experiences with different kinds of bread. Conversely, objects might be verbally distinguished in different ways by the two types of bilinguals.

Weinreich's classification system has been criticized on the grounds that it has been difficult to define the categories operationally in terms of language-acquisition experience and that empirical studies have produced only mixed support for the distinction. Taking such criticisms into account, Lambert (1969) proposed a modified operational definition in terms of early versus late bilingualism, in which compounds are those who have been brought up in a bilingual environment from infancy on, whereas coordinates are those who had learned their second language later than the first, usually after ten years of age and usually outside of the family setting. The distinction was supported by the observation (Lambert, 1969, pp. 108–109) that coordinate bilinguals, so defined, showed less interference on a bilingual version of the Stroop test than did compound bilinguals, as though the former had greater functional separation of the two languages.

The present approach to the problem begins with the general view that it is more useful to think of the compound-coordinate distinction as a matter of degree rather than extreme types. In dual coding terms, bilingual verbal systems have multiple connections to an independent, nonverbal-representational system, some connections converging on a common set of imaginal representations (reflecting a "compound" aspect of bilingual memory), and others activating relatively independent sets (reflecting a "coordinate" aspect). For some individuals and some concepts, the converging connections might predominate, so that *bread* and *pain*, for example, might elicit images of the same kind of bread; for others, the independent connections might predominate, resulting in images of different kinds of bread to the two words. Individuals also could differ in the number and strength of direct associations between translation equivalents in ways not easily encompassed by the compound-coordinate distinction. The different associative patterns would be determined by linguistic and nonlinguistic experiences to which the bilingual had been exposed during language learning.

The relevant empirical evidence is sparse and bears mainly on imagery reactions to a bilingual's two languages. Bugelski (1977) described a personal observation, which he also confirmed with other bilinguals. Bugelski had spoken Polish as a child in Europe before moving to the United States, so he would qualify as a coordinate bilingual for whom the later-acquired language is dominant. He noticed that stimulus words in his two languages elicited quite different imagery: Polish words evoked images of objects and scenes from his childhood, whereas English words experienced in his North American setting did not. Winograd, Cohen, and Barresi (1976) also suggested that such culture-specific differences might occur in the nature of imagery aroused by a bilingual's two languages.

Lambert, Havelka, and Crosby (1958) provided some indirect evidence on possible differences in the imagery experienced by compounds and coordinates. Lambert et al. (1958) had compound and coordinate French-English bilinguals rate a series of translation-equivalent concepts, such as *church* and *église*, on a series of semantic differential scales. They predicted and found that the semantic differential profiles for equivalent terms were more similar for the compound than for the coordinate group. At one point, the authors hinted that equivalent words in the two languages may have evoked somewhat different images (of a typical English church as compared to a French église, for example) as well as different affective reactions among the coordinates. The study warrants replication with more direct measures of imagery reactions.

The results of relevant word-association studies can also be interpreted in terms of the dual coding model. Kolers (1963) found that the word associations of bilingual subjects to translation equivalents differed more than would be expected if the associations were mediated by one memory store, but similar associations also occurred too often to support an absolute independence position. The interesting additional observation was that the common associations occurred more frequently to concrete nouns, such as *table* and its German equivalent *Tisch*, than to abstract nouns (e.g., *freedom-Freiheit*) or affective terms (e.g., *pain-Schmerz*). Kolers suggested that this might be because the referents of concrete terms are likely to be more similar than those of other classes of words. In dual coding terms, the associations to concrete nouns are mediated partly by referent images common to the translation equivalents in each verbal system, whereas associations to abstract terms are determined primarily by the structure of the separate verbal-associative networks of the two languages.

Taylor (1971) reported associative data that can be used to evaluate the dual coding assumption regarding within-language and between-language relational differences. One of her conditions permitted French-English bilinguals to switch languages freely during a continuous association task. She found that subjects were more likely to continue associating in English or French than to switch from one to the other. Taylor interpreted this result to mean that the associative links are stronger within than between languages. The dual coding interpretation is that the associative connections within verbal systems are more numerous and diversified than connections between languages, since the latter occur mainly between translation equivalents. Performance in a continuous association task is accordingly facilitated by the rich intralanguage associations and inhibited by frequent switching because the switch to an associatively related verbal concept in the other language is usually mediated by an implicit translation of a word preceding the switch. For example, *knife* might elicit *fourchette* via *couteau*, the translation of knife. Alternatively, the switch could occur via the mediating image of a knife, which in turn arouses the image of a fork. This process, too, would increase reaction time relative to unilingual associations mediated by connections within the corresponding verbal system.

The results of a variety of naming and translation reaction time experiments have been interpreted as supporting the interdependence or common-coding theory of bilingual representation. To the extent that they do so, they are a challenge to dual coding theory. One series of studies (e.g., Dalrymple-Alford, 1968; Preston & Lambert, 1969) used a bilingual Stroop test in which subjects were asked to name in one language the print colors (e.g., blue) of a color word written in the other language (e.g., rouge). Others have used an auditory version of the task (Hamers & Lambert, 1972) or a picture-naming variant (Ehri & Ryan, 1980) in which the pictures included a distracting (semantically related) word printed in the same language to be used in naming or in the bilingual's other language. Mägiste (1984) investigated the phenomenon using bilinguals who differed in degree of proficiency in the two languages. These studies have typically shown that the distracting words increase naming reaction time relative to control conditions even when they are printed in the language not used in naming. Thus, the bilingual apparently cannot "turn off" the irrelevant language system while responding in the other language, suggesting some form of functional interdependence.

The Stroop-like results do not present any special problem for dual coding theory. The interference effect may occur simply because the stimulus situation contains explicit cues for competing responses in the two languages. The fact that the competition is stronger between translation equivalents or semantically related words than for unrelated ones is explainable in terms of associative probabilities and spreading activation, so that related verbal representations in L_1 and L_2 are more likely to reinforce each other's activation than are unrelated words, given that both have been simultaneously activated by the stimulus cues. The common-conceptual coding hypothesis also accounts for the data, but it is not a compelling alternative.

Potter, So, Von Eckardt, and Feldman (1984) compared reaction times for translating L_1 words into L_2 and naming pictures in L_2, with results taken as support for common conceptual mediation as opposed to a direct word-association hypothesis. Thus, bilingual dual coding theory might also be called in question because it incorporates the possibility of direct connections between translation equivalents. One experiment used proficient Chinese-English bilinguals and a second used nonfluent English-French bilinguals. The bilinguals were required to read words aloud, name pictures, and translate words. The critical finding from both experiments was that it took no longer to name a picture in L_2 than to translate L_1 words into L_2. This finding is inconsistent with the word-association hypothesis described by Potter et al. (1984), according to which access to and from an L_2 word is exclusively via the first language, so that picture naming in L_2 would require that the picture first be named (covertly) in L_1 and then translated into L_2. This process would take more time than translating a printed word into L_2 because picture naming takes longer than reading a printed word. Note, however, that the bilingual dual coding model does *not* assume that picture naming in L_2 must be mediated by L_1. To the extent that L_2 names had been learned in the context of their referents (objects, pictures, images), the bilingual would develop direct referential interconnections between imagens and V_2 logogens. There would be no reason, then, to expect that picture naming in L_2 would take longer than translating a printed word into L_2. Longer naming reaction times would be expected only if L_2 had been learned exclusively through direct word-word translation, which is unlikely to be the case in ordinary language-learning situations. Accordingly, contrary to what was suggested by Potter et al. (1984, p. 34), their results are not difficult to reconcile with dual coding theory.

Our final research examples provide data that are inconsistent with any strong form of the interdependence-conceptual coding hypothesis, whereas they are consistent with the independence hypothesis of bilingual semantic memory and with dual coding theory. Lachman and Mistler-Lachman (1976) had German-English bilinguals name pictures of objects in each of their languages. The same pictures were named on two trials so that some pictures were named twice in the same language and some were named once in one language and once in the other. The relevant finding was that naming latencies on trial 2 were significantly faster for pictures named in the same language than for pictures named in the other language. According to the Lachmans, the result suggests that the internal processes necessary for accessing visual-conceptual content of pictures on the one hand and linguistic information on the other are at least partly independent. Their preferred interpretation is in terms of a model of object naming proposed by R. Lachman (1973), which includes a visual memory component for dealing with identifiable visual patterns, a semantic memory component that links the visual pattern to its conceptual infrastructure and knowledge of the world, and a lexical storage component.

Lachman's model is similar to dual coding if we interpret the semantic memory component of the former in terms of associative structures within the imagery system. However, we need not resort to the associative level nor to its analogue in the Lachman model to explain the results. It suffices instead to assume that referential responding in one language increases the availability of that response on a subsequent trial, but would not similarly augment referential responding in the other language because the verbal-representational systems for the two languages are independent. Cross-language facilitation would occur only if the presentation conditions actually encouraged the subject to name the pictures in both languages, at least covertly. The implication is that such dual referential encoding was not encouraged in the study by the Lachmans, but the authors' report does not include enough procedural details to permit us to evaluate the suggestion.

A similar interpretation is applicable to the following study. Scarborough, Gerard, and Cortese (1984) tested Spanish-English bilinguals in a lexical decision experiment in which the subjects had a series of word-nonword trials in one language, and then had a second series in which words were unexpectedly repeated in the same language for one group, and in the other language for another group. The results showed a priming effect (faster latencies relative to unrepeated words) for the same language repetitions but not for words repeated in the other language. A second experiment showed that bilinguals who were told to respond positively to words of one language responded to real words from the other (nontarget) language as though they were nonwords. Consistent with the bilingual dual coding model, these results suggest that subjects can respond selectively to one language without being influenced by the other when the context does not encourage (or explicitly discourages) immediate translation. When the context does encourage translation, as in the bilingual Stroop-like tasks discussed earlier, or in a priming procedure that forces subjects to translate prior to a lexical decision task or provides items from both languages so that they can be processed in quick succession (Kirsner, Smith, Lockhart, King & Jain, 1984, Experiments 2, 4 and 5), performance is influenced by both languages. The effect is positive if the response is compatible with each verbal system (lexical decision) and negative if incompatible responses are activated (the Stroop task). The next section reviews similar contrasting effects in episodic memory tasks.

Episodic memory implications

Bilingual-episodic memory studies have provided evidence that bears on the two-store versus one-store hypothesis in particular and, more generally, on the independence assumptions of the dual coding approach. The evidence is relevant also to the general assumption that the memory trace includes information from subjective and objective sources (see chap. 8), elaborated now by the idea that different linguistic codes may be represented in that trace along with nonlinguistic information. The present review deals first with findings from studies that were designed specifically to test dual coding theory, and next with other findings in the literature, many of which can be interpreted in terms of the model and some of which remain somewhat problematic.

The most direct support for dual coding theory comes from evidence of additive effects of verbal and nonverbal memory traces on recall performance. One series of experiments extended the unilingual item repetition and image-verbal encoding studies described in chapter 8, in which it was reasoned that mnemonic independence of nonverbal images and verbal codes would be reflected in additive effects when pictures and their names are repeated at zero lag, a condition in which word-word repetition effects are ordinarily less than additive. Similarly, differential encoding instructions or a combination of encodings and item attributes designed to activate different codes should have additive effects. These expectations were consistently and strongly supported by the results of the unilingual experiments, and we shall see that comparable predictions are upheld by some bilingual memory experiments.

Glanzer and Duarte (1971) obtained evidence for the independence of two linguistic codes using a repetition paradigm in which Spanish and English translation equivalents were repeated at different lags, along with within-language repetitions and once-presented items. The relevant results were that bilingually repeated items were recalled better than within-language repetitions at short interitem lags but the two kinds of repetitions converged at long lags. Glanzer and Duarte did not test for independence of repeated items, but their recall patterns indicate that short-lag bilingual repetition effects were more nearly additive than were within-language repetitions, suggesting that the two verbal codes are mnemonically independent.

Two experiments by Paivio and Lambert (1981) specifically tested implications of the bilingual dual coding theory. In one experiment, French-English bilinguals were presented a mixed list of pictures, French words, and English words, to which they responded by writing the English name of each picture, translating the French words into English, and simply copying the English words. They were then given a surprise free-recall test for the English words they had written down. A second experiment reversed the encoding and recall tasks. The subjects were shown only English words and, in response to encoding cues, they imaged and quickly sketched the referents of one-third of the words, translated one-third into French, and copied the remaining third. Then they were asked to recall the English stimulus words they had been shown. Thus, in both experiments, the subjects recalled English words that had been generated by different encoding processes, or words that had been encoded in different ways.

The results of both experiments, presented in Figure 11–2, showed an identical pattern, with recall increasing sharply from the copy condition, to translation, to verbal-nonverbal coding. Approximately twice as many translated items were recalled as copied items, suggesting that the bilingual verbal encodings were at least additive in their effect. The equivalent and substantial further increase from bilingual to verbal-nonverbal encoding is consistent with the dual coding assumptions that verbal and nonverbal episodic trace components are independent and that the nonverbal (imaginal) component is mnemonically stronger than the verbal one. In brief, the results were entirely in agreement with the bilingual version of dual coding theory. Alternative interpretations in terms of processing levels and other

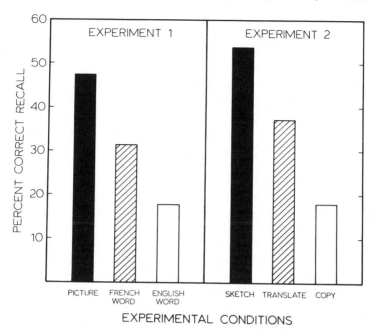

Figure 11–2. Incidental free-recall scores for English words that bilingual subjects in Experiment 1 had generated by naming pictures, translating French words, and copying English words; and for presented English words that subjects in Experiment 2 had coded by sketching the referent, translating, or copying. From "Dual coding and bilingual memory" by Paivio and Lambert, 1981, *Journal of Verbal Learning and Verbal Behavior.* Copyright © 1981 by Academic Press. Reprinted by permission.

theories were considered in the discussion and found wanting for logical and empirical reasons.

A variety of other studies are directly relevant to dual coding theory or can be reinterpreted in its terms. Saegert and Young (1975) paired Spanish and English translation equivalents with different stimuli in the same paired-associates list, so that bilingual subjects had to remember which concept went with each stimulus as well as the language of the concept. In addition, half of the pairs were concrete nouns and half were abstract nouns. Saegert and Young reasoned that the concrete items could be conceptualized in a nonlinguistic (imaginal) form and that this would enhance the probability of translation errors because subjects would be confused about which language code, Spanish or English, was appropriate for a given stimulus when the association had been image mediated. Such confusions would be less likely in the abstract case because they are more likely to be processed in terms of their verbal representations alone. The results were consistent with these predictions.

In a conceptually related study, however, Winograd et al. (1976) obtained the opposite results in that they found memory for input language to be poorer with abstract words than with concrete words. The discrepant results are probably due to procedural differences. Saegert and Young used an associative learning task that was designed to maximize the probability of confusion errors. Winograd et al. (1976) used a free-recall task, which is generally less likely to produce confusion errors. Still, the task difference would not explain why memory for input language was *better* with concrete than abstract items in the Winograd et al. (1976) study. The authors suggested two image-based interpretations. Their "cultural imagery" hypothesis is equivalent to one of the dual coding interpretations of coordinate bilingualism discussed earlier: Bilinguals have different images associated with translation equivalents in their two languages, so the images themselves contain clues to the language of the concrete words from which they were generated. The second suggestion was that the images associated with concrete words may function as effective retrieval cues for phonological and other features of the words themselves. Such interpretations are yet to be investigated.

Bilingual dual coding theory also provides a basis for reinterpreting some findings that have been taken as evidence for a common memory store. Several studies have shown positive transfer effects in a variety of verbal learning tasks when the word lists are switched from one language to the other for bilinguals (e.g., Lopez & Young, 1974; MacLeod, 1976; Young & Saegert, 1966). The effect has been taken to mean that transfer is mediated via common memory representations for the two languages. Dual coding suggests the following reinterpretation. To the extent that the studies used concrete words (as they generally have), positive transfer effects would be expected because the translation equivalents in the two languages would tend to arouse common referent images. Moreover, direct verbal associations could also produce positive transfer if we assume that bilingual subjects sometimes translate words covertly during first- or second-list learning. When such translations occur during first-list learning, they would provide a head start for learning items presented in that language in the second list. The reverse translations during second-list learning could be used to check the correctness of the recall attempts against memories of the already learned first-list responses.

Dual coding and second language learning

We deal finally with the implications of bilingual dual coding theory for second language learning in experimental and natural settings. The general assumptions are that the learner develops (a) a verbal representational system corresponding to the second language, (b) referential interconnections between those representations and old or new nonverbal representations in the image system, and (c) associative interconnections with already established L_1 verbal representations. I will deal briefly with the empirical implications of the approach (for a more detailed review, see Paivio, 1983a).

A major implication is that it is especially important to learn the second language (L_2) in direct association with appropriate nonverbal referents because such referents (objects, events, behaviors, emotions), cognitively represented, constitute the knowledge of the world that L_2 must tap if it is to be used meaningfully. The richer and more direct the referential interconnections, the more efficient L_2 use will be. Referential availability also capitalizes on the powerful mnemonic properties of nonverbal stimuli and imagery, as discussed in preceding chapters. The difference in the present case is that the L_2 verbal units and structures are unfamiliar to begin with.

Relevant evidence comes from studies that have used actual objects, or pictures, or imagery techniques to teach second language vocabulary and, less often, syntactic skills. Many experimental studies (e.g., Kellogg & Howe, 1971; Wimer & Lambert, 1959) have compared native language words with pictures or objects as stimuli for learning word responses in the unfamiliar language. The results have consistently shown that L_2 responses are learned in fewer trials and with fewer errors if nonverbal referents rather than L_1 words serve as stimuli. Imagery-based techniques have also yielded positive results, although qualified by a number of variables.

Most research has been done on the keyword technique, in which a familiar L_1 word is used to establish an acoustic and semantic link between the L_2 target item and its L_1 translation equivalent. For example, the English word cart could serve as the keyword for the Spanish target word *carta*, which means "letter." The acoustic link is established by the similarity in sound between the two words. The semantic link is established by an interactive image of the referents of the words—for example, a huge letter envelope inside a grocery cart. The language learner can be presented the keyword along with pictures or verbal cues for the interactive image, or they can be asked to supply both components on their own. Vocabulary learning is ordinarily measured by a comprehension test in which the learner translated the L_2 item into its L_1 equivalent, presumably via the appropriate mediating steps. Thus, carta serves as a reminder for cart, which in turn redintegrates the interactive image, from which the relevant semantic component (letter) can be retrieved.

The keyword technique has generally, but not always, proven to be more effective than a variety of control conditions (for reviews, see Atkinson, 1975; Paivio & Desrochers, 1981; Pressley, Levin, & Delaney, 1982). The main qualifications are: (a) the technique is effective for learning the meanings of the target items, as measured by an L_2-L_1 translation test, but relatively ineffective when the L_2 item must be recalled as a response to L_1; (b) it is more consistently superior to free-strategy control conditions with children than with adult learners, apparently because adults are more likely to make spontaneous use of keyword-like and other mediating strategies than are children; and (c) its effect is specifically on the associative link between L_2 and L_1, rather than on recall of responses or meanings as independent components.

The dual coding interpretation is that the keyword method explicitly brings into play both verbal and imaginal processes. The acoustic bridge is provided by the phonemic properties of L_1 keyword representations and the sounds of the L_2 target items, which the learner generates from visually presented words or remembers as episodic traces if the items had been presented auditorily. This aspect of the procedure affects the development of V_2 logogens and direct V_1-V_2 links between translation equivalents. The use of the imagery component initiates the development of appropriate referential interconnections between V_2 logogens and the imagery system.

The hook mnemonic is another imagery-based technique which was designed (Paivio, 1978e) to increase the availability of unfamiliar words or larger units as meaningful responses to associative cues presented in the second language itself. Essentially an adaptation of familiar pegword-imagery systems discussed in chapter 8, it has two stages. The first consists of learning an ordered series of mnemonic pegwords or hooks that are easily retrieved by means of a number-consonant code. For example, the numbers 1–4 can be represented by the consonants t, n, m, and r, and pegwords are chosen so that each contains only the relevant pronounced consonant and is easily imaged. Thus, the first four pegs in a French version of the system could be *thé* ("tea"), *noeud* ("knot"—the d is not pronounced), *mât* ("mast"—the t is not pronounced), and *roi* ("king"). Basic consonants are selected for zero and all one-digit numbers. These can be used to generate as many as 100 pegwords containing the relevant consonant sounds—for example, pegword 11, 23, and 34 could be *tête, enemmi,* and *mur,* respectively.

The second stage consists of associating new items from the target language with the already-learned pegwords by means of interactive images, just as in the keyword technique. For example, suppose that the French words *chaise* ("chair"), *arbre* ("tree"), *camion* ("truck"), and *maison* ("house") are the first four items of a vocabulary list. Then referents would be imaged in association with the referents of the first four pegwords as, say, a teapot on a chair, a tree with a knotted rope hanging from it, a truck on top of a ship's mast, and a king building a house. The learner then can attempt to retrieve the items starting with the numbers as cues.

The hook system differs from the keyword technique in a number of ways. One difference is that it does not include an acoustic link between a target item and its translation equivalent. Second, the hook technique uses already learned words in L_2 as retrieval cues for target items in that language, rather than simply translating the target item into its L_1 equivalent. Third, the technique can be used for mental rehearsal of L_2 targets once these are "hooked" to the numbered pegs, without requiring any external cues. Such rehearsal is not possible with the standard keyword technique.

Paivio and Desrochers (1979) first showed that the hook technique greatly facilitated the learning of French vocabulary items relative to a rote-rehearsal control condition. Desrochers (1982, 1983) extended the technique to the learning of French grammatical gender, with qualified positive results. Paivio, Clark, Pressley, and Desrochers (unpublished) compared hook, keyword, and free-strategy control conditions factorially crossed with retrieval conditions appropriate to the two mnemonic strategies. The results showed clearly that the hook technique functioned as intended in that it was superior to both keyword and free-strategy conditions on number-cued, ordered recall tests, but somewhat inferior on translation tests of memory for the meanings of the vocabulary items. A fourth group was taught a combined hook plus keyword strategy. Only those subjects who reported postexperimentally that they had followed the strategy showed the benefits of both techniques in that they had the highest performance scores overall. Those who reported that they resorted to other strategies, apparently because of the complexity of the combined strategy, performed in a manner similar to the hook-strategy group.

The relevant theoretical point is that the hook technique is explicitly based on the bilingual dual coding model in that the associative learning experience requires use of imagery as well as intraverbal connections between the overlearned L_2 pegwords and the new L_2 target items. It thereby promotes the development of verbal-associative interconnections between different V_2 representations, and referential links between the V_2 representations and the imagery system. It also provides a basis for some development of direct V_1-V_2 interconnections in that L_1 translation equivalents must be presented on initial trials to give the meanings of the unfamiliar L_2 items. Retrieval of L_2 items on later trials could be based entirely on such V_1-V_2 connections, or on image-mediated associations between V_1 and V_2, or partly on each. Thus, the technique can be viewed as providing intraverbal- and nonverbal-associative contexts for learning a second language. The nonverbal context in particular is subject-generated and imaginal rather than situational, so its practical usefulness hinges on the degree to which imagery-based learning transfers to language comprehension and production in real-life contexts. That issue has not yet been studied experimentally in any systematic way.

The keyword and hook techniques do not exhaust the mnemonic strategies that could be developed on the basis of dual coding assumptions. For example, Raja Hammoud (1982) used dual coding ideas to develop an associative-field technique in which subjects study L_2 target items in verbal-associative and imagery contexts. Hammoud tested the technique with French-speaking university students who were studying Arabic as a foreign language. The verbal associates were based on association norms to Arabic target items and their French translation equivalents, obtained from native speakers of each language. The subjects learning Arabic as L_2 were presented an Arabic word together with its French translation and a set of associates drawn from both languages, but presented in French. The subjects were asked to construct a mental image to the set of associates and to rehearse the Arabic word silently. The major result was that the associative-field technique resulted in better vocabulary learning than hook, keyword, or control conditions. Learning was measured entirely by translation tests, so the hook technique (which is designed for number-cued retrieval) may have been disadvantaged in the experiment. Nonetheless, the effectiveness of Hammoud's innovative associative-field procedure is quite encouraging. Theoretically, the technique is designed to promote the development of interconnections between L_2 target items and image compounds in which a target's referent is embedded in a context of associated images relevant to both L_1 and L_2. The technique could be further extended to promote the development of rich intraverbal networks by including the associates themselves as to-be-learned L_2 items.

The preceding discussion dealt only with the learning of a second language vocabulary. Vocabulary learning is an important goal in itself—far more important and complex than is generally conceded by teachers of foreign languages. Nonetheless, second language learning obviously entails the learning of a grammatical system as well, and the question that arises in the present context is whether dual coding theory and related empirical procedures have anything to contribute to that goal.

The special relevance of the theory is that it draws attention to the importance of nonverbal-situational, cognitive, and behavioral contexts in the acquisition of all language skills, including syntax. This nonverbal-contextual emphasis is generally consistent with other current approaches that stress the role of experiential and semantic factors in language acquisition (see chap. 5, this volume; Paivio & Begg, 1981, chap. 10). More specifically, in dual coding terms, the development of grammatical skills involves formation of referential interconnections, not only between representations corresponding to objects and their names, but also between the abstract and dynamic attributes of objects (e.g., relations, transformations, actions) and their corresponding verbal descriptions. For example, the propositional relation in the sentence, "the pencil is on the book," maps onto a corresponding real or imaginal situation. Learning to understand and produce such expressions in a first or a second language accordingly requires experiential contiguity between the verbal expression and the situation as perceived or imagined, at least during the initial stage of learning. Later, such structural (grammatical) skills can be strengthened and expanded (generalized) through intraverbal experience alone—that is, new instances may be learned by reference to already developed intraverbal structures.

The empirical implication is that grammar learning should be facilitated by the use of appropriate nonverbal referent situations, pictures, or imagery. Some relevant evidence is available. Recall from chapter 5 that Moeser and Bregman (1973) investigated the learning of a miniature artificial language under conditions in which perceptual referents were provided or were absent. They found that learning was best when sentences constructed from nonsense words were presented along with pictures in which the syntactic constraints of the language were also mirrored in the logical constraints of the pictures. The authors concluded that semantic referents and imagery are necessary for the initial learning of syntax. Consistent with the dual coding view just presented, they also found that subsequent learning of the syntactic class membership of new words could be learned in a purely verbal context.

Another relevant example is the *total physical response strategy* for second language learning as studied by Asher (e.g., 1972). The strategy is aimed at developing listening skills by having learners act out responses to commands. Thus, it is essentially a pragmatic learning strategy in which language is studied in the context of nonverbal behaviors and appropriate situations. A number of second-language learning experiments (e.g., Asher, 1972) have shown that the strategy can be quite effective in comparison with some other standard second-language learning techniques, but its effectiveness needs to be studied further under carefully controlled experimental conditions and in comparison with other experimental strategies, including imagery mnemonics.

With the exception of Desrochers's (1982, 1983) promising application of the hook technique to the learning of French grammatical gender, imagery-based mnemonic strategies have not yet been applied systematically to the learning of grammatical skills. Other possibilities are suggested by my own use of the hook technique in language study. For example, I have used it to rehearse phrase structure, verb forms in sentence contexts, and idiomatic expressions in French. I found that I could represent the grammatical gender of nouns and the appropriate ordering of adjectives and nouns in the structure of mnemonic images, with a high rate of success in recalling long lists of phrases using the numbered hooks as retrieval cues. These personal observations are not a substitute for the experimental studies of the general problem, but they do indicate that such experiments are feasible.

In summary, we have considered a bilingual version of dual coding theory that has implications for the performance of bilingual individuals in a variety of semantic memory and episodic memory tasks that require the individual to respond selectively to pictorial or verbal stimuli.[3] The theory also leads to a strong emphasis on the role of situational contexts and imagery in second language learning. In particular, the theory suggests that language-learning strategies based on the systematic use of referent objects, pictures, activities, and mental imagery would be especially effective in promoting learning. I have interpreted the available research evidence to be generally supportive of the approach but there are discordant notes as well. Moreover, the research has only scratched the surface of the fundamental issues in this domain.

12
Neuropsychological Evidence

We turn finally to neuropsychological evidence concerning representational processes and dual coding theory. The evidence is provided by studies of functional differences between the two cerebral hemispheres and different regions within each hemisphere as inferred from performance on tasks that implicate verbal and nonverbal processes in different degrees. My selective treatment draws on recent experimental studies as well as reviews of the literature on the functional asymmetry of the normal brain (Bryden, 1982), effects of focal lesions (e.g., Milner, 1980), effects of commissurotomy (e.g., Gazzaniga & LeDoux, 1978), and interpretive summaries of the evidence on verbal and imagery processes in particular (Ley, 1983; Paivio & Begg, 1981; Paivio & te Linde, 1982). Studies of psychophysiological correlates of these processes raise a different (though related) set of issues and they are not covered here, though reviews are available elsewhere (e.g., Ley, 1983; McGuigan, 1978; Paivio, 1973; Zikmund, 1972).

The theoretical emphasis is on observations that bear on the verbal-nonverbal symbolic distinction, the more specific sensorimotor systems of which the symbolic systems are comprised, and the different levels of processing within and between systems. We shall also consider evidence relevant to specific functional distinctions, such as sequential as compared to synchronous or parallel processing.

BACKGROUND INFORMATION ON THE BRAIN AND METHODS OF STUDY

The evidence has to do mainly with neuroanatomical distinctions that are correlated with functional differences as revealed by behavioral studies. The general picture is that the two hemispheres of the brain are functionally asymmetrical, and different regions within each subserve different functions. More specifically, for most people, the left hemisphere dominates in the control of speech whereas the right hemisphere has the advantage in certain nonverbal tasks.

Functional asymmetries between the two hemispheres are revealed by studies of people with intact brains as well as patients with unilateral focal lesions, or patients in whom the corpus callosum that connects the two hemispheres has been severed. The intact brain studies are possible because sensory input to the two hemispheres is lateralized. Auditory information from each ear reaches both sides of the brain, but the contralateral input is stronger or more efficient than ipsilateral, so that right-ear input is processed more efficiently by the left hemisphere than by the right hemisphere, and vice versa for left-ear input. The visual pathways involve crossover of half of the sensory neurons from each retina so that an object seen to the right of the central fixation point (the right-visual hemifield) excites visual receiving areas in the left-visual cortex, and, conversely, for the left-visual field. Tactual information from the left and right hands is similarly processed relatively more efficiently by the contralateral hemisphere. Reciprocally, motor control is also contralateral, so that muscles on the right side of the body are controlled by the left hemisphere, and vice versa.

These neuroanatomical arrangements make it possible to present material selectively to either hemisphere for perceptual recognition or other kinds of cognitive processing. Dichotic listening tasks, in which each ear simultaneously receives different information, have been most common in the case of audition, although asymmetries are also revealed by presentations to one ear at a time. Visual studies have primarily relied on tachistoscopic presentation in which items are flashed briefly to one side of the fixation point, so that the stimulus has disappeared before the eyes have time to move. Tactual tasks entail presentation of "feelable" materials to one hand at a time.

The functions of different regions within each hemisphere have been inferred primarily from the results of studies of patients with focal lesions in different parts of one hemisphere or the other, resulting from brain injury or surgery. The best controlled studies have used patients with well-defined lesion resulting from surgery performed to relieve such problems as severe epileptic seizures. Some (mostly confirmatory) evidence has also emerged from studies in which regional activity in the normal brain has been inferred from patterns of electrical activity as measured by the EEG and regional changes in cortical blood flow revealed by radioactive isotopes.

The above summary provides sufficient background for present purposes. Readers wishing more detailed information on methodology can find it in the sources cited earlier. We now turn to the highlights of research findings that bear on the relevant theoretical issues.

INDEPENDENT VERBAL AND NONVERBAL SYMBOLIC SYSTEMS

All sources of evidence support the conclusion that different parts of the brain are specialized for processing verbal and nonverbal information or, more correctly stated, for processing stimulus information verbally or nonverbally. The latter statement is more consistent with the dual coding view that contextual and focal stimulus materials vary in the probability with which they activate verbal and nonverbal (imagery) representations and processes related to them. That interpretation is taken for granted in the following summary.

It is widely accepted that the two hemispheres are functionally differentiated so that, for most people the left hemisphere controls speech and is more efficient than the right hemisphere in a variety of tasks with verbal material, including perceptual recognition, episodic memory performance, and comprehension. Conversely, the right hemisphere has the advantage in certain tasks with nonverbal materials, such as face identification, recognition of nonverbal sounds, and memory for faces and other spatial patterns. These conclusions hold for different sensory modalities—visual, auditory, tactual—thereby justifying the generalization that the distinction is a verbal-nonverbal symbolic one that cuts across sensory modalities.

The correlation of hemispheric functional asymmetries with the verbal or nonverbal nature of materials is important evidence in itself for the general independence assumption of dual coding theory. The independence can be seen most clearly in the case of episodic memory performance among patients with focal lesions in the right- or left-temporal lobes, where a double dissociation is observed so that those with left-temporal lesions show deficits (relative to normal subjects) in verbal memory tasks but not in nonverbal ones, and vice versa for those with right-temporal lesions. However, it is not crucial for dual coding theory that the functional differences be divided neatly between the two hemispheres. Any anatomical-regional correlation with performance on verbal and nonverbal tasks can be equally informative theoretically. In fact, the right-left distinction is qualified in a number of ways that are relevant to dual coding theory.

One of the important qualifications is that pictures of common objects apparently can be perceptually recognized equally well regardless of which hemisphere receives the information. The evidence comes from lateralized presentation to one or the other hemifield of normal subjects as well as split-brain patients. In the case of normals, no asymmetry is observed even when the subjects are required to indicate their recognition by naming the presented picture. In the case of the split-brain subjects, right-hemisphere recognition is indicated by their ability to pick out a corresponding object tactually from a number of alternatives but not by naming, whereas left-hemisphere recognition can be indicated either tactually or by naming. We can conclude from such observations that both hemispheres must contain representational systems necessary for visual recognition of common objects. Note again that this conclusion contrasts with the left-hemisphere superiority typically observed for visually presented verbal material, such as letters or words.

Hemispheric functional asymmetry might also be qualified by word concreteness in a way that is consistent with the above interpretation. A number of tachistoscopic recognition studies have shown that word concreteness and visual field interacted so that abstract words yielded the usual right-field (left-hemisphere) superiority, whereas concrete words were recognized equally well in either field. Strong generalizations are as yet unwarranted because other studies have demonstrated right-field superiority for both concrete and abstract words (e.g., Boles, 1983). Nonetheless, the perceptual asymmetry appears to be less consistent for concrete than for abstract words. This tentative conclusion is buttressed by the finding that so-called deep-dyslexic patients, with wide-spread lesions in the left hemisphere, generally have greater difficulty reading abstract, low imagery words than concrete high imagery words (see Coltheart, Patterson & Marshall, 1980; Paivio & te Linde, 1982), suggesting that the intact right hemisphere somehow permits more efficient visual processing of concrete than abstract words.

Different interpretations have been suggested for the above effects. One is that imagery contributes to right-hemisphere reading of concrete words and that the right hemisphere is superior in imagery processing. Another is that lexical representations are equally available in both hemispheres in the case of concrete but not abstract words (e.g., Ley & Bryden, 1983). I tentatively favor a variant of the second interpretation (cf. Paivio & te Linde, 1982), one that is consistent also with the absence of perceptual asymmetry for pictures of common objects: Representations for high imagery words and the concrete objects to which they refer are available in both hemispheres, whereas representations for low imagery words are more available in the left than the right hemisphere.

The data and the hypothesis concerning object representations need to be reconciled with the observation that episodic memory performance for nonverbal stimuli is impaired by lesions to the right- (but not the left-) temporal lobe. This generalization also needs to be qualified, however, in that the differential hemispheric impairment has been observed for such materials as geometric figures, faces, and nonsense figures, but not familiar objects. For example, a study by Jaccarino (1975, cited in Milner, 1980) showed a slight impairment in immediate free recall of drawings of common objects among patients with left- but not right-temporal lobectomies; on a delayed-recall test 24 hours later, both groups showed pronounced impairment relative to controls. Jaccarino interpreted the immediate recall results in terms of a left-temporal deficit in evoking names, and the delayed-recall results partly in terms of a right-temporal deficit in evoking visual images. The point to be noticed here is that no *differential* right-temporal deficit occurred at either delay, which is consistent with the interpretation that systems for memory processing of common visual objects are available in (or are activated by) the left as well as the right hemisphere. In apparent contrast, Whitehouse (1981) found that patients with anterior right-hemisphere damage had better recognition memory for words than for pictures of nameable objects, whereas left-hemisphere patients did better with pictures than words. Comparing across groups, the right-hemisphere group was superior to the left-hemisphere group with words, but inferior with pictures. The same pattern of results occurred using abstract pictures and abstract words. Whitehouse

(1981) interpreted these and other results from two experiments to be consistent with predictions from dual coding theory. However, we are left somewhat uncertain concerning hemispheric differences in memory for common objects, given the procedural differences that accompanied the different pattern of results in Jaccarino's and Whitehouse's studies.

To summarize the effects of stimulus materials, we find consistent evidence for a selective right-hemisphere role in memory for geometric forms, faces, and nonsense figures, and less consistent evidence for a similar asymmetry in the case of memory for common objects. The pattern is similar to the one that emerges from perceptual recognition studies, in which geometric forms, etc., are recognized better by the right hemisphere, whereas common objects are recognized equally well by each hemisphere. Thus, both hemispheres may be able to deal efficiently with familiar objects in episodic memory tasks as well as in a task (perceptual recognition) that is dependent on the availability of representations in semantic memory. I will discuss the implications of that point further after considering some additional data.

The above generalizations concern effects of stimulus materials. Hemispheric asymmetries have also been obtained with verbal and imagery tasks. Jones-Gotman and Milner (1978) compared a group of right-temporal lobectemy patients and matched controls on paired-associate learning of separate lists of concrete and abstract word pairs. The subjects were instructed to use mediating images to learn the concrete pairs and sentences to link the abstract pairs. The results were that the right-temporal patients recalled significantly fewer responses than the control group with the image-linked concrete pairs, but the two groups performed equally well with the sentence-linked abstract pairs. The authors concluded that the right-temporal deficit found for concrete pairs must be attributed to the visual component of the imagery mnemonic. Thus, although the material was verbal, the right-hemisphere memory deficit under imagery instructions was similar to the selective deficit in memory for nonverbal materials typically observed with such patients. The right-hemisphere deficit also contrasts with the observation that left-temporal lobectomy patients perform more poorly than controls in memory tasks using verbal material (whether concrete or abstract) in the absence of imagery instructions. These and other findings described in the reviews cited earlier (e.g., Bryden, 1982) suggest that the hemispheric asymmetries reflect the manner in which materials are processed rather than differences in the type of material per se, although stimulus materials obviously affect the probability that verbal and nonverbal representations and processes will be activated and thereby affect memory performance.

What about the left-temporal lobe and imagery instructions? Earlier research by Jones-Gotman (Jones, 1974) showed that patients with lesions in the left-temporal lobe were able to improve their performance in a verbal paired-associate learning task when they were instructed to use imagery mnemonics. Thus, they were able to compensate partly for their verbal memory impairment, presumably by tapping the intact episodic memory systems in (or accessed via) the right-temporal lobe. In that study, however, right-temporal lobectomy patients also benefited from imagery instruction. Jones-Gotman and Milner (1978) attributed the failure to demonstrate a right-hemisphere imagery deficit to the use of short lists that did not tax memory processes enough to reveal an imagery deficit, but this interpretation does not seem to account adequately for the *gain* in performance under imagery instructions. We are left with the possibility that the intact left-temporal lobe contributed to the imagery-mnemonic effect, or that the imagery-mnemonic instructions also activated left-hemisphere verbal processes that were effective in mediating recall. These uncertainties remain unresolved at this time and so we cannot be sure of the relative degree to which each hemisphere contributes to the effectiveness of imagery in episodic memory for verbal material, although there is some evidence that the right hemisphere may have a slight advantage.

The above data should not be taken to mean that imagery processing is predominantly a right-hemisphere function, as is often suggested. The findings pertain specifically to the role of imagery in storage and retrieval of episodic memory information. Other aspects of imagery processing may be carried out equally well by each hemisphere, or asymmetries may implicate areas other than the temporal lobes. The imagery-mnemonic studies in fact suggest that imagery encoding can occur in either hemisphere. Specifically, left-temporal and right-temporal lobe patients alike were able to respond appropriately to instructions to construct images of the referents of concrete word-pairs, including being able to describe their images. The right-hemisphere impairment observed by Jones-Gotman and Milner (1978) showed up only in image-mediated retrieval, at least as far as one can tell from the data. The semantic memory representations and processes necessary for *generating* nonverbal-visual images may be available in both hemispheres.

A study by Wilkins and Moscovitch (1978) provides relevant evidence. Patients with their left- or right-temporal lobes removed and normal controls were tested on two semantic memory tasks. One, a variant of the symbolic size-comparison task described in chapter 9, required the patients to classify a series of common objects (some presented as words and others as line drawings) as larger or smaller than a chair. Wilkins and Moscovitch assumed that performance on the size-classification task was mediated by a nonverbal analogue system. The other task, presumably dependent on verbal processing, required the patients to classify objects as living or manufactured. The results showed no impairment in either patient group in the size-classification task, but those with left-temporal removals were inferior to the other subjects in the living-manufactured classification task. These findings suggest that semantic systems that use visual analogue representations are equally represented in each hemisphere, whereas semantic systems that use verbal representations are asymmetrically represented so that the left hemisphere dominates in verbal semantic memory tasks as it does in the case of episodic verbal memory.

Other studies suggest that the parietal and occipital regions of the right hemisphere may be differentially implicated in some tasks that depend on nonverbal semantic memory representations and processes (Paivio & te Linde, 1982, pp. 263–265). Studies of patients with lateralized cerebral lesions have shown that lesions in the posterior regions of the right hemisphere are associated with poor performance (relative to controls) in such tasks as mental rotation, tactual spatial learning, and perceptual closure. Patients with posterior lesions in the left hemisphere and those with lesions in more anterior regions of either hemisphere are unimpaired or less impaired in such tasks. These results suggest that nonverbal-visual imagery processes may be more strongly based in the right-parietal and occipital lobes than in other regions. However, studies that have relied on evidence of conscious imagery as reported by patients have also indicated loss of reported imagery from lesions to the left-occipital lobe. This loss could be taken to mean that imagery information is simply inaccessible to the verbal system because of the left-hemisphere damage, but the preferred interpretation by the researchers who conducted the imagery studies (e.g., Bisiach, Capitani, Luzzatti, & Perani, 1981) is that the neural processes responsible for the generation of visual-spatial images are available in both hemispheres (see also Kosslyn, Holtzman, Farah, & Gazzaniga, 1985).

We can conclude generally that the two hemispheres are differentially implicated in verbal and nonverbal tasks. The left hemisphere dominates in verbal tasks, whether these entail episodic or semantic memory processes, whereas the right hemisphere dominates or both hemispheres contribute equally to performance in nonverbal tasks, including those that implicate conscious imagery. These conclusions are supported as well by evidence from EEG studies and other approaches to the study of brain function (Ley, 1983). The important point for our purposes is that the differing efficiency of the two hemispheres in tasks involving verbal and nonverbal materials or processes is strong evidence for the dual coding assumption that the two symbolic systems are functionally independent. The results also point clearly to the interconnectedness of systems in that sometimes the nonverbal system is activated by verbal input (as in the imagery-mnemonic studies with temporal lobe and other patient groups), and at other times the verbal system is activated by nonverbal input (as in perceptual recognition studies that require object pictures to be named). Evidence on the nature of such interconnections will be examined in more detail following a brief discussion of the relation between sensory modalities and the verbal-nonverbal representation distinction.

SENSORY VERSUS SYMBOLIC MODALITIES

The dual coding assumption that symbolic and sensory modalities are orthogonal implies a functional dissociation whereby different brain areas predominate in processing material presented in different sensory modalities when symbolic modality remains constant, or vice versa. We have already encountered examples of such dissociation. For example, pictures of familiar objects are recognized equally well when presented to either hemisphere whereas their printed names are recognized better when presented to the left hemisphere (right-visual field). Thus, hemispheric functional asymmetry varies with the verbal-nonverbal symbolic distinction when sensory modality is constant. The reverse pattern has also been observed. A variety of nonverbal sounds are recognized better by the left ear (right hemisphere) than by the right ear in a dichotic listening task (see Bryden, 1982). It is especially noteworthy that the asymmetry has been observed for such environmental sounds as a car starting, a toilet flushing, and tooth brushing (Curry, 1967), which are associated with familiar objects. This hemispheric asymmetry in recognition of sounds contrasts with the symmetry observed with visually presented pictures of objects. In this case, therefore, the pattern of asymmetries varies with sensory modality when symbolic modality is held constant.

Yet another pattern has been observed with dichhaptic tasks, in which subjects palpate forms with each hand: A left-hand (right-hemisphere) advantage has been found for the recognition of nonsense forms and other stimuli that are not easily named, and a right-hand (left-hemisphere) advantage for letter forms (Bryden, 1982, pp. 92–98). The dissociation pattern would be more directly relevant here if it could be demonstrated for familiar objects and their haptically presented names (e.g., raised print), but such a study apparently has not been done.

The dissociated patterns of hemispheric asymmetries are consistent with the dual coding assumption that symbolic and sensory modalities are functionally orthogonal. The objection might be raised that variation in sensory modality does not necessarily mean that processing has also varied. Neuropsychologists typically assume, for example, that processing of familiar objects and patterns may show left-hemisphere advantages or no asymmetry, despite their nonverbal nature, because such stimuli are easily named and likely to be processed verbally. In a sense, that interpretation simply restates the dual coding point that the verbal-nonverbal symbolic distinction is independent of (orthogonal to) the sensory modalities. However, dual coding theory goes farther than that, for it also implies that the cognitive representations corresponding to verbal and nonverbal events are themselves functionally specific and variable with respect to sensory modality. Thus, printed words must activate neuronal systems specialized for visual processing of word patterns (visual logogens), whereas spoken words activate systems specialized for auditory processing of word patterns (auditory logogens). These neuronal systems are language related by definition and they are independent in the sense that localized brain damage can affect one without affecting the other, at least to the same degree. For example, a patient may be unable to read words following the occurrence of a focal lesion while remaining relatively unimpaired in comprehension of speech.

The visual and auditory representational systems presumably converge on a common verbal output system. The same analysis applies to nonverbal stimuli: Different brain areas are specialized for processing the different input modalities, and these areas may differ from the corresponding modality-specific verbal ones. The nonverbal-representational sites can also be connected to neural pathways that converge on a verbal output system. This common verbal output system, too, is modality specific (i.e., it is a motor system) and it is the dual coding candidate for the common verbal processing system referred to in the neuropsychological literature. Again, a parallel case can be made for separate nonverbal output systems, which may be more variable in nature than those that control speech.

The above description of independent systems will be clarified further when we consider the neuropsychological evidence relevant to the functional interconnections (traditionally known as association pathways) between the different modality-specific representational systems. The analysis bears directly on the dual coding assumptions concerning functional interconnections and the different levels of processing that they implicate.

REPRESENTATIONAL, REFERENTIAL, AND ASSOCIATIVE INTERCONNECTIONS

The structural and processing levels that are postulated in dual coding theory correspond closely to some traditional distinctions in the neuropsychological literature (e.g., Luria, 1973), which have been based on particular neurological syndromes and which continue to be supported by recent observations. We deal briefly with the representational level and then more fully with the correlates of the other two levels.

Recall that representational processing refers to the activation of logogens or imagens by corresponding verbal and nonverbal stimuli. The operational behavioral specification of such processing is the recognition of a stimulus. Neurologically, such representational processing implicates sensory pathways from the relevant receptors to the representational sites in the cortex. The neuropsychological evidence for representational processing is the selective failure to recognize specific classes of stimuli that follows damage to the representational sites or the pathways leading to them. For example, lesions of the parieto-occipital regions of the left hemisphere may impair the recognition of written language without similarly affecting object recognition and, conversely, lesions in corresponding zones of the right hemisphere can lead to selective impairments in face recognition, the ability to draw, and so on (Luria, 1973, pp. 237–239).

Referential and associative interconnections can be inferred from functional losses that occur when the brain damage leaves stimulus recognition intact while impairing further processing by another system. These disturbances are commonly described as functional dissociations or disconnection syndromes (Geschwind, 1965; Luria, 1973). One of the most common examples is anomia, the loss of ability to name objects that the patient can recognize (as indicated, for example, by appropriate use of the object), and despite the fact that the patient can also produce the names to printed words or in appropriate intraverbal contexts. The symptoms may also include disturbances of the ability to produce visual images to words as revealed, for example, by the patient's inability to draw named objects while retaining the ability to copy pictured objects (Luria, 1973, pp. 145–146). Associated with lesions of the posterior regions of the left-temporal lobe, such syndromes constitute clear evidence for referential interconnections. The following studies show that such between-system neurological and functional interconnections can be distinguished from within-system (associative) connections.

Beauvois (1982) described a particularly clear case of optic aphasia or visual anomia, which she characterized as "a disturbance between visual semantics and verbal semantics, both of which operate normally" (p. 35). The inference was based on a carefully constructed series of tests that were designed to reveal the level of the process that was impaired. Thus, some tests were intended to be purely verbal in the sense that the test items were presented verbally and the answer depended on verbal-associative knowledge (e.g., "What color-name is generally associated with envy?"). The brain-damaged patient performed very well on these tests, indicating that she did not suffer from aphasia for color-names. In dual coding terms, verbal-representational and verbal-associative levels of processing were intact.

Other tests were purely visual (nonverbal) in that the stimulus, the response, and the inferred mediating process required to perform the task were visual. Toward this end, the patient was discouraged from verbalizing, and the tests were designed so that they could be completed without any verbal processing. For example, one test required color matching and another required the patient to point to the correctly colored picture of an object (e.g., a traffic sign) from a set of five pictures of the same object. In these tests, too, the patient performed almost at ceiling, indicating that her nonverbal color and associated object processing systems were unimpaired. In dual coding terms, nonverbal-representational and associative levels of processing systems were intact.

A third series consisted of visuo-verbal tests in which the stimulus and response differed in modality. In one version, the patient was required to name colors presented alone or as attributes of objects, and in the other, to point to a color when asked to do so (e.g., "Show me what color a cherry is"). Her performance on these tests was "drastically impaired" (29% correct as compared to almost 100% correct on the visual tests), indicating that referential processing systems had suffered damage.

Impaired referential processing was also revealed by tests in which the stimuli and responses were both verbal or both visual-nonverbal, but where verbal-nonverbal processing was induced by the nature of the test question or processing instructions. It was assumed, for example, that a correct answer to the question, "Tell me what color a gherkin is," would require visual imagery. Similarly, instructions to "imagine a beautiful snowy landscape" should induce an imagery strategy when answering the question, "Tell me what color snow is." Again, performance under such cross-modal processing conditions was significantly lower than when similar questions could be answered by means of a verbal strategy alone (e.g., "What do people say when they are asked what color snow is?").

In summary, the results reported by Beauvois can be taken as neuropsychological evidence for the different kinds of interconnections and levels of processing assumed in dual coding theory. Specifically, referential processing in both the verbal-visual (nonverbal) and visual-verbal direction was affected by neurological damage, whereas verbal-associative processing and visual- (nonverbal) associative processing were not similarly affected. Analogous crossmodal syndromes have been described for tactile and auditory modalities (see Beauvois, 1982, pp. 38–39), suggesting that verbal-nonverbal functional interconnections are differentiated by sensory modality as well.

The empirical and theoretical picture would be complete if neuropsychological research also provided clear evidence that verbal-associative and nonverbal-associative processing can be selectively impaired independent of the referential level and each other. The evidence would have to show, for example, that nonverbal associations are disrupted, whereas object naming and verbal-associative abilities remain unimpaired. Clear data of this kind are lacking, although some results are at least suggestive of the appropriate patterns. Luria (1973, pp. 239–240) described a form of a syndrome called associative mental blindness, observed among patients with lesions of the parieto-occipital areas of the right hemisphere, which is characterized by the inability to relate objects to experiences normally associated with them. These patients manifest an "uncontrollable emergence of irrelevant associations" that suggests a disruption of nonverbal-associative systems, although we cannot be sure that the disturbance was nonverbal because the inference was based partly on verbal responses.

Some recent experimental studies provide some evidence for selective associative disturbances. Whitehouse, Caramazza, and Zurif (cited in Caramazza & Berndt, 1978, pp. 906–907) compared aphasics with anterior or posterior hemispheric damage on a task that required the patients to name pictures that were variants of a modal cup, so that some looked like bowls and others like glasses. The interesting result was that the anterior aphasics were like normal speakers in that they named clear examples consistently and borderline ones inconsistently, whereas posterior aphasics named all items inconsistently or based their name selection on one feature, such as the presence or absence of a handle. The authors concluded that the naming difficulty demonstrated by the posterior aphasics was due to their inability to differentiate among members of the semantic category, food containers, rather than a failure to activate intact word representations to the stimuli. Accordingly, their problem could be interpreted as a disruption of processing at the nonverbal-associative level rather than the referential level. Since the problem manifested itself in naming difficulty, however, the referential and associative levels are not clearly differentiated. Other data summarized by Caramazza and Berndt (1978) are suggestive of impairments in verbal semantic (verbal-associative) processing, but nonverbal-associative and referential processes may be implicated as well.

SEQUENTIAL VERSUS SYNCHRONOUS PROCESSING

This section reviews neuropsychological evidence relevant to the dual coding distinction between sequential and synchronous processing. Recall from chapter 4 that the sequential processing capacity of the verbal system is assumed to be linked particularly to auditory-motor verbal representations and processes so that, even in the case of printed words and visually imaged words, verbal processing is sequentially constrained despite the visual character of the target representation. Conversely, synchronous processing implicates visual and haptic modalities, particularly as applied to spatial processing of nonverbal stimuli, although visual letters can also be treated as spatial objects. One important characteristic of synchronous processing is relative freedom from sequential constraints. Another is that relatively complex representational information can be processed as an integrated unit—commonly referred to as holistic or gestalt processing in the neuropsychological literature, and even more appropriately as simultaneous synthesis in Luria's (1973) analysis.

A general association between verbal mechanisms and sequential processing has been demonstrated by the finding that patients with damage to left-hemisphere speech areas are also impaired in tasks requiring temporal discriminations even when the stimuli are nonverbal events such as light flashes and sounds (e.g., Efron, 1963). A similar conclusion is justified by dichotic listening studies, which show that discriminations of temporal order and duration are more accurate when the stimuli are presented to the right ear (left hemisphere) than when presented to the left ear (Mills & Rollman, 1979, 1980). Such studies suggest that the sequential processing capacity of the verbal system derives from a more general temporal processing capacity for which the left hemisphere is somehow specialized. The left-temporal lobe in particular appears to be crucial in the sequential organization of speech, probably through a combination of motor and acoustic control processes (Kimura, 1982).

Other results suggest that the frontal lobes play a special role in episodic memory for the temporal order of events. Corsi (described in Milner, 1973) found that patients with damage to the left-frontal lobe were selectively impaired in their ability to remember the temporal order in which two words had been presented. Conversely, right-frontal lobe patients were impaired in a comparable task with abstract nonverbal stimuli. Neither group was impaired in recognition memory for the items themselves. In contrast, patients with lesions in the left- or right-temporal lobe showed no impairment in memory for sequential order but did show their usual material-specific deficits in memory for items.

Complications aside, the evidence as a whole suggests that anterior regions of the left hemisphere are functionally dominant in a variety of tasks that require sequential processing, particularly in the case of speech and perceptual and memory processing of verbal stimuli. Thus, consistent with dual coding theory, the verbal system appears to be represented in part by sensory and motor structures that are specialized for sequential processing.

The contrasting synchronous processing functions of the brain appear to be associated with posterior regions of both hemispheres. Luria (1973, chap. 5) reported that structures located in the parieto-temporal-occipital boundary regions of the cortex are crucial to what he described as the organization of complex simultaneous (spatial) syntheses, including integration of information from different sensory modalities ("inter-analyser syntheses"). Such functions are suggested by a complex group of disorders of spatial organization among patients with lesions in those areas. These functions appear to pose a problem for dual coding theory because they implicate verbal as well as nonverbal abilities. Thus, some patients with posterior lesions are unable to distinguish such logico-grammatical relations as "the father's brother," "cross below square," and "spring before summer" from their reversals (e.g., "the brother's father"). This apparent inconsistency with dual coding theory can be reconciled by assuming that prepositional relations and many other verbally expressed logical relationships are based on nonverbal spatial cognition (cf. H. Clark, 1973). Consistent with such a view, Luria noted that a disturbance in the ability to understand such logical constructions involves a "defect of perception of simultaneous spatial structures, but transferred to a higher (symbolic) level" (1973, p. 154).

Although both hemispheres contribute to synchronous processing, there is increasing evidence of lateralization of such functions. Thus, effects of lateralized presentation of materials to normal subjects as well as selective performance effects among split-brain patients or ones with focal brain lesions suggest that the right (posterior) hemisphere dominates in perceptual recognition, memory, and other cognitive tasks that require processing of spatial information. In some tasks this asymmetry is specific to certain classes of nonverbal stimuli, whereas in others it appears to be more general. For example, the right hemisphere appears to excel in the case of visual recognition of faces, particularly their holistic or gestalt properties (Sergent, 1984), but not other familiar objects. The right-hemisphere superiority appears to be more general in such spatial memory tasks as memory for geometric figures, faces, and nonsense figures, as well as in learning of tactile and visual mazes (see Paivio & te Linde, 1982). Right-hemisphere superiority has also been shown from performance in perceptual closure and spatial manipulation tests. Such asymmetrical effects occur for tactile as well as visual tasks. The pattern recognition, closure, and manipulation tasks implicate the right-parietal and temporo-occipital regions in particular.

In summary, the right-hemisphere functions are suggestive of representational and processing systems that are specialized for dealing with synchronously organized structural information that is simultaneously available for processing, or on which simultaneously (synchronously) functioning processes operate. These functions are often contrasted with verbal, sequential, and analytic functions ascribed to the left hemisphere. The descriptive contrasts have additional connotations as well, but their core component is consistent with the synchronous-sequential functional contrast of dual coding theory.

REPRESENTATION OF EMOTION

The dual coding view as presented in chapter 4 was that affective and emotional reactions become associated primarily with the nonverbal-representational system because they are learned in the context of nonverbal events. Accordingly, learned affective reactions to stimuli are generally mediated by imagens with high probability connections to primary affective systems. It was also suggested, however, that words could acquire generalized affect-arousing qualities analogous to referential meaning, in which the referential reaction is a particular emotion. The analysis was based mainly on such data as reaction time for comparisons of pictures and words on pleasantness (see chap. 9). Here we consider relevant neuropsychological findings.

Bryden and Ley (1983) reviewed various kinds of evidence suggesting that the right hemisphere is particularly involved in the perception and expression of emotion. Their own research using visual and auditory lateralized presentation procedures suggested that the right hemisphere is superior to the left in tasks requiring the subject to match emotional facial expressions, categorize the emotional tone of musical passages, and judge the emotional tone of sentences. A linkage with right-hemisphere imagery systems was suggested by a priming study. Subjects first memorized a list of high imagery or low imagery words that also varied in affective value. This procedure was intended to induce the subjects to think about emotional material and thereby produce activity in the right hemisphere. The subjects then participated in a face-recognition or dichotic listening experiment using affective material. The results were that studying either positive or negative word lists resulted in relative improvement in left-visual field (right-hemisphere) recognition of emotional facial expressions and in the left-ear (right-hemisphere) recognition of dichotically presented emotional words. Moreover, the right-hemisphere enhancement was greater when the memorized (priming) word list consisted of high imagery words than when it consisted of low imagery words.

Bryden and Ley suggested that the priming results become quite explicable if they are analyzed in terms of dual coding theory combined with Zajonc's (1980) views concerning affective components of stimuli. Thus,

> Study of a high-imagery list of emotional words leads to a representation of the word list that includes not only verbal coding mechanisms that presumably are represented in the left hemisphere, but also imagery-based and affective components that are localized to the right hemisphere. Thus, relative to a neutral word list, there is greater activity in the right hemisphere than in the left when either high-imagery or highly emotional words have been presented. This increased right-hemispheric activity makes the right hemisphere more receptive to incoming stimuli, and consequently produces relatively better performance in the left visual field or at the left ear, performance better than that which is observed when word lists not having imagery or affective components are studied. (1983, p.38)

I would add only a cautionary note concerning the implication that imagery is a right-hemisphere phenomenon. The evidence reviewed earlier suggested that imagery activity could occur in either hemisphere. Accordingly, the Bryden and Ley results should be interpreted to mean that affective imagery in particular is a right-hemisphere function. In any case, the operational link between affect, imagery, and right-hemisphere efficiency is consistent with aspects of the dual coding approach to emotion. The evidence is less strong in regard to the possibility of direct affective arousal by abstract verbal representations.

GENERAL THEORETICAL IMPLICATIONS

The evidence reviewed in this chapter provides considerable support for the major assumptions of dual coding theory. The assumption of functionally independent verbal- and nonverbal-representational and processing systems is supported by material and task-specific functional asymmetries of the two cerebral hemispheres. That the independent systems are nonetheless interconnected is supported by studies with split-brain patients and those with lesions in certain brain areas who are able to recognize and remember objects without being able to identify their names, or are able to use words in verbal contexts without being able to associate them consistently with their referents. Such data also constitute partial support for the distinctions between representational, referential, and associative processing in that the interconnections are inferred from impairments that specifically affect referential processing without affecting representational or within-system associative levels of processing to the same degree. Some observations are also consistent with the assumption that the verbal-nonverbal symbolic distinction is orthogonal or partly orthogonal to sensory systems. More generally, the data that support the orthogonality assumption indicate a high degree of modality specificity in the representational and processing functions of different brain regions.

How do theories of the propositional-computational type fare in light of the neuropsychological evidence? Not very well at first sight, for it is difficult to see how the assumption of a unimodal (or amodal) representational system could account for the high degree of functional specialization of different parts of the brain, correlated with distinctions in sensory as well as symbolic modalities. There also seems to be no clear neuropsychological evidence for a completely amodal representational system.

Still, propositional theories are so flexible that they can be accommodated to the data. J. R. Anderson, for example, suggested that studies on hemispheric specialization are indecisive because it can always be argued that propositions encoding visual information or procedures for processing such information are stored in the right hemisphere and propositions encoding verbal information or relevant procedures are stored in the left hemisphere (1978, pp. 271–272). However, such an argument amounts to redefining the dual coding distinction in a way that makes the propositional view formally equivalent to dual coding theory, which assumes representational and functional (procedural) distinctions at the outset. The redefinition proposed by Anderson is entirely terminological, without any special predictive or explanatory consequences that would differentiate it from dual coding theory unless the propositional version also includes assumptions about the informational content and procedures associated with visual-spatial and verbal propositional systems that differ from those associated with the present (nonpropositional) dual coding theory. This has not yet been done in any systematic way. Propositional theories have been based instead on the assumption of an absence of distinctions in representational information and procedures where dual coding draws sharp distinctions, as in tasks contrasting verbal and nonverbal stimuli or processing modes. The neuropsychological evidence is clearly more consistent with the latter view than with the former.

NEUROPSYCHOLOGICAL THEORIES AND COGNITION

We end this final chapter and the book with a brief consideration of neuropsychological theories as they pertain to cognition in general and dual coding theory in particular. A number of specific hypotheses have been mentioned, such as the functional distinctions between the two hemispheres, the role of the hippocampus in episodic memory, the sequential processing function associated with the region of the left hemisphere that deals with motor and acoustic aspects of language stimuli and behavior, and so on. Such hypotheses are directed at aspects of brain organization and processing mechanisms but they are not general neuropsychological theories of cognition. The best known systematic attempt at such a general theory is Hebb's (1949, 1980) cell-assembly model, in which phenomena ranging from perception of simple figures or qualities to abstract ideas, encompassing imagery and language in their scope, are interpreted in terms of the activity of hierarchically organized neural systems in memory, association, and motor areas of the cortex. The theories proposed by Arnold (1960), Beritoff (1965), and Pribram (1971) are also relevant because imagery is one of the problems they are intended to explain. An attempt by Parkins (1982) to synthesize the available neuropsychological information into a general theory of brain and mind is even more relevant because it distinguishes between two basic forms of representation that are functionally analogous to the nonverbal and verbal systems in dual coding theory. Parkins's approach is too speculative as yet to warrant a detailed discussion here, but it exemplifies the kind of analysis and synthesis that might be required for a comprehensive neuropsychological theory of mental representations and processes.

TOWARD A NEUROPSYCHOLOGICAL DUAL CODING MODEL

This chapter aimed primarily to review evidence relevant to dual coding rather than to develop a neuropsychological dual coding model, but a tentative outline of those theoretical aspects that implicate the cerebral hemispheres can be suggested in a way that serves also to summarize the data.

The representational and processing levels of the two symbolic systems along with organizational distinctions form the basis of the theory. Multimodal cognitive representations that store information about nonverbal objects and events become established in posterior and central cortical areas closely associated with the primary sensory systems. Their multimodal character is a result of repeated and varied sensory and motor experiences that create synchronously organized or integrated cortical representations in which component information in any modality (visual, auditory, haptic, olfactory, gustatory) can activate a larger holistic representation. Association pathways also develop between different representations within and between hemispheres, so that activation of one representation can activate another with greater or lesser probability, depending on the nature of contextual sensory information. Such representations and associations develop in both hemispheres, but one hemisphere (usually the right) becomes more proficient in integrative, associative, and transformational activities involving those representations. Accordingly, posterior regions in particular play a basic functional role in perceptual tasks dependent on the availability and use of visual information and integrative processing of spatial information in long-term memory. Activity in those cortical-representational systems also forms the basis of consciously experienced visual imagery.

Modality-specific systems that represent and process verbal information are similarly established in the auditory-motor areas of the cortex, particularly in the left hemisphere. The internal organization of these representations is sequential in the sense that their activation is sequentially constrained. Similarly, interunit associative activity is successive and reflects the sequential constraints of linguistic experience, which in turn are based on the temporal and sequential aspects of acoustic patterns and motor activity. Their neuroanatomical location is necessarily distinct from those for nonverbal-visual representations because different modalities are involved, and because the organizational properties of the representational systems are basically incompatible with each other. Distinct visual representations corresponding to printed words also develop in more posterior areas, and their processing is partly constrained by their associative cortical links with the auditory-motor verbal system so that they are more readily processed in a left-to-right spatial order, although they can also be processed as spatial entities.

Verbal-nonverbal referential experience results in the development of associative pathways between the visual-spatial nonverbal neural representations located in postcentral regions and the more frontal auditory-motor verbal representations, primarily in the left hemisphere. Functional connections also develop between verbal representations and nonverbal representations corresponding to other sensory modalities (auditory, haptic) located more centrally. These interconnections make it possible for words and descriptions to evoke nonverbal perceptual imagery in whatever modality, and to initiate relevant organizational and transformational activity (e.g., image rotation). Conversely, objects or images experienced in different modalities can be named or described. The multimodal nature of the referential interconnections is enriched still further by the integrative neural associations between the different sensory components of nonverbal objects as represented in either hemisphere, so that referential activity could occur via indirect pathways between and within the two hemispheres if more direct pathways are damaged.

Episodic memory functions are subserved by different brain areas, with the temporal lobe (and hippocampus in particular) being a crucial site for item memory—the left, for verbal items and the right, for nonverbal items. Thus, whatever information is necessary for remembering specific nonverbal perceptual events or linguistic events is somehow transmitted to (or recoded in) hippocampal and related structures and stored there for a time. Alternatively, the hippocampus might play a crucial role in the retrieval of such information from other storage systems, or may facilitate encoding in other areas of the brain (for a review of various possibilities, see Moscovitch, 1979). Information generated from long-term memory representations, such as images aroused by words or names aroused by objects, would be similarly transmitted to the hippocampal episodic memory system. That is, mental images and mental words are themselves neural events that can be stored and retrieved (see the earlier discussion in chap. 8).

In contrast to the item-specific episodic memory functions of the temporal lobes, the frontal lobes seem to be more crucial in memory for the sequential order of discrete items, again with the hemispheres being functionally differentiated in terms of the verbal-nonverbal contrast. This frontal specialization for sequential memory may be a neuroanatomical convenience, representing an extension of the sequential organizational properties of the motor cortex anterior to the central fissure.

This theoretical sketch emphasizes functions related to neuroanatomical regions in the cortex. It says nothing about other structures that might play a role in representational activity. It also passes over the representational and processing functions of patterns of neuronal activity and biochemical factors associated with different regions. A detailed neuropsychological theory of cognitive representations and processes that incorporates all of the available brain information remains to be written.

References

Alba, J. W., & Hasher, L. (1983). Is memory schematic? *Psychological Bulletin, 2,* 203–231.

Algom, D., Wolf, Y., & Bergman, B. (in press). Integration of stimulus dimensions in perception and memory: Composition rules and psychophysical relations. *Journal of Experimental Psychology: General.*

Allport, F. H. (1955). *Theories of perception and the concept of structure.* New York: Wiley.

Anderson, J. R. (1978). Arguments concerning representations for mental imagery. *Psychological Review, 85,* 249–277.

Anderson, J. R. (1983). *The architecture of cognition.* Cambridge, MA: Harvard University Press.

Anderson, J. R., & Bower, G. H. (1973). *Human associative memory.* Washington, DC: Winston.

Anderson, R. C., Goetz, E. T., Pickert, H. M., & Halff, H. M. (1977). Two faces of the conceptual peg hypothesis. *Journal of Experimental Psychology: Human Learning and Memory, 3,* 142–149.

Anderson, R. C., & Hidde, J. L. (1971). Imagery and sentence learning. *Journal of Educational Psychology, 62,* 526–520.

Anderson, R. C., & McGaw, B. (1973). On the representation of the meanings of general items. *Journal of Experimental Psychology, 101,* 301–306.

Anderson, R. C., & Ortony, A. (1975). On putting apples into bottles—a problem in polysemy. *Cognitive Psychology, 7,* 167–180.

Anderson, R. C., & Pichert, J. W. (1978). Recall of previously unrecallable information following a shift in perspective. *Journal of Verbal Learning and Verbal Behavior, 17,* 1–12.

Anderson, R. E. (1976). Short-term retention of the where and when of pictures and words. *Journal of Experimental Psychology: General, 105,* 378–402.

Anderson, R. E. (1984). Did I do it or did I only imagine doing it? *Journal of Experimental Psychology: General, 113,* 594–615.

Anisfeld, M., & Knapp, M. (1968). Association, synonymity, and directionality in false recognition. *Journal of Experimental Psychology, 77,* 171–179.

Annett, J. (1982). Action, language and imagination. In L. Wankel & R. B. Wilberg (Eds.), *Psychology of sport and motor behavior.* Edmonton, Alberta: University of Alberta Printing Services.

Arnheim, R. (1969). *Visual thinking.* Berkeley & Los Angeles: University of California Press.

Arnold, M. B. (1960). *Emotion and personality: Vol. 2. Neurological and physiological aspects.* New York: Columbia University Press.

Asch, S. E. (1958). The metaphor: A psychological inquiry. In R. Tagiuri & L. Petrullo (Eds.), *Person perception and interpersonal behavior.* Stanford: Stanford University Press.

Asher, J. J. (1972). Children's first language as a model for second language learning. *The Modern Language Journal, 56,* 133–139.

Atkinson, R. C. (1975). Mnemotechnics in second-language learning. *American Psychologist, 30,* 821–828.

Atkinson, R. C., & Shiffrin, R. M. (1968). Human memory: A proposed system and its control processes. In K. W. Spence & J. T. Spence (Eds.), *The psychology of learning and motivation: Advances in research and theory (Vol. 2).* New York: Academic Press.

Attneave, F. (1974, July). How do you know? *American Psychologist,* pp. 493–499.

Attneave, F., & Pierce, C. R. (1978). Accuracy of extrapolating a pointer into perceived and imagined space. *American Journal of Psychology, 91,* 371–387.

Babbit, B. C. (1982). Effect of task demands on dual coding of pictorial stimuli. *Journal of Experimental Psychology: Learning, Memory, and Cognition, 8,* 73–80.

Baddeley, A. D. (1978). The trouble with levels: A reexamination of Craik and Lockhart's framework for memory research. *Psychological Review, 85,* 139–152.

Baddeley, A. D., Grant, S., Wight, E., & Thomson, N. (1974). Imagery and visual working memory. In P. M. A. Rabbitt & S. Dornic (Eds.), *Attention and performance* (Vol. V). London: Academic Press.

Baggett, P. (1979). Structurally equivalent stories in movie and text and the effect of the medium on recall. *Journal of Verbal Learning and Verbal Behavior, 18,* 333–356.

Bahrick, H. P., & Bahrick, P. (1971). Independence of verbal and visual codes of the same stimuli. *Journal of Experimental Psychology, 91,* 344–346.

Baker, L., & Santa, J. L. (1977). Context, integration, and retrieval. *Memory & Cognition, 5,* 308–314.

Bandura, A. (1977). *Social learning theory.* Englewood Cliffs, NJ: Prentice-Hall.

Banks, W. P. (1977). Encoding and processing of symbolic information in comparative judgements. In G. H. Bower (Ed.), *The psychology of learning and motivation* (Vol. 11). New York: Academic Press.

Banks, W. P., & Flora, J. (1977). Semantic and perceptual processes in symbolic comparisons. *Journal of Experimental Psychology: Human Perception and Performance, 3,* 278–290.

Bartlett, F. C. (1932) *Remembering.* Cambridge, England: Cambridge University Press.

Battig, W. F., & Montague, W. E. (1969). Category norms for verbal items in 56 categories: A replication and extension of the Connecticut category norms. *Journal of Experimental Psychology Monographs, 80*(3, Pt. 2).

Baum, D. R., & Jonides, J. (1979). Cognitive maps: Analysis of comparative judgments of distance. *Memory & Cognition, 7,* 462–468.

Baylor, G. W. (1972). *A Treatise on the mind's eye: An empirical investigation of visual mental imagery.* Doctoral dissertation, Carnegie-Mellon University, Pittsburgh. (Ann Arbor, MI: University Microfilms No. 72–12)

Beauvois, M. F. (1982). Optic aphasia: A process of interaction betwen vision and language. *Philosophical Transactions of the Royal Society of London, 298,* 35–47.

Beech, J. R., & Allport, D. A. (1978). Visualization of compound scenes. *Perception, 7,* 129–138.

Begg, I. (1971). Recognition memory for sentence meaning and wording. *Journal of Verbal Learning and Verbal Behavior, 10,* 176–181.

Begg, I. (1972). Recall of meaningful phrases. *Journal of Verbal Learning and Verbal Behavior, 11,* 431–439.

Begg, I. (1973). Imagery and integration in the recall of words. *Canadian Journal of Psychology, 27,* 159–167.

Begg, I. (1976). Acquisition and transfer of meaningful function by meaningless sounds. *Canadian Journal of Psychology, 30,* 178–186.

Begg, I. (1978). Imagery and organization in memory: Instructional effects. *Memory & Cognition, 6,* 174–183.

Begg, I. (1982). Imagery, organization, and discriminative processes. *Canadian Journal of Psychology, 36,* 273–290.

Begg, I., & Clark, J. M. (1975). Contextual imagery in meaning and memory. *Memory & Cognition, 3,* 117–112.

Begg, I., & Paivio, A. (1969). Concreteness and imagery in sentence meaning. *Journal of Verbal Learning and Verbal Behavior, 8,* 821–827.

Begg, I., & Robertson, R. (1973). Imagery and long-term retention. *Journal of Verbal Learning and Verbal Behavior, 12,* 689–700.

Begg, I., & Sikich, D. (1984). Imagery and contextual organization. *Memory & Cognition, 12,* 52–59.

Begg, I., Upfold, D., & Wilton, T. D. (1978). Imagery in verbal communication. *Journal of Mental Imagery, 2,* 165–186.

Belmore, S. M., Yates, J. M., Bellack, D. R., Jones, S. N., & Rosenquist, S. E. (1982). Drawing inferences from concrete and abstract sentences. *Journal of Verbal Learning and Verbal Behavior, 21,* 338–351.

Beritoff, J. S. (1965). *Neural mechanisms of higher vertebrate behavior* (W. T. Liberson, Ed. & Trans.). Boston: Little, Brown & Co.

Besner, D., & Coltheart, M. (1979). Ideographic and alphabetic processing in skilled reading of English. *Neuropsychologia, 17,* 467–472.

Betts, G. H. (1909). *The distribution and functions of mental imagery.* New York: Teacher's College, Columbia University.

Bever, T. G., Fodor, J. A., & Garrett, M. (1968). A formal limitation of associationism. In T. R. Dixon & D. L. Horton (Eds.), *Verbal behavior and general behavior theory.* Englewood Cliffs, NJ: Prentice-Hall.

Biederman, I., Rabinowitz, J. C., Glass, A. L., & Stacey, E. W., Jr. (1974). On the information extracted from a glance at a scene. *Journal of Experimental Psychology, 103,* 597–600.

Bierwisch, M. (1970). Semantics. In J. Lyons (Ed.), *New horizons in linguistics.* New York: Penguin.

Billow, R. M. (1975). A cognitive developmental study of metaphor comprehension. *Developmental Psychology, 11,* 415–423.

Binet, A. (1894). *Psychologie des grands calculateurs et joueurs d'échec* [Psychology of great calculators and chess players]. Paris: Hachette.

Bisiach, E., Capitani, E., Luzzatti, C., & Perani, D. (1981). Brain and conscious representation of outside reality. *Neuropsychologia, 19,* 543–551.

Black, J. B., Turner, T. J., & Bower, G. H. (1979). Spatial reference points in language comprehension. *Journal of Verbal Learning and Verbal Behavior, 18,* 187–198.

Black, M. (1962). Metaphor. In M. Black (Ed.), *Models and metaphors.* Ithaca, NY: Cornell University Press.

Boles, D. B. (1983). Dissociated imageability, concreteness, and familiarity in lateralized word recognition. *Memory & Cognition, 11,* 511–519.

Bousfield, W. K. (1953). The occurrence of clustering in recall of randomly arranged associates. *Journal of General Psychology, 49,* 229–240.

Bower, G. H. (1967). A multicomponent theory of the memory trace. In K. W. Spence & J. T. Spence (Eds.), *The psychology of learning and motivation* (Vol. 1). New York: Academic Press.

Bower, G. H. (1970). Imagery as a relational organizer in associative learning. *Journal of Verbal Learning and Verbal Behavior, 9,* 529–533.

Bower, G. H. (1972). Mental imagery and associative learning. In L. Gregg (Ed.), *Cognition in learning and memory.* New York: Wiley.

Bower, G. H. (1981). Mood and Memory. *American Psychologist, 36,* 129–148.

Bower, G. H., & Glass, A. L. (1976). Structural units and the redintegrative power of picture fragments. *Journal of Experimental Psychology: Human Learning and Memory, 2,* 456–466.

Bower, T. G. R. (1966). The visual world of infants. *Scientific American, 215,* 80–92.

Bower, T. G. R., & Paterson, J. G. (1973). The separation of place, movement, and object in the world of the infant. *Journal of Experimental Child Psychology, 15,* 161–168.

Bowerman, M. (1973). *Early syntactic development.* New York: Cambridge University Press.

Braine, M. D. S. (1963). On learning the grammatical order of words. *Psychological Review, 70,* 323–348.

Brainerd, C. J. (1983). Working memory systems and cognitive development. In C. J. Brainerd (Ed.), *Recent advances in cognitive-developmental theory: Progress in cognitive development research.* New York: Springer-Verlag.

Brainerd, C. J., Desrochers, A., & Howe, M. L. (1981). Stages-of-learning analysis of picture-word effects in associative memory. *Journal of Experimental Psychology: Human Learning and Memory, 7,* 1–14.

Bransford, J. D., Stein, B. S., Vye, N. J., Franks, J. J., Auble, P. M., Mezynski, K. J., & Perfetto, G. A. (1982). Differences in approaches to learning: An overview. *Journal of Experimental Psychology: General, 3,* 390–398.

Bregman, A. S. (1977). Perception and behavior as compositions of ideals. *Cognitive Psychology, 9,* 250–292.

Bregman, A. S., & Campbell, J. (1971). Primary auditory stream segregation and perception of order in rapid sequences of tones. *Journal of Experimental Psychology, 89,* 244–249.

Bremner, J. G. (1982). Object localization in infancy. In M. Potegal (Ed.), *Spatial abilities.* New York: Academic Press.

Brewer, W. F. (1975). Memory for ideas: Synonym substitution. *Memory & Cognition, 3,* 458–464.

Brewer, W. F., & Pani, J. R. (1984). The structure of human memory. In G. H. Bower (Ed.), *The psychology of learning and motivation: Advances in research and theory* (Vol. 17). New York: Academic Press.

Bridgman, P. W. (1928). *The logic of modern physics.* New York: Macmillan.

Broadbent, D. E. (1958). *Perception and communication.* London: Pergamon Press.

Brooks, L. R. (1967). The suppression of visualization in reading. *The Quarterly Journal of Experimental Psychology, 19,* 289–299.

Brooks, L. R. (1968). Spatial and verbal components of the act of recall. *Canadian Journal of Psychology, 22,* 349–368.

Brooks, L. R. (1978). Nonanalytic concept formation and memory for instances. In E. Rosch & B. B. Lloyd (Eds.), *Cognition and categorization.* Hillsdale, NJ: Lawrence Erlbaum Associates.

Brown, I. Jr. (1979). Language acquisition: Linguistic structure and rule-governed behavior. In G. J. Whitehurst & B. J. Zimmerman (Eds.), *The functions of language and cognition.* New York: Academic Press.

Brown, R. W. (1958). *Words and things.* Glencoe, IL: The Free Press.

Brown, R. W. (1973). *A first language: The early stages.* Cambridge, MA: Harvard University Press.

Bryden, M. P. (1982). *Laterality: Functional asymmetry in the intact brain.* New York: Academic Press.

Bryden, M. P. & Ley, R. G. (1983). Right-hemispheric involvement in the perception and expression of emotion in normal humans. In K. M. Heilman & P. Satz (Eds.), *Neuropsychology of human emotion.* New York: Guilford.

Bucci, W. (1984). Linking words and things: Basic processes and individual variation. *Cognition, 17,* 137–153.

Bucci, W., & Freedman, N. (1978). Language and hand: The dimension of referential competence. *Journal of Personality, 46,* 594–622.

Bugelski, B. R. (1970). Words and things and images. *American Psychologist, 25,* 1002–1012.

Bugelski, B. R. (1971a). The definition of the image. In S. J. Segal (Ed.), *Imagery: Current cognitive approaches.* New York: Academic Press.

Bugelski, B. R. (1971b). *The psychology of learning applied to teaching.* Indianapolis: Bobbs-Merrill.

Bugelski, B. R. (1974). The image as mediator in one-trial paired-associate learning: III. Sequential functions in serial lists. *Journal of Experimental Psychology, 103,* 298–303.

Bugelski, B. R. (1977). The association of images. In J. M. Nicholas (Ed.), *Images, perception, and knowledge.* Boston: D. Reidel.

Bugelski, B. R. (1982). Learning and imagery. *Journal of Mental Imagery, 6,* 1–192.

Caplan, D., & Chomsky, N. (1982). Linguistic perspectives on language development. In D. Caplan (Ed.), *Biological studies of mental processes.* Cambridge, MA: MIT Press.

Caramazza, A., & Berndt, R. S. (1978). Semantic and syntactic processes in aphasia: A review of the literature. *Psychological Bulletin, 85,* 898–918.

Carpenter, P. A., & Just, M. A. (1975). Sentence comprehension: A psycholinguistic processing model of verification. *Psychological Review, 82,* 45–73.

Carr, T. H., McCauley, C., Sperber, R. D., & Parmelee, C. M. (1982). Words, pictures, and priming: On semantic activation, conscious identification, and the automaticity of information processing. *Journal of Experimental Psychology: Human Perception and Performance, 8,* 757–777.

Carroll, J. B. (1962). The prediction of success in intensive foreign language training. In R. Glaser (Ed.), *Training and education research.* Pittsburgh: University of Pittsburgh Press.

Carroll, J. B. (1976). Psychometric tests as cognitive tasks: A new "structure of intellect". In L. B. Resnick (Ed.), *The nature of intelligence.* Hillsdale, NJ: Lawrence Erlbaum Associates.

Carroll, J. B. (1983). Studying individual differences in cognitive abilities: Through and beyond factor analysis. In R. F. Dillon & R. S. Schmeck (Eds.), *Individual differences in cognition* (Vol. 1). New York: Academic Press.

Cartwright, D. (1959). Lewinian theory as a contemporary systematic framework. In S. Koch (Ed.), *Psychology: A study of a science* (Vol. 2). New York: McGraw-Hill.

Case, R. (1978). Intellectual development from birth to adulthood: A neo-Piagetian interpretation. In R. S. Siegler (Ed.), *Children's thinking—What develops?.* Hillsdale, NJ: Lawrence Erlbaum Associates.

Chafe, W. L. (1970). *Meaning and the structure of language.* Chicago: University of Chicago Press.

Chafe, W. L. (1975). The recall and verbalization of past experience. In R. W. Cole (Ed.), *Current issues in linguistic theory.* Bloomington: Indiana University Press.

Chase, W. G., & Clark, H. H. (1972). Mental operations in the comparison of sentences and pictures. In L. Gregg (Ed.), *Cognition in learning and memory.* New York: Wiley.

Chevalier-Girard, N., & Wilberg, R. B. (1980). The effects of image and label on the free recall of organized movement lists. In P. Klavora & J. Flowers (Eds.), *Motor learning and biomechanical factors in sport.* Toronto: Canadian Society for Psychomotor Learning and Sport Psychology.

Chi, M. T. H. (1976). Short-term memory limitations in children: Capacity or processing deficits? *Memory & Cognition, 4,* 559–572.

Chomsky, N. (1957). *Syntactic structures.* The Hague: Mouton.

Chomsky, N. (1959). [Review of *Verbal behavior* by B. F. Skinner]. *Language, 35,* 26–58.

Chomsky, N. (1965). *Aspects of the theory of syntax.* Cambridge, MA: MIT Press.

Chomsky, N. (1968). *Language and mind.* New York: Harcourt, Brace, and World.

Chomsky, N. (1982). *Some concepts and consequences of the theory of government and binding.* Cambridge, MA: MIT Press.

Christian, J., Bickley, W., Tarka, M., & Clayton, K. (1978). Measures of free recall of 900 English nouns: Correlations with imagery, concreteness, meaningfulness, and frequency. *Memory & Cognition, 6,* 379–390.

Clark, H. H. (1969). Linguistic processes in deductive reasoning. *Psychological Review, 76,* 387–403.

Clark, H. H. (1973). Space, time, semantics, and the child. In T. E. Moore (Ed.), *Cognitive development and the acquisition of language.* New York: Academic Press.

Clark, J. M. (1978). *Synonymity and concreteness effects on free recall and free association: Implications for a theory of semantic memory.* Unpublished doctoral dissertation, University of Western Ontario, London.

Clark, J. M. (1983). Representational memory: Paivio's levels of meaning as experiential model and conceptual framework. In J. C. Yuille (Ed.), *Imagery, memory, and cognition: Essays in honor of Allan Paivio.* Hillsdale, NJ: Lawrence Erlbaum Associates.

Clark, J. M. (1984). Concreteness and semantic repetition effects in free recall: Evidence for dual-coding theory. *Canadian Journal of Psychology, 38,* 591–598.

Clark, J. M., & Paivio, A. (1984, May). *Associative mechanisms in cognition.* Paper presented at the annual meeting of the Canadian Psychological Association, Ottawa, Ontario, Canada.

Clark, J. M., & Paivio, A. (unpublished paper). Cognitive foundations for empiricist views of science: Observations and theory.

Clark, R. W. (1975). *The life of Bertrand Russell.* London: J. Cape.

Collins, A. M., & Loftus, E. F. (1975). A spreading-activation theory of semantic processing. *Psychological Review, 82,* 407–428.

Colpo, G., Cornoldi, C., & De Beni, R. (1977). Competition in memory between high and low imagery value stimuli and visual stimuli: Temporal conditions for occurrences of interference effects. *Italian Journal of Psychology, 4,* 387–402.

Coltheart, M., Patterson, K., & Marshall, J. C. (Eds.). (1980). *Deep dyslexia.* London: Routledge & Kegan Paul.

Conlin, D., & Paivio, A. (1975). The associative learning of the deaf: The effects of word imagery and signability. *Memory & Cognition, 3,* 335–340.

Cooper, L. A. (1975). Mental rotation of random two-dimensional shapes. *Cognitive Psychology, 7,* 20–43.

Cooper, L. A., & Shepard, R. N. (1973). Chronometric studies of the rotation of mental images. In W. G. Chase (Ed.), *Visual information processing.* New York: Academic Press.

Cornoldi, C. (1976). *Memoria e immaginazione.* Bologna: Patron.

Cornoldi, C., & Paivio, A. (1982). Imagery value and its effects on verbal memory: A review. *Archivio di Psicologia Neurologia e Psichiatria, 2,* 171–192.

Craik, F. I. M., & Lockhart, R. S. (1972). Levels of processing: A framework for memory research. *Journal of Verbal Learning and Verbal Behavior, 11,* 671–684.

Craik, F. I. M., & Tulving, E. (1975). Depth of processing and the retention of words in episodic memory. *Journal of Experimental Psychology: General, 104,* 268–294.

Crowder, R. G. (1976). *Principles of learning and memory.* Hillsdale, NJ: Lawrence Erlbaum Associates.

Curry, F. K. W. (1967). A comparison of left-handed and right-handed subjects on verbal and non-verbal dichotic listening tasks. *Cortex, 3,* 343–352.

D'Agostino, P. R., O'Neill, B. J., & Paivio, A. (1977). Memory for pictures and words as a function of level of processing: Depth or dual coding? *Memory & Cognition, 5,* 252–256.

Dalrymple-Alford, E. C. (1968). Interlingual interference in a color naming task. *Psychonomic Science, 10,* 215–216.

Das, J. P., Kirby, J., & Jarman, R. F. (1975). Simultaneous and successive syntheses: An alternative model for cognitive abilities. *Psychological Bulletin, 82,* 87–103.

Day, J. C., & Bellezza, F. S. (1983). The relation between visual imagery mediators and recall. *Memory & Cognition, 11,* 251–257.

Deese, J. (1962). On the structure of associative meaning. *Psychological Review, 69,* 161–175.

Deese, J. (1965). *The structure of associations in language and thought.* Baltimore: Johns Hopkins Press.

Deffenbacher, K. A., Carr, T. H., & Leu, J. R. (1981). Memory for words, pictures, and faces: Retroactive interference, forgetting, and reminiscence. *Journal of Experimental Psychology: Human Learning and Memory, 7,* 299–305.

de Groot, A. M. B. (1983). The range of automatic spreading activation in word priming. *Journal of Verbal Learning and Verbal Behavior, 22,* 417–436.

del Castillo, D. M., & Gumenik, W. E. (1972). Sequential memory for familiar and unfamiliar forms. *Journal of Experimental Psychology, 95,* 90–96.

Dell, G. S., & Reich, P. A. (1981). Stages in sentence production: An analysis of speech error data. *Journal of Verbal Learning and Verbal Behavior, 20,* 611–629.

den Heyer, K., & Barrett, B. (1971). Selective loss of visual and verbal information in STM by means of visual and verbal interpolated tasks. *Psychonomic Science, 25,* 100–102.

Denis, M. (1979). *Les images mentales* [Mental images]. Paris: Presses Universitaires de France.

Denis, M. (1982a). Imaging while reading text: A study of individual differences. *Memory & Cognition, 10,* 540–545.

Denis, M. (1982b). On figurative components of mental representations. In F. Klix, J. Hoffmann, & E. van der Meer (Eds.), *Cognitive research in psychology.* Berlin: Verlag der Wissenschaften.

Denis, M. (1984). Imagery and prose: A critical review of research on adults and children. *Text, 4,* 381–401.

Denis, M. (in press). Visual imagery and the use of mental practice in the development of motor skills. *Canadian Journal of Applied Sport Sciences.*

Denis, M., & Carfantan, M. (in press). People's knowledge about images. *Cognition.*

DeRenzie, E., & Spinnler, H. (1967). Impaired performance on color tasks in patients with hemispheric damage. *Cortex, 3,* 194–217.

DeSoto, C., London, M., & Handel, S. (1965). Social reasoning and spatial paralogic. *Journal of Personality and Social Psychology, 2,* 513–521.

Desrochers, A. (1982). Imagery elaboration and the recall of French article-noun pairs. *Canadian Journal of Psychology, 36,* 641–654.

Desrochers, A. (1983). Effect of instructions and retrieval cues on the recall of French article-noun pairs. *Human Learning, 2,* 295–311.

deVilliers, J. G., & deVilliers, P. A. (1978). *Language acquisition.* Cambridge, MA: Harvard University Press.

Dilley, M. G., & Paivio, A. (1968). Pictures and words as stimulus and response items in paired-associate learning in young children. *Journal of Experimental Child Psychology, 6,* 231–240.

Di Vesta, F. I., Ingersoll, G., & Sunshine, P. (1971). A factor analysis of imagery tests. *Journal of Verbal Learning and Verbal Behavior, 10,* 471–479.

Dosher, B. A., & Russo, J. E. (1976). Memory for internally generated stimuli. *Journal of Experimental Psychology: Human Learning and Memory, 2,* 633–640.

Downs, R. M., & Stea, D. (1973). *Image and environment: Cognitive mapping and spatial behavior.* Chicago: Aldine.

Dubin, R. (1969). *Theory building.* New York: Collier-Macmillan.

Duhem, P. (1974). *The aim and structure of physical theory.* New York: Atheneum.

Durso, F. T., & Johnson, M. K. (1980). The effects of orienting tasks on recognition, recall, and modality confusion of pictures and words. *Journal of Verbal Learning and Verbal Behavior, 19,* 416–429.

Dyer, J. C., & Meyer, P. A. (1976). Facilitation of simple concept identification through mnemonic instruction. *Journal of Experimental Psychology: Human Learning and Memory, 2,* 767–773.

Ebbinghaus, H. (1964). *Memory: A contribution to experimental psychology* (Ruger & Bussenius, Trans.). New York: Dover. (Original work published 1885)

Eddy, J. K., & Glass, A. L. (1981). Reading and listening to high and low imagery sentences. *Journal of Verbal Learning and Verbal Behavior, 20,* 333–345.

Edwards, D. (1973). Sensory-motor intelligence and semantic relations in early child grammar. *Cognition, 2,* 395–434.

Efron, R. (1963). Effects of handedness on the perception of simultaneity and temporal order. *Brain, 86,* 261–284.

Ehri, L. C., & Ryan, E. B. (1980). Performance of bilinguals in a picture-word interference task. *Journal of Psycholinguistic Research, 9,* 285–302.

Eich, J. M. (1982). A composite holographic associative recall model. *Psychological Review, 89,* 627–661.

Ellson, D. G. (1941). Hallucinations produced by sensory conditioning. *Journal of Experimental Psychology, 28,* 1–20.

Epstein, W., Rock, I., & Zuckerman, C. B. (1960). Meaning and familiarity in associative learning. *Psychological Monographs, 74* (4, Whole No. 491).

Erdelyi, M. H. (1974). A new look at the new look: Perceptual defense and vigilance. *Psychological Review, 81,* 1–25.

Ericsson, K. A., & Simon, H. A. (1984). *Protocol analysis: Verbal reports as data.* Cambridge, MA: MIT Press.

Ernest, C. H. (1977). Imagery ability and cognition: A critical review. *Journal of Mental Imagery, 1,* 181–216.

Ernest, C. H. (1980). Imagery ability and the identification of fragmented pictures and words. *Acta Psychologica, 44,* 51–57.

Ernest, C. H., & Paivio. A. (1971). Imagery and verbal associative latencies as a function of imagery ability. *Canadian Journal of Psychology, 25,* 83–90.

Eysenck, H. J. (1967). Intelligence assessment: A theoretical and experimental approach. *British Journal of Psychology, 37,* 81–98.

Farah, M. J. (1985). Psychophysical evidence for a shared representational medium for mental images and percepts. *Journal of Experimental Psychology: General, 114,* 91–103.

Farah, M. J., & Kosslyn, S. M. (1981). Structure and strategy in image generation. *Cognitive Science, 4,* 371–383.

Feltz, D. L., & Landers, D. M. (1983). The effects of mental practice on motor skill learning and performance: A meta-analysis. *Journal of Sport Psychology, 5,* 25–57.

Ferguson, G. A. (1954). On learning and human ability. *Canadian Journal of Psychology, 8,* 95–112.

Ferguson, G. A. (1956). On transfer and the abilities of man. *Canadian Journal of Psychology, 10,* 121–131.

Fernald, M. R. (1912). The diagnosis of mental imagery. *Psychological Monographs* (Whole No. 58).

Field, T. (1982). Infancy. In R. Vasta (Ed.), *Strategies and techniques in child study.* New York: Academic Press.

Fillenbaum, S., & Rapoport, A. (1971). *Structures in the subjective lexicon.* New York: Academic Press.

Fillmore, C. J. (1968). The case for case. In E. Bach & R. T. Harms (Eds.), *Universals in linguistic theory.* New York: Holt, Rinehart, and Winston.

Fillmore, C. J. (1977). The case for case reopened. In P. Cale, & J. Sadock (Eds.), *Syntax and semantics.* New York: Academic Press.

Finke, R. A. (1980). Levels of equivalence in imagery and perception. *Psychological Review, 87,* 113–132.

Finke, R. A. (1985). Theories relating mental imagery to perception. *Psychological Bulletin, 98,* 236–259.

Finke, R. A., & Shepard, R. N. (in press). Visual functions of mental imagery. In L. Kaufman & J. Thomas (Eds.), *Handbook of perception and human performance.* New York: Wiley.

Fleishman, E. A., Roberts, M. M., & Friedman, M. P. (1958). A factor analysis of aptitude and proficiency measured in radio-telegraphy. *Journal of Applied Psychology, 42,* 129–135.

Fleishman, E. A., & Rich, S. (1963). Role of kinesthetic and spatial-visual abilities in perceptual-motor learning. *Journal of Experimental Psychology, 66,* 6–11.

Flexser, A. J., & Tulving, E. (1978). Retrieval independence in recognition and recall. *Psychological Review, 85,* 153–171.

Fodor, J. A. (1965). Could meaning be an r_m? *Journal of Verbal Learning and Verbal Behavior, 4,* 73–81.

Fodor, J. A. (1975). *The language of thought.* New York: Thomas Y. Crowell.

Fodor, J. A. (1983). *The modularity of mind.* Cambridge, MA: MIT Press.

Foltz, G., Poltrock, S., & Potts, G. (1984). Mental comparison of size and magnitude: Size congruity effects. *Journal of Experimental Psychology: Learning, Memory, and Cognition, 10,* 442–453.

Forisha, B. D. (1975). Mental imagery verbal processes: A developmental study. *Developmental Psychology, 11,* 259–267.

Foss, D. J., & Harwood, D. A. (1975). Memory for sentences: Implications for human associative memory. *Journal of Verbal Learning and Verbal Behavior, 14,* 1–16.

Fraisse, P. (1960). Recognition time measured by verbal reaction to figures and words. *Perceptual and Motor Skills, 11,* 204.

Fraisse, P. (1968). Motor and verbal reaction times to words and drawings. *Psychonomic Science, 12,* 235–236.

Friedman, A. (1978). Memorial comparisons without the "mind's eye". *Journal of Verbal Learning and Verbal Behavior, 17,* 427–444.

Friedman, A., & Bourne, L. E., Jr. (1976). Encoding the levels of information in pictures and words. *Journal of Experimental Psychology: General, 105,* 169–190.

Friedman, W. J. (1983). Image and verbal processes in reasoning about the months of the year. *Journal of Experimental Psychology: Learning, Memory, and Cognition, 9,* 650–666.

Frost, N. (1972). Encoding and retrieval in visual memory tasks. *Journal of Experimental Psychology, 95,* 317–326.

Fry, P. S. (Ed.). (1984). Changing conceptions of intelligence and intellectual functioning: Current theory and research. *International Journal of Psychology, 19,* [Special issue], 457–474.

Gage, D. F., & Safer, M. A. (1985). Hemisphere differences in the mood state-dependent effect for recognition of emotional faces. *Journal of Experimental Psychology: Learning, Memory, and Cognition, 11,* 752–763.

Galton, F. (1883). *Inquiries into human faculty and its development.* London: Macmillan.

Garner, W. L., Hake, H. W., & Eriksen, C. W. (1956). Operationism and the concept of perception. *Psychological Review, 63,* 149–159.

Garner, W. R. (1974). *The processing of information and structure.* Potomac, MD: Lawrence Erlbaum Associates.

Garrett, M. F. (1975). The analysis of sentence production. In G. H. Bower (Ed.), *Psychology of learning and motivation* (Vol. 9). New York: Academic Press.

Gazzaniga, M. S., & LeDoux, J. E. (1978). *The integrated mind.* New York: Plenum Press.

Gernsbacher, M. A. (1984). Resolving 20 years of inconsistent interaction between lexical familiarity and orthography, concreteness, and polysemy. *Journal of Experimental Psychology: General, 113,* 256–281.

Geschwind, N. (1965). Disconnexion syndrome in animals and man. *Brain, 88,* 237–294, 585–644.

Gibson, E. J. (1969). *Principles of perceptual learning and development.* New York: Appleton-Century-Crofts.

Gibson, J. J. (1966). *The senses considered as perceptual systems.* Boston: Houghton Mifflin.

Gibson, J. J. (1979). *The ecological approach to visual perception.* Boston: Houghton-Mifflin.

Gildea, P., & Glucksberg, S. (1983). On understanding metaphor: The role of context. *Journal of Verbal Learning and Verbal Behavior, 22,* 577–590.

Gillund, G., & Shiffrin, R. M. (1984). A retrieval model for both recognition and recall. *Psychological Review, 91,* 1–67.

Glanzer, M., & Duarte, A. (1971). Repetition between and within languages in free recall. *Journal of Verbal Learning and Verbal Behavior, 10,* 625–630.

Glass, A. L., Eddy, J. K., & Schwanenflugel, P. J. (1980). The verification of high and low imagery sentences. *Journal of Experimental Psychology: Human Learning and Memory, 6,* 692–704.

Glass, A. L., Millen, D. R., Beck, L. G., & Eddy, J. K. (1985). Representation of images in sentence verification. *Journal of Memory and Language, 24,* 442–465.

Glucksberg, S. (1984). Commentary: The functional equivalence of common and multiple codes. *Journal of Verbal Learning and Verbal Behavior, 23,* 100–104.

Glucksberg, S., Trabasso, T., & Wald, J. (1973). Linguistic structures and mental operations. *Cognitive Psychology, 5,* 338–370.

Goldman-Eisler, F. (1961). Hesitation and information in speech. In C. Cherry (Ed.), *Information theory.* London: Butterworths.

Goldman-Eisler, F. (1968). *Psycholinguistics: Experiments in spontaneous speech.* New York: Academic Press.

Goodale, M. A. (1983). Vision as a sensorimotor system. In T. E. Robinson (Ed.), *Behavioral approaches to brain research.* New York: Oxford University Press.

Goodnow, J. J. (1977). *Children's drawing.* London: Open Books.

Gordon, R. (1949). An investigation into some of the factors that favour the formation of stereotyped images. *British Journal of Psychology, 39,* 156–167.

Graesser, A. C., Gordon, S. E., & Sawyer, J. D. (1979). Recognition memory for typical and atypical actions in scripted activities: Tests of a script pointer plus tag hypothesis. *Journal of Verbal Learning and Verbal Behavior, 18,* 319–332.

Greenwald, A. G. (1970). Sensory feedback mechanisms in performance control. *Psychological Review, 77,* 73–99.

Griffin, D. R. (1976). *The question of animal awareness.* New York: Rockefeller University Press.

Groninger, L. D., & Groninger, L. K. (1982). Function of images in the encoding-retrieval process. *Journal of Experimental Psychology: Human Learning and Memory, 8,* 353–358.

Groninger, L. D., & Groninger, L. K. (1984). Autobiographical memories: Their relation to images, definitions, and word recognition. *Journal of Experimental Psychology: Learning, Memory, and Cognition, 4,* 745–755.

Guenther, R. K. (1980). Conceptual memory for picture and prose episodes. *Memory & Cognition, 8,* 563–572.

Guilford, J. P. (1967). *The nature of human intelligence.* New York: McGraw-Hill.

Guilford, J. P. (1974). Rotation problems in factor analysis. *Psychological Bulletin, 81,* 498–501.

Guilford, J. P. (1982). Cognitive psychology's ambiguities: Some suggested remedies. *Psychological Review, 87,* 48–59.

Guilford, J. P., & Hoepfner, R. (1971). *The analysis of intelligence.* New York: McGraw-Hill.

Haber, R. N. (1979). Twenty years of haunting eidetic imagery: Where is the ghost? *The Behavioral and Brain Sciences, 2,* 583–629.

Haber, R. N., & Haber, R. B. (1964). Eidetic imagery: I. Frequency. *Perceptual and Motor Skills, 19,* 131–138.

Hall, C. R. (1980). Imagery for movement. *Journal of Human Movement Studies, 6,* 252–264.

Hall, C. R. (in press). The role of mental practice and imagery ability in motor skill performance. *Canadian Journal of Applied Sport Sciences.*

Hall, C. R., & Buckolz, E. (1983). Imagery and the recall of movement patterns. *Imagination, Cognition, and Personality, 12,* 251–260.

Halliday, M. A. K., & Hasan, R. (1976). *Cohesion in English.* London: Longman.

Hamers, J. F., & Lambert, W. E. (1972). Bilingual interdependencies in auditory perception. *Journal of Verbal Learning and Verbal Behavior, 11,* 303–310.

Hammoud, R. (1982). *Utilisation de l'image mental et du champ d'associations dans l'enseignement du vocabulaire arabe à des débutants adultes francophones* [Use of mental imagery and associative fields in the teaching of Arabic vocabulary to adult francophone beginners]. Unpublished doctoral dissertation, Laval University, Quebec, P.Q., Canada.

Hampson, P. J., & Duffy, C. (1984). Verbal and spatial interference effects in congenitally blind and sighted subjects. *Canadian Journal of Psychology, 38,* 411–420.

Hanley, G. L., & Levine, M. (1983). Spatial problem solving: The integration of independently learned cognitive images. *Memory & Cognition, 11,* 415–422.

Harnad, S. (1982). Metaphor and mental duality. In T. W. Simon & R. J. Scholes (Eds.), *Language, mind, and brain.* Hillsdale, NJ: Lawrence Erlbaum Associates.

Harris, P. L. (1975). Development of search and object permanence during infancy. *Psychological Bulletin, 82,* 332–344.

Harris, P. L. (1983). Infant cognition. In P. H. Mussen (Ed.), *Handbook of child psychology: Vol. II. Infancy and developmental psychobiology.* New York: Wiley.

Hasher, L., Riebman, B., & Wren, F. (1976). Imagery and the retention of free-recall learning. *Journal of Experimental Psychology: Human Learning and Memory, 2,* 172–181.

Hatakeyama, T. (1981). Individual differences in imagery ability and mental rotation. *Tohoku Psychologica Folia, 40,* 6–23.

Hayes-Roth, B. (1977). Evolution of cognitive structures and processes. *Psychological Review, 84,* 260–278.

Hayes-Roth, B., & Hayes-Roth, F. (1977). The prominence of lexical information in memory representations of meaning. *Journal of Verbal Learning and Verbal Behavior, 16,* 119–136.

Head, H. (1920). *Studies in neurology.* New York: Oxford University Press.

Healy, A. F. (1975). Coding of temporal-spatial patterns in short-term memory. *Journal of Verbal Learning and Verbal Behavior, 14,* 481–495.

Healy, A. F. (1977). Pattern coding of spatial order information in short-term memory. *Journal of Verbal Learning and Verbal Behavior, 16,* 491–437.

Hebb, D. O. (1949). *The organization of behavior.* New York: Wiley.

Hebb, D. O. (1961). Distinctive features of learning in higher animal. In J. F. Delafresnage (Ed.), *Brain mechanisms and learning.* New York: Oxford University Press.

Hebb, D. O. (1980). *Essay on mind.* Hillsdale, NJ: Lawrence Erlbaum Associates.

Hebb, D. O., Lambert, W. E., & Tucker, G. R. (1971). Language, thought, and experience. *The Modern Language Journal, 55,* 212–222.

Heidbreder, E. (1946). The attainment of concepts: I. Terminology and methodology. *Journal of General Psychology, 35,* 173–189.

Hermelin, B., & O'Connor, N. (1982). Spatial modality coding in children with and without impairments. In M. Potegal (Ed.), *Spatial abilities.* New York: Academic Press.

Hilgard, E. R. (1977). *Divided consciousness: Multiple controls in human thought and action.* New York: Wiley.

Hintzman, D. L., & Block, R. A. (1971). Repetition and memory: Evidence for a multiple-trace hypothesis. *Journal of Experimental Psychology, 88,* 297–306.

Hintzman, D. L., & Ludlam, G. (1980). Differential forgetting of prototypes and old instances: Simulation by an exemplar-based classification model. *Memory & Cognition, 8,* 378–382.

Hintzman, D. L., O'Dell, C. S., & Arndt, D. R. (1981). Orientation in cognitive maps. *Cognitive Psychology, 13,* 149–206.

Hockett, C. F. (1963). The problem of universals in language. In J. H. Greenberg (Ed.), *Universals of language.* Cambridge, MA: MIT Press.

Hoffman, R. R., & Nead, J. M. (1983). General contextualism, ecological science, and cognitive research. *The Journal of Mind and Behavior, 4,* 507–560.

Hoffmann, J., Denis, M., & Ziessler, M. (1983). Figurative features and the construction of visual images. *Psychological Research, 45,* 39–54.

Hollan, J. D. (1975). Features and semantic memory: Set-theoretic or network model? *Psychological Review, 82,* 154–155.

Holland, P. C. (1983). Representation-mediated overshadowing and potentiation of conditioned aversions. *Journal of Experimental Psychology: Animal Behavior Processes, 9,* 1–13.

Holmes, V. M., & Langford, J. (1976). Comprehension and recall of abstract and concrete sentences. *Journal of Verbal Learning and Verbal Behavior, 15,* 559–566.

Holyoak, K. J. (1977). The form of analog size information in memory. *Cognitive Psychology, 9,* 31–51.

Holyoak, K. J., Dumais, S. T., & Moyer, R. S. (1979). Semantic association effects in a mental comparison task. *Memory & Cognition, 7,* 303–313.

Honeck, R. P., Riechmann, P., & Hoffman, R. R. (1975). Semantic memory for metaphor: The conceptual base hypothesis. *Memory & Cognition, 3,* 409–415.

Horn, J. L., & Knapp, J. R. (1973). On the subjective character of the empirical base of Guilford's structure-of-intellect model. *Psychological Bulletin, 80,* 33–43.

Horowitz, L. M., & Prytulak, L. S. (1969). Redintegrative memory. *Psychological Review, 76,* 519–531.

Howe, M. L. (1985). The structure of associative memory traces. *Canadian Journal of Psychology, 39,* 34–53.

Hubel, D. H., & Wiesel, T. N. (1962). Receptive fields, binocular interaction, and functional architecture in the cat's visual cortex. *Journal of Physiology, 160,* 106–154.

Hudson, J., & Nelson, K. (1984). Play with language: Overextensions as analogies. *Journal of Child Language, 11,* 337–346.

Huey, E. B. (1908). *The psychology and pedagogy of reading.* New York: Macmillan. (Reprinted 1968, Cambridge, MA: MIT Press)

Hunt, E. B. (1978). Mechanics of verbal ability. *Psychological Review, 85,* 109–130.

Hunt, E. B., Frost, N., & Lunneborg, C. (1973). Individual differences in cognition: A new approach to intelligence. In G. Bower (Ed.), *The psychology of learning and motivation* (Vol. 7). New York: Academic Press.

Hunt, J. McV. (1961). *Intelligence and experience.* New York: Ronald.

Hunter, W. S. (1913). The delayed reaction in animals and children. *Behavior Monographs, 2,* (Serial No. 6).

Huttenlocher, J. (1968). Constructing spatial images: A strategy in reasoning. *Psychological Review, 75,* 550–560.

Huttenlocher, J., & Kubicek, L. F. (1983). The source of relatedness effects on naming latency. *Journal of Experimental Psychology: Learning, Memory, and Cognition, 9,* 486–496.

Intons-Peterson, M. J. (1983). Imagery paradigms: How vulnerable are they to experimenters' expectations? *Journal of Experimental Psychology: Human Perception and Performance, 9,* 394–412.

Intraub, H., & Nicklos, S. (1985). Levels of processing and picture memory: The physical superiority effect. *Journal of Experimental Psychology: Learning, Memory, and Cognition, 11,* 284–298.

Irwin, D. I., & Lupker, S. J. (1983). Semantic priming of pictures and words: A levels of processing approach. *Journal of Verbal Learning and Verbal Behavior, 22,* 45–60.

Jaccarino, G. (1975). *Dual-coding in memory: Evidence from temporal lobe lesions in man.* Unpublished Master's thesis, McGill University, Montreal.

Jacoby, L. L. (1978). On interpreting the effects of repetition: Solving a problem versus remembering a solution. *Journal of Verbal Learning and Verbal Behavior, 17,* 649–667.

Jakobson, R., Fant, G. M., & Halle, M. (1951). *Preliminaries to speech analysis.* Cambridge, MA: MIT Press.

James, C. T., Thompson, J. G., & Baldwin, J. M. (1973). The reconstructive process in sentence memory. *Journal of Verbal Learning and Verbal Behavior, 12,* 51–63.

Janssen, W. H. (1976). Selective interference in paired-associate and free recall learning: Messing up the image. *Acta Psychologica, 40,* 35–48.

Jenkins, J. J., & Palermo, D. S. (1964). Mediation process and the acquisition of linguistic structures. In U. Bellugi & R. W. Brown (Eds.), *The acquisition of language: Monographs of the Society for Research in Child Development, 29,* 141–169.

Jenkins, J. J., & Russell, W. A. (1952). Associative clustering during recall. *Journal of Abnormal and Social Psychology, 47,* 818–821.

Johnson, M. K. (1983). A multiple-entry, modular memory system. In G. H. Bower (Ed.), *The psychology of learning.* New York: Academic Press.

Johnson, M. K., Kahan, T. L., & Raye, C. L. (1984). Dreams and reality monitoring. *Journal of Experimental Psychology: General, 113,* 329–344.

Johnson, M. K., & Raye, C. L. (1981). Reality monitoring. *Psychological Review, 88,* 67–85.

Johnson, P. (1982). The functional equivalence of imagery and movement. *Quarterly Journal of Experimental Psychology, 34A,* 349–365.

Johnson-Laird, P. N. (1972). The three-term series problems. *Cognition, 1,* 57–82.

Johnson-Laird, P. N. (1983). *Mental models.* Cambridge, MA: Harvard University Press.

Jolicoeur, P., & Landau, M. J. (1984). Effects of orientation on the identification of simple visual patterns. *Canadian Journal of Psychology, 38,* 80–93.

Jones, M. K. (1974). Imagery as a mnemonic aid after left temporal lobectomy: Contrast between material-specific and generalized memory disorders. *Neuropsychologia, 12,* 21–30.

Jones-Gotman, M., & Milner, B. (1978). Right temporal lobe contribution to image-mediated memory. *Neuropsychologia, 16,* 61–71.

Jonides, J., Kahn, R., & Rozin, P. (1975). Imagery instructions improve memory in blind subjects. *The Bulletin of the Psychonomic Society, 5*(5), 424–426.

Jorgenson, C. C., & Kintsch, W. (1973). The role of imagery in the evaluation of sentences. *Cognitive Psychology, 4,* 110–116.

Just, M. A., & Carpenter, P. A. (1976). Eye fixations and cognitive processes. *Cognitive Psychology, 8,* 441–480.

Kammann, R. (1968). Associability: A study of the properties of associative ratings and the role of association in word-word learning. *Journal of Experimental Psychology Monographs, 78* (Whole No. 4, Pt. 2).

Katz, A. N. (1978). Differences in the saliency of sensory features elicited by words. *Canadian Journal of Psychology, 32,* 156–179.

Katz, A. N. (1983). What does it mean to be a high imager? In J. C. Yuille (Ed.), Imagery, memory, and cognition: Essays in honor of Allan Paivio. Hillsdale, NJ: Lawrence Erlbaum Associates.

Katz, A. N., & Denny, P. (1977). Memory-load and concreteness in the order of dominance effect for verbal concepts. *Journal of Verbal Learning and Verbal Behavior, 16,* 13–20.

Katz, A. N., & Paivio, A. (1975). Imagery variables in concept identification. *Journal of Verbal Learning and Verbal Behavior, 14,* 284–293.

Kaufmann, F. (1980). *Imagery, language, and cognition.* New York: Columbia University Press.

Keil, F. C. (1981). Constraints on knowledge and cognitive development. *Psychological Review, 88,* 197–227.

Kelley, H. P. (1964). Memory abilities: A factor analysis. *Psychometric Monographs (Whole No. 11).*

Kellogg, G. S., & Howe, M. J. A. (1971). Using words and pictures in foreign language learning. *Alberta Journal of Educational Research, 17,* 87–94.

Kerr, N. H. (1983). The role of vision in "visual imagery" experiments: Evidence from the congenitally blind. *Journal of Experimental Psychology: General, 112,* 265–277.

Kerst, S. M., & Howard, J. H., Jr. (1977). Mental comparisons for ordered information on abstract and concrete dimensions. *Memory & Cognition, 5,* 227–234.

Kerst, S. M., & Howard, J. H., Jr. (1978). Memory psychophysics for visual area and length. *Memory & Cognition, 6,* 327–335.

Kieras, D. (1978). Beyond pictures and words: Alternative information-processing models for imagery effects in verbal memory. *Psychological Bulletin, 85,* 532–554.

Kimura, D. (1982). Left-hemisphere control of oral and brachial movements and their relation to communication. *Philosophical Transactions of the Royal Society of London, 298,* 135–149.

King, D. L. (1973). An image theory of classical conditioning. *Psychological Reports, 33,* 403–411.

Kintsch, W. (1974). *The representation of meaning in memory.* Hillsdale, NJ: Lawrence Erlbaum Associates.

Kintsch, W., & van Dijk, T. A. (1978). Toward a model of text comprehension and production. *Psychological Review, 85,* 363–394.

Kirby, J. R., & Das, J. P. (1976). Comments on Paivio's imagery theory. *Canadian Psychological Review, 17,* 66–68.

Kirsner, K., Smith, M. C., Lockhart, R. S., King, M. L., & Jain, M. (1984). The bilingual lexicon: Language-specific units in an integrated network. *Journal of Verbal Learning and Verbal Behavior, 23,* 519–539.

Kiss, G. R. (1973). Grammatical word classes: A learning process and its simulation. In G. H. Bower (Ed.), *The psychology of learning and motivation.* New York: Academic Press.

Kiss, G. R. (1975). An associative thesaurus of English: Structural analysis of a large relevance network. In A. Kennedy & A. Wilkes (Eds.), *Studies in long term memory.* New York: Wiley.

Klee, H., & Eysenck, M. W. (1973). Comprehension of abstract and concrete sentences. *Journal of Verbal Learning and Verbal Behavior, 12,* 522–529.

Klix, F. & Metzler, P. (1982). Structural coding of pictures in human memory and its relation to the representation of concepts. In F. Klix, J. Hoffman, & E. van der Mier (Eds.), *Cognitive research in psychology.* Berlin: Verlag der Wissenschaften.

Koen, F. (1965). An intra-verbal explication of the nature of metaphor. *Journal of Verbal Learning and Verbal Behavior, 4,* 129–133.

Kolers, P. A. (1963). Interlingual word association. *Journal of Verbal Learning and Verbal Behavior, 2,* 291–300.

Kolers, P. A. (1973). Remembering operations. *Memory & Cognition, 1,* 347–355.

Kolers, P. A. (1978). On the representation of experience. In D. Gerver & W. Sinaiko (Eds.), *Language interpretation and communication.* New York: Plenum Press.

Kolers, P. A., & Brison, S. J. (1984). Commentary: On pictures, words, and their mental representations. *Journal of Verbal Learning and Verbal Behavior, 23,* 105–113.

Kolers, P. A., & Gonzales, E. (1980). Memory for words, synonyms, and translations. *Journal of Experimental Psychology: Human Learning and Memory, 6,* 53–65.

Kolers, P. A., & Roediger, H. L. (1984). Procedures of mind. *Journal of Verbal Learning and Verbal Behavior, 23,* 425–449.

Kolers, P. A., & Smythe, W. E. (1979). Images, symbols, and skills. *Canadian Journal of Psychology, 33,* 158–184.

Kolers, P. A., & Smythe, W. E. (1984). Symbol manipulation: Alternatives to the computational view of mind. *Journal of Verbal Learning and Verbal Behavior, 23,* 289–314.

Kolers, P. A., & von Grünau, M. (1976). Shape and color in apparent motion. *Vision Research, 16,* 329–335.

Kosslyn, S. M. (1973). Scanning visual images: Some structural implications. *Perception & Psychophysics, 14,* 90–94.

Kosslyn, S. M. (1980). *Image and mind.* Cambridge, MA: Harvard University Press.

Kosslyn, S. M. (1981). The medium and the message in mental imagery: A theory. *Psychological Review, 88,* 46–66.

Kosslyn, S. M., Holtzman, J. D., Farah, M. J., & Gazzaniga, M. S. (1985). A computational analysis of mental image generation: Evidence from functional dissociations in split-brain patients. *Journal of Experimental Psychology: General, 114,* 311–341.

Kosslyn, S. M., Pinker, S., Smith, G. E., & Schwartz, S. P. (1979). On the demystification of mental imagery. *The Behavioral and Brain Sciences, 2,* 535–581.

Kosslyn, S. M., & Pomerantz, J. R. (1977). Imagery, propositions, and the form of internal representations. *Cognitive Psychology, 9,* 52–76.

Kroll, J. F., & Potter, M. C. (1984). Recognizing words, pictures, and concepts: A comparison of lexical, object, and reality decisions. *Journal of Verbal Learning and Verbal Behavior, 23,* 39–66.

Krueger, T. H. (1981). *Imagery pattern in creative problem solving: A study of visualizing.* Las Cruces, NM: Encina Press.

Kuiper, N. A., & Paivio, A. (1977). Incidental recognition memory for concrete and abstract sentences equated for comprehensibility. *Bulletin of the Psychonomic Society, 9,* 247–249.

Lachman, R. (1973). Uncertainty effects on time to access the internal lexicon. *Journal of Experimental Psychology, 99,* 199–208.

Lachman, R., & Mistler-Lachman, J. (1976). Dominance lexicale chez les bilingues [Lexical dominance in bilinguals]. *Bulletin de Psychologie* [Special issue], 281–288.

Lakatos, I. Proofs and refutations (I). (1963–1964). *The British Journal for the Philosophy of Science, XIV*, 1–117.

Lakoff, G. (1971). On generative semantics. In D. D. Steinberg & L. A. Jacobovits (Eds.), *Semantics*. Cambridge, England: Cambridge University Press.

Lakoff, G. (1977). Linguistic gestalts. In *Papers from the thirteenth regional meeting*. Chicago: Chicago Linguistic Society.

Lambert, W. E. (1969). Psychological studies of the interdependencies of the bilingual's two languages. In J. Puhvel (Ed.), *Substance and structure of language*. Los Angeles: University of California Press.

Lambert, W. E., Havelka, J., & Crosby, C. (1958). The influence of language acquisition contexts on bilingualism. *Journal of Abnormal and Social Psychology, 56*, 239–244.

Lambert, W. E., & Paivio, A. (1956). The influence of noun-adjective order on learning. *Canadian Journal of Psychology, 10*, 9–12.

Lang, P. J. (1979). A bio-informational theory of emotional imagery. *Psychophysiology, 16*, 495–512.

Langer, S. K. (1948). *Philosophy in a new key*. New York: Mentor Books. (Original work published 1942)

Lay, C. H., & Paivio, A. (1969). The effects of task difficulty and anxiety on hesitations in speech. *Canadian Journal of Behavioural Science, 1*, 25–37.

Lazarus, R. S. (1984). On the primacy of cognition. *American Psychologist, 39*, 124–129.

Lederman, S. J., Klatzky, R. L., & Barber, P. O. (1985). Spatial and movement-based heuristics for encoding pattern information through touch. *Journal of Experimental Psychology: General, 114*, 39–49.

Leeper, R. (1935). A study of a neglected portion of the field of learning—The development of sensory organization. *Journal of Genetic Psychology, 46*, 41–75.

Leeper, R. (1951). Cognitive processes. In S. S. Stevens (Ed.), *Handbook of experimental psychology*. New York: Wiley.

Leight, K. A. & Ellis, H. C. (1981). Emotional mood states, strategies, and state-dependency in memory. *Journal of Verbal Learning and Verbal Behavior, 20*, 251–275.

Leuba, C. (1940). Images as conditioned sensations. *Journal of Experimental Psychology, 26*, 345–351.

Leventhal, H. (1980). Toward a comprehensive theory of emotion. In L. Berkowitz (Ed.), *Advances in experimental social psychology* (Vol. 13). New York: Academic Press.

Levin J. R. (1982). Pictures as prose-learning devices. In A. Flammer & W. Kintsch (Eds.), *Discourse processing*. Amsterdam: North-Holland.

Levine, M., Jankovic, I. N., & Palij, M. (1982). Principles of spatial problem solving. *Journal of Experimental Psychology: General, 111*, 157–175.

Ley, R. G. (1983). Cerebral laterality and imagery. In A. A. Sheikh (Ed.), *Imagery: Current theory, research, and application*. New York: Wiley.

Ley, R. G., & Bryden, M. P. (1983). Right hemispheric involvement in imagery and affect. In E. Perecman & J. Brown (Eds.), *Cognitive processing in the right hemisphere*. New York: Academic Press.

Light, L. L., & Berger, D. E. (1974). Memory for modality: Within-modality discrimination is not automatic. *Journal of Experimental Psychology, 103*, 854–860.

Light, L. L., Berger, D. E., & Bardales, M. (1975). Trade-off between memory for verbal items and their visual attributes. *Journal of Experimental Psychology: Human Learning & Memory, 104*, 188–193.

Lockhart, R. S., Craik, F. I. M., & Jacoby, L. (1976). Depth of processing, recognition, and recall. In J. Brown (Ed.), *Recall and recognition*. New York: Wiley.

Lockhead, G. R. (1972). Processing dimensional stimuli: A note. *Psychological Review, 79*, 410–419.

Lockhead, G. R. & Evans, N. J. (1979). Emmert's imaginal law. *Bulletin of the Psychonomic Society, 13*, 114–116.

Loftus, E. F., & Loftus, G. R. (1980). On the permanence of stored information in the human brain. *American Psychologist, 35,* 409–420.

Lohr, J. M. (1976). Concurrent conditioning of evaluative meaning and imagery. *British Journal of Psychology, 67,* 353–358.

Lopez, M., & Young, R. K. (1974). The linguistic interdependence of bilinguals. *Journal of Experimental Psychology, 102,* 981–983.

Lowes, J. L. (1927). *The road to Xanadu.* London: Constable.

Lupker, S. J. (1979). The semantic nature of response competition in the picture-word interference task. *Memory & Cognition, 7,* 485–495.

Lupker, S. J., & Katz, A. N. (1981). Input, decision, and response factors in picture-word interference. *Journal of Experimental Psychology: Human Learning and Memory, 7,* 269–282.

Lupker, S. J., & Katz, A. N. (1982). Can automatic picture processing influence word judgments? *Journal of Experimental Psychology: Learning, Memory, and Cognition, 8,* 418–434.

Luria, A. R. (1961). *The role of speech in the regulation of normal and abnormal behavior.* New York: Liveright.

Luria, A. R. (1973). *The working brain: An introduction to neuropsychology.* New York: Penguin.

MacCorquodale, K., & Meehl, P. E. (1954). Edward C. Tolman. In W. K. Estes, S. Koch, K. MacCorquodale, P. E. Meehl, C. G. Mueller, W. N. Schoenfeld, & W. S. Verplanck (Eds.), *Modern learning theory.* New York: Appleton-Century-Crofts.

MacLeod, C. M. (1976). Bilingual episodic memory: Acquisition and forgetting. *Journal of Verbal Learning and Verbal Behavior, 15,* 347–364.

MacLeod, C. M., Hunt, E. B., & Mathews, N. N. (1978). Individual differences in the verification of sentence-picture relationships. *Journal of Verbal Learning and Verbal Behavior, 17,* 493–507.

Macnamara, J. (1972). Cognitive basis of language learning in infants. *Psychological Review, 79,* 1–13.

Madigan, S. (1983). Picture memory. In J. C. Yuille (Ed.), *Imagery, memory, and cognition: Essays in honor of Allan Paivio.* Hillsdale, NJ: Lawrence Erlbaum Associates.

Mägiste, E. (1984). Stroop tasks and dichotic translation: The development of interference patterns in bilinguals. *Journal of Experimental Psychology: Learning, Memory, and Cognition, 10,* 304–315.

Malgady, R. G., & Johnson, M. G. (1976). Modifiers in metaphors: Effects of constituent phrase similarity on the interpretation of figurative sentences. *Journal of Psycholinguistic Research, 5,* 43–52.

Mandler, G. (1975). *Mind and emotion.* New York: Wiley.

Mandler, G. (1980). Recognizing: The judgment of previous occurrence. *Psychological Review, 87,* 252–271.

Mandler, J. M. (1983). Representation. In P. H. Mussen (Ed.), *Handbook of child psychology: Cognitive development* (Vol 3). New York: Wiley.

Mandler, J. M. (1984). *Stories, scripts, and scenes: Aspects of schema theory.* Hillsdale, NJ: Lawrence Erlbaum Associates.

Mandler, J. M., & Parker, R. E. (1976). Memory for descriptive and spatial information in complex pictures. *Journal of Experimental Psychology: Human Learning and Memory, 2,* 38–48.

Marks, D. F. (1972). Individual differences in the vividness of visual imagery and their effect on function. In P. Sheehan (Ed.), *The function and nature of imagery.* New York: Academic Press.

Marks, D. F. (1973). Visual imagery differences in the recall of pictures. *British Journal of Psychology, 64,* 17–24.

Marmor, G. S. (1975). Development of kinetic images: When does the child first represent movement in mental images? *Cognitive Psychology, 7,* 548–559.

Marmor, G. S. (1977). Mental rotation and number conservation: Are they related? *Developmental Psychology, 13,* 320–325.

Marmor, G. S., & Zaback, L. A. (1976). Mental rotation by the blind: Does mental rotation depend on visual imagery? *Journal of Experimental Psychology: Human Perception and Performance, 2,* 515–521.

Marschark, M. (1978). *Prose processing: A chronometric study of the effects of imagibility.* Unpublished doctoral dissertation, University of Western Ontario, London.

Marschark, M. (1979). The syntax and semantics of comprehension. In G. Prideaux (Ed.), *Perspectives in experimental linguistics.* Amsterdam: John Benjamins B. V.

Marschark, M. (1983). Semantic congruity in symbolic comparisons: Salience, expectancy, and associative priming. *Memory & Cognition, 11,* 192–199.

Marschark, M., & Hunt, R. R. (in press). On memory for metaphor. *Memory & Cognition.*

Marschark, M., Katz, A. N., & Paivio, A. (1983). Dimensions of metaphor. *Journal of Psycholinguistic Research, 12,* 17–40.

Marschark, M., & Paivio, A. (1977). Integrative processing of concrete and abstract sentences. *Journal of Verbal Learning and Verbal Behavior, 16,* 217–231.

Marschark, M., & Paivio, A. (1979). Semantic congruity and lexical marking in symbolic comparisons: An expectancy hypothesis. *Memory & Cognition, 7,* 175–184.

Mathews, N. N., Hunt, E. B., & MacLeod, C. M. (1980). Strategy choice and strategy training in sentence-picture verification. *Journal of Verbal Learning and Verbal Behavior, 19,* 531–548.

May, J. E., & Clayton, K. N. (1973). Imaginal processes during the attempt to recall names. *Journal of Verbal Learning and Verbal Behavior, 12,* 683–688.

McClelland, D. C. (1961). *The achieving society.* Princeton, NJ: D. Van Nostrand.

McCormack, P. D. (1977). Bilingual linguistic memory: The independence-interdependence issue revisited. In P. A. Hornby (Ed.), *Bilingualism: Psychological, social, and educational implications.* New York: Academic Press.

McCune-Nicolich, L. (1981). The cognitive bases of relational words in the single word period. *Journal of Child Language, 8,* 15–34.

McFarland, C. E., Jr., Frey, T. J., & Rhodes, D. D. (1980). Retrieval of internally versus externally generated words in episodic memory. *Journal of Verbal Learning and Verbal Behavior, 19,* 210–245.

McGee, M. G. (1982). Spatial abilities: The influence of genetic factors. In M. Potegal (Ed.), *Spatial abilities.* New York: Academic Press.

McGonigle, B., & Chalmers, M. (1984). The selective impact of question form and input mode on the symbolic distance effect in children. *Journal of Experimental Child Psychology, 37,* 525–554.

McGuigan, F. J. (1978). *Cognitive Psychophysiology: Principles of covert behavior.* Englewood Cliffs, NJ: Prentice-Hall.

McKennell, A. C. (1960). Visual size and familiar size: Individual differences. *British Journal of Psychology, 51,* 27–35.

McNeill, D. (1979). *The conceptual basis of language.* Hillsdale, NJ: Lawrence Erlbaum Associates.

Mervis, C. B., & Pani, J. R. (1980). Acquisition of basic color categories. *Cognitive Psychology, 12,* 496–522.

Miller, A. I. (1984). *Imagery in scientific thought: Creating 20th century physics.* Boston: Birkhauser.

Miller, G. A. (1956). The magical number seven plus or minus two: Some limits on our capacity for processing information. *Psychological Review, 63,* 81–97.

Miller, G. A. (1962). Some psychological studies of grammar. *American Psychologist, 17,* 748–762.

Miller, G. A. (1979). Images and models, similes and metaphors. In A. Ortony (Ed.), *Metaphor and thought.* New York: Cambridge University Press.

Mills, L., & Rollman, G. B. (1979). Left hemisphere selectivity for processing duration in normal subjects. *Brain and Language, 7,* 320–335.

Mills, L., & Rollman, G. B. (1980). Hemispheric asymmetry for auditory perception of temporal order. *Neuropsychologia, 18,* 41–47.

Milner, B. (1973). Hemispheric specialization: Scope and limits. In F. O. Schmitt & F. G. Worden (Eds.), *The Neurosciences: Third study program.* Cambridge, MA: MIT Press.

Milner, B. (1980). Complementary functional specializations of the human cerebral hemispheres. In R. Levi-Montalcini (Ed.), *Nerve cells, transmitters, and behavior.* Vatican City: Pontificia Academia Scientiarum.

Minsky, M. (1975). A framework for representing knowledge. In P. Winston (Ed.), *The psychology of computer vision.* New York: McGraw-Hill.

Mistler-Lachman, J. L. (1975). Queer sentences, ambiguity, and levels of processing. *Memory & Cognition, 3,* 395–400.

Moar, I., & Bower, G. H. (1983). Inconsistency in spatial knowledge. *Memory & Cognition, 11,* 107–113.

Moar, I., & Carleton, L. (1982). Memory for routes. *Quarterly Journal of Experimental Psychology, 34A,* 381–394.

Moeser, S. D., & Bregman, A. S. (1972). The role of reference in the acquisition of a miniature artificial language. *Journal of Verbal Learning and Verbal Behavior, 11,* 759–769.

Moeser, S. D., & Bregman, A. S. (1973). Imagery and language acquisition. *Journal of Verbal Learning and Verbal Behavior, 12,* 91–98.

Moran, T. (1973). *The symbolic imagery hypothesis: A production system model.* Unpublished doctoral dissertation, Carnegie-Mellon University.

Mori, K., & Moeser, S. D. (1983). The role of syntactic markers and semantic referents in learning an artificial language. *Journal of Verbal Learning and Verbal Behavior, 22,* 701–718.

Morris, P. E., & Hampson, P. J. (1983). *Imagery and consciousness.* New York: Academic Press.

Morris, P. E., & Stevens, R. (1974). Linking images and free recall. *Journal of Verbal Learning and Verbal Behavior, 13,* 310–315.

Morrow, D. G. (1985). Preposition and verb aspects in narrative understanding. *Journal of Memory and Language, 24,* 390–404.

Morton, J. (1969). Interaction of information in word recognition. *Psychological Review, 76,* 165–178.

Morton, J. (1979). Facilitation in word recognition: Experiments causing change in the logogen model. In P. A. Kolers, M. Wrolstead, & H. Bouma (Eds.), *Processing of visible language* (Vol. 1). New York: Plenum Press.

Moscovitch, M. (1979). Information processing and the cerebral hemispheres. In M. S. Gazzaniga (Ed.), *Handbook of behavioral neurobiology: Vol. 2. Neuropsychology.* New York: Plenum Press.

Mowrer, O. H. (1960). *Learning theory and the symbolic processes.* New York: Wiley.

Moyer, R. S. (1973). Comparing objects in memory: Evidence suggesting an internal psychophysics. *Perception & Psychophysics, 13,* 180–184.

Moyer, R. S. & Bayer, R. H. (1976). Mental comparisons and the symbolic distance effect. *Cognitive Psychology, 8,* 228–246.

Moyer, R. S., Bradley, D. R., Sorensen, M. H., Whiting, J. C., & Mansfield, D. P. (1978). Psychophysical functions for perceived and remembered size. *Science, 200,* 330–332.

Moyer, R. S., & Dumais, S. T. (1978). Mental comparison. In G. H. Bower (Ed.), *The psychology of learning and motivation.* New York: Academic Press.

Murdock, B. B., Jr. (1974). *Human memory: Theory and data.* Potomac, MD: Lawrence Erlbaum Associates.

Murdock, B. B., Jr. (1982). A theory for the storage and retrieval of item and associative information. *Psychological Review, 89,* 609–626.

Murray, D. J. (1982). Rated associability and episodic memory. *Canadian Journal of Psychology, 36,* 420–434.

Neisser, U. (1967). *Cognitive Psychology.* New York: Appleton.

Neisser, U., & Kerr, N. (1973). Spatial and mnemonic properties of visual images. *Cognitive Psychology, 5*, 138–150.

Nelson, D. L. (1981). Many are called but few are chosen: The influence of context on the effects of category size. In G. H. Bower (Ed.), *The psychology of learning and motivation, 15*, 129–162.

Nelson, D. L., & Brooks, D. H. (1973). Functional independence of pictures and their verbal memory codes. *Journal of Experimental Psychology, 98*, 44–48.

Nelson, D. L., Reed, V. S. & Walling, J. R. (1976). Pictorial superiority effect. *Journal of Experimental Psychology: Human Learning and Memory, 2*, 523–528.

Nelson, K. (1974). Concept, word, and sentence: Interrelations in acquisition and development. *Psychological Review, 81*, 267–285.

Nelson, K. (1977). The syntagmatic-paradigmatic shift revisited: A review of research and theory. *Psychological Bulletin, 84*, 93–116.

Newell, A., & Simon, H. A. (1972). *Human problem solving.* Englewood Cliffs, NJ: Prentice-Hall.

Nickles, T. (1982). Introductory essay: Scientific discovery and the future of philosophy of science. In T. Nickles (Ed.), *Scientific discovery, logic, and rationality.* Boston: D. Reidel.

Nisbett, R. E., & Wilson, T. D. (1977). Telling more than we can know: Verbal reports on mental processes. *Psychological Review, 84*, 231–259.

Noble, C. E. (1952). An analysis of meaning. *Psychological Review, 59*, 421–430.

Norman, D. A., & Rumelhart, D. E. (1975). *Explorations in cognition.* San Francisco: W. H. Freeman.

O'Connor, N., & Hermelin, B. (1972). Seeing and hearing and space and time. *Perception & Psychophysics, 11*, 46–48.

O'Connor, N., & Hermelin, B. (1978). *Seeing and hearing and space and time.* New York: Academic Press.

Oldfield, R. C. (1966). Things, words, and the brain. *Quarterly Journal of Experimental Psychology, 18*, 340–353.

Olson, D. R. (1970). Language and thought: Aspects of a cognitive theory of semantics. *Psychological Review, 77*, 257–273.

Olson, D. R., & Bialystok, E. (1983). *Spatial cognition: The structure and development of mental representations of spatial relations.* Hillsdale, NJ: Lawrence Erlbaum Associates.

Olson, D. R., & Filby, N. (1972). On comprehension of active and passive sentences. *Cognitive Psychology, 3*, 361–381.

O'Neill, B. (1971). *Word attributes in dichotic recognition and memory.* Unpublished doctoral dissertation, University of Western Ontario, London.

O'Neill, B. J. (1972). Defineability as an index of word meaning. *Journal of Psycholinguistic Research, 1*, 287–298.

O'Neill, B. J., & Paivio, A. (1978). Semantic constraints in encoding judgments and free recall of concrete and abstract sentences. *Canadian Journal of Psychology, 32*, 3–18.

Ortony, A. (1975). Why metaphors are necessary and not just nice. *Educational Theory, 25*, 45–53.

Ortony, A. (1979). The role of similarity in similes and metaphors. In A. Ortony (Ed.), *Metaphor and thought.* New York: Cambridge University Press.

Osgood, C. E. (1953). *Method and theory in experimental psychology.* New York: Oxford University Press.

Osgood, C. E. (1963). Language universals and psycholinguistics. In J. H. Greenberg (Ed.), *Universals in language.* Cambridge, MA: MIT Press.

Osgood, C. E. (1971). Where do sentences come from? In D. D. Steinberg and L. A. Jakobovits (Eds.), *Semantics: An interdisciplinary reader in philosophy, linguistics, and psychology.* New York: Cambridge University Press.

Osgood, C. E. (1973). The discussion of Dr. Paivio's paper. In F. J. McGuigan & R. A. Schoonover (Eds.), *The psychophysiology of thinking: Studies of covert processes.* New York: Academic Press.

Osgood, C. E., & Ervin, S. (1954). Second language learning and bilingualism. In C. E. Osgood & T. A. Sebeok (Eds.), *Psycholinguistics. Journal of Abnormal and Social Psychology, 49,* 139–146.

Osgood, C. E., Suci, G. J., & Tannenbaum, P. H. (1957). *The measurement of meaning.* Urbana, IL: University of Illinois Press.

Owens, J., Dafoe, J., & Bower, G. (1977). *Taking a point of view: Character identification and attributional processes in story comprehension and memory.* Paper presented at the Convention of the American Psychological Association, San Francisco.

Paivio, A. (1963). Learning of adjective-noun paired-associates as a function of adjective-noun word order and noun abstractness. *Canadian Journal of Psychology, 17,* 370–379.

Paivio, A. (1965a). Abstractness, imagery, and meaningfulness in paired-associate learning. *Journal of Verbal Learning and Verbal Behavior, 4,* 32–38.

Paivio, A. (1965b). Personality and audience influence. In B. A. Maher (Ed.), *Progress in experimental personality research* (Vol. 2). New York: Academic Press.

Paivio, A. (1966). Latency of verbal associations and imagery to noun stimuli as a function of abstractness and generality. *Canadian Journal of Psychology, 20,* 378–387.

Paivio, A. (1968). A factor-analytic study of word attributes and verbal learning. *Journal of Verbal Learning and Verbal Behavior, 7,* 41–49.

Paivio, A. (1969). Mental imagery in associative learning and memory. *Psychological Review, 76,* 241–263.

Paivio, A. (1971). *Imagery and verbal processes.* New York: Holt, Rinehart, and Winston. (Reprinted 1979, Hillsdale, NJ: Lawrence Erlbaum Associates)

Paivio, A. (1972). Symbolic and sensory modalities of memory. In M. E. Meyer (Ed.), *The third Western symposium on learning: Cognitive learning.* Bellingham, WA: Western Washington State College.

Paivio, A. (1973). Psychophysiological correlates of imagery. In F. J. McGuigan & R. A. Schoonover (Eds.), *The psychophysiology of thinking.* New York: Academic Press.

Paivio, A. (1974a). Language and knowledge of the world. *Educational Researcher, 3,* 5–12.

Paivio, A. (1974b). Spacing of repetitions in the incidental and intentional free recall of pictures and words. *Journal of Verbal Learning and Verbal Behavior, 13,* 497–511.

Paivio, A. (1975a). Coding distinctions and repetition effects in memory. In G. H. Bower (Ed.), *The psychology of learning and motivation* (Vol. 9). New York: Academic Press.

Paivio, A. (1975b). Imagery and synchronic thinking. *Canadian Psychological Review, 16,* 147–163.

Paivio, A. (1975c). Neomentalism. *Canadian Journal of Psychology, 29,* 263–291.

Paivio, A. (1975d). Perceptual comparisons through the mind's eye. *Memory & Cognition, 3,* 635–647.

Paivio, A. (1976a). Concerning dual-coding and simultaneous-successive processing. *Canadian Psychological Review, 17,* 69–72.

Paivio, A. (1976b). Imagery in recall and recognition. In J. Brown (Ed.), *Recall and recognition.* New York: Wiley.

Paivio, A. (1977). Images, propositions, and knowledge. In J. M. Nicholas (Ed.), *Images, perception, and knowledge.* The Western Ontario Series in the Philosophy of Science. Boston: Reidel.

Paivio, A. (1978a). Comparison of mental clocks. *Journal of Experimental Psychology: Human Perception and Performance, 4,* 61–71.

Paivio, A. (1978b). Dual coding: Theoretical issues and empirical evidence. In J. M. Scandura and C. J. Brainerd (Eds.), *Structural/process models of complex human behavior.* Leiden, The Netherlands: Nordhoff.

Paivio, A. (1978c). Imagery, language, and semantic memory. *International Journal of Psycholinguistics, 5,* 31–47.

Paivio, A. (1978d). Mental comparisons involving abstract attributes. *Memory & Cognition, 6,* 199–208.

Paivio, A. (1978e). On exploring visual knowledge. In B. S. Randhawa & W. E. Coffman (Eds.), *Visual learning, thinking, and communication.* New York: Academic Press.

Paivio, A. (1978f). The relationship between verbal and perceptual codes. In E. C. Carterette & M. P. Friedman (Eds.), *Handbook of perception: Vol. IX. Perceptual processing.* New York: Academic Press.

Paivio, A. (1979). Psychological processes in the comprehension of metaphor. In A. Ortony (Ed.), *Metaphor and thought.* New York: Cambridge University Press.

Paivio, A. (1980). On weighing things in your mind. In R. W. Klein & P. W. Jusezyk (Eds.), *The nature of thought: Honoring D. O. Hebb.* Hillsdale, NJ: Lawrence Erlbaum Associates.

Paivio, A. (1982a). Individual differences in coding processes. In F. Klix, J. Hoffmann, & E. van der Meer (Eds.), *Cognitive research in psychology: Recent approaches, designs, and results.* Amsterdam: Elsevier, North-Holland.

Paivio, A. (1982b). The Hebbian perspective on mind-brain relations: A review of *Essay on Mind* by D. O. Hebb. *Canadian Journal of Psychology, 36,* 543–547.

Paivio, A. (1983a). Strategies in language learning. In M. Pressley & J. R. Levin (Eds.), *Cognitive strategies research: Educational applications.* New York: Springer-Verlag.

Paivio, A. (1983b). The empirical case for dual coding. In J. C. Yuille (Ed.), *Imagery, memory, and cognition: Essays in honor of Allan Paivio.* Hillsdale, NJ: Lawrence Erlbaum Associates.

Paivio, A. (1983c). The mind's eye in arts and science. *Poetics, 12,* 1–18.

Paivio, A. (in press). Cognitive and motivational functions of imagery in human performance. *Canadian Journal of Applied Sport Sciences.*

Paivio, A., & Begg, I. (1971). Imagery and comprehension latencies as a function of sentence concreteness and structure. *Perception & Psychophysics, 10,* 408–412.

Paivio, A., & Begg, I. (1974). Pictures and words in visual search. *Memory & Cognition, 2,* 515–521.

Paivio, A., & Begg, I. (1981). *The psychology of language.* Englewood Cliffs, NJ: Prentice-Hall.

Paivio, A., & Bleasdale, F. (1974). Short-term memory: A methodological caveat. *Canadian Journal of Psychology, 28,* 24–31.

Paivio, A., Clark, J. M., & Digdon, N. (unpublished paper). Dual-coding theory and individual differences: Empirical investigations.

Paivio, A., Clark, J. M., Pressley, M., & Desrochers, A. (unpublished paper). Imagery mnemonic and control strategies in second-language vocabulary learning.

Paivio, A., & Cohen, M. (1979). Eidetic imagery and cognitive abilities. *Journal of Mental Imagery, 3,* 53–64.

Paivio, A., & Csapo, K. (1969). Concrete-image and verbal memory codes. *Journal of Experimental Psychology, 80,* 279–285.

Paivio, A., & Csapo, K. (1973). Picture superiority in free recall: Imagery or dual coding? *Cognitive Psychology, 5,* 176–206.

Paivio, A., & Desrochers, A. (1979). Effects of an imagery mnemonic on second language recall and comprehension. *Canadian Journal of Psychology, 33,* 17–28.

Paivio, A., & Desrochers, A. (1980). A dual-coding approach to bilingual memory. *Canadian Journal of Psychology, 34,* 390–401.

Paivio, A., & Desrochers, A. (1981). Mnemonic techniques in second-language learning. *Journal of Educational Psychology, 73,* 780–795.

Paivio, A., & Harshman, R. A. (1983). Factor analysis of a questionnaire on imagery and verbal habits and skills. *Canadian Journal of Psychology, 37,* 461–483.

Paivio, A., & Lambert, W. (1981). Dual coding and bilingual memory. *Journal of Verbal Learning and Verbal Behavior, 20,* 532–539.

Paivio, A., & Marschark, M. (1980). Comparative judgments of animal intelligence and pleasantness. *Memory & Cognition, 8,* 39–48.

Paivio, A., & Okovita, H. W. (1971). Word imagery modalities and associative learning in blind and sighted subjects. *Journal of Verbal Learning and Verbal Behavior, 10,* 506–510.

Paivio, A., & O'Neill, B. J. (1970). Visual recognition thresholds and dimensions of word meaning. *Perception & Psychophysics, 8,* 273–275.

Paivio, A., Philipchalk, R., & Rowe, E. J. (1975). Free and serial recall of pictures, sounds, and words. *Memory & Cognition, 3,* 586–590.

Paivio, A., & Rowe, E. J. (1970). Noun imagery, frequency, and meaningfulness in verbal discrimination. *Journal of Experimental Psychology, 85,* 264–269.

Paivio, A., & Rowe, E. J. (1971). Intrapair imagery effects in verbal discrimination and incidental associative learning. *Canadian Journal of Psychology, 25,* 302–312.

Paivio, A., & te Linde, J. (1980). Symbolic comparisons of objects on color attributes. *Journal of Experimental Psychology: Human Perception and Performance, 6,* 652–661.

Paivio, A., & te Linde, J. (1982). Imagery, memory, and the brain. *Canadian Journal of Psychology, 36,* 243–272.

Paivio, A., & Yarmey, A. D. (1966). Pictures versus words as stimuli and responses in paired-associate learning. *Psychonomic Science, 5,* 235–236.

Paivio, A., & Yuille, J. C. (1969). Changes in associative strategies and paired-associate learning over trials as a function of word imagery and type of learning set. *Journal of Experimental Psychology, 79,* 458–463.

Paivio, A., Yuille, J. C., & Madigan, S. A. (1968). Concreteness, imagery, and meaningfulness values for 925 nouns. *Journal of Experimental Psychology Monographs, 78*(1, Pt. 2).

Palermo, D. S., & Jenkins, J. J. (1964). *Word association norms: Grade school through college.* Minneapolis: University of Minnesota Press.

Palmer, S. E. (1975). Visual perception and world knowledge: Notes on a model of sensory-cognitive interaction. In D. A. Norman & D. E. Rumelhart (Eds.), *Explorations in cognition.* San Francisco: Freeman.

Palmer, S. E. (1978). Fundamental aspects of cognitive representations. In E. Rosch & B. B. Lloyd (Eds.), *Cognition and categorization.* New York: Lawrence Erlbaum Associates.

Paradis, M. (1980). Language and thought in bilinguals. In H. J. Izzo & W. C. McCormack (Eds.), *The sixth Lacus forum.* Columbia, SC: Hornbeam Press.

Parkins, E. J. (1982). *Brain/mind.* Lancashire, England: E. J. Parkins.

Pellegrino, J. W., & Goldman, S. R. (1983). Developmental and individual differences in verbal and spatial reasoning. In R. F. Dillon & R. R. Schmeck (Eds.), *Individual differences in cognition* (Vol. 1). New York: Academic Press.

Pellegrino, J. W., Rosinski, R. R., Chiesi, H. L., & Siegal, A. (1977). Picture-word differences in decision latency: An analysis of single and dual memory models. *Memory & Cognition, 5,* 383–396.

Pellegrino, J. W., Siegal, A. W., & Dhawan, M. (1975). Short-term retention of pictures and words: Evidence for dual coding systems. *Journal of Experimental Psychology, 104,* 95–102.

Perfetti, C. A. (1983). Individual differences in verbal processes. In R. F. Dillon & R. R. Schmeck (Eds.), *Individual differences in cognition.* New York: Academic Press.

Peterson, L. R., Holsten, J., & Spevak, P. (1975). Spatial coding of auditory signals. *Memory & Cognition, 3,* 243–246.

Peterson, M. J. (1975). The retention of imagined and seen spatial matrices. *Cognitive Psychology, 7,* 181–193.

Peterson, M. J., & Graham, S. E. (1974). Visual detection and visual imagery. *Journal of Experimental Psychology, 103,* 509–514.

Peterson, M. J., & McGee, S. H. (1974). The effects of imagery instruction, imagery ratings, and the number of dictionary meanings upon recognition and recall. *Journal of Experimental Psychology, 102,* 1007–1014.

Philipchalk, R. P. (1971). *The development of imaginal meaning in verbal stimuli.* Unpublished doctoral dissertation, University of Western Ontario, London.

Philipchalk, R. P., & Rowe, E. J. (1971). Sequential and nonsequential memory for verbal and nonverbal auditory stimuli. *Journal of Experimental Psychology, 91,* 341–343.

Piaget, J. (1926). *The language and thought of the child.* New York: Harcourt, Brace.

Piaget, J. (1980). The psychogenesis of knowledge and its epistemological significance. In M. Piattelli-Palmarini (Ed.), *Language and learning: The debate between Jean Piaget and Noam Chomsky*. Cambridge, MA: Harvard University Press.

Piaget, J., & Inhelder, B. (1966). L'image mentale chez l'enfant. Paris: Presses Universitaires de France. (English translation published 1971 [*Mental imagery in the child: A study of the development of imaginal representations*]. London: Routledge & Kegan Paul)

Piattelli-Palmarini, M. (Ed.). (1980). *Language and learning: The debate between Jean Piaget and Noam Chomsky*. Cambridge, MA: Harvard University Press.

Pike, R. (1984). Comparison of convolution and matrix distributed memory systems for associative recall and recognition. *Psychological Review, 91*, 281–294.

Pinker, S. (1984). *Language learnability and language development*. Cambridge, MA: Harvard University Press.

Podgorny, P., & Shepard, R. N. (1978). Functional representations common to visual perception and imagination. *Journal of Experimental Psychology: Human Perception and Performance, 4*, 21–35.

Posner, M. I., & Keele, S. W. (1968). On the genesis of abstract ideas. *Journal of Experimental Psychology, 77*, 353–363.

Posner, M. I., & Warren, R. E. (1972). Traces, concepts, and conscious constructions. In A. W. Melton & E. Martin (Eds.), *Coding processes in human memory*. New York: Winston-Wiley.

Postman, L., & Burns, S. (1973). Experimental analysis of coding processes. *Memory & Cognition, 1*, 503–507.

Postman, L., & Burns, S. (1974). Long-term retention as a function of word concreteness under conditions of free recall. *Memory & Cognition, 2*, 703–708.

Potter, M. C., & Faulconer, B. A. (1975). Time to understand pictures and words. *Nature, 253*, 437–438.

Potter, M. C., So, K., Von Eckardt, B., & Feldman, L. B. (1984). Lexical and conceptual representation in beginning and proficient bilinguals. *Journal of Verbal Learning and Verbal Behavior, 23*, 23–38.

Potter, M. C., Valian, V. V., & Faulconer, B. A. (1977). Representation of a sentence and its pragmatic implications: Verbal, imagistic, or abstract? *Journal of Verbal Learning and Verbal Behavior, 16*, 1–12.

Premack, D. (1983). The codes of man and beasts. *The Behavioral and Brain Sciences, 6*, 125–167.

Prentice, J. L. (1968). Intraverbal associations in sentence behavior. *Psychonomic Science, 10*, 213–214.

Pressley, M. (1977). Imagery and children's learning: Putting the picture in developmental perspective. *Review of Educational Research, 47*, 585–622.

Pressley, M. (1982). Elaboration and memory development. *Child Development, 53*, 296–309.

Pressley, M., & Levin, J. R. (1978). Developmental constraints associated with children's use of the keyword method of foreign language vocabulary learning. *Journal of Experimental Child Psychology, 26*, 359–372.

Pressley, M., Levin, J. R., & Delaney, H. D. (1982). The mnemonic keyword method. *Review of Educational Research, 52*, 61–92.

Preston, M. S., & Lambert, W. E. (1969). Interlingual interference in a bilingual version of the Stroop color-word task. *Journal of Verbal Learning and Verbal Behavior, 8*, 295–301.

Pribram, K. H. (1971). *Languages of the brain: Experimental paradoxes and principles in neuropsychology*. Englewood Cliffs, NJ: Prentice-Hall.

Pylyshyn, Z. W. (1973). What the mind's eye tells the mind's brain: A critique of mental imagery. *Psychological Bulletin, 80*, 1–24.

Pylyshyn, Z. W. (1978). Imagery and artificial intelligence. In W. Savage (Ed.), *Minnesota studies in the philosophy of science* (Vol. 9). Minneapolis: University of Minnesota Press.

Pylyshyn, Z. W. (1979a). Metaphorical imprecision and the "top-down" research strategy. In A. Ortony (Ed.), *Metaphor and thought*. Cambridge, MA: Cambridge University Press.

Pylyshyn, Z. W. (1979b). The rate of "mental rotation" of images: A test of holistic analogue hypothesis. *Memory & Cognition, 7,* 19–28.

Pylyshyn, Z. W. (1981). The imagery debate: Analogue media versus tacit knowledge. *Psychological Review, 88,* 16–45.

Pylyshyn, Z. W. (1984). *Computation and cognition.* Cambridge, MA: MIT Press.

Ratcliff, R. (1978). A theory of memory retrieval. *Psychological Review, 85,* 59–108.

Ratcliff, R., & McKoon, G. (1981). Does activation really spread? *Psychological Review, 88,* 454–462.

Reed, H. B. (1918). Associative aids: III. Their relation to the theory of thought and to methodology in psychology. *Psychological Review, 25,* 378–401.

Reed, S. K., Hock, H. S., & Lockhead, G. R. (1983). Tacit knowledge and the effect of pattern configuration on mental scanning. *Memory & Cognition, 11,* 137–143.

Reese, H. W. (1970). Imagery and contextual meaning. In H. W. Reese (Chair), Imagery in children's learning: A symposium. *Psychological Bulletin, 73,* 404–414.

Rescorla, R. A., Grau, J. W., & Durlach, P. J. (1985). Analysis of the unique cue in configural discriminations. *Journal of Experimental Psychology: Animal Behavior Processes, 11,* 356–366.

Reynolds, A., & Paivio, A. (1968). Cognitive and emotional determinants of speech. *Canadian Journal of Psychology, 22,* 164–175.

Reynolds, J. H. (1968). Cognitive transfer in verbal learning: II. Transfer effects after prefamiliarization with integrated versus partially integrated verbal-perceptual structures. *Journal of Educational Psychology, 59,* 133–138.

Richardson, A. (1969). *Mental imagery.* New York: Springer.

Richardson, J. T. E. (1975). Imagery, concreteness, and lexical complexity. *Quarterly Journal of Experimental Psychology, 27,* 211–223.

Richardson, J. T. E. (1978). Reported mediators and individual differences in mental imagery. *Memory & Cognition, 6,* 376–378.

Richardson, J. T. E. (1980). *Mental imagery and human memory.* London: Macmillan.

Roberts, W. A. (1984). Some issues in animal spatial memory. In H. L. Roitblatt, T. G. Bever, & H. S. Terrace (Eds.), *Animal cognition.* Hillsdale, NJ: Lawrence Erlbaum Associates.

Robins, C., & Shepard, R. N. (1977). Spatio-temporal probing of apparent rotational movement. *Perception & Psychophysics, 22,* 12–18.

Rock, I. (1975). *An introduction to perception.* New York: Macmillan.

Roediger, H. L. III. (1980). Memory metaphors in cognitive psychology. *Memory & Cognition, 8,* 231–246.

Rogers, T. B. (1983). Emotion, imagery, and verbal codes: A closer look at an increasingly complex interaction. In J. C. Yuille (Ed.), *Imagery, memory, and cognition: Essays in honor of Allan Paivio.* Hillsdale, NJ: Lawrence Erlbaum Associates.

Rohwer, W. D., Jr. (1970). Images and pictures in children's learning: Research results and instructional implications. In H. W. Reese (Chair), Imagery in children's learning: A symposium. *Psychological Bulletin, 73,* 393–403.

Rohwer, W. D., Jr. (1973). Elaboration and learning in childhood and adolescence. In H. W. Reese (Ed.), *Advances in child development and behavior* (Vol. 8). New York: Academic Press.

Roitblatt, H. L. (1982). The meaning of representation in animal memory. *The Behavioral and Brain Sciences, 5,* 353–406.

Rosch, E. (1975a). Cognitive reference points. *Cognitive Psychology, 7,* 532–547.

Rosch, E. (1975b). Cognitive representations of semantic categories. *Journal of Experimental Psychology: General, 104,* 192–233.

Rosenberg, S. (1967). The relation between associations on lexical selection and syntactic arrangement in production. *Language and behavior: Progress report V.* Ann Arbor: University of Michigan Center for Research on Language and Language Behavior.

Rosenberg, S. (1969). The recall of verbal material accompanying semantically well-integrated and semantically poorly-integrated sentences. *Journal of Verbal Learning and Verbal Behavior, 8,* 732–736.

Rosenberg, S., & Simon, H. A. (1977). Modelling semantic memory: Effects of presenting semantic information in different modalities. *Cognitive Psychology, 9,* 293–325.

Rosenfeld, J. B. (1967). *Information processing: Encoding and decoding.* Unpublished doctoral dissertation, Indiana University.

Rosinski, R. R. (1977). Picture-word interference is semantically based. *Child Development, 48,* 643–647.

Rowe, E. J., & Cake, L. J. (1977). Retention of order information for sounds and words. *Canadian Journal of Psychology, 31,* 14–23.

Rowe, E. J., & Paivio, A. (1971). Imagery and repetition instructions in verbal discrimination and incidental paired-associate learning. *Journal of Verbal Learning and Verbal Behavior, 10,* 668–672.

Royce, J. R., Kearsley, G. P., & Klare, W. (1978). The relationship between factors and psychological processes. In J. M. Scandura & C. J. Brainerd (Eds.), *Structural/process models of complex human behavior.* Alphen aan den Rijn, The Netherlands: Sijthoff & Noordhoff.

Rubin, D. C. (1980). 51 properties of 125 words: A unit analysis of verbal behavior. *Journal of Verbal Learning and Verbal Behavior, 19,* 736–755.

Rucker, R. (1982). Master of the incomplete. *Science 82, 3*(8), 56–60.

Rugg, H. (1963). *Imagination.* New York: Harper & Row.

Rumelhart, D. E., & Ortony, A. (1977). The representation of knowledge in memory. In R. C. Anderson, R. J. Spiro, & W. E. Montague (Eds.), *Schooling and the acquisition of knowledge.* Hillsdale, NJ: Lawrence Erlbaum Associates.

Runquist, W. N. (1971). Stimulus coding and interference in paired-associate learning. *Journal of Experimental Psychology, 87,* 373–377.

Runquist, W. N., & Blackmore, M. (1973). Phonemic storage of concrete and abstract words with auditory presentation. *Canadian Journal of Psychology, 27,* 456–463.

Sadoski, M. (1983). An exploratory study of the relationship between reported imagery and the comprehension and recall of a story. *Reading Research Quarterly, 19,* 110–123.

Sadoski, M. (in press). The natural use of imagery in story comprehension and recall: Replication and extension. *Reading Research Quarterly.*

Saegert, J., & Young, R. K. (1975). Translation errors for abstract and concrete responses in a bilingual paired-associate task. *Bulletin of the Psychonomic Society, 6,* 429.

Salthouse, T. A. (1977). Number of memory representations in perceptual concepts. *Journal of Experimental Psychology: Human Learning and Memory, 3,* 18–28.

Saltz, E., & Nolan, S. D. (1981). Does motoric imagery facilitate memory for sentences? A selective interference test. *Journal of Verbal Learning and Verbal Behavior, 20,* 322–332.

Santa, J. L. (1977). Spatial transformations of words and pictures. *Journal of Experimental Psychology: Human Learning and Memory, 3,* 418–427.

Scarborough, D. L., Gerard, L., & Cortese, C. (1984). Independence of lexical access in bilingual word recognition. *Journal of Verbal Learning and Verbal Behavior, 23,* 84–99.

Schank, R. C. (1972). Conceptual dependency: A theory of natural language understanding. *Cognitive Psychology, 3,* 552–631.

Schank, R. C., & Abelson, R. (1977). *Scripts, plans, goals, and understanding.* Hillsdale, NJ: Lawrence Erlbaum Associates.

Schwanenflugel, P. J., & Shoben, E. J. (1983). Differential context effects in the comprehension of abstract and concrete verbal materials. *Journal of Experimental Psychology: Learning, Memory, and Cognition, 9,* 82–102.

Segal, A. U. (1976). *Verbal and nonverbal encoding and retrieval differences.* Unpublished doctoral dissertation, University of Western Ontario, London.

Seidenberg, M. S., Waters, G. S., Sanders, M., & Langer, P. (1984). Pre- and postlexical loci of contextual effects on word recognition. *Memory & Cognition, 12,* 315–328.

Selfe, L. (1983). *Normal and anomalous representational drawing ability in children.* New York: Academic Press.

Sergent, J. (1984). Configural processing of faces in the left and the right cerebral hemispheres. *Journal of Experimental Psychology: Human Perception and Performance, 10,* 554–572.

Seymour, P. H. K. (1973). A model for reading, naming, and comparison. *British Journal of Psychology, 64,* 35–49.

Shaver, P., Pierson, L., & Lang, S. (1974). Converging evidence for the functional significance of imagery in problem solving. *Cognition, 3,* 359–375.

Sheehan, P. W. (1967). A shortened form of Betts' questionnaire upon mental imagery. *Journal of Clinical Psychology, 23,* 386–389.

Sheffield, F. D. (1961). Theoretical considerations in the learning of complex sequential tasks from demonstration and practice. In A. A. Lumsdaine (Ed.), *Student response in programmed instruction* (NAS-NRS Publication No. 943). Washington, DC: National Academy of Sciences—National Research Council.

Sheikh, A. A., & Jordan, C. S. (1983). Clinical uses of mental imagery. In A. A. Sheikh (Ed.), *Imagery: Current theory, research, and application.* New York: Wiley.

Shepard, R. N. (1962). The analysis of proximities: Multidimensional scaling with an unknown distance function. *I. Psychometrika, 27,* 125–140.

Shepard, R. N. (1978). The mental image. *American Psychologist, 33,* 125–137.

Shepard, R. N. (1984). Ecological constraints on internal representation: Resonant kinematics of perceiving, imagining, thinking, and dreaming. *Psychological Review, 91,* 417–447.

Shepard, R. N., & Chipman, S. (1970). Second-order isomorphism of internal representations: Shapes of states. *Cognitive Psychology, 1,* 1–17.

Shepard, R. N., & Judd, S. A. (1976). Perceptual illusion of rotation of three-dimensional objects. *Science, 191,* 952–954.

Shepard, R. N., & Metzler, J. (1971). Mental rotation of three-dimensional objects. *Science, 171,* 701–703.

Simon, H. A. (1972). What is visual imagery? An information-processing interpretation. In L. W. Gregg (Ed.), *Cognition in learning and memory.* New York: Wiley.

Simon, H. A., & Feigenbaum, E. A. (1964). An information-processing theory of some effects of similarity, familiarization, and meaningfulness in verbal learning. *Journal of Verbal Learning and Verbal Behavior, 3,* 385–396.

Sinclair-de Zwart, H. (1973). Language acquisition and cognitive development. In T. E. Moore (Ed.), *Cognitive development and the acquisition of language.* New York: Academic Press.

Singer, J. L. (1966). *Daydreaming: An introduction to the experimental study of inner experience.* New York: Random House.

Singer, J. L. (1974). *Imagery and daydream methods in psychotherapy and behavior modification.* New York: Academic Press.

Singer, J. L., & Antrobus, J. S. (1972). Daydreaming, imaginal processes, and personality: A normative study. In P. W. Sheehan (Ed.), *The function and nature of imagery.* New York: Academic Press.

Skinner, B. F. (1953). *Science and human behavior.* New York: Macmillan.

Skinner, B. F. (1957). *Verbal behavior.* New York: Appleton-Century-Crofts.

Skinner, B. F. (1963). Behaviorism at fifty. *Science, 140,* 951–958.

Skinner, B. F. (1975). The steep and thorny way to a science of behavior. *American Psychologist, 30,* 42–49.

Slack, J. M. (1983). Imagery effects and semantic similarity in sentence recognition memory. *Memory & Cognition, 11,* 631–640.

Slamecka, N. J. & Graf, P. (1978). The generation effect: Delineation of a phenomenon. *Journal of Experimental Psychology: Human Learning and Memory, 4,* 592–604.

Sloman, A. (1971). Interactions between philosophy and artificial intelligence: The role of intuition and non-logical reasoning in intelligence. *Artificial Intelligence, 2,* 209–225.

Smith, E. E., Shoben, E. J., & Rips, L. J. (1974). Structure and process in semantic memory: A featural model from semantic decisions. *Psychological Review, 81,* 214–241.

Smith, E. E., & Medin, D. L. (1981). *Categories and Concepts.* Cambridge, MA: Harvard University Press.

Smythe, P. C. (1970). *Pair concreteness and mediation instructions in forward and backward paired-associate recall.* Unpublished doctoral thesis, University of Western Ontario, London, Ontario, Canada.

Snodgrass, J. G. (1984). Concepts and their surface representations. *Journal of Verbal Learning and Verbal Behavior, 23,* 3–22.

Snodgrass, J. G., Burns, P. M., & Pirone, G. U. (1978). Pictures and words and space and time: In search of the elusive interaction. *Journal of Experimental Psychology: General, 107,* 206–230.

Snodgrass, J. G., & Vanderwart, M. (1980). A standardized set of 260 pictures: Norms for name agreement, image agreement, familiarity, and visual complexity. *Journal of Experimental Psychology: Human Learning and Memory, 6,* 174–215.

Solso, R. L. & Raynis, S. A. (1979). Prototype formation from imaged, kinesthetically, and visually presented geometric figures. *Journal of Experimental Psychology: Human Perception and Performance, 5,* 701–712.

Sperling, G. (1960). The information available in brief visual presentations. *Psychological Monographs, 74,* (Whole No. 498).

Spurgeon, C. F. E. (1935). *Shakespeare's imagery and what it tells us.* New York: Cambridge University Press.

Staats, A. W. (1961). Verbal habit families, concepts, and the operant conditioning of word classes. *Psychological Review, 68,* 190–204.

Staats, A. W. (1968). *Learning, language, and cognition.* New York: Holt.

Steckol, K. L., & Leonard, L. B. (1981). Sensorimotor development and the use of prelinguistic performatives. *Journal of Speech and Hearing Research, 24,* 262–268.

Stein, B. S., & Bransford, J. D. (1979). Constraints on effective elaboration: Effects of precision and subject generation. *Journal of Verbal Learning and Verbal Behavior, 18,* 769–777.

Steinfeld, G. J. (1967). Concepts of set and availability and their relation to the reorganization of ambiguous pictorial stimuli. *Psychological Review, 74,* 505–522.

Sternberg, R. J. (1980). Representation and process in linear syllogistic reasoning. *Journal of Experimental Psychology: General, 109,* 119–159.

Sternberg, R. J. (1984). Toward a triarchic theory of human intelligence. *Behavioral and Brain Sciences, 7,* 269–315.

Sternberg, R. J., & Weil, G. M. An aptitude-strategy interaction in linear syllogistic reasoning. *Journal of Educational Psychology,72,* 226–234.

Sternberg, S. (1967). Two operations in character recognition: Some evidence from reaction-time measurements. *Perception and Psychophysics, 2,* 45–53.

Strømnes, F. J. (1973). A semiotic theory of imagery processes with experiments on an Indo-European and a Ural-Altaic language. Do speakers of different languages experience different cognitive worlds? *Scandinavian Journal of Psychology, 14,* 291–304.

Strømnes, F. J. (1979). The problem of the image: Can there be information in propositions? *Communications, 4,* 259–275.

Stroop, J. R. (1935). Interference in serial verbal reactions. *Journal of Experimental Psychology, 18,* 643–661.

Suinn, R. M. (1983). Imagery and sports. In A. A. Sheikh (Ed.), *Imagery: Current theory, research, and application.* New York: Wiley.

Tapley, S. M., & Bryden, M. P. (1977). An investigation of sex differences in spatial ability: Mental rotation of three-dimensional objects. *Canadian Journal of Psychology, 31,* 122–130.

Tatum, B. C. (1976). Stimulus imagery effect in associative learning: Differentiation or mediation? *Journal of Experimental Psychology: Human Learning and Memory, 2,* 252–261.

Taylor, I. (1971). How are words from two languages organized in a bilingual's memory? *Canadian Journal of Psychology, 25,* 228–239.

te Linde, J. (1982). Picture-word differences in decision latency: A test of common-coding assumptions. *Journal of Experimental Psychology: Learning, Memory, and Cognition, 8,* 584–598.

te Linde, J., & Paivio, A. (1979). Symbolic comparisons of color similarity. *Memory & Cognition, 3,* 635–647.

Terrace, H. S. (1985). In the beginning was the "name." (1985). *American Psychologist, 40,* 1011–1028.

Thorndyke, P. (1977). Cognitive structures in comprehension and memory of narrative discourse. *Cognitive Psychology, 9,* 77–110.

Tolman, E. C. (1948). Cognitive maps in rats and men. *Psychological Review, 55,* 189–208.

Triesman, A. (1979). The psychological reality of levels of processing. In L. S. Cermak & F. I. M. Craik (Eds.), *Levels of processing in human memory.* Hillsdale, NJ: Lawrence Erlbaum Associates.

Tulving, E. (1972). Episodic and semantic memory. In E. Tulving & W. Donaldson (Eds.), *Organization of memory.* New York: Academic Press.

Tulving, E. (1983). *Elements of episodic memory.* New York: Oxford University Press.

Tversky, A. (1977). Features of similarity. *Psychological Review, 84,* 327–352.

Tversky, B. (1969). Pictorial and verbal encoding in a short-term memory task. *Perception & Psychophysics, 6,* 225–233.

Tversky, B. (1981). Distortions in memory for maps. *Cognitive Psychology, 13,* 407–433.

Tversky, B., & Hemenway, K. (1984). Objects, parts, and categories. *Journal of Experimental Psychology: General, 113,* 169–193.

Underwood, B. J. (1965). False recognition produced by implicit verbal responses. *Journal of Experimental Psychology, 70,* 122–129.

Underwood, B. J. (1969). Attributes of memory. *Psychological Review, 76,* 559–573.

Underwood, B. J. (1975). Individual differences as a crucible in theory construction. *American Psychologist, 30,* 128–134.

Underwood, B. J., & Schulz, R. W. (1960). *Meaningfulness and verbal learning.* Chicago: Lippincott.

van Dijk, T. A., & Kintsch, W. (1983). *Strategies of discourse comprehension.* New York: Academic Press.

van Fraassen, B. C. (1980). *The scientific image.* New York: Oxford University Press.

Vanderwart, M. (1984). Priming by pictures in lexical decision. *Journal of Verbal Learning and Verbal Behavior, 23,* 67–83.

Verbrugge, R. R., & McCarrell, N. S. (1977). Metaphoric comprehension: Studies in reminding and resembling. *Cognitive Psychology, 9,* 494–533.

Wallace, B. (1984). Apparent equivalence between perception and imagery in the production of various visual illusions. *Memory & Cognition, 12,* 156–162.

Warren, M. W. (1977). The effects of recall-concurrent visual-motor distraction on picture and word recall. *Memory & Cognition, 5,* 362–370.

Warren, R. M., Obusek, C. J., Farmer, R. M., & Warren, R. P. (1969). Auditory sequence: Confusion of patterns other than speech or music. *Science, 164,* 586–587.

Watson, J. B. (1913). Psychology as the behaviorist views it. *Psychological Review, 20,* 158–177.

Weber, R. J., & Harnish, R. (1974). Visual imagery for words: The Hebb test. *Journal of Experimental Psychology, 102,* 409–414.

Weinreich, V. (1953). *Languages in contact.* New York: Linguistic Circle of New York.

Wexler, K., & Culicover, P. W. (1980). *Formal principles of language acquisition.* Cambridge, MA: MIT Press.

Whitehouse, P. J. (1981). Imagery and verbal encoding in left and right hemisphere damaged patients. *Brain and Language, 14,* 315–332.

Wickens, D. D. (1970). Encoding categories of words: An empirical approach to meaning. *Psychological Review, 77,* 1–15.

Wicker, F. W., Thorelli, I. M., & Saddler, C. D. (1978). Stimulus concreteness, response characteristics, and the recognition-recall method in paired-associate learning. *Journal of Experimental Psychology: Human Learning and Memory, 4,* 136–145.

Wilkins, A., & Moscovitch, M. (1978). Selective impairment of semantic memory after temporal lobectomy. *Neuropsychologia, 16,* 73–79.

Wilson, K. (1980). *From associations to structure.* Amsterdam: North-Holland.

Wimer, C., & Lambert, W. E. (1959). The differential effects of word and object stimuli on the learning of paired associates. *Journal of Experimental Psychology, 57,* 31–36.

Winnick, W. A., & Kressel, K. (1965). Tachistoscopic recognition thresholds, paired-associate learning, and immediate recall as a function of abstractness-concreteness and word frequency. *Journal of Experimental Psychology, 70,* 163–168.

Winograd, E., Cohen, C., & Barresi, J. (1976). Memory for concrete and abstract words in bilingual speakers. *Memory & Cognition, 4,* 323–329.

Wiseman, S., MacLeod, C. M., & Lootsteen, P. J. (1985). Picture recognition improves with subsequent verbal information. *Journal of Experimental Psychology: Learning, Memory, and Cognition, 11,* 588–595.

Wollen, K. A., Weber, A., & Lowry, D. H. (1972). Bizarreness versus interaction of mental images as determinants of learning. *Cognitive Psychology, 3,* 518–523.

Wolpe, J. (1958). *Psychotherapy by reciprocal inhibition.* Stanford: Stanford University Press.

Woodworth, R. S. (1938). *Experimental psychology.* New York: Holt.

Yarmey, A. D. (1974). Effect of labelling-latency of pictures in associative learning of pictorial representations and their word labels. *Canadian Journal of Psychology, 28,* 15–23.

Yates, F. A. (1966). *The art of memory.* London: Routledge & Kegan Paul.

Young, R. K., Overbey, G., & Powell, G. D. (1976). Is there sequential information in a mental image? *Journal of Experimental Psychology: Human Learning and Memory, 2,* 663–670.

Young, R. K., & Saegert, J. (1966). Transfer with bilinguals. *Psychonomic Science, 6,* 161–162.

Yuille, J. C. (1973). A detailed examination of mediation in PA learning. *Memory & Cognition, 1,* 333–342.

Yuille, J. C. (1983). The crisis in theories of mental imagery. In J. C. Yuille (Ed.), *Imagery, memory, and cognition: Essays in honor of Allan Paivio.* Hillsdale, NJ: Lawrence Erlbaum Associates.

Yuille, J. C. & Catchpole, M. J. (1973). Associative learning and imagery training in children. *Journal of Experimental Child Psychology, 16,* 403–412.

Yuille, J. C., & Paivio, A. (1969). Abstractness and recall of connected discourse. *Journal of Experimental Psychology, 82,* 467–471.

Yuille, J. C., & Steiger, J. H. (1982). Nonholistic processing in mental rotation: Some suggestive evidence. *Perception & Psychophysics, 31,* 201–209.

Zajonc, R. B. (1980). Feeling and thinking: Preferences need no inferences. *American Psychologist, 35,* 151–175.

Zajonc, R. B. (1984). On the primacy of affect. *American Psychologist, 39,* 117–123.

Zikmund, V. (1972). Psychophysiological correlates of visual imagery. In P. W. Sheehan (Ed.), *The function and nature of imagery.* New York: Academic Press.

Zimler, J., & Keenan, J. M. (1983). Imagery in the congenitally blind: How visual are visual images? *Journal of Experimental Psychology: Learning, Memory, and Cognition, 9,* 269–282.

Zimmer, H. D., & Engelkamp, J. (1985). An attempt to distinguish between kinematic and motor memory components. *Acta Psychologica, 58,* 81–106.

Zimmerman, B. J., & Rosenthal, T. L. (1974). Observational learning of rule-governed behavior by children. *Psychological Bulletin, 81,* 29–42.

Author Index

Abelson, R., 27
Alba, J. W., 28, 149
Algom, D., 179
Allport, D. A., 71
Allport, F. H., 120
Anderson, J. R., 11, 41, 43, 44, 46, 48, 49, 52, 81, 125, 129, 159, 163, 171, 196, 214, 273
Anderson, R. C., 132, 154, 167, 171, 224
Anderson, R. E., 151, 173
Anisfeld, M., 148
Annett, J., 208
Antrobus, J. S., 208
Arndt, D. R., 204–5
Arnheim, R., 201
Arnold, M. B., 80, 274
Asch, S. E., 234
Asher, J. J., 257
Atkinson, R. C., 38, 253
Attneave, F., 59, 178
Auble, P. M., 145

Babbit, B. C., 160
Baddeley, A. D., 70, 145, 156
Baggett, P., 226
Bahrick, H. P., 158
Bahrick, P., 158
Baker, L., 169
Baldwin, J. M., 231
Bandura, A., 86
Banks, W. P., 184, 189, 192
Barber, P. O., 204
Bardales, M., 150
Barresi, J., 246, 251–52
Barrett, B., 156
Bartlett, F. C., 27, 28, 38, 70
Battig, W. F., 122
Baum, D. R., 180, 181
Bayer, R. H., 180
Baylor, G. W., 50
Beauvois, M. F., 267–68
Beck, L. S., 222
Beech, J. R., 71

Begg, I., 86, 104, 142, 148, 150, 154, 159, 168–71, 218, 220, 223, 229, 232, 239, 256, 258
Bellack, D. R., 219
Bellezza, F. S., 169, 170
Belmore, S. M., 219
Berger, D. E., 150
Bergman, B., 179
Beritoff, J. S., 86, 274
Berndt, R. S., 268–69
Besner, D., 191
Betts, G. H., 101, 117
Bever, T. G., 11
Bialystok, E., 46
Bickley, W., 159
Biederman, I., 165
Bierwisch, M., 29
Billow, R. M., 236
Binet, A., 37
Bisiach, E., 264
Black, J. B., 225
Black, M., 237
Blackmore, M., 150
Bleasdale, F., 143, 148
Block, R. A., 181
Boles, D. B., 127, 261
Bourne, L. E. Jr., 132
Bousfield, W. K., 38, 70
Bower, G. H., 11, 24, 39, 41, 43, 44, 48, 80, 81, 129, 141, 159, 166, 171, 203, 214, 224–25
Bower, T. G. R., 88
Bowerman, M., 217
Bradley, D. R., 178
Braine, M. D. S., 92, 216
Brainerd, C. J., 84, 168
Bransford, J. D., 70, 145
Bregman, A. S., 19, 27, 28, 42, 94, 175, 256
Bremner, J. G., 88
Brewer, W. F., 140, 154
Bridgman, P. W., 13
Brison, S. J., 139
Broadbent, D. E., 38
Brooks, D. H., 158

307

Subject Index